D1879181

MANAGING DEVELOPMENT FOR FUTURE
A Study in Transition and Change Management

MANAGING DEVELOPMENT FOR FUTURE
A Study in Transition and Change Management

SATISH C. SETH

GYAN

GYAN PUBLISHING HOUSE
New Delhi-110002

MANAGING DEVELOPMENT FOR FUTURE
A Study in Transition and Change Management
[*Management*]

ISBN: 81-212-0678-2 (Set)
ISBN: 81-212-0736-3 (Vol. I)

© SATISH C. SETH
14th March, 1932
Painting on Front Cover: Satish C. Seth

All rights are reserved. No part of this book may be reproduced in any manner without written permission.

Published in 2001 in India by
Gyan Publishing House
5, Ansari Road
New Delhi 110 002
Phones: 3261060, 3282060, Fax: 3285914
e-mail: gyanbook@del2.vsnl.net.in
visit our website at: http://www.gyanbooks.com

Laser Typeset at: Alphabet, Delhi
Printed at: Mehra Offset Printers, New Delhi.

To

My Wife, Padma Seth

for her continued support
and guidance

Contents

PREFACE

The two decades of 70's and 80's have been a momentous period of unbelievable shift in the public and private sectors management in India. It is a pity that no serious attempt has been made to capture and measure in depth manifold features of this transition. This book is a humble attempt to do that to a limited extent.

It has been a part of the worldwide managerial folk-lore to pick one or the other mega trends to explain all kinds of development or progress. Some would attribute it to the information technology (IT) and others may recite prayers for the new training inputs, as brought out by behavioural science. For many Indian corporate thinkers, the key transition has been the family based business acquiring some resemblance of professionalism. One can multiply a hundred such "choices" and "emphasis", as holding the secret of change that has led to a slow but steady-almost incremental transformation in the public and private sectors domain.

All this is true. But we miss here the key factor of this transition which has been the engine and the key motivator of the mega-transformation of the industrially developed world. It lies in their concern and scientific understanding of future. Their systems were forced to work towards optimization and for high productivity. But they constantly also kept asking a simple question! What next? What next; What next? This query indeed paved the way to progress and the sophistication in technology in its diversified application to the various man-made systems, be it transportation, communication, housing, health, etc. The internalization of technological prowess came from the world of science and research: yesterday's science has become today's technology. It was not a one-time exercise. Every managerial subdivision, be it production or processing, placement or profit-making, every activity was subjected to and backed by scientific research which guaranteed results through ever new "product" development. To some extent consumerism too accelerated change. In many sectors the technology related Research Development and Design (RD&D) activities did become the bed-rock because of which India too became a conscious and active global partner in many fields. Much of this indeed happened during the two decades mentioned above. This is a period of momentous change *par excellence*. India's leap into information and atomic era; its success in agriculture, space and ocean research and micro-electronics are a case in point. Alas, a commitment to Research and future consciousness is not yet integral to many systems, institutions and thinking of all people of India.

In the context of the Industry management's and the public administrative system of India, our educational *status quo* still continued as the dominant negative element. Change, if any, is still sought through the colonial practice of setting up of Commissions and Committees. As we have seen in the past in the public domain, these Commission's learned views for reform emerge after months of deliberations. By the time the concerned authorities of the Government accepted or rejected recommendations received, it was too late in awakening, leading to inappropriate policy changes; since most systems and the socio-economic landscape, surrounding them do alter considerably. In the private sector domain, change still remains on an *ad hoc* decision making process caught as it exists between the governmental fiats and the market forces.

Even though these two decades were a time of transition, yet a recognition that humans should shape their individual future in whatever field they are was neither an accepted value nor a public policy. The decision making process laid more emphasis on precedent (past) rather than on consequence (future). The fact of socio-economic dependency and feudal culture did not provide any scope or space to individual creative thinking.

By exception, some practitioners of management accepted the fact that whenever we make decisions it is critically important to take the future into account. However, long range thinking was seldom integral to the planning process in the public domain. If for government a Five-Year Plan was the vehicle of change, the corporate sector did not think beyond the budgetary one year. For the Indian subsidiaries of the Multinationals, long range thinking was done by their Principals. On the whole, Indian managerial culture remained rigid, narrow, cautious, where loyalty was a higher value and concepts like creativity, idea generation, productivity, technology, forecasting, systems analysis were mere theoretical notions which, like R&D, were never thought of as major contributors to profit making. The captains of Indian industry and public administration could not quite emerge out of and remained caught with the colonial ethos.

Any suggestion that decisions made with adequate foresight is essential to guide us to go for tomorrow's technologies and to develop a vast range of new products did not quite impress the industry since, they were comfortable with the fact that everything sells. The official policy of license and controls had sealed for a long time the arrival of a certain future, although now many of these sleepy policy makers do pretend to usher in a different India into the 21st century. Nobody suggests that we should not deal with day to day problems; but does anyone prevent us from also looking ahead and preparing for future problems and opportunities in order to manage change.

Notwithstanding such a past looking management functioning in India, it is also in these very decades that system by system, a silent awakening arose that "future" too needs to be taken seriously, that we need to understand the significant trends in the emerging global, Hi-tech society and to study the implications as to where these trends may lead; also that this thinking constitutes the dominant lever of change and offers the right framework for good decision making; that it is important to gather foresight information and to think creatively about the future both professionally and personally in that if we could know where we are and whither we are tending. If we can have this professional glimpse in advance, we could better judge what to do and how to do it. Besides, when we move towards the new millennia, we do need to acquire a set of mental tools, to prefer and manage "change".

India is not an easy country. Its complexity needs to be understood with a great deal of sympathy to appreciate why well intentioned measures for "Change" do not yield quick and desired results. To appreciate this, we need to look, amongst others at five significant factors: (i) India is a large human system of over one billion people, (ii) India harbours abject and unending poverty, (iii) India's development in its internal geographical context is unhomogeneous, (iv) India lives at the same time in several centuries and thus displays a unique cultural plurality, and finally (v) India always displays a technological plurality too, unlike the developed countries where a new technology, by and large, displaces the old technology; it is not so in India. Its technologies encompass an alive array of bullock cart (a great contributor to its economy) to the ultimate current technological frontiers well established in the satellite era. The simple truth is that, even now only a few gifted Indians alone ask the question: what next? And seek an answer to it, system by system. There are millions of other Indians who do not want any change; who are quite happy and feel secure, as they are, where they are while seeking their ultimate solace in the question "What was Yesterday? They are doubly happy for they know its answer. Their past, is thus, also their future. This indeed is the true Indian dilemma, be it in politics, management or socio-economic change.

Future is change. Every page of this book advocates the paramount need to assess the 'need -spectrum' of Indians, be it for food, housing, transportation, rural or urban development or education, etc., now and what would it be in the next twenty odd years (it is only a 7000 days time span); and then how we can remould our existing delivery systems in terms of new technology, new management and new education.

One more word about transition: There are an accountable number of changes that are taking place whether they be in architecture, medicine or micro electronics. We cannot comprehensively catalogue all of them here. In fundamental terms, world over, five major transitions are influencing every man-made system, they are: (i) the world is moving from an oil based civilization to a non-oil based civilization; (ii) all systems are transiting, at a low or high speed from traditional management towards Hi-tech modern management; (iii) all societies are heading towards an information era and finally (iv) the character of knowledge has significantly got altered from a single subject — Linear mode to intersubject, inter-disciplinary, nonlinear, lateral, knowledge base. During early seventies there were only eight major recognized areas in Physics. Today there are over seventy recognized areas in Physics such as Astro-physics, Geo-physics, Bio-physics and so on. This is happening to the knowledge base in every subject.

Indian development of the preceding decades of transition in India thus needs to be seriously studied. We also need to collect the required foresight and wisdom to prepare ourselves in terms of bringing about technological, managerial or human resource development and educational fine tuning to cope with the growing spectrum of myriad needs of a billion plus Indian populace. In this book thus, a passionate plea is being made, through its select readings, to impress upon our policy makers and corporate world captains, not to discount future; instead, they should accommodate future needs, demands, supply obligation and pressure on our various serving systems in the current day decisions. A great deal of this book is thus concerned with Future-Scan and Anticipatory Management in explaining its alphabets, methodologies and paramount relevance for the socio-economic development of India as it enters the 21st century.

A few select readings included here had earlier appeared in two prestigious and internationally known quarterly journals published by the Indian Council of Management and Future (ICMF) namely *Indian Administrative and Management Review* and *Indian Review of Management and Future*. I was Editor-in-Chief for full twenty years (1970-90) encompassing the passage of this transition time duly recorded here. In this book's second volume appendices and select editorials have also been included to impart its contemporaneous flavour. And this information to date is most important documentation of the Futurology Movement in India.

Finally, this period of "Transition" has certainly thrown forth several issues concerning change: whose perception of change? which method of change and achievement; and, how to do it; in what time-frame (the corporate myopic, profit centered, time frame or the governmental inert system of *do not rock the boat;* laid back languid bureaucratic time-frame? We can multiply such pertinent questions.

It is my firm belief that different sections of this book, amongst other things, shall stimulate and help the readers to envision in an analytical mode to think creatively and to generate several innovative ideas concerning change management, system by system, to provide a billion Indians a certain quality of life. I further believe that thinking and dreaming has never harmed either an individual or a corporate entity or a nation. No matter what views one may hold, the 21st century shall belong only to a people of 'vision' and those who care for future.

Satish C. Seth

PART ONE

The Alphabets of Future

1

FUTURE AND ITS ALPHABETS

Satish C. Seth

The alphabets of future are indeed shrouded in deep mystery. Nevertheless, individuals have been colonizing the future in terms of their own imagery and personal preferences pertaining to a host of 'Private futures'. Even if it be so, it is common knowledge that most of our thinking process remains dominated by a certain linearity. The Linear thinking draws its justification from the 'past' as well as from our own individual set of experiences. We, thus, either as an individual entity or as a collectivity, seem to move with a 'self-conditioning' both of thoughts and actions. This 'linearity' provides an unconscious extension of the past into the future even on the societal level, since most social sanction acts and norms glorify the 'past' and justify the present to a point where linearity and conformity triumphs over non-linearity and non-conformism. Thus, as an ongoing social process, we tend to avoid change both in thinking and in action.

When any society is so set with non-linear thinking and action, it denies itself creative and innovative and experimental opportunities. It solidly stands for a pre-determined future to the point of doing all it can to prevent the emergence of yet another kind of future. Linearity in thought and action, offers people a false sense of security. They use it as a weapon to cope with the 'fear of change' and to 'avoid all uncertainty' that is so characteristic of future. Even though tomorrows do not repeat yesterdays, yet most people and most societies try not only to perpetuate yesterday's, but unconsciously, even carry them forward into their tomorrows. All thinking men and women should instead be asked if they are turning their tomorrows into yesterdays? If so, why?

The second level where the blossoming attributes of future get compromised is connected with 'System Preservation'. Man to protect himself, builds systems around needs and aspirations be it for defence or food needs or for education. All systems set certain boundary conditions. They thus ensure security, since they contribute to the status-quo. Within a system's confines we feel secure. So confined, we move towards future, little realising, that no system can ever remain static. It is in the nature of a 'System' to experience constant disequilibrium. But it is through 'Management' that we try to restore the equilibrium, only to find again that all systems suffer an on-going turbulence. In fact, it is this 'turbulence' which creates the inner dynamics in a given system. If we can understand this dynamics, we can turn a given system's turbulence to our advantage to build afresh another kind of future.

There is yet a third aspect. The individual with his linear thinking and action on the one hand, and 'Systems' with their boundary conditions and rigidity on the other, whether we like it or not, stand further enveloped by a highly dynamic socio-political, economic, cultural and national and global environment.

And, therefore, whether or not an individual changes or whether or not a given system redefines its boundaries, the external environment, today and in future, is changing and will change so fast enough, that no individual or system for sheer survival shall have little choice but to go to Non-Linearity of thought and action, think of acquiring bigger understanding of the 'Systems-dynamics.'

Once this is done, it is easy for us to understand the alphabets of future.

Can We Choose a Future?

If the alphabets of 'Future' have to be spelled out in terms of change, uncertainty, perceptions of time, System dynamics, Corporate Survival growth and 'Strategic Normative Envisionment', then the prime question, we can ask is: Can we choose a future? Before we can answer it by saying both yes and no, let us examine two additional factors.

The first is the varying perceptions of time. No inquiry into future can ignore the fact that people of different cultures have a perception of 'time', which has a specificity of its own. One culture may prefer to seek instant change, but this may not be a desirable value for some other culture. For example, professional mobility in America is considered as a sign of progress, whereas in Japan, mobility is looked as a negative quality.

The second aspect relates to our individual or cultural attitude towards change: If Future is change: what makes some individuals and societies covet change and some others fear it or even reject it?

Today we have a body of knowledge, which through inquiry, can enable us to forecast certain trends and happenings and non-happenings of certain events to a confidence level which may go up to 60-70 per cent of near accuracy. This is realistic as 30-40 per cent is that part of future which still may remain 'obscure' and 'fuzzy'.

The social turbulence and developments in the field of Science & Technology (S&T) and the intensity with which they are helping and hitting human societies on the planet earth, hardly leaves any choice to individuals, organizations and societies to understand the imperatives of changing future. We have to change whether we like it or not? But future as a process, to some extent, can be pre-determined, or at any rate be influenced to our liking. We, therefore, need to search those options, alternates and choices that can possibly influence and shape the coming events to ensure for us a living in a kind of 'future' that we prefer. This is what the entire planning process is all about.

In any case, the rest of our lives we have to live in the future. So should we not prefer to be concerned for it? Such a concern, therefore, further compels us to make use of all such details of inquiry and analysis which make us understand the System turbulence, inter-sectoral interactions to identify the growth options for the system, and in turn for our individual work, education, lifestyle, etc.

An allied question could be : How far into future should we look? The important aspect of this question is firstly that we look as far as we possibly can quantitatively and qualitatively assess it, and, secondly it better be a 'foresight' function, as far as possible free from the grip of the historical forces. And thus, 'future' for perspective planning purposes can be seen for the next 20-25 years time-frame. This is more so, because the historical forces once unleashed do not fade out in a lesser time-frame. And, therefore, we have to identify certain directions of change, free from the grip of the past. In seeking this new orientation to life and to synergistically live with change, one thing that is, therefore, absolutely clear is that we need to induct in our learning systems and processes, positive orientation and informal or formal 'study of-future' in our schools, colleges and Universities.

If we had a reasonable analytical ability to understand 'futures' and to probe into its mysteries, then we can exercise our options, alternates and choices. The real problems of change and future do not lie with 'technology' but with the 'value' systems. The technology - society interface and the value-spectrum provide a complication which is not easy to untangle. How to choose a future thus, for all the advocacy that we futurists and forecasters can command, still remains a difficult question. In the third world context, however, where societies have not yet quite conquered even the basic needs 'Survival' and search for a certain 'quality of life' ought to be the sole criteria to search 'our perspectives'.

Concluding Questions

For an inquiring mind and for an alert system, consideration for and about future do hold some serious connotations. We need to pose, illustratively and not exhaustively, some of the following questions :

1. Do we know our direction of change?
2. Do we have a preference for change?
3. Can we influence that change? If so, how?
4. In the case of organizations, the key question *inter alia* could be: Are we going towards self-destruction or growth? Are we relating ourselves to the internal and the external environmental forces?
5. Do individuals/organizations know what they will be doing or what should be their business after 20 years?
6. Do societies know what 'value-shifts' they are facing or are going to face in future?
7. Are people ready to absorb such future shocks?
8. Is our educational system a vehicle only to disseminate the stereotyped thinking of the last 5000 years? Or, does it care to prepare its 'pupils' at all levels for the long-range complexities of future? Do our educational programmes inspire students and scholars (i) to probe deep into future (ii) to understand the implications of technology and (iii) to learn how to consciously, through 'foresight and 'Anticipatory Management', redesign society?

9. Are we, as people, turning our tomorrows into yesterdays?
10. Does our organizational network promote non-linear thinking and non-conformism? Or, it resents change and creativity? (Where is creativity anyhow in the Indian educational system?)
11. Are we consciously or by neglect doing this today in our Teaching and Policy making whereby we are compromising the future of the coming generation (our children and grandchildren)?
12. Does our Technical or Social Science education help us to look critically at technology; to learn to:
    (a) Forecast it,
    (b) And through 'Technology Assessment, understand its long-range implications for Man, Nature and Society. (Who is doing impact studies and with what visibility?)
    (c) Do we have a mechanism whereby we gather information of the environmental turbulence and analyse it for a given system?
    (d) And, further analyse the 'Trends' to generate alternative futures scenarios for the benefit of the various systems.
    (e) What analytical tools, if any, do we use to understand future? (Application and use of Forecasting tools is different than the use of Committee Systems).

One can ask many questions. If we have to spend the rest of our lives in future; if tomorrows do not necessary repeat yesterdays and today; if we have the ability and knowledge to shape and influence future, to a very large extent both at the individual as well as at the social level, then, it is our professional duty to enquire and analyse the mankind's concerns of the future. Some of these concerns, *inter alia*, are primarily as follows:

(i) How to evolve a future oriented—a new and dynamic—educational policy?

(ii) How to introduce Anticipatory Management to usher innovative managerial excellence; and finally

(iii) How do we do all that needs to be done to usher in an understanding of what S&T can do for us, not as our master but as our aid, a tool and as an ally.

It is only through the study of the future, in its informal or formal mode that we can push the country towards the 21st century with some strength to usher in an era of a certain quality of life for millions of our countrymen. And regrettably, in India it still remains a neglected area looking for a "Policy" directive from powers that be.

India Towards 21st Century

It was a Policy statement from the very top which enthused and invigorated every sector, to take such steps which can fulfil the Indian Prime Minister's exhortation that each system in the country should speedily usher itself into the 21st century.

What does this really imply? The first thing that "India towards 21st Century" implies is that we should view "future" more seriously than we normally do as a tradition bound society.

After all, a majority of us will be living in the "future" and will be individually, collectively and as a nation achieving things in the "future".

The question, therefore, arises is: Do we know what kind of future we as individuals and as a social collectivity are seeking?

The second implication of the slogan "India towards 21st Century" is whether we have an individual or a corporate "view" of the future? If so, we better begin to prepare for it from today onwards.

Thus, all corporate entities, Public or Private, have an obligation to undertake a long-range perspective planning.

At the individual level it is a "call" for becoming an innovative and a creative person.

In terms of the managerial culture, it means that we need not constantly be backward looking. We need not wait for "events" to overtake us or to hit us while we are unprepared for the future "crisis" or the future "opportunity". In short, all systems from today onward should commit resources based on a long-range view of the future and their respective "direction of change".

The third important implication lies in developing

professional groups who know how to 'scan' and 'interpret' the likely future. They have to be trained to pay full time attention to "scan" the future.

Undoubtedly today, some such activities are being carried out by a dozen private and public organizations in India. But not all functionaries carry out or use the right forecasting methodologies and techniques. A long-range plan is not just an "Activity Calendar".

The first basic requirement of looking into the future is to broadbase and reorganize the Information and Data Base in a given organization—what we now call the Management Information System (MIS).

The second thing is that each organization should set-up an expert group consisting of persons who are well-versed in interpreting data, carrying out Trend analysis; who know how to apply statistical methods for a time frame. This group should also be well conversant with systems analysis, forecasting and programming. Such groups would constitute an Early Warning System (EWS).

The combination of MIS and EWS then ideally constitutes that professional unit, which can help an organization to draw perspective plans and to identify, sector by sector, the real building blocks on which each sector can intelligently, conscientiously, and, in the context of a preferred future, move towards the 21st Century.

In the governmental sector, what the planning process provides as the only vehicle of change is the Five Year Plan.

Apparently, when the Indian Prime Minister suggested that all systems should think in futuristic terms and should move speedily towards the 21st century, he was in no unmistakable terms demanding that the professional world of this country, sector by sector, should set-up :

(a) the future scanning groups; and
(b) draw up long-range perspective plans; and
(c) the Indian educational and training network should have educational courses to train and develop forecasting groups for the different organizations.

All this also implies that the current-day investments, be they for an Annual Plan or a Five Year Plan, should be made only after sufficient effort has been made towards environmental scanning, using Future scan techniques.

In other words, in the public administrative context, the options for the forthcoming Five Year Plans would have to be based on a "vision" and full awareness of the expectations of a given system's likely expansion and growth for the next 20 years, to encompass the time-frame of the Eighth, Ninth, Tenth or the Eleventh Five Year Plan. The Four Five Year Plans for the period 1988-2008 AD do constitute the major period of "transition". It is implied here that each plan should become the foundational building block for the succeeding plans to enable this nation to realize certain preferred future for India as it marches towards the 21st century.

Secondly, it also implies that considering that our national resources are finite in nature, we need to draw up the material balance statement, to examine our national requirements, to develop the infrastructure and to gear all systems to work to fulfil tomorrow's needs of a billion Indians who will be with us in less than 7000 days.

Finally, it need not be said that whatever else may be important for those who swear so much by "past" and "day-to-day" current obligations, no dynamic and alert system can survive without paying attention to the future. The message of the slogan "Towards 21st Century" clearly indicates a heavy leaning towards treating Future as a resource hereafter. Thus, all sectors have to work in a systematic and a planned manner and that the time has come for a massive effort to be launched in three spheres.

Firstly, in our schools and colleges, in our universities, we should introduce formal or non-formal education in Technology Forecasting, Technology Assessment and future-related studies understanding the "Social - Systems-dynamics".

Secondly, that all systems, as in many other countries, must draw their perspective plans for the next 20 years. The current choice for physical and fiscal outlays should emerge out of such a future-based analysis.

And, finally, systems which have become too rigid and inflexible must promote a great deal of experimentation and innovation to encourage creative efforts at the individual and the collective levels within the broad National guidelines.

A question, that still remains to be answered is, what indeed is the relevant norm for Creativity, Change and Future.

Creativity, Change and Future: Search of a Relevant Norm

Creativity

One of the missing elements in the Indian educational and the organized sector is the absence of "Creativity". It is understood that all education has within it, elements of creativity. It is equally believed that any industrial production is necessarily a reflection of the creative endeavour. However, both these opinions are totally erroneous. Creativity can be understood in many ways such as: to create is to make; it can be inspiration; innovation; improvization; colour pattern; awareness; sensitivity; beauty, truth, an arrangement; satisfaction or fulfilment; a bridge; horizon or approach to touch new heights; growth; development; quality not quantity; a composition; a combination (say of sounds, words, or colours); reorganization; design or redesign; softness; a beautiful manoeuvre; a tackle or a harmony; it is also personality development; it could be concentration; and experiment; learning; a brilliant execution; originality; analysis, reaction and response to environment; projection of the self; unburdening of one's soul; portrayal of visible and invisible; contemplation; a dream; a vision; a method; a system; unearthing or description of relationship of sub-systems in a system; a new approach; a new idea; a shining pattern; objectivity incarnate; subjectivity of a higher order; formal education; non-formal education; informal education; free expression; a right to differ; the total system; right to challenge; conformity expressed anew; non-conformity; a function and product of training; an interpretation, ability to evolve new modes; modules; methods; an aspect of a system; the learning process; a human ability; a change of attitude; an opportunity; reflection of continuous encouragement and above all, looking at "Future"—as a resource.

Like this, we can endlessly search social indicators which shall define creativity. Ultimately, however, I think creativity is a function and product of liberalized, innovative experiment finding, on the one hand, and on the other hand creativity, is a way of approximating future, since it is the hallmark of a change process and since it is the search of new ideas, new alternatives, which is what the concern for future indeed is: a large-scale "Idea Generation".

Change

Likewise turning to change one should first ask what is change? Is it something different. Is it a fulfilment; a goal; a target; a value; a norm; a state of flux; a movement; a method; a system; a mode or a mobility aggregation or disaggregation; a bundle of tears; security; insecurity, endless hell, a practice or a challenge; thesis, anti-thesis of synthesis order or disorder; progress; growth; development, or is it resistance and desire to be different; a decision; an all agreed solution or a democratic design of national a mamtesto, a document, an alternative one of many, or is it the shape of things to come in this sense. I believe, change is an essential part of the future.

What then is future? Future consists of uncertain events, some of these we would like to see happen, such as 100 per cent literacy; 100 per cent employment ; food for all, health and educational facilities for all and so on. Then the events we would not like to see happen, such as unemployment, disease, hunger, poverty, flood, famine, war, etc. To arrive creatively to a changed life, that is into the Future, it is necessary, perhaps, to prefer events that we desire to take place. We need to set norms and goals for this.

It is also necessary, that we try to understand the logic and imperatives of the Future for our society; in the light of which we shall have to evolve a criteria for creativity, change and progress.

In the Indian context, the implications of future arise from our paramount concern for the welfare of a large human system. (800 million plus or minus now and 1000 million plus or minus by the turn of the century). Besides, the second parameter to be taken into consideration is the fact of value plurality. Indian society simultaneously coexists in several centuries. In the same household, different people have different value frames, both in the horizontal and in the vertical sense. In India, we have to deal with multiple technology. Uneven growth of Indian society and the fact that India simultaneously also lives in the stage of agraria, industria and post-industria, we are compelled not to cut-off any technology from use. Here no technology goes into disuse, we are thus simultaneously in the bullock-cart age as well as in the jet or space age. Considering these factors, what then should be our criteria to judge creativity and change?

It is clear that creativity and change can be ushered in only through educational management and technological interventions. Apparently, therefore, the real norm to judge whether or not an activity justifies actions amounting to creativity and change shall depend on the consequences of future in as much as whether that action or activity firstly, promotes a society which is knowledge and information based and secondly, whether we can usher in a participative culture. And finally, an action is creative and is promoting change, if it serves the welfare not of a few but of many in our case several millions indeed.

Obviously, the crises that India faces today is basically an institutional crises where institutions are consciously obstructing creativity and change and which are primarily catering to the needs of a few-elitist or otherwise. And thus, essentially they have really become totally redundant to usher in better social futures.

If we wish to safeguard our future, it is high time that all those who are running the Government bureaucracy, education and industry and are thus concerned with creativity and change took a second look at their style and evolve appropriate work-methods upholding the new norm of promoting creativity and total change—if not a revolution. It might help us a bit from preventing India turning into a disaster area even before future arrives.

THE SPATIAL VIEW OF FUTURE AND ALLIED CONSIDERATIONS

Satish C. Seth

The concept of future as we have examined it so far, is a segment of the time-continuum of past, present and future. It has indeed *inter alia* a spatial characteristic. We can have a glimpse of it against a number of indices. For understanding the cognative futures the following five parameters should suffice:

These are :

(a) Perception of Change
(b) Threshold of Existence
(c) Command on Resources
(d) Number and Needs and
(e) Happiness Scale (See Annexure 1).

It is apparent that if we looked at the local, national and global situation, against the above paradigm, we shall come across a bewildering mosaic of perceptions, needs, aspirations, crises and opportunities.

If the key characteristic of future is change, then the second most important facet, at any given point of time, could be viewed in terms of instruments of change viz. (i) educational status (skills, concepts and learning systems for skills and rational thinking) (ii) technological status (Technique, how to do aids, artefacts, systems, tools, machines and automation, etc.) (iii) Management Status (Traditional, specialization, feudal, professionalism, skilled, trained manpower, electronic office, etc.)

Illustratively, if we looked closely, we shall find that in the spatial context the outlook towards future, stands predetermined by the "Existential mode" rather than by a "Normative-mode" preferred through a traditional and a deliberate choice function. In spatial terms, we can even say that 'Future' is partly something given by others, say from top to the grass roots and in the Indian context from the Centre to a Block.

Let us look at the spatial features in Tables 1.

TABLE - 1

OUTLOOK TOWARDS THE FUTURE: THE SPATIAL CONTEXT

	Local	*National*	*Global*
Education	Literacy 5-15 per cent Skills-Traditional based on knowledge of past experience on the familiar and known.	Literacy-40 per cent Skills-Both traditional and Modern Knowledge-A little more based on Science (Regional and analytical mould)	Rational-Scientific Mode dominates the world of Education with proliferation of INTER-DISCIPLINARITY (Advancing knowledge explosion).
Technology	Traditional Crafts predominant; Poverty coexists with excellence.	Technology Plurality Bullock-cart-to-space.	What Next: Culture Hi Tech. based on Technology Forecasting, Systems and Analytical Enquiring mode.
Management	Native Wisdom and Feudalistic Mobilization of Manpower for Agricultural Pursuits/ Crafts (exploitative mode) dominates.	Colonial Mould though acquiring new gloss here and there; Bureaucratic delays persists with dawn of computer culture.	Management modes dominated by Industrial and post Industrial society specialization and electronic computer dominated information-cybernatic culture.
Lifestyle	Nature-dominated; Run by Customs; Faith Folk-Tradition; Future opportunity Growth cell, sought more from the past. Flow of information is opening aspiration spectrum.	Urbanization Westernized living; Faith still dominates so does the hold of Tradition. Opportunity and growth cells lie in new technology— a new recent 20 years phenomenon.	Institutionalism Hi-Tech Rationalised systems; Here and there articulated with Fundamentalism and Social fragmentation; war psychosis, Nuclear Family Alternative Lifestyle.

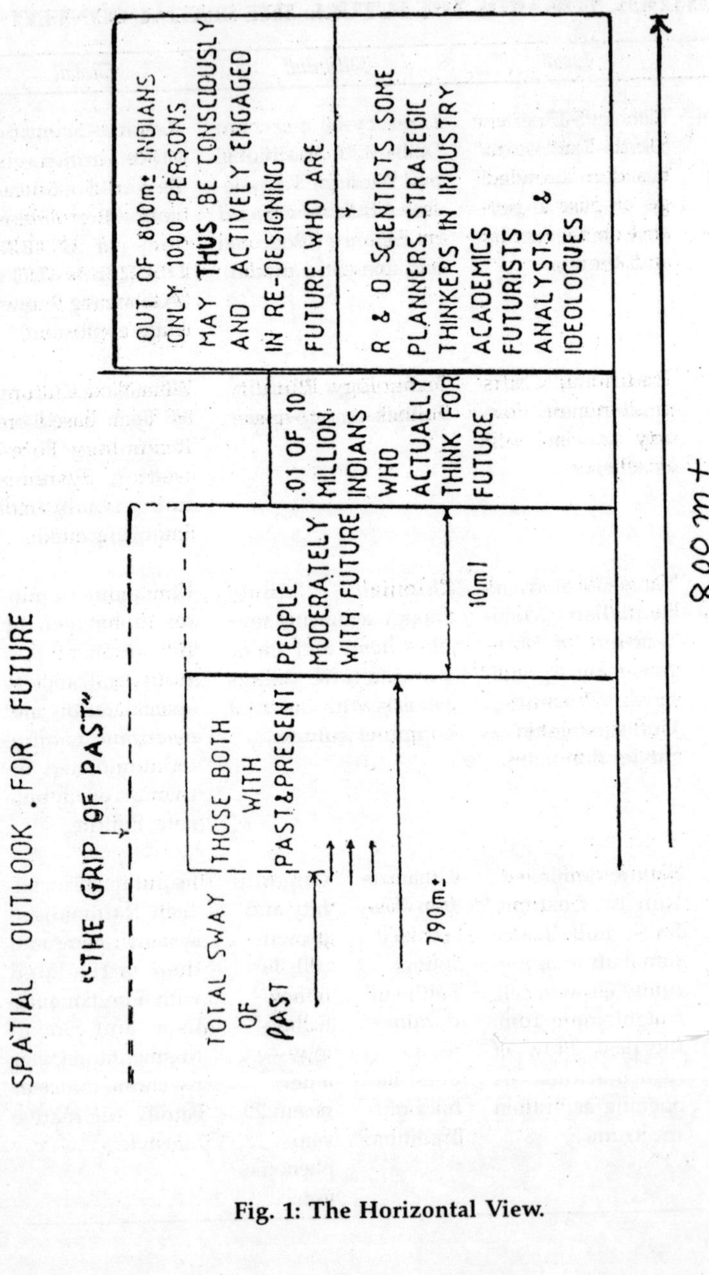

Fig. 1: The Horizontal View.

Table 1 *inter alia* does indicate the following few facts:

(i) Across the Indian societal horizon, out of a population of 800 million (–), the majority, about more than 600-790 millions, whether rural or urban, are still living a life where the grip of the past, in terms of their beliefs, social customs, culture and practices, economic activity, and living standards is still not much different form, let us say, what it was a few centuries ago. For them, the right direction towards the future is one wherein, they must in their own interest, carry the 'past' forward.

(ii) Secondly, the modernization and the advent of the S&T in the Indian society as it has helped its prime economic activity viz., Agriculture and Industry is relatively a recent phenomenon dating back only to a few decades. However, it does not yet possess an even spread. Hence, the incidence of technological plurality prevails; the bullock cart exists with the Jet and the Space age. Naturally, therefore, even though India is trying its best to force an entry into the Frontier areas of S&T, Future oriented perspective, hardly emerges with any well focussed clarity. Ours is indeed a very mixed up scene.

(iii) Finally, therefore, the spatial outlook towards the future does not pin-point to the Growth Cells for Societal re-design. On the other hand this kind of thinking as understood, in terms of the Indian planning and socio-economic development processes in the public administrative system even if it be considered a 'Future' related design work with an exception in only a few areas is something still being done more by a 'few' for the 'many'.

It can hardly be described as a long-range planning which is the product of intense systems analysis or arrived at through the use of techniques of Technology Forecasting and Technology Assessment.

If the spatial outlook implies what it is, clearly three important questions arise :

Q. What is the Percolation mode of Future Related Thinking in India- if any? (See Annexure 2).

Q. Is it (i) Science and Technology; (ii) Education; (iii) Information Networks; (iv) Travel; (v) Media; or (vi) Consumer Products; or (vii) Other factors? Which lie in the sphere of futuristic thinking?

Q. Should futuristic thinking be merely an elitist phenomenon?

Whatever be the answers to the above questions, the truth of the matter is the concerns of future to stand compromised because of the (a) dominant grip of the past (b) the fear of change and (c) the paucity of consciously introduced filter which can enable the percolation from (i) the top to base and of (ii) sensoring system which can gauge the "future-sensitivity and perceptions of change" from the base and (iii) A conscious instrumentality to use Future-scan and opt for Anticipatory Management.

Annexure 1

Envisioning Future: (Technology-Culture: Reactions-Interactions)

Indicators	*Developed Society (USA, USSR)*	*Developing Society (India and some others)*
1. Perceptions individual and societal mores, norms, values, belief, etc.	Change: A high cultural value both personal and societal (Hence favours experimentation innovation: Society committed to an external quest for something new).	Change: It is something that individuals and the society want to avoid; conformity, preservation are higher values: change arouses emotions of insecurity; even fear. Dominant cultural trait. Glorification of the past. Concern of future takes secondary place, if any.
	Education, management and technology are deemed as holding the key for fulfilment and continued enrichment of individual and societal goals, (promoting values such as, freedom, more choice to people, etc.)	Hold of traditions also dominates and effects societal attitude governing choice of technology.
	Notwithstanding social cost and consequences attributed to technology, is still deemed to	Key characteristic is the presence of an ambivalent attitude towards technology:

(Continued on next page)

(Annexure 1 Continued)

(1)	*(2)*	*(3)*
	have the capability to overcome unwanted consequences. Hence for these countries future lies with technological advancement.	so lack of clear-cut technology policy; (Hence its need and that of long-range planning). — lack of direction for the future not clearly visible. If, however, society could permit experimentation and the free development of an indigenous approach, a framework can then emerge to shape future (e.g. China).
2. Threshold Agraria Industria Post-Industria.	Dominant culture pattern corresponds to industria and post industria and not agraria. — Professionalism — Science and Technology orientation — Rejection of undesirable tradition — Mobility — Individualism State-cum-Social controls — Homogenity of lifestyles — Clear vision of Future.	Agraria value-frame dominates societal norms, mores, values — Strong rural-urban contrast — Steep socio-economic differences — Heterogeneous lifestyles — Immitation of Western mores — Industrial culture and allied value-frame-emerging in several pockets. — Blurred vision of future.
3. Resource uneven distribution and resource imbalance.	Control of resources governs cultural and technological options. (USA: 6 per cent of world's population consumes 42 per cent of world's resources). — The dominant resource is energy (oil, atomic). — It governs everything: industrial infrastructure lifestyle. — Society and people display a frontiers spirit. — Emphasis on knowledge and information network. — Grabbing of resource dominant motive. — Thus in these countries future lies in increased exploitation of space and ocean for more and more resources.	Inadequate exploitation of physical and human resources (Feeble economies see export-import picture). — Poor knowledge levels (see literacy figures). — Extreme poverty condition (getting worse overtime) — Ambivalent attitude towards technology have allowed down possibilities of a quantum jump into future. (Great need for an information and data base).

(Continued on next page)

(Annexure 1 Continued)

(1)	(2)	(3)
4. Numbers desires-life-style.	Societies characterized by small population. (Sweden 9 million people only). Low population growth rate (Some countries even have negative growth rate). — Certain quality and standard of life has been given to most people. — Welfare programmes, Unemployment benefit, social security system, etc. — What would constitute a 'desire' in a less developed country is in a developed society integral to the needs and welfare spectrum (Private car is a case in point). — High rate of literacy. — Commitment to preserve a certain lifestyle (Major setback comes from the energy angle : the oil crisis). Hence search for substitutes: Hence cultural dynamics geared to technological growth and concomitant future possibilities.	Large unmanageable societies, multi-religious, multi-ethnic human needs (India 800 million now, 1000 million in 2000 AD); (Calcutta : A (single) city of 9+ million people). — Low standard life. Large numbers dilute the quality of life. — Illiteracy: Social and cultural degradation visible. — Institutional network elitist welfare network not reaching masses. — Need of new delivery systems to reach welfare-packages to people. — Basic minimum needs for all not yet ensured. — Need for a better management to fulfil needs of a large human system. — A bleak future awaits those societies where structural changes in the society are not ensured. — Need for community participation. — Need for social mobilization to ensure a better future.
5. The Happiness Scale (Too difficult to codify)	Happiness lies in getting more and more goods for more and more people. — Achievement oriented societies. — Expolitive societies — Wasteful societies — Cultural erosion visible (Highest number of mental cases in USA & USSR; Highest rate of divorce too).	Happiness lies in reducing one's wants (A virtue little practised though. Also, this is not a value shared by everyone in the Indian society). — Steep inequalities. — Non-achieving societies (Indian: Concept of Maya: Purposelessness of life of all achievements etc.). — Management failures. Characterise these societies. — Overdependence on God.

(Continued on next page)

(Annexure 1 Continued)

(1)	(2)	(3)
	— High speed of technological development may ultimately lead to the emergence of State lead control over total human life, privacy, freedom may suffer. — Arms Race - A Negative feature. — Loss of individuality visible — Needs emphasis to eliminate. consumerism tone down lifestyle and equitable sharing of resources.	— People may have high survival value in spite of poverty; may be they are more contented than their Western counterparts yet they are non-recipient of the basic goods of welfare: health services, education, etc. Emphasis on sharing and community living offers a natural alternative to create a better future.
Conclusion	For better future: Need for social redesign.	For better future: Need for social redesign.

ANNEXURE 2

Note

In preparing future related scenarios we need Teams/Task forces of a minimum of five people. A documentation/information scientist; a statistician; a system/trend analyst; a forecaster and a computer programmer: they will constitute Management Information System-Early Warning System (MIS-EWS) Group. Every Indian Forecast exercise should relate itself to the Indian society.

The critical Indian Societal Features are as follows :

(i) Large Human System (1988 AD: 800 m - 2000 AD: 1 Billion)

(ii) Acute Poverty conditions

(iii) Uneven state of development (Agraria, Industria and Post - industria)

(iv) Value Plurality

(v) Technological Plurality

Importance of Technological Forecasting

What is the importance of technological forecasting? What it can do? Research has covered well what technological forecasting can do, and Bright, lists Nine useful purposes. (See J.R. Bright,

"Can We Forecast Technology?" Industrial Research, March, 1968. p. 56).

1. Assists in the planning of research programmes; the amount, direction, scientific skills needed, and so forth;
2. Guides engineering programmes towards the use of new technology and the adjustment to new technical demands.
3. Identifying areas where product improvement will be needed and revealing the need for new products.
4. Setting quantitative performance standards for new products, processes and materials.
5. Helping to establish the timing of new technology.
6. Assisting and identifying the economic potentials and impact of technological progress.
7. Guiding technological planning and its contribution to long-range planning.
8. Helping to identify major opportunities and threats in the technological environments.
9. Identifying possible political developments arising out of technological advances.

A, B, C OF FUTURE-SCAN AND ANTICIPATORY MANAGEMENT

Author

We all know that to manage is to do things in a better way. Over the years, man has found various new approaches to achieve this experience of work, of fulfilling targets, and attaining the organizational goals, have all provided several lessons which are usually kept in mind while making management decisions.

The interdisciplinary approach has also brought in numerous new inputs to distribute workload to devise new work methods and to measure the same, both quantitatively and in terms of the quality of performance. The disciplines of economics, psychology and sociology apart from the statistical and mathematical inputs, individually and in combination, have also provided in good measure, newer and yet newer tools and techniques of managing and evaluating work.

The body of knowledge of management theory and practice is indeed growing by leaps and bounds and even through its absorption, application and appreciation, down the line, in any given system is still questionable. The development in the field of management education, training and of skill formations yet remain an area for further research and demands ongoing teaching innovations.

Essentially, in business of management, the key concern is with the decision making process. After all, no matter what we manage, we are in doing so, constantly making judgements at the operational levels be it to set-up a mill or to learn how best to push a Hand-cart.

The corporate and the public policy judgements, however, do constitute a different kettle of fish. Different organizations have their individualistic stance, their own comprehension of change and the speed with which they move towards future. In short, they also display their own managerial culture, distinct but not necessarily superior to others. Such value judgements are usually extraneous to the system. Why should the management of Birlas and Tatas let themselves be judged by the norms of producing goods and generating wealth by the norms used by the Ford Motors or Du Pont or Imperial Chemical Industry. Be it as it may, the twin goals of all systems can be summed up in two terms: Survival and Growth. It is in the making or unmaking of these two principal goals that the relevance or irrelevance, the need or the lack of it, of new ways of doing and evaluating things, surfaces along with several question marks? And thus the questions of "good management" or "bad management" irrespective of passive or active shareholders loom-larger and attracts a "time" aspect.

It is further apparent that such days are gone by when an organization, a private company or a public undertaking could extol its past achievements and could gleefully sit on its oars. In a highly competitive world, no corporate or public agency can now afford to be self-complacent or afford to blissfully live in the 'past' unmindful of and·what "future" holds for it.

Today, the professional manager, as well as the Board members, have to learn to scan the social, economic, technological and even political environment around them. In fact, in order (i) to survive and (ii) to grow, they need to constantly ask the question: what next? An alert, dynamic and successful manager of a corporation or a public agency, is verily one who manages things, not merely with reference to the past, instead, who also looks ahead deep into the future. The study of future has since arrived as an important, powerful tool and an aid to management both in the corporate as well as in the development sector.

In the English speaking countries the interdisciplinary probe into future has been titled as Futurology, Futures Research, Futuristics, Futurism or Futures Studies. The French call it Futuribles. The Russians and the East European countries use the term 'Prognestics'.

The key question that managers have to ask themselves is whether or not they have the tools to scan and map out likely developments in their business, profession, technology, political developments and societal change. Do they know the direction of change for themselves and for their organization? More than that, do they also know why should they prefer a certain kind of

Future? And above all, do they know how to 'manage' that change, and realize, their preferred future.

During the years 1974-88, almost for over a full decade it had been my privilege, in India to interact with the Central and State Governments, the Universities, the IIT's, the Indian Institutes of Managements and the Indian Industry, both in the private and the public sector, besides interacting, as a short-term consultant, to a couple of UN agencies, to motivate professionals to learn to appreciate the importance of Futures Analysis and to learn how to scan future, and above all, to acquire a new consciousness, that good decision making is not a repetitive process of carrying forward the past decisions into the present and the future. Good management, indeed is one that lays equal emphasis on the 'precedence' (past) as well as on 'consequence' (future). A good manager is one who not merely reacts to 'event' but who also knows how to 'anticipate' and prefer them; shape them; and at least, influence the likely events and happenings.

In these interactions, what I discovered most, is an obvious but none the less extraordinary fact. Every manager and administrator acknowledged that thinking about 'future' is important. But whether an executive came from the public administrative system or the private sector, they also unanimously proclaimed that their key concern is with the 'urgent'. In our current management systems in India, thus the 'urgent' (today) invariably triumphs over what is 'important' (tomorrow).

A time has perhaps come when all administrative and industrial executives realized that the 'growth' and 'survival' is not possible without a thorough and scientific understanding of the likely future developments. They need to learn and practice more and more what I have termed the 'Anticipatory Managerial Culture'.

Most productive systems go into the 'Future' of a country influencing people's future; they need constantly to readjust themselves to the new challenges. Thus, Futurology or the study of Future is not an escape function. As with the Defence system, it seeks a managerial attitude of constant preparedness. A scientific probe into future and generation of long-term perspectives do help us to get ready to overcome the future crises as well as to grab the future 'opportunities' and, above all to accommodate future demands, through the current day's policy.

In this sense 'Future is today'. Any investment, any managerial decision, any choice of Technology made today does commit us to a certain kind of future, even if it be short-term, because most decisions made once are usually irreversible in character, at least, in the fiscal and the physical terms.

It is, therefore, strongly suggested that all managers, not merely planners, need to acquire a genuine concern and a new corporate attitude to think, analyse and 'anticipate' future. For this they need to have an internal group consisting of forecasters, programmers and Future Scanners. They can indeed scan the Environment in order to give important inputs to an organization's long-range corporate strategic plan. A bird's eye view of the important elements and allied aspects that are involved here has been provided as follows:

We Study Future because

(1) It helps us to prepare ourselves for it.

(2) We can and we should influence and control the times (future) we wish to live in.

(3) It gives the sheer joy of knowing the unknown.

(4) All our opportunities will come to us only in future.

(5) It is a tool for a planned, purposive and creative existence.

Certain Facts about Future

(1) Future is a stage in the flow of time.

(2) Future is where things shall happen.

(3) Future can be glimpsed through two kinds of events:
- — Events which we would like to see happen - A fulfilment (opportunity);
- — Events which we would not like to see happen - A crisis (threat).

(4) Past is gone. We can do nothing about it.

(5) We can act in the present. Take decisions:
- — Make judgements on or about things which may take place over a time - in future.

(6) We can, perhaps, influence future; even shape it; at least, we can prefer a future:

(a) for our society (social future),

(b) for ourselves (private futures).

(7) In sense "Future is Today". Whatever we do today has an impact on the Future.

(8) The study of future is thus a powerful Tool of Management.

(9) Do all Managers and Development Administrators know how to anticipate future? - Futurology enables them to do so.

(10) Futurology is the interdisciplinary body of knowledge and analytical tool which can help scan and map out Future.

(11) It is, thus, an important input to planning since it generates ideas and alternatives for decision makers by studying long-range future - as against short-range - the long-range possibilities.

March Towards Future is full of Breaks & Disconti nuities

FUTURE : THE CONCEPT

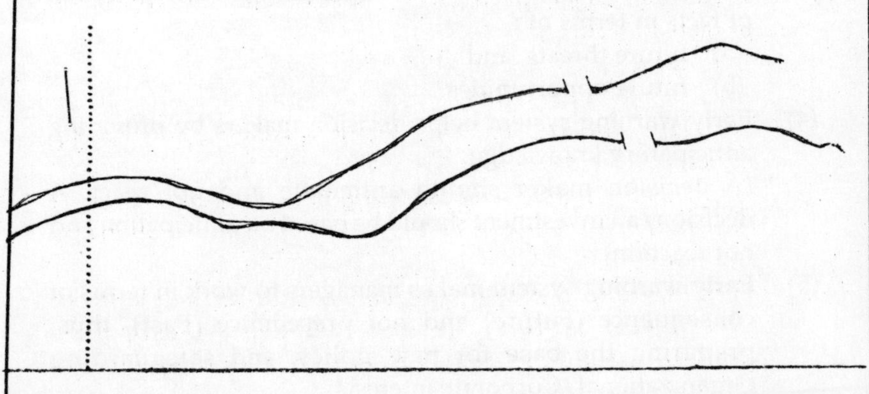

Other Characteristics of Future

(1) Future is change (Do we know our direction of change?).

(2) Tomorrow does not necessarily repeat today.

(3) We cannot in a linear fashion walk up to future. It is full of breaks and discontinuities. It is a state of uncertainty.

(4) There are no *a priori* future facts. Individuals can colonize future with their individualistic and private thoughts about future. (What we need to evolve is societal thinking?).

(5) Future oriented thinking can be of two types:
  (a) Deterministic
  (b) Normative

(6) In social terms concern of future is with the needs (as distinct with desire) of people of today and the needs of coming generation.

(7) Future is anticipatory imaginering and its management and realization.

Future Scanning Needs an Early Warning System

(1) Future oriented studies and anticipatory activities require sound information and data base.

(2) Anticipatory function is a highly skilled and analytical exercise.

(3) Early warning system records signals of future events. It needs both data and research besides detailed interpretation of facts in terms of :
  (a) future threats, and
  (b) future opportunities.

(4) Early warning system helps decision makers by providing anticipatory knowledge.
(A decision maker should anticipate and not react. A decision/an investment should be based on anticipation and not reaction).

(5) Early warning system makes managers to work in terms of consequence (Future) and not precedence (Past), thus, preparing the base for new policy, and safeguarding Organizational/Corporate interests.

EWS: Threat and Opportunity Inventory

(1) A futurist has to catalogue likely future threats and likely future opportunities.

(2) This requires, amongst other things rigorous Trend Analysis.

(3) The study of a trend calls for system analysis both of the internal and external sub-sets and socio-economic environment as well as of their interrelationships.

(4) EWS combined with systems analysis can help prepare threat/opportunity inventories.

(5) A policy maker can use such inventories to capitalise on:

(a) opportunities and to prepare the organization/system to cope with or eliminate the

(b) Crisis

(Future scan is, thus, an exercise in preparedness and not an escape function).

Future-Scan gives us Two kinds of Foresight—Extrapolative and Normative Futures

(1) Extrapolative Futures are deterministic in character. Here we assume that all the variables in a given development system will continue to change at the same rate and in the same direction over the years.

(2) In Normative approach it is emphasized that the future is not fixed; many things may occur and administrators and managers and policy makers should explore the various possibilities and then set a norm/goal — choose and prefer a future — and try to relive it.

The essence of Futurism lies in generating alternatives in preferring future even inventing them, if possible, emphasis is not on Forecasting but fulfilling and achieving future (anticipated and preferred).

Methodologies for Future Scanning

Note 1: No single technique of anticipation by itself is foolproof. It should be judiciously combined with others.

Note 2: There are more than 100 Forecasting Methodologies in use. Only a few illustrative anticipatory techniques are mentioned here.

1. *Brainstorming*:

It is an elementary approach wherein groups can be inspired to conjure images for future on any topic followed by discussion how to realise the same.

2. *Trend-Extrapolation*:

It involves plotting of historical values of a factor and extrapolation of past phenomena into the future.

3. *Delphi*:

   Assessment of future based on intuitive knowledge and judgement of a matter in hand through a confidential group field feedback process of experts geographically distantly located to determine consensus, if any. It is an improvement on the Committee system.

4. *Simulation Modelling*:

   It is based on the interaction between three concepts: Systems, mathematical modelling and simulation. It helps provide judgement on the validity of alternative course of action/ policies.

5. *Cross-Impact Analysis*:

   Here one assesses the expected impacts and probabilities of occurrence of individual events upon each other. One develops a matrix of possibilities. This technique helps in policy analysis / strategic planning, where alternative courses of action may be evaluated in the context of a complex, interacting environment.

6. *Scenario Building*:

   A scenario is a sequence of events. Scenarios are narrative and/or mathematical manifestations of a future state of affairs. It helps to grasp the vision of the future. There can be four kinds of scenarios:

   (i) Macro level (Societal and Global)
   (ii) Micro level (Organizational/Corporate)
   (iii) Forecasting Scenario (Description of probable future).
   (iv) Design scenario (Creative/normative image).

Types of scenarios (Illustrative listing)

(1) Business — As usual scenario
(2) Moderating enhanced (Energy or quality of life) scenario
(3) National — Socio-economic development scenario

Definitions of Futurology

Futurology encompasses applications of technology forecasting, social forecasting and technology assessment.

(1) *Technology Forecasting*: Its simple definition is elusive. Various researchers see different meanings at different levels of

planning. For example, E. Jantsch sees three planning levels and defines technological forecasting at each of these levels:

At policy planning level: technological forecasting is the clarification of scientific-technological elements determining the future boundary conditions for corporate (or generally, institutional) development.

At strategic planning level: technological forecasting is the recognition and comparative evaluation of alternative technological options or in other words, the preparation of the technological decision - agenda.

At operational or tactical planning level: technological forecasting is the probabilistic assessment of future technology transfer.

(2) *Social Forecasting*: realizes on techniques of social science research and use of social indicators.

(3) *Technology Assessment*: is a thorough and balanced analysis of all significant primary, secondary, indirect and delayed consequences or impacts, present and foreseen, of a technological innovation on society, the environment or the economy. (See E.B. Sheldon and W.B. Moore, Ed., *Indicators of Social Change*, Russel Sage Foundation, NY, 1968).

Other Forecasting Methodologies

There are several other techniques drawn from the disciplines of mathematics, statistics, operations research which should be used selectively according to the area under scrutiny. These are: Regression analysis, Time-series smoothing, Sales-force composite, use of Index numbers, Box-leaking approach, Econometric models, Input models, Simulation model, Life cycle analysis. There has been a further spurt in the development of a wide-range of other forecasting methods by the late 1970s which have been used by many scholars the world over. These are: Mean forecasts, Moving averages, Exponential smoothing, Naïve forecasts, Linear smooth, Adaptive filtering, Auto-regressive moving averages, Simple regression Life-cycle curves, Multiple regression, Multivariate auto-regressive moving averages, Decomposition, Census II, Foran, Delphi, Historical analogies, Morphological research, Relevance trees, Systems analysis, etc. Different organizations have to define for themselves the place and scope of forecasting function for their organizations. The important point is that, forecasting ought to be fitted into an organization and integrated with other activities. Since forecasting is not yet a career in the Indian private and public sectors, it lies on a periphery and is used very little if at all. It should also be realized that forecasting which provides quantitative data based on environmental scanning, both within and outside of the organization is not an end in itself. Spyros Makridkis and Steven C Wheel-wright in their paper on "Forecasting on Organization's Future" rightly observe: "the application of a specific method and the obtaining of a numerical output is only one step, albeit an important one in the process of forecasting: It is like trying to melt an iceberg by heating the tip: when forecasting accuracy is slightly improved, other managerial problems of implementation rise to the surface to prevent the full realization of forecasting's promise. To achieve systematic and substantial performance improvement, decision makers who rely on forecasts should have a broader understanding of forecasting and the factors essential to its execution."

Key Message of Future

Every corporate entity (Public or Private) and every decision maker (Political or managerial) must relate to the following: Indian societal realities

(Population in millions)

	*1988	2000 AD
	800 ±	1000 ±
A large human system		
Poverty condition		
Unhomogenous development	Agraria, industria and post-industria causes problems of change	
Value plurality		
Technological plurality	affects decisions for technology	

Global Threats and Opportunities Future Threats

1. Food shortages in various parts of the world.
2. High cost of energy : development of many resources : old and new.
3. Exploitation/transfer of mineral resources.
4. Environmental degradation and climatic changes (Ozone/CO_2).

5. International terrorism (Piracy at sea and in space).
6. Value crisis/social fragmentation/industrial unrest and youth unrest.
7. Nuclear war (Probability is one not zero).

Future Opportunities: Seven Technologies for 80's and 90's

(They will have greatest impact upon the man-on-the-street)

Productivity Improving Technologies

- Lasers
- Optics
- Robotics
- Micro-processors

Energy Technologies

- Solar photo voltaics
- Fuel cells
- Coal conversion — Electric power through combustion, gasification, liquefaction.
- Fusion

Five Transitions

First Transition	20 — to — Frozen to reserves (Coal, Oil, Gas)	30 years near depletion of stored energy	Time Frame non-oil alternatives and civilization
Second Transition	Tradition to—		Modernity, people technology, management, systems
Third Transition	Fruits of excellence: (From few) - (to many)		Rising expectations Elitist concepts yielding to egalitarianism
Fourth Transition	Limited information base		Exponential information explosion
Fifth Transition	Linear and conventional set boundary & mode		To non-linear interdisciplinary base of knowledge and creativity.

FUTURE SHOULD BE GLIMPSED THROUGH A SYSTEM VIEWING

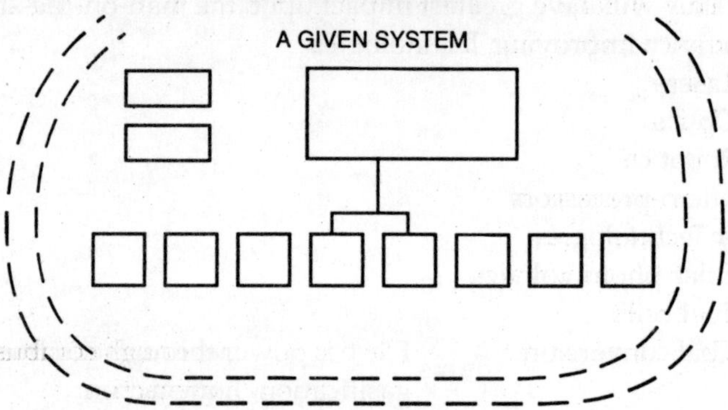

ASPECTS OF MANAGEMENT PERSPECTIVES IN SOCIAL FORSTRY (An Illustration)

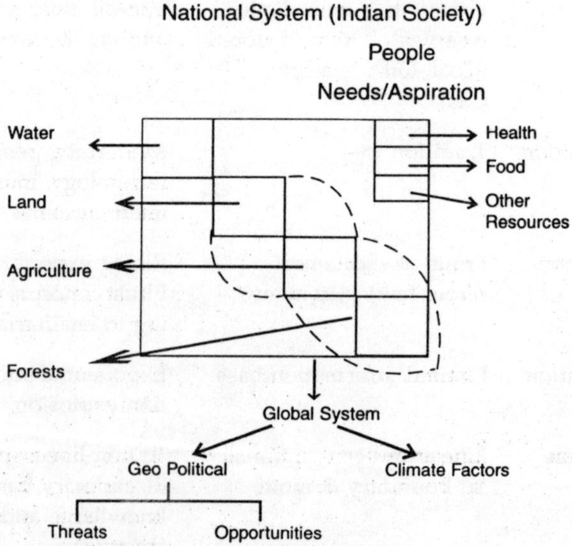

Attributes of Future

- Future is a state of uncertainty.
- Future is change.
- Consideration of future are assessment of tomorrow's needs and current decision to accommodate tomorrow.
- Future will not just happen with just wishes.
- Future requires decisions-now.
- Future imposes risk-now.
- Future requires action-now.
- Demands of allocation of resources, human resources-now.
- It requires work-now.
- In short future is :
  - — Whatever we do today influences future in a certain direction.
  - — Do we know our direction of change?
  - — All corporate entities have a date with future.
  - — Let us prefer a future.

Future Oriented Management

- Today's managements have no choice but to anticipate the future.
- We should attempt to mould it (we can).
- We should balance short-range and long-range goals.
- There are no divine guidelines in these matters.
- It is managerial challenge to confront uncertainty with reasonable certainty.
- We can generate several alternatives.
- Do we simply react to situation.

or

- We know how to anticipate?
- Futurology (the study of future) teaches us to become "anticipatory managers".
- And face future with greater confidence.
- Corporate management's image of future guides its actions and policies of the present.
- It is necessary to shape "this image" more reliably and systematically.
- This is made possible by futurology/futuristics.
- Future scanning/systems analysis.

- Futurism/futuribles/prognostics/forecasting.
- To achieve this we need MIS-EWS Units.

Is Our Decision Making Geared to Past or Future?

- Are our managers anticipatory planners?
- Are they consciously sloughing up yesterday?
- Do they ask following questions?
  - — Will our present commitment be relevant for tomorrow?
  - — Are we well prepared for tomorrows crisis and opportunities?
  - — Do we take decision based on precedence? (Past only).
  - — Do we take decisions in terms of consequence (Future)?
- What new and different things we have to do and when?
- How do we arrive at our goals?
- Scenario development helps clarify our goals.

Planning : Two Stage Process

1. Specification of goals.
2. Specification of plans.

Planning in simple terms means the assessment of:

- What must be done to achieve an aim/goal/objective/target.
- It is a process of devising methods/ways/schemes/programmes of doing a given task.

All plans have a time-frame and one can go for either:

- a short-range plan.

  or
- a long-range plan.
- it is advisable to evolve short-range plans out of a long-range futuristic consideration.
- this way a plan can accommodate future needs also.

- Planning through forecasting links up the internal controllable events to external uncontrollable events.

Long-Range Planning

- What is the characteristic of long-range planning?
- What is our business now?
- What should we do and what should our business be? As opposed to what is our business?

- What will it be?
- Long-range planning is not extension of present trends into future.
- It is not the defence of yesterday today's products, services, markets and technology need not be tomorrow's products, services, markets and technology.
- It gives us the glimpse of the unknown.

How Forecasting Helps

Futurology does not try to eliminate risk. It does help to identify likely future threats and likely future opportunities.

Does your organization or you have a threat inventory/an opportunity inventory?

Do you have facilities to forecast technologies relevant to your corporations?

- Is your R&D system responding to tomorrow's technologies?
- Do you have several blueprints for organizational redesign?
- What are your future strategies and structures?
- Or, are you turning your tomorrows into yesterdays?

What is Strategic Planning?

- It is the continuous process of making present entrepreneural (Risk taking) decisions.
- Systematically and with the greatest knowledge of their farsightedness: organising systematically the efforts needed to carry out these decisions; and measuring the results of these decisions against the expectations through organized systematic feedback.
- It is the organized performance of old task. The task will rarely get done unless organized. Above all, it will rarely become achievement unless done purposefully.

Aspect of Corporate Strategic Planning

- Every basic management decision is a long-range decision.
- Ten years is a rather short time span these days. Every major management decision takes years before it is really effective.

- It has to be productive for years thereafter to pay off investments of men and money.
- All managers, therefore, need to be skilled in making decisions with long futurity on a systematic basis.

Corporate Goal Setting

Goals: What is important? What is not important?

Question 1: Is our goal specification being
— done defensively?
— hastily?
— to reduce the psychological costs of genuine uncertainty?

Question 2: Is our goal specification
— a premature statement?
In the context of
(a) organization
(b) environment
What do scenario writers provide: scenarios: they clarify goals by providing
(a) Broad theories
(b) Concepts
(c) Information
(d) Provides foresight - provision and
(e) Breaks stereotyped thinking in the organization.

All About Scenario

Scenario Building: A Tool of Anticipatory Management

- Scenario is a sequence of events:
- An instrument of forecasting
- It helps us understand future
- It improves the planning and processing

Use Seth-Harva Scenario Development Technique

Step 1: Survey of the present state of art in.....
(Identify various indicators)

Step 2: Develop a trend scenario for 2006 AD.
(Deterministic scenario)

(i) Identify 2-3 crisis points; and
(ii) 2-3, points of fulfilment.

Step 3: Envisage the future Indian society as the group would like it to emerge in the 21st century.

Step 4: Now develop a preferred future in ... ... based on your picturization as given by you for Step 3.

Step 5: Based on your preferred future scenario (The Normative future) prepare an Action Plan (This will be Recommendations of this Workshop).

Uses of Scenario Writing

• An instrument forecasting	Alive to possibility not certainty.
• A rough mapping of the future (Gives us the feel of future events)	Can put an organization wise of the "risks" *vis a vis* the alternative chosen—so they help minimize "risks".
• An aid to strategic planning and decision making	Aid to future-scan will deal with complexities

Importance of Technological Forecasting

What is the importance of technological forecasting? What can it do? Research has covered well what technological forecasting can do, and Bright, lists ten useful purposes. (See J.R. Bright, "Can we Forecast Technology?" Industrial Research, March 1968, p. 56).

1. Assisting in the planning of research programs, the amount, direction, scientific skills needed, and so forth.
2. Guiding engineering programs toward the use of new technology and the adjustment to new technical demands.
3. Identifying areas where product improvement will be needed and revealing the need for new products.
4. Setting quantitative performance standards for new products, processes, and materials.
5. Helping to establish the timing of new technology.
6. Assisting and identifying the economic potentials and impact of technological progress.
7. Guiding technological planning and its contribution to long-range planning.

8. Helping to identify major opportunities and threats in technological environment.
9. Identifying the social impact of technological progress on employment, skills, educational needs, etc.
10. Identifying possible political developments arising out of technological advances.

How to Choose a Future

1. Choosing a future is the most difficult thing.
2. Whose perception of future should one take into account.
3. The answer lies in clear understanding of the following:
   (i) National Resources/Facts;
   (ii) National Goals/Values, or, Organizational;
   (iii) National Development Theory/Strategies.

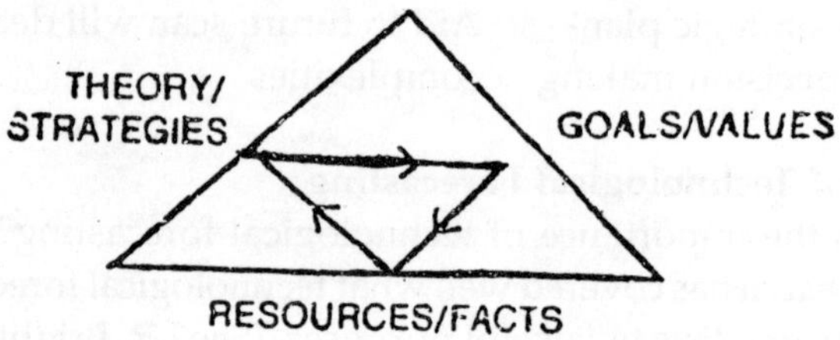

Corporate Message from Future

- Diversify or perish
- Managers should obtain fore-knowledge about:
  — Tomorrow's demands/needs.
  — Tomorrow's technologies
  — Tomorrow's resources
    * Human
    * Fiscal
    * Raw material
  — Tomorrow's organizational structures Identify today
- What they shall or should be doing during and after the next 7000 days.

Annexure 1

The Indian Societal Considerations: Threat and Opportunity Inventory

Indian Societal Features (Co-existence and Continuation into Future of Agraria, Industria and Post-Industria	*Early Warning Signals and Corporate Sector. Likely future threats and future opportunities/ possibilities. (It is only an illustrative and not an exhaustive 1 list).*	
	Future Threats	*Future Opportunities*
(1)	*(2)*	*(3)*
1. Large Human System (1988 AD : 800 m+ : 2000 AD : 1 billion)	1. Resource Depletion: Demand-Supply Imbalance. 2. System Overload and Sectoral Breakdown in commodity supply in services etc. 3. Erosion and Malfunctioning in the systems for both justice and the distributive justice. 4. Others : Not identified here.	Large India population is an asset provided we succeed to turn it into a resource: (1) Ample Manpower (2) Adequate internal market.
2. Acute Poverty conditions	1. Ethnic decay due to malnutrition. From 1985 onward beginning of slow and lingering death of 500 m people due to malnutri-tion in South East Asia- (Messorovich and Pestel Forecast). 2. Urban overload (1981 AD : 130m+) (2000 AD: 330m+) due to mass migration from rural to urban area. (Water, Housing, traffic breakdown and sharp decline in the quality of life in urban areas) 3. Others.	Increased S&T applications coupled with management and delivery systems can avert future crisis and can raise physical quality of life. (1) Augmentation of Internal R&D Base. Quantum-Jump. (2) Modernisation by taking to Tomorrow's Technology in

(Contd...)

(Annexure 1 Contd.)

(1)	(2)	(3)
3. Uneven state of development	1. Accentuation of Rural Urban divide leading to social-rift and tensions. 2. Environmental degradation (Forest depletion; Likelihood of the occurrence of Fuel famine and fuel riots in some parts of India: Acute paper crisis). 3. Others.	(1) Food and Water (2) Health (3) Agriculture (4) Industry (5) Communications.
4. Value Plurality	1. Crisis arising from awkward unhomogenous social change and lifestyle disparities. 2. Increased labour and youth unrest (Partly due to politicisation of labour and now of the student community). 3. Emergence of anti-social forces mainly due to traditional social malaise arising from caste, language, religion, sects and inadequate management know-how in administering a highly socially fragmented society. 4. Others.	
5. Technological Plurality	1. India enters 21st century with sophisticated technology in several areas but without a technological culture. (Also continued co-existence of Bullock-cart age with Space age). 2. Inadequate horizontal diffusion of Technology. 3. Increased failure of Maintenance system both in the private and the public sector. 4. Others.	Development of inter-sectoral linkages and setting up various socio-techno modules and national grids. Cybernetic development made possible.

Annexure 2

Future-related Quiz on developing futures scanning and idea industry: discussion points

Given below are a few illustrative questions which every Industrialist/Business Executive and a Corporate Policy Planner should ask and find suitable answers thereto:

Q. 1. What is the period for which you plan in your Company/Organization/Undertaking?

Q. 2. Why is it difficult for you to plan for the next 20 years?

Q. 3. Do you know what your company would be doing after 20 years?
- (i) Do you know your raw-material requirements after 20 years? Will they be available?
- (ii) Do you know your product line after 10 years-after 20 years?
- (iii) Do you know your Future markets? Where will they be?
  - (a) Domestic
  - (b) External

Q. 4. Have you ever tried to scan the national and international environment and the economic, political and societal angles, if not, why not?

Q. 5. In the context of your Company Organization's context, what Geo-political factors you think will affect your industry and corporate growth?

Q. 6. What are your perceptions of technology of today and tomorrow in the context of your enterprise?

Q. 7. Do you have any mechanism whereby you get information based on the scanning of technological development in the engineering sector and in the specific context of your own products?

Q. 8. Do you have an R&D unit? Do you believe in R&D at all? Can you intellectually relate R&D to profits?

Q. 9. Does the apex body in your industry sector offer you any early warning advice? If the answer is yes:
- (i) in what form and
- (ii) how many times in a year? Do you pay any attention to it?

Q. 10. Where do you draw your ideas from? Do you encourage your subordinates in your organizations to give new ideas?

Q. 11. Do you promote venture research? Would you allow some budgetary provision for your staff members to pursue exotic ideas which may have some future possibility. Where do you think your corporate opportunity lies? In the past or in the future?

Q. 12. What importance do you give to future? If any, or do you treat future as an irrelevant facet of time which is obscure, fuzzy and uncertain? What makes it so difficult for you to believe in future? After all you will spend rest of your individual and professional life only in future?

Q. 13. Do you have any preference for future?

(i) your self growth,

(ii) growth of your employees,

(iii) the growth of your company

(iv) the growth of the nation.

Q. 14. Have you set-up at the level of your undertaking a MIS-EWS System? Or, would you rather have your apex organization do this for its constituent units?

Q. 15. How keen are you to spend money for receiving ideas?

Q. 16. Are you satisfied with the corporate goals of your organization which were decided 10 years ago?

Q. 17. Where do your goals come from? Have you ever thought of the future corporate goals for your organization? If so, what are your new strategic policies to fulfil those goals?

Q. 18. Have you ever tried to introduce Anticipatory Managerial culture in your organizations, if no, why not?

Q. 19. Do you believe in Diversification? If not why? Can you think and diversify outside your current line (Do you indulge in non-linear thinking)?

Q. 20. Do you understand the meaning of the terms (i) Quantum-jump (ii) Technology Forecasting (iii) Systems Analysis (iv) Creative thinking and Creative Management and (v) Social obligation.

Q. 21. Discuss: "Future is Today".

RELEVANCE OF FUTURISTIC THINKING FOR SOCIO-ECONOMIC CHANGE

Satish C. Seth

Futurology/Futures Research and Systems Analysis/Futuribles or Futurism is primarily the study of the interplay between resource and demand. We are also concerned here with technological and social prognostics. When we are looking for new alternatives and options for the future of India, we have also to take into account the needs, the aspirations and the lifestyle that our people wish to have both in the rural as well as in the urban areas. Such an exercise, thus, eventually acquires a normative character since we have to provide a wholesome answer to the question: what kind of society are we going to create in the year 2000 AD?

The relevance of futuristic studies essentially lies in our deliberate attempt to look "beyond our nose" to study numerous known and unknown limits to growth, to establish systems which will help build a new society based on a philosophy of development which goes beyond the concept of "business as usual". Any single view or a combination of different views of future that we may foresee does, however, imply that action on them should commence now. In this sense, one can aptly say what shall happen in future starts today. Thus, a concern for prognostics is not entirely an utopian exercise. It is intimately tied to a nation's efforts for preparedness.

What is the Message of Future?

The message of future lies in offering a challenge to mankind to explore the character of uncertainty that characterizes it. Future consists of two kinds of events: Events one would like to see happen and events which we would like to see not happen. Thus, the additional challenge for us is to so plan the national life that we are able to realize the "futures" that we prefer. In so far as the global and national futures go, three things are certain. These are:

(1) Future of every nation in intimately linked and will directly correspond to its advancements in the field of science and technology. It is through science and technology alone that poverty can be eradicated; ill-health conquered and a quality of life ensured. Therefore, it will be an erroneous step to have an ambivalent attitude towards 'science and technology'.

(2) Secondly future lies with those individuals, organizations and nations which are heavily drawing upon information which promotes a knowledge-based society and which has trained manpower. Human resource on the one hand and a vast pool of information on the other, will definitely help any nation to meet the future with ease. Apparently, therefore, heavy investments in the field of data collection, information retrieval and information processing for current day decision making processes will go a long way to safeguard our future interest.

(3) The third message of future is that the future lies with the strong, be it an individual, an organization or a nation. Weakness has no place in the life of a society. The strength, however, does not indicate possession of an arsenal of armaments. The strength of a society emerges from its social resilience to change. If we have an adaptive and participative culture and, if we are an open society, we then definitely have a bright future.

Indian Societal Features

In the Indian context the implications of future arise from our paramount concern for the welfare of a large human system. (630 million plus or minus now and 960 million plus or minus by the turn of the century). Besides, the second parameter to be taken into consideration is the fact of value plurality. Indian society simultaneously coexists in several centuries. In the same household different people have different value frames: both in the horizontal and in the verticle sense. In India we have to deal with multiple technology. Uneven growth of Indian society and the fact that India simultaneously also lives in the state of agraria, industria and post-industria, we are compelled not to cut-off any technology from use. Here no technology goes into disuse; we are thus simultaneously in the bullock-cart age as well as in the jet or space age.

The Key-Question

The key question pertaining to India is: How does one change and open up a traditional society which has centuries old customs? And which is socially highly fragmented? One thus asks, Do we have, here in India, a theory of social change? If so, what is it? One also asks if we are "non-change-oriented" are we the masters of *status quo*? Is our administrative system designed for how not to change? And if it be so, then how does one open up this society? How does one reach millions of people with this message of change. Or, how does one inspire them to change, to look for new values and new designs for life? Besides, one would like to know how can this be done - through force? Or it be done through persuasion? What technological approach needs to be adopted to reach millions with the right message? One feels baffled when we have seen that both force and persuasion have met with a failure. Our efforts in the field of family planning and welfare being a case in point. What then is the third alternative?

India is a unique society in as much as the agraria, industria and the post-industria simultaneously coexist here and shall do so for centuries to come. However, our poverty, the paucity of resources, the population explosion do deny an equitable satisfaction of needs. On a per capita basis, we may not be able to satisfy human needs for a long time to come. And, therefore, one of the most important criteria for assessing any technology in the Indian context for the welfare of the millions of people of this country - compels us to opt for the 'technology' which satisfies the need of 'many' rather than a 'few'. Whereas factors like environmental degradation and other well-catalogued consequences of technology — now familiar enough — should be studied though Indian research in this area is still negligible. What is needed more is that Indian education, industry and Government should take a very long-range vision in choosing those technologies which can collapse time, bridge a gap of decades and be of use for larger sections of society. The welfare and service criteria should take precedence over the "scale" and sophistication that characterizes "technology".

In conclusion, firstly I must categorically reject toying with the romantic idea of a return to a pastoral living and a life of idyllic happiness. The times have changed. The logic of world history indicates the direction towards which we should be speedily moving now. India has once missed the 'Industrial Revolution. India cannot afford to miss the 'Technological Revolution'. We cannot turn away from technology. What we need today is to learn and institutionalize a system to decide how best we can manage our affairs for the 'maximum good of maximum number' ensuring the basic needs today and ushering a better future tomorrow.

Where does one start solving India's problems? It is almost like asking how does one eat an elephant. We may bite it anywhere and yet we can merely scratch it here and there. A total reorganization, if not a revolution, can release human energy to work for regional and local developmental programmes. This in itself is a great management task — a challenge both for the present and the future.

The Threat Inventory

There are many important threats that face us but five of these are significant indeed and deserve attention:

(1) *Biological Decay*

First, in terms of futuristic thinking, the future of our children stands heavily compromised and scientific evidence exists to suggest that the present state of nutrition available to the vulnerable section of society could, by the turn of the century, bring forth 60 per cent or more of India's population as that of mentally retarded people. It could usher a genetic loss.

(2) *The Energy Crisis*

Second is the energy crisis. It has to be seen both in terms of the escalation of the price of oil and the scarce availability of the middle distillates like kerosene and diesel: and secondly it has to be looked at in terms of the non-availability of the domestic fuel particularly for the vulnerable sections of society. This can cripple our industry and precipitate civil disorder.

(3) *Institutional Redundance*

The third crisis arises from the mis-match of 19th century institutions to the 21st century challenge. Many of our institutions today, which were good enough to serve the interest of a few seem redundant when it comes to place on them the demand and interests of many. With the present work style, these institutions cannot serve the interests of the millions of people. The educational institutions are a classic case in point. They serve for instance, only 30 per cent of our population. Such institutions have thus become stagnant and do not promote creativity and change. Their management style only support the 'process' and not the 'substance'. Most of them are anyhow elitist in character. These institutions, if not drastically overhauled, will fail to usher better social futures for India.

(4) *Non-Participative Culture*

India is still a non-participative culture and its organized sector feudalistic in character. Without people's participation, the effort made by the Government cannot today reach, with the fruits of welfare, to millions of our countrymen. People's participation takes many forms, it involves community action and joint participation of the people with the governmental programme. In the industrial sector it takes the shape of participative management and industrial democracy. This is an area which deserves an innovative look. Failure to serve people and to introduce participative element will cripple our administration and managerial efforts.

(5) *Crisis Arising from Short-term Planning and Lack of Anticipatory Management Culture*

Short-term planning leads to short-range decision and yields mainly short-range results. Resources once committed, investments once made — all these spring from decisions which are irreversible in character. And this commits us towards a future without providing for it. Our planning should accommodate future needs today. Thus, without taking recourse to long range-planning we would be steadily compromising our financial investments and fail to cope with the demands of future.

The Need of the Hour

It is apparent that we need to generate a massive awareness within the country to bring about futures consciousness. People on the one hand and the organized sector on the other, should think of all those areas where they can make a quantum leap into future.

We need to invent future in every walk of life.

Since time is against us, we cannot afford the luxury of slow march towards future.

Structural changes will have to be brought about and social systems introduced ensuring long-range investments in the basic need areas.

In our schools and colleges we shall have to create a new innovative and creative culture whereby our children and our youth acquire a vested interest in the future since they are going to be the beneficiaries of such an outlook.

Future rests on political goodwill and understanding and consensus. Ultimately, however, all decisions have a political character. It is high time that a political dialogue amongst all concerned, to evolve national consensus on policies and programmes is initiated in the interest of Indian society and its future.

DEMOCRACY, SOCIETAL TRANSFORMATIONS IN THE SYSTEMS AGE AND ADVANCED ECONOMIC SYSTEMS*

*Robley E. George***

Democracy is inevitable, in a scientific sense, according to Harvey Wheeler's *Democracy in a Revolutionary Era* (1970). "Democracy" Wheeler writes, "has always drawn its meaning from the stage of development at which it finds expression. For at each stage the form of despotism is different and so is the form of democracy. Accordingly, democracy's substantive ingredients change, and must change, from place to place with different stages of development, even though its inner logic remains the same. What is this abiding inner logic of democracy? There are three basic elements: scientific, organizational, and philosophic. Each one is irrefutable. Because of this, democracy will always be mankind's most valid political idea as well as the permanent reservoir from which its revolutionary impulses are drawn".

Democracy is technologically trivial, as was argued years ago by the undisputedly competent technologist, Simon Ramo (1970). Of course, numerous others before and after Ramo have also argued persuasively for new expressions of democracy. Evidently democracy is desirable and indeed desired by many.

These and other considerations suggest, among other things, that the democratization of society would provide a fertile area for futures and cybernetics research. For, while folklore abounds, there is not, unfortunately, much of what might properly be called scientific understanding of the properties and possibilities of democracy. An important portion of our understanding is typified by Dennis Muellers's excellent introduction to Social Choice theory entitled *Public Choice* (1979) and A.K. Sen's delightful *Collective Choice and Social Welfare* (1970).

---

* Presented at the 20th Anniversary meeting of the American Society for Cybernetics, October 1983.

** Centre for the Study of Democratic Societies POB 475 Manhattan Beach, CA 90266, USA.

"The deficiencies of democratic government viewed humanistically, are of three interacting types" according to Russel Ackoff's *Redesigning the Future: A System's Approach to Societal Problems* (1974). "First, the legislative (decision making) bodies are not sufficiently representative. Second, they do not address themselves to many critical issues and thus are less than perfectly responsive to the needs and desires of the governed. Finally, the quality of candidates for public office is frequently so low as to deprive the electorate of responsible and effective representation and meaningful choice".

A major deterrent to the more widespread employment of democracy is the present lack of a procedure by which each citizen of a society can individually indicate his particular preference for an amount of something in question, with the democratically determined amount unequivocally resulting. Accordingly, whole classes of societal questions cannot now be democratically resolved.

Yet the mathematical economists Duncan Black, in his classic *Theory of Committees and Elections* (1958), and later Kenneth Arrow with *Social Choice and Individual Values* (1963), have provided a theory which justifies use of a precise yet simple mathematical procedure to accomplish this — assuming the common "one participant, one-vote; majority rule" decision making process. The familiar result is that median value of the participants' preference distribution is the amount the democratic society as a whole is "for". This is because the median is the only value which could command a majority's favour in pair-wise voting with all other amounts. This result will be used later.

Let us next make a few simple yet sufficient observations concerning societal transformations in the Systems Age. We begin with the assumption that humanity is now indeed proceeding through a fundamental and profound transformation. Suffice it to say Willis Harman's *Incomplete Guide to the Future* (1976) is an articulate and interesting discussion of the matter.

Depending upon one's perspective, these profound societal transformations could, should or ultimately will enjoy societal sanctions. Likewise, these societal transformations could, should or ultimately will enjoy scientific sanctions. In as much as the transformation evidently does not respect university departmental boundaries, and is taking place in the Systems Age, it may be anticipated that systems science will necessarily play an important role in understanding and supporting the revolutionary transformation.

Writing of a new knowledge paradigm, Harman (1976) asserts that this renewed and invigorated science ".... would aim toward vastly different goals, namely to guide individuals and society in their efforts to discover new realms of experience and potentiality and to foster actively the growth and evolution of society and individuals. The priorities, methods, and the overall cultural role of such a science would be very different from today's. Instead of being an eager servant of industry and the military, the new science would actively assist society in formulating new dominant goals for the whole culture".

The necessity of a general systems viewpoint has been much discussed. Ackoff (1974) tells us that "the synthetic mode of thought when applied to systems problems, is called the systems approach. In this approach a problem is not solved by taking it apart but by viewing it as a part of a larger problem. This approach is based on the observation that when each part of a system performs as well as possible relative to the criteria applied to it, the system as a whole seldom performs as well as possible relative to the criteria applied to it". Again Ackoff emphasizes (1974) "the solution to a mess (a system of problems) can seldom be obtained by independently solving each of the problems of which it is composed".

Earlier, Ludwig von Bertalanffy, in *General Systems Theory* (1968) quite confidently put it this way. "Social science is the science of social systems. For this reason, it will have to use the approach of general systems science (emphasis in original)."

Finally, let us consider advanced economic systems to accompany, complement and facilitate desirable societal transformation. If, as Harman asserts (1976), "The whole system must change and nothing less than that will meet the challenges of our time ((emphasis in the original)" then clearly the economic systems of the world must change. It is time to stop learning and instead start knowing this.

Numerous others have also stated the need for alternative

and improved economic systems. Among these are the ten Nobelists including economists Gunnar Myrdal and Kenneth Arrow (1975), who issued a call for the scientific study of economic alternatives.

The late R. Buckminster Fuller, speaking at the first Integrity Day Conference (1983), so designated by California Governor George Deukmejian and Los Angeles Mayor, Thomas Bradley, observed that "since about 1970 it has been clear that the basic working assumption of all political economies, namely, that there isn't enough to go around for all humanity, was false. Both the savage and sophisticated struggle for the little this planet offered its people was no longer necessary and indeed was detrimental to realizing the potential well-being of all. Integrity includes publicly acknowledging this simple scientific and technological fact and working effectively to realize this already possible state of affairs."

For a variety of reasons, it is, therefore, appropriate and indeed necessary to examine the nature of advanced and improved economic systems. It is respectfully suggested that cyberneticists and systems thinkers can play a key role in the solution to this essential control problem.

In the "old" days, the process which involves appropriate use of various scientific principles, facts and theories to develop specific systems to accomplish specific goals subject to specific constraints, was called engineering.

In his pioneering work *Automation, Unemployment and the Distribution of Income*, Keith Roberts (1983) defines the subject. "Economic engineering is the discipline that is concerned with the design of model economic systems to meet specified requirements, and with the prediction and evaluation of the performance of such systems."

As Roberts (1983) puts it, "in addition to the existing disciplines of pure and applied economic science one should, therefore, recognize the new discipline of economic engineering, the task of it being to design and analyse, in detail, alternative model economies to meet appropriate specifications, and to put them forward as options for public discussion and political decision."

As an important example of economic engineering, Robert

(1963) discusses one possible model: "....a dual form of economy in which personal income is distributed by two separate routes:

1. a national dividend (ND), allocated uniformly to all adults... at a level that is sufficient to provide basic subsistence;
2. additional forms of income (wages, salaries, investment income, private pensions) that are subject to classical market forces."

Roberts examines the nature of such a system from the perspective of a set of Principles, for example, indefinite exponential growth is impossible, and Specifications, such as there is to be basic income for all with positive incentives to work. He describes some of the major benefits derived from ND. He compares and contrasts the ND scheme with the Negative Income Tax (NIT) proposals put forth by economics Nobelists Milton Friedman (1962) and Paul Samuelson (1970) and numerous others including Robert Theobald (1963; 1966; 1968), Daniel Moynihan (1973), Leonard Greene (1981) and Wil Albeda (1983).

Now, if we are serious about democracy, fundamental societal transformation, systems thinking and the need for advanced economic systems, we can easily arrive at an improved model. We conclude by briefly describing socioeconomic democracy, as a fundamentally democratic and just alternative economic system which appears to possess many desirable and somewhat unique features. The system has been described in more detail by this writer in, the paper "Socioeconomic Democracy and General Systems Research" presented at the Society for General Systems Research 1983 annual meeting.

Two primary concerns of the science of economics are the distributions of income and wealth in a society. The socioeconomic democracy (SeD) model is an economic system in which there is a guaranteed minimum income for all as well as a maximum allowable personal wealth limit, with both these bounds set democratically. By democratic is meant employing the simple yet mathematically correct procedure described by Black.

To the set of 7 Principles and 11 Specifications suggested by Roberts as a tentative basis for the design of improved economic systems, SeD includes the following important additions. First, it is fundamentally democratic. It is also fundamentally just, in the sense of John Rewls' Seminal Theory of Justice (1971). It further overcomes the two major acknowledged obstacles to the realization of all past guaranteed income of when and how should it be financed. Observe that if, for any reason, a particular participant in this democratic economic system were opposed to governmentally guaranteed income for all, that participant could vote to place the lower limit on guaranteed income at zero. Likewise, any participant who would be opposed to a finite bound on allowable personal wealth could vote to place that upper limit on allowable wealth at Infinity. Subsequent votes on these questions could, of course, change the magnitudes of these bounds.

It is noted that wide variations in societies, all of which would still be democratic, could be possible with SeD. Such a system could exist with or without a number of contemporary taxes and exist with varying amounts of private or central societal planning. Some societies might democratically decide to have a nonzero lower bound on guaranteed personal income yet no bound on allowable personal wealth, while others might democratically desire an upper bound on allowable personal wealth but reject a lower limit on guaranteed personal income. Yet again, a democratic society could adopt or reject both bounds. Quantitative differences in the magnitudes of the bounds would provide further variety.

Elsewhere, it has been shown that the SeD model has powerful desirable implications for a wide range of contemporary societal problems. Among others, it has favourable ramifications for all economies, industrialised or not, inflation, involuntary unemployment, involuntary employment, untamed technology and automation, pollution, crime, labour strife, women's and minority's liberation, bureaucracy, international conflict, contempt for, or disinterest in, present political processes and much more.

Summarizing, we have observed that new forms of democracy are inevitable, trivially implementable, and evidently desirable. Further there exists a simple yet mathematically correct procedure by which society can democratically decide "how much" of something it desires. As we all presumably agree, the profound societal transformations presently taking place could and should be assisted by systems science. The acknowledged need for alternative, improved and advanced economic systems has been discussed. The new discipline of economic engineering has been introduced. Finally, a particular advanced economic system model which is at once democratic, just and capable of simultaneously resolving a large number of serious contemporary societal problems has been described.

REFERENCES

1. Russell Ackoff, *Redesigning the Future: A Systems Approach to Social Problems* (New York: John Wiley and Sons, 1974).
2. Wil Albeda, *Social Progress for World Solidarity: Reflections on the Future of Full Employment* (Geneva: World Social Prospects Study Association, 1983).
3. Kenneth Arrow, *Social Choice and Individual Values* (New York: John Wiley and Sons, 2nd ed., 1963).
4. Duncan Black, *The Theory of Committees and Elections* (London: Cambridge University Press, 1958).
5. Milton Friedman, *Capitalism and Freedom* (Chicago: University of Chicago Press, 1962).
6. R. Buckminster Fuller, Integrity Day Conference (Los Angeles Convention Center, 26 February, 1983).
7. Robley George, "Socioeconomic Democracy and General Systems Research", in George Lasker's (ed), *The Relation Between Major World Problems and Systems Learning* (Seaside), (CA: Intersystems Publications, 1983).
8. Leonard Greene, *Free Enterprise Without Poverty* (New York: W.W. Norton, 1981).
9. Willis Harman, *An Incomplete Guide to the Future* (San Fransisco: San Fransisco Book Co., 1976).
10. Daniel Moynihan, *The Politics of a Guaranteed Income: The Nixon Administration and the Family Assistance Plan* (New York: Random House, 1973).
11. Dennis Muller, *Public Choice* (London: Cambridge University Press, 1979).
12. Gunnar Myrdal et al, *Nobel Laureates Call for Economic Alternatives* (New York: Democratic Socialist Organizing Committee Second National Convention, 24-26 January, 1975).
13. Simon Ramo, *Century of Mismatch* (New York: David McKay, 1970).
14. John Rawls, *A Theory of Justice* (Cambridge: Harvard University Press, 1971).

15. Keith Roberts, *Automation, Unemployment and the Distribution of Income* (Maastricht: European Centre for Work and Society, 1983).
16. Paul Samuelson, *Economics* (New York: McGraw-Hill Book Co, 8th ed., 1970).
17. Amartya Sen, *Collective Choice and Social Welfare* (Amsterdam: North-Holland, 1970).
18. Robert Theobald, *Free Men and Free Markets* (New York: Clarkson N. Potter, 1963), *The Guaranteed Income* (New York: Doubleday, 1966) and *Committed Spending* (New York: Doubleday, 1968).
19. Harvey Wheeler, *Democracy in a Revolutionary Era* (Santa Barbara: Centre for the Study of Democratic Institutions, 1970).

THE FUTURE OF EDUCATION: EDUCATIONAL FUTURES

*Pierre Bertaux**

The future of education is interesting in two different ways.

(i) first of all in itself,

(ii) but also from the point of view of future studies in general, their methods and the critique of these methods, especially concerning the use of models and the danger of extrapolation (the naive projection into the future of existing trends).

First question: how important is the future of education?

There is little agreement on this subject.

Some consider it most important. A report of the British Ministry of Education (1963) is entitled : "Half our Future". The report quotes Disraeli as saying: "On the education of the people of this country its future depends... Our pupils will eventually become half the citizens of this country, half the workers, half the mothers and fathers, half the consumers... Half the future is in their hands, we must see that it is in good hands." The British report concludes that everything has to be done to develop the school-system of Great Britain, whatever the cost may be.

But on the other hand many well-known specialists of future studies seem to give little or no consideration to the future of education.

Let us look at *The Year 2000, a Framework for Speculation on the Next Thirty-three Years* of Herman Kahn and Anthony Wiener. The word education occurs only twice:

Let us look at the second report of the Club of Rome (Mesarovic-Pestel). I have not been able to find one single mention to the subject. The word "education" seems to be totally absent.

Between these two extreme points of view we will probably all of us agree in saying: the future of education deserves something more than no consideration at all.

---

* The author is at the Institute D' Allemind, University of Paris 111 94, Avenue des Gresillons, 92-Asniers.

My second question : what sort of consideration?

We find here, once again, two completely opposite approaches to the subject.

The first is the traditional one. It is best represented by the recent report of the "Fondation europeenne de la culture" entitled "Creative Education" in the frame of the "Plan Europe 2000" (Brussels). Very roughly speaking, the idea is that what Europe needs is more schooling, better schooling; in other words, a development of the educational system (both quantitative and qualitative) to meet the educative needs and demands, which, we suppose, are growing.

The implication is that before the year 2000 more people will be engaged in teaching than in food-producing agriculture;

— by adding teachers and learners, half the European population will be in some way active in educational process.

I found most encouraging the title adopted recently by a group of young researchers: "Does education have a future ?" If you ask me, I would answer : No, education has no future, at least in the frame of the concepts actually conveyed by the word "education".

We are forgetting all the time that education means, not an aim. For an aim, the purpose, can be attained- and better attained- by other means than teaching and why not ? I have contemplated entitling these considerations briefly: "teaching vs. learning". You see the idea: more teaching and even better teaching, does not solve the problem. We have to consider the problem the other way round: from the learning end of the process.

I have quoted the words of my colleagues. Perhaps I may now say a few words from my own experience.

I am an educationalist myself, and so to say I was born in the teaching branch. My father was an educationalist, and so was my grandfather: he was one of the founders of the school-system of the French Republic at its beginnings a century ago. I do not agree, as far as France is concerned, with the assertion of Alvin Toffler saying that the modern school-system of mass education was "the ingenious machine constructed by industrialism to produce the kind of adults it needed". In our country, the aim was a different one; it was to educate citizens for a democratic community. Our whole teaching-system was at that aim designed to "make citizens". Be it right or wrong, this was our idea — for three generations.

I must confess that, without overlooking by any means this ideal of ours, I have now reached a stage of "agonizing reappraisal". I am not convinced that the teaching-system is able to attain this aim any more. We expect too much of it, overloading it and expecting from it something which the system is not able to carry out.

I am in the situation of a priest or a monk having lost his faith- certainly not lost his faith in God, but lost his belief, that the church as a human institution is on the right way. He asks himself if, for "Gods" sake, the church he serves has not to be thrown overboard. He is very tempted to say: yes, it has to be.

The first shock I experienced was connected with the development in the Third World (Africa, Indonesia). We had assumed, twenty years ago, that two ways were open to developing countries, and that we should help them if we could;

— one way was that of industrialization (I personally never shared that belief):
— the second way was that of education-massive education. In that I believed for some time, and I am ready to go on believing as far as the Third World is concerned.

But the hard fact we are facing now is that the development of the Third World passes neither through industrialization nor through education, but through militarization. The school of the people-at least in the Third World is the Army. Even if nobody dares to say so, it is a fact. A fact which a sociologist would easily explain, if he but cared or dared to.

The second shock I received was as a university professor. It came to me long before the troubles of 1968 in the French Universities.

To put it simply and plainly: I have made and encouraged, for many years and decades, every effort to teach better and better, especially in my own field: the teaching of foreign languages and foreign cultures. But I not only tried to teach, I tried to follow closely the results of teaching—my teaching and the teaching of my colleagues. As a fan of cybernetics, I tried to develop personally some sort of an information feedback on the outcome of our action: a sort of information badly needed in the educational system because of an obvious reason. As teachers, we have been so to say, the true believers of our time. Our mission was in a way a holy one, and we were sacred persons. If the results of our action proved poor, it was none of our fault, and we cared little. Our moral conscience was at ease in so far as we had done our best to teach. If some scruple entered our mind — which very often happened — we thought that perhaps the teaching we had given was not enough, or not good enough. We tried and tried again to improve the functioning of our Church, the sacred system of Education, by giving more teaching and better teaching.

The results appeared to be worse and worse. The more we were teaching, the less they were learning. Can you explain that?

Is there perhaps some sort of link between the two terms?

I happened to read an old book by Freud, now fifty years old, called *The Future of an Illusion* By "illusion" he meant religion. But already at that time he explicitly said that there were other illusions of that kind, without mentioning explicitly what he was alluding to.

It seemed to me that one of these other illusions, our own one, was what I would call the pedagogical illusion, i.e. the illusion that the school-system is the whole of the educational system, and that by developing and improving the school-system we will be automatically progressing towards better education.

This illusion seemed to me to be linked now with the technological illusion, i.e. the illusion that technological devices will solve our problems (I especially appreciated the conclusion of the above-quoted Philips-report saying that "We should not cherish false hope with regard to technical solutions".)

John Galtung once said: "Education is like the part of the iceberg that shows; a much greater part is less visible".

The educational institution is the visible part of the iceberg, and by far the smaller part to it. But even of that visible part we mostly take into consideration only one side, that of teaching. In fact, more than half of what a child learns at school is the effect not of the teaching he receives, but of the learning effect of playmates and of the peergroup.

Then there is the part of the iceberg that is under water; what is called socialization. This part of education we receive:

(1) from the family: father and mother, brothers and sisters;
(2) from the peergroup, the playmates in school and out of school;
(3) from sexual relations one's sexual partners;
(4) from newsmedia, advertising, entertainment, especially TV;
(5) from travelling abroad and participating in other ways of life.

All these aspects of the socialization-process pour now on young people a quantity, a mass a flood of information that can, in no way be compared with any former situation throughout the history of mankind. The problem of young people now is not to acquire information (as it was at a time when information was scarce, a costly "good" in itself, now information is everywhere in the environment, in the very latest costly and most penetrating forms) but to protect themselves against the excess of information, i.e. to reduce the information affluence of the social environment.

The teaching-system is now placed in a competitive situation with regard to the socializing part of education; and the teaching-institution is definitely losing the competition. School-children in France already spend more time looking at the TV than sitting in school and TV is much more entertaining, more convincing.

The result is that pupils leave school mostly ignorant of the things that have been taught to them—though not ignorant on the whole because they know a lot of other things, perhaps more than any teacher ever dreamed of.

The tendency of the school-system is to compensate its inefficiency with more teaching. Did a physician ever try to cure a sick stomach by stuffing it with more food? This describes exactly what our school-system is trying to do. Hence the failure.

I will not attempt to say what should be done. I don't know. What I know is that what we will be doing, if we go on in this way, is wrong. What I would like to submit for discussion is the following:

1. Education — as far as we mean by that word the schooling system, the pedagogic institution—has little or no future as such. As it is now, the costs are soaring, the returns diminishing (there seems to be, matters of education as well in matters of industry, a law of diminishing returns). The wastage is enormous—a fantastic wastage of money, of time, of efforts, a wastage that cannot be afforded very long.
2. The role of teaching pedagogics has to be taken over by some sort of "learning pedagogics". The question is: how to convert a teaching process in a learning process? We know very little about learning process.
3. No educational system can work if it does not take into account the rest of the educating process as a whole, i.e. socialization, as it is now. But what do we know about it?
4. It is for me quite clear that, as the last decades have been marked by the sexual liberation initiated by Freud, the decades to come will be marked by the acknowledgement of the play instinct and the taking into account, in every model of future societies, of the 'homo ludens', who will develop fully in the leisured society into which we are entering by the backdoor.

SOCIETAL ASPECTS OF FUTURE SCANNING FOR LONG TERM EDUCATIONAL POLICIES AND PLANNING

*Satish C. Seth**

Over the years long-term planning has acquired tremendous global importance and acceptance both by various Governments and in the Institutes of Advanced Learning in different fields and sectors, such as, agriculture, industry, health, education, etc. Even though the concern for the future of societies and the questions of societal redesign are not yet part of an average man's thinking, yet questions of future, in terms of future needs and demands, have become integral to a variety of building blocks, not merely that of a demographer, but also of the planners and policy makers. Today, there are more than 50 countries and almost over a thousand organizations world-over which are working in the field of futures research. Several agencies of the United Nations, such as, UNITAR, UNESCO, WHO and FAO are actively engaged scientifically looking at the future of mankind in their respective areas of concern. Thus, futurology/futures research/futures analysis/future scanning is today a well-established and organized academic activity both for the teaching and for the research in order to provide numerous alternatives for the long-term planning and policy making.

Here, therefore, we find two trends: First constitutes a bald fact that very few people are interested or care for future. They consider future as something which is illusive in more than one sense. In the second trend we find that there are people who are strongly of the belief that 'in our life if we can exercise any control whatsoever, it can only be in trying to shape and hopefully influence things that lie ahead in the future. Such people now treat future as an object of deepening concern. As the speed and complexity of modern life abound, it is now universally realized that the potential grows both for disaster as well as for advancement. Mature societies further recognize that catastrophy and opportunity have to be foreseen if we are to survive well. We must gain, it is argued, the clearest conception of what does—and can—lie ahead in time. Using newly-developed forecasting techniques futurist's work to improve anticipation. A fuller comprehension of things to come leading to better plans and more appropriate action, is the primary aim of futures research. Scholars are continuously trying to improve upon the methodologies and approaches whereby the techniques of exploring the future can lead to a comprehensive understanding of the forces that govern or shall shape transition from today to tomorrow. They are vitally alive to the need to discover an integrated view of the future and a repertoire of ways for confronting it.

Notwithstanding the above two contrary views, an important question is: How does one scan or map out at least some, if not all, features of uncertainty that characterizes future? The search for long-range option is usually approached in two ways. Firstly, we can make a quantitative projection extrapolating the known trends over a given range of time. This will give us the idea of future possibilities in the context of what is possible, if the present trends continue as they are, without any special intervention either in the 'concept' or in the 'practice'. This approach predominantly happens to be quantitative in character.

The second approach is the normative approach where we can think of a 'perspective' or a 'vision' or a 'preferred future' in a given sector. In such a normative approach the long-range planning, exercise is cast in a creative and innovative mould, where there is a conscious attempt to invent or seek a certain preferred future, through conscious interventions and discontinuities, deliberately engineered to achieve certain predetermined goals of the future.

The long-range considerations in any sector require a clear provision or statement of the direction in which a society, a people or a region wishes to move. Thus, in any exercise of future scanning, the societal goals of the future play a very important role. Here one needs to possess a sensitive instrument, be it people or a people's assembly, to scan future or act as an Early Warning Signal mechanism to acquaint us, in howsoever, feeble or strong terms, of the likely Threats and opportunities that await us in the future. After all, future is nothing but simply two kinds of events. Events we would like to avoid, like war, famine, unemployment or illiteracy; or, events we would like, to see happen, over a time, such as, 100 per cent literacy, 100 per cent employment or `peace' and freedom from want and hunger for all people of every society, etc.

The Societal Aspects

However, each society does need someone to define the long-term objectives which can spell out the kind of society one wants to see emerge after 20-25 years.

— Should it be a knowledge-based society?
— An information-based society.
— A democratic society with participative culture.
— Society with a citizenry which is both able and willing to deal with complex long-range kinds of issues.
— A society which preserves its national heritage.
— A society where creativity, innovation and experimentation is encouraged and honoured.
— A forward looking society.
— A change-oriented society.
— A society imbued with a culture which is not reactive but is anticipatory and proactive.

The Educational Aspect

Having determined and taken into account the societal considerations we have to go to instrumentalities and interventions. Education is one of them. Before we embark in identifying long-term goals, we have to ask what are the key objectives of education?

— Is education for knowledge and skills?
— Or, is it for employment?
— Or, is it for societal transformation?
— Are educational goals and development goals congruent? Is it so today? Should education be past and present bound?
— Or, a key to prepare one for the future—for change—for adaptavity.

What is the Message of Future?

Once the broad objectives of education are clear, it is easy to set long-range goals and targets. Here, however, it is important to understand the message of future so that the long-range goals and targets are realistic on the one hand and sufficiently creative and innovative and futuristic on the other.

What is the message of future?

- — Future matters socially, politically and educationally.
- — Future is where things can happen.
- — Future is change.
- — Future is concern for needs of coming generation.
- — Future is search of new ideas.
- — Future, even though it is a state of uncertainty, embraces both crisis and opportunities.

The next question we need to answer is how does one co-relate education, society and future?

- — Future indicates that social reality is that today life is changing too fast than was the case in the past.
- — It indicates that most societies, in their own context, are going to be a large human system.
- — It indicates that present day educational system is too *status quo* oriented. It is based on the 19th century wisdom.
- — It is ill-equipped to prepare children for the challenges of 21st century.
- — The message of education is that it establishes the image both of the social reality and also establishes the image of the future.
- — Both education and the concept of future are powerful organisational concepts for change.
- — The gap between the social reality of today and tomorrow can be bridged up by a future-oriented education which requires three things:
    - (a) Change curricula;
    - (b) Change the internal structure of educational institutes, and
    - (c) Link education to external community/ environment.

What is required, therefore, is that since future oriented education is key to adaptivity and since education cannot be divorced from the aspirations, needs and motivations of the learner, since they have to develop abilities to live, cope with and grow towards a high changed society. We should:

(i) reassess societal values (society is the end and the ultimate thing—education is only a means and intervention).

(ii) restore to educational system its rightful place in order to overcome the gradual loss of its legitimacy.

(iii) Search:
- (a) New educational structures;
- (b) New educational methodologies;
- (c) New Modes of organisation of knowledge.

(iv) In order to serve society better the educational policy be such as to serve the four clients of education:
- (a) The individual students;
- (b) The society as a whole;
- (c) The institution of education; and
- (d) Individuals, teachers, educators, administrators, planners, technologists, policy makers, etc.

Educational overhaul in the context of long-range planning, therefore, will have to satisfy its client and accommodate the challenges of the future.

— The key question is: Is our educational system merely providing an education for unreality? Is it un-responsive to individual ends? Is it repressive of innovative initiative?

— What would then constitute education for reality?

Thus, its goals and practices need to be examined.

The major question is not whether the educational system will survive, but rather what its character is to be whether it will further increase social alination or diminish it, whether it will continue to foster unreality or prepare people of the real world for the 21st century?

The Use of Anticipatory Techniques

Finally, we come to various anticipatory techniques and methodologies that we shall have to use to scan the future prior to providing future oriented inputs towards educational change in the context of long-range planning. These techniques are drawn from both social sciences as well as hard sciences. It involves not merely the generation of several ideas but also identifying the need element in the long-range context. Professional groups can use Brain-storming sessions, adopt Delphi methods, undertake quantitative trend analysis, indulge in Scenario building exercises, simulate models in addition to the use of cross impact analysis, Relevance tree-technique, Morphological analysis and the use of various statistical and other methodologies, integral to technology forecasting. The use of "Seth-Harva" Method for scenario building exercise leading to the development of policy options is also recommended. (See Annexure 1).

The key point that should be remembered here is that in any attempt of future scanning to delineate long-term educational policies, the identification of a social paradigm or a social criteria in order to fully understand and decode the early warning signals in terms of threats and opportunities is a prerequisite of Future Scanning. This has to be society specific and culture specific.

As an illustration, in the context of Third World societies, the key societal factors that shall constitute such a paradigm, in the context of Future, will *inter alia* include: (a) Emergence of a large human system; (b) Acute poverty conditions; (c) Uneven state of development; (d) Value Plurality; and (e) Technological Plurality.

To sum up, Future Scanning, even though it is an exercise to unravel the nature, of a state of 'uncertainty' can, through the use of Social Indicators, Tools and Techniques of Technology Forecasting and Social Forecasting and making use of Technology Assessment (understanding the First order, Second order and Third order long-range impact and consequences of Technology on Man, Nature and Society) help us identify several of its features in terms of Future crisis and Future opportunities. Having done some such mapping, we can then 'prefer' or 'invent' a certain future of our choice. Normative approach to build anew a society and its institutions, in a long-range context, is the ideal first step. It is the prerequisite to search new policies and plans for a satisfactory, long-range future in education.

ANNEXURE 1

INDIAN SOCIETAL FEATURES AND SCANNING OF FUTURE IN THE CONTEXT OF THE EDUCATIONAL SYSTEM

Indian Societal Features (Co-existence and Continuation into future of Agraria, Industria and Post-Industria	*Early Warning Signals Likely Future Threats (it is not an exhaustive list)*	*Signals of Future Opportunities/Possibilities (an illustrative list only)*	*Policy Implications for Educational System*
(1)	*(2)*	*(3)*	*(4)*
1. Large Human System (1981 AD: 680m +: 2000 AD: 1 Billion). **Illustration**: The implications for education of a large human system can be understood with reference to one illustration, namely, that of educational needs of children between the age group 6-14. We have a Directive Principle of State Policy to give universal compulsory free education to the children between this age group. According to an estimate for the Union Ministry	1. Resource depletion: Demand-Supply imbalance. 2. System overload and Sectoral Breakdown in supply and services. 3. Total disenchantment with educational programmes at all levels; Rejection of the educational system by the youth; collapse of teacher's authority.	The large Indian population can be made an asset and a resource provided we know how to turn it into a resource. We need to search new modes of turning the Indian population into an asset and a resource.	1. Need for preparing a long-range and perspective planning. Long-range Educational Development Plans can not be mere trend extrapolation of the past. We should prefer and invent futures. 2. Need for a highly alert educational and learning information management system. 3. Need to develop administrative systems for handling problems of educating large population.

(Continued till Page No. 80)

(1)	(2)	(3)	(4)
of Social Welfare there will be 120 m ± children during the year 1982-83 in the age group 6-14. By the turn of the century we will have 145 m ± children in this age group. If we follow the traditional educational technology to cope with these children's educational needs we need to open a school every tenth minute for 250 pupils and keep on going so round the clock for the next 20 years employing today 1 per cent of India's population, i.e. 6¼ m± primary school teachers.			(see the contrast: Sweden: A big country population 9 m. people; Calcutta : A city: Population 9 m. people.
Discussion Points: *(Illustrative, not exhaustive)* (1) Do we have enough resources both physical (school buildings), financial (funds), academic (trained teachers) and other resources (text-books, teaching material) to	**Discussion Points:** Q. 1. Are the threats real? Q. 2. Does the Indian Educational System have an Early Warning System? Q. 3. How does the Future oriented	**Discussion Points:** Q. What are the chances of a hardware and software combination for learning supported by ground force (teachers and teaching equipment) as an	**Discussion Points:** 1. Who is doing creative innovative thinking for educational change in India? 2. Are innovative educational experiments permitted today? If so, where?

cope with the requirements of the traditional educational system for a large human system? This demand will be overwhelming if we also include other sections of the society, those who go to the established organisations for general and science courses and for the educational needs of adults and other specialised categories like the handicapped, etc. How do we then meet this demand? Do we have enough managerial capability to provide for this size of educational needs of all? Can we achieve it within the next 5,000 days? (2) Should we not redefine education? May be education for, towards and of future will be different than what we understand by the term education today. If so, in what	Monitoring in the Indian Educational net-work function and how well?	alternative to current day traditional educational modes? Q. Do you believe that India today has a grand opportunity to make a quantum jump into future? If so, how? And in what directions in (a) Communications (b) Learning Systems (i) Formal (ii) Non-formal (iii) Others	3. Can a teacher develop his own curricula syllabus in any State in India? If not, why not? 4. What global educational change experiments have relevance to India? 5. Are Indians averse to change? Why can't we plan for 20 years? Is to do this wrong? Why? Or, is it that we don't know tools and techniques of long-range planning.

(1)	(2)	(3)	(4)
way will it be different? Discuss the concepts and new methodologies of communication and learning? (3) Is future a linear trend? What discontinuities, if any, do we foresee with reference to the Indian educational system over the next 20 years? React to the following social indicators: (i) Values (ii) Employment (iii) Skills (iv) Power (v) Equality/Inequality (vi) Culture (vii) Science and Technology (viii) Choose any other Indicator			
2. Acute Poverty Conditions. **Explanation:** The document on Sixth Plan 1980-85 which has just been	1. Ethnic decay due to malnutrition. (From 1985 onwards beginning of slow and	Increased S&T applications coupled with new management and delivery systems can avert future crisis.	

released gives the latest official estimates of the proportion of the poor based on the 32nd Round of NES. Adopting the nutritional norms of 2400 (rural) and 2100 (urban) calories per person per day, the poverty line is Rs. 76 in rural areas and Rs. 88 in urban areas in 1979-80 prices. The estimates are that in 1977-78, 50.8 per cent of the rural population of 495.2 million and 38.2 per cent of the urban population of 133.8 million were in poverty. In absolute numbers, 251.7 million were the rural poor and 51.2 million were the urban poor. In the total population of 629 million, 48.1 per cent or 302.8 million were under the poverty line. Their average per capita monthly expenditure was Rs. 45 in rural areas and Rs. 54 in urban areas.	lingering death of 500 m ± people due to malnutrition in South-East Asia—Messorovich and Pestel)	
	2. Inability to Pay for Services, Health, Transportation, Education, etc.	We can if we are innovative and non-traditional raise the physical quality of life.
	3. Migration from Rural to Urban areas will go on unabated.	(For this innovative communication and learning processes are important).
	4. Causing urban overload 1981 AD 130 m ± (Water, Housing, Traffic breakdowns and sharp decline in the quality of life in urban areas). (2000 AD: 330 m ± in urban sector). We will then have more islands of educational literacy surrounded by a sea of illiteracy and backwardness.	As we move towards future there is a possibility of increase in employment opportunities and the purchasing power of the vulnerable sector. Future may predominantly be an age of "Visual Literacy".

(1)	(2)	(3)	(4)
	Discussion Points: Q. What is your concept of the schools of future? Will the school continue as it is? (Do you believe in the concept of deschooling society?) Or, will it be a multipurpose centre? Q. Can rural or region specific community needs of health services, educational services, agricultural extension services, local industry and technology services be made integral to a school's role? If you don't agree with this concept, why not? Q. What part of migration from rural to urban areas is partly because of education and training?	**Discussion Points:** Q. If the future society is going to be a participative society and would be one where human inputs and humanism will play an increased role than the exploitative order offers, the growth of such values. And if we are moving towards an age where technology, particularly communication technology, is going to play a vital role. In this context, have we developed sufficient imaginative programmes to herald an age of "cultural literacy" and "visual literacy" discuss. Q. Future lies with self-learning and not with	**Discussion Points:** 1. Each educational campus in India is today crisis borne. We should give training in the various educational programmes for crisis management. 2. We should also give training in Anticipatory Management. 3. We should train decision making from young age and this training should include how to take decisions which are future oriented. 4. In the context of the present Indian societal framework, 90 per cent of Indian population has *de facto* no consumer personality. It cannot buy health or education. We need to develop programmes in which there is increased involvement of

Q. In the urban context it costs 7 times more to maintain a person than in the rural context. The city of Mumbai has Corporation run schools in thousands for primary school children upto Class VII. Enrolement is of the order of 8 to 10 lakhs against a budget of Rs. 33 crores. (Of course, Maharashtra teachers are paid better than elsewhere). Is this cost justifiable? What are the alternatives where the same educational and learning message can be shared with children at 50 per cent of the cost.	regimented inflexible learning? Will it be the case in India?	the community/citizenry of the Governmental sponsored educational programmes. 5. It should, however, be noted that a single approach is not relevant for a large country like India: each region should develop its own region specific, cultural specific even language specific educational response. 6. In the non-formal system, we need to innovate further in developing and in searching new administrative ways to introduce appropriate educational programmes for the vulnerable sections of the society. Some of these programmes will be functional in character. 7. There is need to develop linkages between the

(1)	(2)	(3)	(4)
			educational programme and the employment opportunities in the country and other related sectors. 8. There is need to delink degrees from job. (This view is now almost like an ancient saying). 9. There is need to delink examinations from the educational institutions. Let examinations be conducted by Central Examining Organisations. This may restore some peace on our disturbed campus: Let those who wish to take an exam. go for it? 10. There is need to introduce community activities which should be graded like other subjects. 11. There is need to diversify offering several groups of educational subjects/

			programmes at the High School stage itself. (9th and 10th Classes in particular). Today there is no choice for young students who are subjected to a monolithic rigid package of education and examination. We should offer at the High School stage whole range of options and choices, providing new learning opportunities in rural; folk; region specific science and technology oriented and performing arts oriented subjects should be deemed as important as we give importance to mathematics or English language.
3. Uneven state of development.	**(Future Threats)**	**(Future Possibilities)**	**(Policy Implications)**
Illustration This is characteristic of most developing societies. This	1. Accentuation of Rural-Urban divide leading	1. We have a unique opportunity to develop	Other policy implications based on a long-range

(1)	(2)	(3)	(4)
uneven state of development can be glimpsed both from the viewpoint of a Geographer as well as of a Sociologist. There is an additional environmental angle also. A broad distinction of course is between the rural side and the urban side. But in pure physical terms too each territory displays unhomogenous development. Take the example of our land and water resources. In India 175 million hectare, out of the country's total land area of 304 million hectare, for which record exists, are prone to environmental problem through serious water and wind erosion (150 mh); shifting cultivation (3 mh); area affected by waterlogging, salinity and alkalinity (13 mh); and other cultivable waste land etc. (9 mh). The losses which the country is bearing on	to social-rifts and tensions. 2. Environmental degradation (Forest depletion: Likelihood of the occurrence of Fuel famine and fuel riots in some parts of India: Acute paper crisis). 3. Accentuation of spatial imbalance in available educational services as well as other services. **Discussion Points:** 1. Do you see any direct or indirect corelations between the educational system and uneven state of development in the countries in the Third World? 2. What are the new inputs necessary to bring about a new educational awareness	a variety of rural-urban linkages. This shall promote developmental homogeneity. **Discussion Points:** 1. What kind of linkages can be thought of to minimise rural-urban rift? 2. Does homogenous development demand new educational outlook and policy. **Discuss:** 1. Futurology is not an escape function. It is an exercise in preparedness. **Comment:** 2. Long-range planning is not a one time job. It is a continuous ongoing Exercise replete with several midcourse corrections.	assessment of Asian societies, point towards the following: 1. Achievement of 100 per cent literacy (we will not at this time go into the polemics surrounding the definition of 'Literacy'). 2. Education to be free upto secondary level; for higher levels and professional education gradual reduction of costs over the years. 3. 'Cafeteria' system of education where one has a greater freedom in choosing areas of ones interest and time schedules that do not require rigid sequential stages of school and college attendance with fixed hours in the day time for 'acquiring' knowledge. 4. Flexible syllabus and course content to ensure greater creativity and less curricula

account of the continuing degradation of its land resources according to B.B. Vohra, Chairman, National Committee on Environmental Planning, Department of Environment, are of staggering dimensions and constitute one of the important threats to our economic progress. As for the paucity of India's forest cover, one should note that of the 75 million hectares classed as forest lands, less than half is actually under adequate tree cover, and as much as about 20 million hectares of forest land is estimated to be affected by erosion. No more than about 12 per cent of the country's land surface is actually under adequate tree cover as against the target of 33 per cent prescribed by the National Forest Policy of 1952. Although

at all levels of education towards our land management, forest's and environment?

3. "Future is Today": Comment.
4. Identify some examples of syllabus overhaul both in the school and the higher educational programme.
4. What new inputs in the form of special courses are necessary to safeguard the societal dangers arising out of uneven state of development?

Discussion Point:

Comment:

1. "Life Long education has become part of the discussion concerning the democratization of

burden on the pupils.

5. Assessment to be made in terms of performance credits and not necessarily written examinations.
6. Degrees to be valid over a limited time-frame. To overcome knowledge obsolescence degrees shall have to be 'renewed'.
7. Mode of education: "Study-work-study" in all fields with increased emphasis on `creativity' at all levels.
8. Educational content to have relevance to life, society, ethics, socio-economic imperatives and culture.
9. Compulsory teaching of history of science, history of civilization, world geography, international institutions and comparative religion.

(1)	*(2)*	*(3)*	*(4)*
13 million hectares are classed as "Permanent Pastures", these areas are in fact generally without any vegetation on account of either overgrazing or encroachments. As for the cities and the metropolitan towns are concerned. Uneven state of development is literally of astonishing and depressing character. It is a little known fact that of all our human settlements only 8 cities can boast of satisfactory sewerage and sewage treatment plants. All our rivers, lakes and ponds are heavily polluted by the discharge into them of untreated sewage and industrial effluents. Even the supply of safe drinking water which is not available to thousands of villages, has now become a problem even in our	our post-industrial society" (Pierre Future in *The Planner and Life Long Education*, UNESCO, IIEP, Paris (1977). 2. With reference to your own respective societies, develop two opposite scenarios on "Education for All" (1981-2001 AD).		10. Compulsory work experience in rural development and military training. 11. An increasing larger portion of the total outlay for education to be devoted to building the infrastructure and the software needed for non-formal education. 12. Conventional higher educational opportunities to be provided only for highly meritorious students in the normal run; and, specialised training in narrow specialities to be open to one and all. 13. Technical education to have a much larger 'practical' component. 14. Industry to be called upon to bear a share of the cost of technical education since they are the biggest

biggest towns which can be judged how even cities like Delhi and Mumbai are visited by epidemics of jaundice and other water-borne diseases every now and then. All these are aspects for which there is neither public awareness nor requisite educational response.			beneficiaries of the products of technical education. 15. Delinking of degree requirements from jobs and linking jobs to work experience and work credits. 16. Increased use of new educational technologies Audio-Visual aids, SITE, correspondence courses and open universities.
4. Value Plurality. **Explanation:** Any society is characterized by its culture which reflects certain values which it cherishes most. The passage of time has led to the emergence of new values replacing the old ones. However, in the Third World's context one notices coexistence of sharply divided value outlook amongst people in a given society. An outlook towards future is intimately linked with its outlook towards	1. Crisis arising from awkward unhomogeneous social change, and lifestyle disparities. 2. Increased labour and youth unrest (Partly due to politicalisation of labour and now that of student community). 3. Emergence of anti-social forces mainly	We have opportunities and Syllabii change in non-technical subjects and goal oriented mass education and mass communication programmes, using most modern technology, shall avert these difficulties in the future.	17. Vocational stream to commence from Class VIII onwards. 18. Special emphasis on education of interest groups such as women, handicapped persons, tribal and hill people and nomads, etc. 19. New educational structures: Greater autonomy for academic institutions.

(1)	(2)	(3)	(4)
values. There are futurists who believe that future redesign is possible only if there is some "value shift". The value plurality of the Third World countries, however, inhibits change. What constitutes the right direction of change is a very difficult question for which there is no single answer. Education is intimately linked both with questions of 'values' and questions of 'change'.	due to traditional social malaise typical to caste, language, religion, sects and inadequate management know-how of administering a highly socially fragmented society. (Value plurality and concomitant conflicts breed social fragmentation and tensions).		20. Increased student participation in determining course content and running of educational administration. 21. Gradual emergence of common school system.
5. Technological Plurality. **Explanation:** **Comment:** The future, many people, believe, lies with Technology. (Herman Kahn and others). Can the Third World countries make a quantum leap into future? (Or must they walk on two legs always)? **Note:** 97 per cent of the	(Future Threats) 1. India and many Third World countries enter 21st century with sophisticated technology in several areas but without a corresponding technological culture. (Also continued co-existence of bullock-cart age (traditional	(Future Opportunities) If we embrace technology (Hardware-Software mix) judiciously, we can develop due linkage provided we introduce various innovative, real life oriented, problem solving and creativity and rigidity) (as against conformity - generating socio-techno modules).	

world's R&D is carried out in the developed countries and 3 per cent in the less developed countries. (Do we know what per cent of this is for Education and Educational Technology)?

village school) with the space-age (IIT's).

2. Inadequate horizontal diffusion of technology.
3. Increased failure of Maintenance systems both in the private and in the public sector.
4. Others, e.g., Value-Assault.

Discussion Note:

Which factors would lay greater emphasis in the three function paradigm presented in *Alternatives and Decisions in Educational Planning* by John D. Montgomery (UNESCO, ITEP, Paris 1976).

Sub-system	*Aims*	*Objective*	*Means*
Technology			
Organisation			
Motivation			

Would you agree with the view that "There are still gaps between `technology' systems and social requirements in the educational sector in most countries"?

CREATING TECHNOLOGY FOR THE 21ST CENTURY

*Indira Gandhi**

The inauguration of the Science Congress by the Prime Minister has become routine, yet this does not detract from the privilege of addressing such a distinguished gathering and sharing thoughts with our eminent scientists, for the political and human points of view are of relevance to scientists too.

At every Science Congress, whatever subject, I have stressed the vital urgency of strengthening the base while we attempt the climb. We have climbed and I congratulate our scientists but I do not know whether we shall be able to sustain the momentum vertically and horizontally, because of the inadequacies of base facilities. We do need to reach out to the frontiers of knowledge, and the scientific community is aware of my deep interest in such subjects and attainments, but I am somewhat disappointed that our scientists have not been sufficiently enthused to work for the needs of average people, especially the poor who must earn their pittance through avoidable drudgery. Also, we have not paid adequate attention to the development of available renewable sources of energy or other local resources.

In 1958 the Government of India adopted a Scientific Policy Resolution to harness science for the people's welfare. The Resolution has been a kind of charter for our scientists. It is time now and appropriate that we evaluate the experience gained, recognize accomplishments, and identify shortcomings before planning the future.

For worthwhile results the goals must be clear-cut. We have a strong base in agriculture and in industry and a significant scientific infrastructure in terms of numbers, range of skills and quality. The foundation for self-reliance has been built.

---

* Inaugural address delivered at 70th Annual Session of the Indian Science Congress, Tirupati, 3 January 1983.

For some years the Indian Science Congress has followed the useful practice of focusing the attention of scientists from different disciplines and backgrounds on one central theme of national importance. This year it is the ocean, its resources and development. We are the only country with the privilege of having an ocean named after us. We have a long coast and our maritime traditions go back to ancient times, yet because of our large land base we become accustomed to thinking of ourselves as, and are regarded by others as, land-lubbers. The Indian Ocean has hardly been explored by those who live around it. Incursions by outside military powers have suddenly opened our eyes to the significance of the sea around us for our security and development.

The adoption, by an overwhelming majority of nations, of the Convention of the UN Conference on the Law of the Seas is a major new development. Apart from territorial waters, national authority now stretches to an economic jurisdiction ranging from 200 to 350 nautical miles from our coastline. In this area we have the exclusive right to utilize living and non-living resources. The most prized resources of the continental shelf are hydrocarbons. India has now been recognized as a "pioneer investor" in ocean-mining, giving it the exclusive right to operate in an area of up to 150,000 square kilometres in the high seas for the recovery and processing of polymetallic nodules. This is a direct result of our past oceanographic research.

Apart from this, the Indian Ocean makes our weather. Here it is that both the life-giving monsoon and the cyclones that cause devastation arise. Meteorological studies over the Indian Ocean and an understanding of the interaction between the ocean and the atmosphere are thus of the greatest importance to our farmers and others.

The bounty of food in the ocean is rich in protein. A mere dozen or so countries, which have extensive technological capabilities to locate living marine resources and to understand physical, chemical and biological oceanography, monopolize more than three-quarters of the total global harvest of fish and operate major fishing fleets with storage facilities at great distances.

We have undertaken a variety of oceanographic activities under the Council of Scientific and Industrial Research, the Oil &

Natural Gas Commission, the Geological Survey of India, the Department of Space, the Indian Meteorological Department, the Ministries of Agriculture, Defence and Shipping and Transport and universities. The Department of Ocean Development will provide the focal point for coordinated progress and our Ocean Policy statement will guide their endeavour, harnessing this tremendous potential.

Our ancient books speak of *Agni* (fire) springing from the sea. Offshore wells have given reality to this allegory. Our literature calls the ocean a treasure-house of gems. We certainly hope that this also will become true for our economy. Treasure is not to be squandered but must be husbanded most carefully. Hence our insistence on the conservation of the marine environment. Too often has science exploited fragile and vanishing resources, careless of consequent scarcity and other results.

Last year our first Indian Scientific Expedition set foot on Antarctica. It brought back experiences of conditions at sea and on land regarded as the coldest, driest, windiest, least accessible and most inhospitable of all the continents. Above all, the expedition reminded us that India has not lost its daring and its competence, and that it is capable of undertaking systematic work on the Southern Ocean and Antarctica. Our Second Expedition has just landed there.

The Antarctica, the deep oceans outside the exclusive economic zone of coastline nations and outer space are the common heritage of humankind. We feel strongly that they should not be subject to the rule of "first come first served". A few countries have not signed the Convention of the Law of the Seas, blatantly refusing to recognize this common human right. We hope that they will reconsider their stand but this makes it all the more necessary for us to build our own self-reliant capabilities. We are neither expansionist nor aggressive and we do not wish to go beyond our rights but those rights must be safeguarded.

1982 gave a fair example of our capabilities and limitations. INSAT-IA vindicated the concept of a multifunctional satellite to suit our developmental needs. Like all progress, science is built on ceaseless learning and an ever increasing, determined effort at doing better. May I on your behalf and my own wish our space scientists the fullest success with INSAT-IB on which they have begun work?

We have a long way to go "to secure for the people of the country all the benefits that can accrue from the acquisition and application of scientific knowledge". By no means are we at the end of problems. On the contrary, they have grown in number and complexity here as in other countries. At the same time the nature of the benefits keeps changing. What was a luxury just a few years ago has become a necessity. The shadow of the affluent hovers over us. It is evident that our scientific capabilities must be meshed more closely with our major developmental efforts. Every sector of our economic activity must have firmer scientific underpinning. The scientific infrastructure already built must serve the priority areas of national investment. But increasing technological complexity in industry and agriculture calls for hardheaded assessments of technological costs and opportunities, no less than the social, economic and political factors.

Technological development need clear guidelines especially as regards the growth of indigenous technology and the acquisition of technology from outside. I should like to take this opportunity to place our Technology Policy Statement before the nation. We believe that technology must be based on our own culture and personality. The Statement underlines the premise that for a country of our size and endowments, self-reliance is inescapable and that the use and development of technology must relate to the people's needs and aspirations. At the same time it is vital to take advantage of advances elsewhere to conserve our own time and resources as well as to aid the expansion and diversification of our technology.

The main aims outlined by the Technology Policy Statement are:

(a) attain technological competence and self-reliance to reduce vulnerability, particularly in strategic and critical areas, making the maximum use of indigenous resources;

(b) provide the maximum gainful and satisfying employment to all strata of society, with emphasis on the employment of women and weaker sections of society;

(c) use traditional skills and capabilities, making them commercially competitive;

(d) ensure the correct mix between mass production technologies and production by the masses;

(e) ensure maximum development with minimum capital outlay;

(f) identify obsolescence of technology in use and arrange for modernization of both equipment and technology;

(g) develop technologies which are internationally competitive, particularly those with export potential;

(h) improve production speedily through greater efficiency and fuller utilization of existing capabilities, and enhance quality and reliability of performance and output;

(i) reduce demands on energy, particularly energy from non-renewable sources;

(j) ensure harmony with the environment, preserve the ecological balance, and improve the quality of the habitat; and

(k) recycle waste material and make full utilization of by-products.

Any policy will succeed only to the extent to which it evokes the enthusiasm, and involvement of our scientists and technologists, and imbues the people as a whole with greater self-assurance and pride in national achievement.

We welcome suggestions, especially from scientists. The immense challenge before them is to convince our people that our science and technology are for them and must unlock their creative potential. Science has grown in the West not only because of the flashes of insight combined with the hard work of a few brilliant brains but because each succeeding generation is tangibly higher in scientific knowledge and familiarity with technology.

Technology is a child of science, yet it has outpaced it and, if one is to believe the reams written on this subject, will soon be on its own. In this race we are far behind. We are overwhelmed by fast developments outside. How do we of the developing countries, who struggled so hard to industrialize in the early 50s, now break the chains of obsolete machinery and technology and step in line with contemporary trends to move into the future?

In India and abroad young Indian technocrats and others interested in these issues have been meeting me. Obviously we cannot change overnight but the advanced countries are moving so fast and the most undeveloped, who have no infrastructure, are thinking of starting off at this much higher level. So where does that leave us? Employment opportunities will not grow by keeping to the present situation. We must convince our workers and even more so, our people of the business and industry and those who often provoke them that although any change does cause dislocation, the larger interest of workers and of greater employment opportunities lie in flexibility and ability to adapt to change, if possible to create necessary changes ourselves. Our capacity to safeguard the interests of groups who resist development in technology which are inexorably forging ahead, sweeping aside the old, will be limited. In the early days of Independence I used to give the example of those who tried to stick to horse-drawn carriages when the motor car had come on the market. Only those coachmen and others concerned who learned to drive or became mechanics and so on, had a chance of continued employment. That is one of the problems of job-oriented education. It should not bind a young person to only one type of job. It is far more important to have good grounding, training to think, to be open to ideas and sensitive to developments and most important, to be able to rise above pettiness and the here and now. Problems and situations must be seen and solutions found in the wider context of the whole.

And lastly, the main question, disturbing or exciting, depending on your nature and attitude, is what of human beings themselves? You the eminent scientists know better than I of the fantastic work in all spheres, none more astounding than that in genetic engineering. Will this not change the usage of some of our bodily functions? The story of species is a story of evolution, adaptation and change. Those who did, survived; those who resisted faded out. So, what will be the human of the future? A master of his own brain children or their victim? Never before has our race faced such a challenge. Will we be equal to it?

Recently my attention was drawn to Le Corbusier's words, "There is no such thing as a primitive man; there are only primitive means." Our farmers astonished Westerners when they so readily took to new methods! So will other villagers if given a chance. Our scientists must think of somehow introducing the most advanced means into our villages, bring professionalism into traditional systems of information, health and so on. Can we think of using micro-electronics and micro-computers? To the question of whether we can afford new techniques and equipment, I counter with another: can we afford to be stuck with obsolete ones? Above all there must be far quicker decision-making at all levels. We must also rid ourselves of the colonial hangover of looking to the West for models, when those become outdated almost as soon as we can acquire or copy them.

The West has concentrated on the sharpening of the intellect. India has always respected qualities of the mind; yet alongside there has run a stream of insight and intuition whose value is getting greater recognition in today's Western science. Unlike the West, our philosophy has flexibility, our myths provide parallels for practically every situation and modern idea. Why don't we use them for such purposes? Gandhiji did. That is how his words went straight to the hearts of our peasants. How can we ever make up for lost time unless we begin now to create technology for the 21st Century?

Prof. Ayensu has sent me an article on the subject. Since he echoes some of the ideas that have been buzzing in my mind — some I have mentioned above — I should like to quote one phrase. He says: "To sell or buy computers may be in a sense to deal with any survivability", and suggests that village mini-computerization should be given high prestige and high priority.

Telugu and other southern languages sing of the metaphorical meaning of the ascent of the Seven Hills. Faith draws millions to Tirupati. Our pilgrimage is towards self-reliance and national strength, so that we can protect the interests of all sections of our people and of our country. Scientific search, indeed life itself, is a steep uphill path. Untouched by the spirit's higher values, science has generated fear and uncertainty. Let it be an ally of life, a friend and guide, imbued with faith in our people and in our future.

Tirumala on the hills is celebrated for its *Suprabhatam* — the hymn of the auspicious dawn. May the dawn of this new year bring good fortune to each of you and to our nation.

MANAGEMENT OF RESEARCH AND DEVELOPMENT

*A. Ramachandran**

Management of Research and Development demands the highest qualities of management, for research scientists and engineers are by nature, sensitive and tend to regard control of any kind, whether it be hierarchical, financial or otherwise as inhibitive to their creativity.

It will be my attempt during this seminar to focus some of the creative aspects of R&D and the special features of its management. It is not my intention to belittle the usual quantitative techniques or to say that these have no place in R&D management. On the contrary, during the project selection stage and the pre-implementation period, techniques such as the evaluation of uncertainties (i.e. Decision Tree Methods), sensitivity analyses, Value Analysis, Network Techniques, Design of Experiments, etc., could make the critical difference between the eventual success or failure of a project.

It should also be appreciated at the very outset, that we shall be talking about commercial, goal oriented projects, time targeted and directed to fulfil corporate desires. Basic and fundamental research are assumed to be the purview of the universities and IIT's or wherever pools of research excellence exists. Such projects do not lend themselves to management control, their output is highly un-predictive and spin offs may come several years or even decades after the work has started. For companies that can afford the luxury of such long-term research, my suggestion is that you identify the individual scientist (or team), allow him a certain percentage of your R&D budget, give him a conducive environment and then leave them strictly alone.

To you as the middle and higher executives or managers of your respective companies, my message is very straightforward that R&D is a very essential part of your corporate lives. We in the

---

* The author was the Secretary to the Government of India in the Department of Science and Technology.

Government have ensured that suitable climate exists. I shall elaborate some of the features which the Government has taken up and implemented.

1. Fiscal incentive exist for scientific research. In addition to allowing for complete writing off of all expenditure incurred on scientific research including acquisition of capital equipments in the years of its expenditure, provisions also exist for amounts paid to scientific and research institutions. These fiscal measures taken as a whole could be regarded as, perhaps, the most generous in the world today.
2. Licensing laws have been liberalized for establishing production of items based on indigenous research and development activities. Provision also exists for expansion of capacities also based on indigenous R&D activities. Industry based on indigenous technology developed in CSIR laboratories and those approved by DST do not require a licence.
3. The requirements of equipments and raw materials needed for R&D activities involving imports have been liberalized. The latest Import Trade Control Policy also provides for import of such items upto a value of Rs. one lakh without an import licence. Provision also exists in which the larger requirements are processed in the Department of Science and Technology facilitating their import.
4. Requirement of full-scale units in the form of prototypes can also be imported for research and development work and in cases where the value of the prototype is less than Rs. one lakh the imports can be effected without consideration of the indigenous availability.
5. Manpower and skills of very high level have been made available for the nation and vast infrastructure of the national laboratories system could now be taken advantage of for sponsoring research against weighted tax deduction (133 per cent).
6. Test and instrumentation centres have been created on a region-wise basis for specialized and support services to various industries.

Interaction between Management and R&D Department

It is the duty of higher management to determine the corporate strategy for and commitment to R&D. Thus, clear directions must be given to the R&D Department and this direction from the Board should incorporate the following:

(i) The new products that are desirable;

(ii) The areas of technology the company wants to be in;

(iii) The new markets that are to be entered;

(iv) The products and processes that are not desired anymore, therefore, related R&D programmes should be stopped;

(v) For companies multiple areas of operation, the desirable rate of expansion for each field.

This list should be examined by the technical staff, i.e. R&D, Marketing, Production, Sales, etc. and based upon the opinions expressed, amended.

Such an exercise in corporate planning for R&D is essential so that development work is programmed correctly. It is important to foresee the times when the company's resources, i.e. production capacity, sales effort, finances, etc., will be idle. New products should, therefore, be developed and this development timed to exploit these idle resources.

Another guideline especially for capital intensive industries, is to ensure that those projects that aim at the maximum utilization of the plant capacity are stressed. The surest way of reducing the overhead that each unit of production will carry is to have the factory producing its maximum output.

It is also the responsibility of higher management to promote an appropriate cultural environment for R&D. Feeling such as those of production and sales staff that R&D personnel are an unnecessary addendum to the company and are in essence a non-productive drain on the company's finances should be discouraged, so should be the counter argument that R&D personnel sometimes indulge in, viz. that production and sales whilst essential are really for lesser intellects. Some of these prejudices can be very simply minimized by a weekly discussion headed by someone of the level of Managing Director, where R&D, production and marketing are represented, problems and achievements discussed and strategies evolved.

The concept that R&D personnel should be real world oriented and should interact with other departments is usually satisfied by using the R&D men for production, troubleshooting and routine testing problems. There are inherent dangers in such a policy, for R&D is really concerned with the next generation of products and it would be a short-sighted management which would strengthen one department at the expense of another. If production problems exist beyond the usual 'teething' period then obviously the crux lies elsewhere because the industrial engineering of the product and process has been done and none or very few innovative inputs are now necessary.

The environment in which R&D is to take place governs both its quality and quantity. Research, development and design are the essential basis for the prosperity of a company and in a larger context, of the nation. They must be integrated into the whole business with a skill and care that calls for the highest qualities of management.

Project Selection

As mentioned earlier sophisticated and quantitative management techniques can be applied to R&D Management also. This is especially true whenever a choice has to be made between projects (due to financial, equipment or manpower constraints, etc.).

The standard methods of project appraisal such as the cost / benefit ratios may be used for comparison. Sensitivity Analysis to study the response of a project to variations in its inputs (e.g. alternate technologies) and market conditions. The use of linear programming to predict the comparative contributions of various projects to the company's prosperity can also be employed. For large corporations with multi-divisional activities, Operations Research Techniques such as dynamic programming have been used to apportion funds between divisions.

The use of Statistical Design of Experiments once a project is selected is another well-known technique as is the use of PERT/ CPM for project management with which I am sure you are all familiar.

Enclosed, is a simple methodology to develop a project index which will rank the alternatives and provide an easy guideline for decisions *vis-a-vis* R&D projects.

Simple Example of Scoring for a Project Rating

Parameter	*Attribute*	*Score*
Probability of success	Unpredictable	1
	Fair	2
	High	3
Anticipated Time duration	Greater than 3 years	1
	1 to 3 years	2
	Less than 1 year	3
Cost	Greater than 2 lakhs	1
	0.5 to 2 lakhs	2
	Less than 0.5 lakhs	3
End use, i.e., need	No obvious market will maintain or	1
	Expand business	2
	Will fulfil company objectives	3
Increased sales	Less than 0.5 lakhs	1
	0.5 to 5 lakhs	2
	Greater than 5 lakhs	3
Maximum score	3 to power 5 = 243	
	1 to power 5 = 1	

This methodology is obviously not the end and be all of decision-making for R&D. Each organization (or company) will have to develop his own refinements such as number of attributes can be increased so can the number of parameters, weighted scores may be given to certain parameters depending upon the company situation and strategy.

Specific Criteria for Evaluation of Research Projects

The feasibility of an industrial project has to be judged from several points of view : technical, engineering, marketing, economic and managerial. Before a project is accepted from a sponsor or authorized for in-house work, it would be given preliminary scrutiny from these five aspects. The R&D unit's technical staff are usually competent to decide on technical feasibility. They may and often do have the qualifications to make judgements on engineering, marketing and economic feasibility; but, if possible, they should get the marketing personnel to agree with their evaluations. Decisions as to managerial feasibility must rest with the top management or the client, who can alone decide whether to implement a project on a commercial scale or use the resources in some other way. They should be made aware of the risks involved and skills required.

Technical Feasibility

Technical evaluation is concerned with the suitability of processes and products. It involves such points as availability and cost of raw materials, feasibility of manufacturing steps and equipment and product characteristics within the range felt to be suitable for the market. This type of evaluation is usually made by an experienced technologist familiar with the industry to which the project relates.

Engineering Feasibility

Engineering feasibility studies are made by engineers, who consider such matters as types and availability of equipment, flow of materials through the operation, process control procedures, wastes, by-products and hazards. They make estimates of the cost of purchasing and operating plant and equipment including overheads. They prepare drawings of plants layout and specifications for equipment, materials handling devices, construction material and instrumentation for process control. They estimate minimum economic plant size when this is a pertinent consideration. They prepare drafts of manuals dealing with plant operation and process control.

Marketing Feasibility

Marketing feasibility is usually called market research. "Marketing" is used here in the broad sense of consumption capacity and would include, for example, a survey to estimate the demand for fertilizers in order to meet a national target of greater agricultural production. A market study deals with the volume of demand, suitable price structure and requirements of distribution channels, including packaging. It also includes an evaluation of present and potential competition and should provide estimates of marketing costs such as expenses for direct sales, advertising and promotion.

Comprehensive Economic Feasibility Review

After the process engineers and market research specialists have prepared their estimates, it is necessary to make an economic analysis of the whole project in order to prepare the data for entrepreneurial decision. Such an analysis may be carried out by joint efforts of the process engineering and market research groups, or it may be done by a separate group working closely with them. In either case, a sum for working capital is included in the estimate of the total investment required for the project. The rate of return on sales and investment and the cash flow are projected. The study may include the method of financing and the effect on the national economy. The report thus constitutes a summary of the financial results that may be expected from the commercial application of the project.

Managerial Feasibility

As was stated earlier, the management of the private or public enterprise sponsoring the project must make the final decision regarding its commercial application. On the basis of the information provided on technical engineering, marketing and economic feasibility, the advantages of a commercial operation must be weighed against alternative uses of resources. For, even if it is assumed that the feasibility studies are all favourable, there still remain questions that can be answered only by the management of an enterprise. Is the undertaking in line with existing policy and plans for future growth? If it is not, is it still so attractive that it warrants revision of these general objectives? If so, the particular project should then be compared with other options that can be considered if the criteria are revised. Does the organization possess adequate managerial talent to launch the new venture successfully? If it should later expand in scope, would it force the enterprise into new raw material commitments, types of processing or marketing areas beyond its capacity? If the management has already worked out systematic criteria on which to base policy decisions, these questions should have been raised at earlier stages so that work on doubtful projects can be cut short. It is advisable that the R&D units programme make provisions for bench mark evaluation at major stages of the project. Nevertheless before the final decision is reached, the proposed commercial application should be reviewed once more in its entirety to make sure that it conforms to the enterprise's broad objectives for expansion and growth.

Industrial R&D Units

Technical activities often grow very rapidly. This is particularly true if the R&D units wishes to obtain at least some of its income from sponsored projects; in developing countries, clients are more likely to be interested in projects that lead to rapid commercial applications than in the classical type of product and process development for which the institute was often founded in the first place. The reason for this is that time is saved by acquiring existing technology and know-how from some source, rather than by obtaining it through research and development.

Speedy industrial growth seems particularly desirable in developing countries. Hence, if a new operation can be put into effect by using foreign technology, this course is likely to be adopted. The important point that the country will need improved technology in the future or technology better adapted to its requirements is often overlooked. When an up-to-date plant has been installed and the local operating personnel have been trained, it is often assumed that the technology will remain static for the life of the plant. Sooner or later, however, improved technology will have to be discovered to handle different raw materials, to satisfy changing patterns of consumption, or to meet altered economic patterns. This new technology to meet local conditions cannot be easily and rapidly obtained. The enterprise must provide it through its own staff, outside consultants or turn to an industrial R&D institute with its pool of diversified talents.

Short-Term Activities

Information Service

Digests of technical information are of value to industrial managers. R&D units regularly publish technical summaries or abstracts of important papers. This activity has the advantage of creating goodwill and contacts among those on the distribution lists and is a way of drawing attention to the work of the unit. To reach smaller companies most effectively, special publications are needed, relating to particular fields and written from a very practical point of view; some industrial associations may be willing to share the cost of such publications.

In addition, the R&D unit usually offers to provide information on specific problems from its library or its specialized personnel. The information service is normally an overhead expense of the unit. It is a valuable promotional activity that often leads to sponsored projects. Occasionally an assignment is received that requires an extensive study; a charge may then be made to recover part of the expense.

Analysis, Testing and Quality Control

The testing section of an R&D unit is a valuable service to local manufacturing establishments, a great many of which cannot carry out such work themselves. Part or all of the costs may be recovered by appropriate fees; charges for the service are a wise safeguard against requests for analysis that are not justified. Where possible, the R&D units should encourage clients to submit samples in a form suitable for standard testing; otherwise, the laboratory staff will have to work out special procedure to meet the case, and it may be difficult for the R&D unit to charge for the extra time involved.

It is sometimes possible to establish a regular system of quality control for purchases by the Government, industrial associations or individual establishments. The volume of such work obviously justifies making a charge for the service. Regular standard tests of this sort that make efficient use of staff and equipment reduce the average cost of analysis.

Analysis and quality control in the past did not enjoy high professional prestige because the work done was routine and was performed chiefly by non-professionals and professionals. As more advanced techniques have been developed using sophisticated instrumentation and interpretation, this work has become much more attractive to well-trained scientists.

Technical Services

Often called "troubleshooting", technical services deal with a wide range of practical problems encountered in manufacturing. They may involve recommendations on selecting or handling raw materials, controlling operations, adjusting equipment, training and supervising operatives, storing and packaging products, or dealing with complaints or inquiries from customers.

It is difficult to develop a system of charges that will cover the expense, although, when the problem requires several days to solve, a charge on a cost-incurred basis may be made. Troubleshooting is, however, a very valuable service to industry and one that broadens the experience of the staff. It is the policy of many R&D units to devote a fair percentage of their domestic budgets to this activity. Technical services create goodwill and help to reveal more important problems, which may ripen into sponsored or in-house projects.

Standardization

Standardization is a valuable service carried out by some industrial research units either by checking samples against specifications, working out technical procedures for checks, or even conducting the entire procedure of selecting, establishing and publishing specifications and assisting industry to attain them. It is often subsidized by government agencies or industrial associations, and the cost of evaluating individual samples may be charged to those submitting them.

Standardization is important for government purchasing operations for upgrading the technical quality of an industry and for producing goods of acceptable export quality. In a number of countries standardization is the responsibility of an independent organization. In such cases, staff members of the institute serve on the technical committees set-up to formulate national standards, and the institute can undertake many technical investigations for the National Standardization Institution.

Medium-Term Activities

Exploratory Researches

Exploratory researches are often required to determine the technical parameters of a concept for a new product, process, or use for a raw material. They provide information upon which it is possible to base an ordered plan for a project to reach a defined objective. To make the best use of technical skills, the project outlined should be drawn up as soon as sufficient information is available; otherwise, man-hours may be wasted. As stated earlier, many industrial research units find it advantageous to set a limit on the amount of time expended on a given idea before a project outline is prepared.

Long-Term Activities

Product Evaluation

Product evaluation is usually conducted by specialists, often from the analytical section, who are skilled in the development and application of test procedures, including those of the analytical type but also some which simulate performance under conditions of use. The work involves systematic study of the proposed product and critical comparison with competitive products, including price.

In addition, field tests need to be carried out. For industrial products, these are usually small-scale tests in the plants of potential industrial customers. For products sold to the general public, consumer-testing procedures are used. These investigations will either confirm the preliminary product specifications or show that modification is required.

Applied Research

Applied research projects are carried out to provide a preliminary definition of a product or process. On the basis of the information obtained from exploratory work, the investigations are undertaken to confirm that known raw materials can be converted by laboratory techniques into specimen products that could be readily utilized. This work may be carried out by scientists or technologists; in larger organisations, it is often assigned to an applied research section.

Product Development

Product development, carried out by technologists who have specialized in the products manufactured or used by a particular sector of industry, is required to refine the definition of useful products reached through applied research, to explore systematically the merits of various modifications of formulations and select the most promising, to develop methods of testing their relative efficiency, to set preliminary product specifications, to confirm the preferred forms of available raw materials, and to demonstrate the proposed method of production.

Process Development

Process development, which may partly overlap the product development project, is conducted to evaluate the proposed sequence of operations in terms of manufacturing practicability. It is best carried out by technologists with experience in the type of manufacture concerned. Its object is to prepare a preliminary process definition in which raw material specification are set, equipment and optimum operating conditions for each major step are described, process and quality control procedures are proposed and preliminary estimates of plant investment are prepared. The scheme of operations is usually shown in a process flow diagram. Finally, the preferred process is carried out in a large laboratory on a pre-pilot scale to produce sufficient quantities of the product for critical evaluation.

By-Product and Waste Utilization

Studies on by-product and waste utilization may be carried out to make manufacturing operations more economical or to abate nuisances. The investigations may require the entire sequence of stages described previously in this section or they may begin with product and process development. Special attention should be paid to the future volume and composition of the waste or by-product in the light of possible changes in raw material or process.

Engineering Development

Studies on engineering development are carried out to verify the results of process development work. They require rigorous analysis of the suitability of the process for scaling up to a commercial operation. They involve complete process design, final specifications for equipment and auxiliaries, and firm estimates of operating costs and plant investment. Frequently they also include the preparation of drafts of operating manuals. They may require establishment of criteria for selecting new plant sites and specifications for new buildings. They provide data on operating costs for managerial decisions. Engineering assistance of this type may be required throughout the design, erection and initial operation of commercial plants.

Pilot Plants

Pilot plants are semi-commercial scale prototypes of large plants. Although they are expensive to install, they should be used, if necessary, to confirm the information from process development studies. Where feasible, however, only part of the entire process should be piloted as an economy measure. Pilot plants are nearly always below minimum economic size and are, therefore, also expensive to operate as small production units unless the products can initially command premium prices, in developing countries, pilot plants often provide an effective means of training operatives from individual establishments in new or improved techniques.

The inflationary spiral to which the economy had been subjected to, has now been largely curbed. In fact, the time for a major technological thrust in the industrial sector based on an intensive in-house R&D drive is on. At the moment, more than 300 in-house R&D units have been recognized whose estimated expenditure on research is claimed to be of the order of Rs 40 crores per annum. What is necessary now is the corporate will to exploit these circumstances and the vision to invest in the future.

FORECASTING FOR THE PURPOSES OF SCIENCE POLICY

*Karol I Pelc**

The increasing social importance of science as a sphere of activity necessitates systematic management of its development. Scientific research conducted on an ever larger scale requires the engagement of more and more material resources and cooperation of interacting research groups and institutions. Contemporary scientific activity has a social character which can be viewed in two aspects: (1) because of collective character of work, the division of labour and resulting social structure in the scientific community; (2) because of its impact on the life conditions and development of the whole society which invests definite resources in scientific activity.

The effectiveness of management of science and optimization of utilization of the results of scientific research for the sake of the society depend, among other factors on whether it is possible, and to what extent, to forecast and assess the potentials, perspectives and social consequences of the actions undertaken in the sphere of science. The necessity of governmental interference in this field is nowadays acknowledged in all the countries. This interference brings positive results, if and only if, it is being accomplished in accordance with the principles of science policy. Comparative studies on science policy carried out in various countries, mainly under the auspices of UNESCO, have provided many interesting results and allowed for the definition of basic terms, distinction of main elements and formulation of some general principles of science policy. A review of these issues is presented in papers of Y.de Hemptinne [7] and I. Malecki [15]. The practice of management of scientific activity in socialist countries required the formulation of the principles of science policy within the context of a centrally

---

* The author heads the Forecasting Research Centre at the Technical University of Wroclaw, Wroclaw (Poland).

planned economic system in accordance with basic ideological concepts accepted in these countries. The description of these principles has been presented in works by J.Kaczmarek [10] and J. Gvishiani [6]. All the authors mentioned above emphasize the necessity of utilization of forecasts to programming of scientific activity and consider forecasting as one of the means of a widely understood science policy. On the other hand, methodological studies referring to forecasting [16], lead to the conclusion that forecasts of scientific development can and should perform a few functions in the system of management of science and technology.

These forecasts can be considered:

(a) as supplementary information for the formulation of science policy of the country, and in particular for the selection of goals of R&D, for setting up the priorities of the development of specific scientific disciplines, determination of optimal size of scientific manpower, etc.;

(b) as a factor influencing scientific community toward better correlation between scientists own research proposals and the State's scientific research programmes. This influence results from the fact that in the course of forecast elaboration, a confrontation of opinion occurs between representatives of scientific community and decision makers. This confrontation aids in the identification of trends of development in various scientific disciplines and domains of technology;

(c) as a constitutive part of the overall system of forecasts which shapes mutual relations between socio-economic development and scientific and technological progress.

We shall deal in a detailed way only with the first of the three functions presented above.

In order to determine the scope of forecasting for the purposes of science policy it is necessary to define what information relating to the future is needed for science policy making. Aiming at the establishment of the complete information, we are going to deal with three main subjects of science policy:

(i) goal formulation for R&D, determination of required effects of this activity on a social scale, of the hierarchy of goals and criteria for evaluation of R&D activity;

(ii) selection of the objects for R&D, formulation of problems and determination of size of R&D undertakings;

(iii) determination of resources aiming at goal achievement, including programming of development and localization of scientific manpower, funds allocation, shaping of the organizational structure.

Each of the three items mentioned above must be solved at the national scale taking into account various interrelations between the sphere of science and other elements of socio-economic system, in the conditions of a changing world scene in particular disciplines of science and in relation to time characteristics of all the processes determining the scale and level of scientific development in the country.

Forecasting studies should contribute to the improvement of decision making, especially in the cases where long time horizons are involved. Therefore, they should enable formulation of alternatives and the assessment of consequences of particular decisions.

1. Goals of R&D Activity

The goals to be set-up for R&D in a given time period/so-called external goals can be rationally defined if one disposes of the following forecasting information in the course of decision making:

(a) assessment of future objectives to be set-up for science by the society and their hierarchization;

(b) assessment of internal trends of the development of particular scientific disciplines and their inter-relationships.

The basis for the assessment of future objectives should be the analysis of structure of social needs and technological possibilities of satisfying them. On this ground it becomes possible to determine probable conflict areas between needs and opportunities/natural resources available, known and feasible technologies, information systems, etc. Moreover, the dynamics of changes in the model of needs should be defined, changes being quantitatively evaluated in order to permit the specification of goals. These goals can be expressed in terms of required changes of level of satisfaction of all the needs categories. Methodological foundation of R&D planning on the basis of goals formulated by means of the so-called model of needs has been a subject of investigation for the last few years in Poland [11], [12], [14]. The principles of operational formulation of goals for R&D activity have been treated in many publications, most interesting of which are those by D. Beckerhoff [2] and P.M.S. Jones [9].

Forecasting studies referring to internal trends of the development of particular scientific disciplines should cover the assessment of probable structural changes occurring in these disciplines, evaluation of the stage of development of a given discipline and evaluation of future importance of research problems for the development of a given discipline. It necessitates undertaking of forecasting study with reference to particular disciplines using morphological analysis as a method of research with simultaneous application of expert opinion [1] when dividing a given discipline into sub-discipline and problem areas it is possible to distinguish the components more or less dynamically developing in a given period of time. Also relations between the components of a given discipline can be submitted to evaluation.

The assessment of mutual interactions between particular sub-disciplines and of their impact on the changes within the discipline treated as a whole can permit to discover the problems of crucial importance for the development of this discipline. A historical example of such an analysis can be Janiszewski's Table [8] presenting the state-of-the-art and development trends of mathematics at the beginning of the 20th century. It should be emphasized that forecasting of scientific disciplines should have a worldwide scope and at the same time should enable to evaluate the level of development of a given discipline in a given country compared with its world status.

2. Selection of the Objects for R&D

The search for an evaluation of R&D projects may be improved by the appropriate forecasting studies which should provide the following information:

— assessment of time period needed to solve the problems currently set-up,

— listing of new scientific and technological problems,
— assessment of the dynamics of technological innovation process.

Forecasting studies driving at the assessment of the time period needed to solve current scientific problems and of probability of success in research have the longest tradition. The main tool in this case is the Delphi technique and investigation based on the experts opinions. Most interesting studies in this domain are Japanese Forecast for Science and Technology up to AD 2000 [18] and, the analysis of priorities for national science policy in FRG [13] and [19]. It seems that forecasts of this type should be worked out both on a national and international scale. Evaluations obtained in this way should link the time parameters with the resources allotted to scientists. Methodology of these studies should be further improved, particularly towards formation of overall problem systems covering the whole range of scientific, technological and social issues.

From the forecasting practice developed in different countries it can be seen that forecasting provides the inspiration for the discovery and classification of new scientific problems. For example, a systematic analysis of the development of particular branches of technology allows for the formulation of new problems appealing to such scientific disciplines as physics, chemistry, biology, etc. Heuristic methods of forecasting are of utmost importance here, these include scenario technique and opinions of a panel of experts. Most promising in this respect seems to be an analytical approach based on Glushkov graph developed in USSR. This approach uses a formal language of the graph theory and applies the opinions of a group of experts. The principles of application of a forecasting technique of this kind for the purposes of R&D planning and the selection of objects for research have been presented in works by G.M. Dobrov and his co-authors [4], [5].

Assessment of the dynamics of technological innovation process requires a model analysis. Such models should simulate the properties of economic systems, characteristics of information channels, and characteristics of couplings between the sphere of economy and science. Methodology of this kind of investigations is not yet developed to the extent permitting to obtain useful information. Nevertheless it seems that it is desirable to use the experience already acquired in modelling of the innovation processes at the level of corporations, for the purposes of forecasting of similar processes at the national level. The main tool of those forecasting studies are computerized dynamic models enabling the simulation of complex technological and economic systems. Particularly interesting in this field are the studies by Roberts [17] and Blackmann [3].

3. Planning and Allocation of Resources

Resources allocated by the state for the purpose of R&D depend on the dynamics of economic change. The range of forecasting issues in this field is wide and covers the following problems:

— assessment of future structure of scientific manpower,
— assessment of dynamics of resources for R&D,
— assessment of future organizational structure in the sphere of science and advanced professional training.

Forecasting of manpower training can be divided into:

(1) assessment of changing demand for scientific staff; and
(2) assessment of maximum training capacity existing in the country.

Also a problem of mobility of scientific personnel should be accounted for, both in the sense of transfer from one discipline to another and in the sense of geographical displacement. The experience shows that dynamic modelling permits to achieve positive results in forecasting of quantitative indices of manpower development. Dynamic models enable checking of various decision alternatives and determination of their future consequences taking into account natural lags of the education process. Forecasts of scientific manpower should be based on international comparisons. In case of short-term forecasts it is also possible to use the trend extrapolation technique.

Characteristics of the dynamics of resources for R&D and forecasts concerned with financing and technical equipment require the study of models describing such relationships as : resources - manpower, resources - results of research, resources - R&D cycles, etc. Since an analytical description of these relations has not yet been established, it is necessary to apply comparative and statistical techniques, trend analogy, correlation techniques.

Forecasting of change in the organizational structure of scientific institutions and establishments for higher education permits to formulate the premises for a future model of such institutions. Systems analysis seems to be most adequate to cope with this problem. The majority of forecasting studies in this field have however the form of scenarios that are based on personal experience of the authors and combination of this experience with observations of changes occurring in social and scientific life. The improvement of methodology of forecasting of changes in organizational structure is closely linked with the necessity for further progress in the domain of sociology of science, psychology of scientific creativity, and the theory of organization and management.

REFERENCES

1. R.U. Ayres, *Technological Forecasting and Long-Range Planning* 1969, McGraw Hill Inc.
2. D. Beckerhoff, Goal Systems for Governmental R&D Planning, *Technological Forecasting* 1970, Nr 1, 363-69.
3. A.W. Blackmann, "New Venture Planning: The Role of Technological Forecasting", *Technological Forecasting and Social Change* 1973, V. 5. Nr 1, 25-50.
4. G.M. Dobrov, Programno-celewyje principy uprawlenia nauczno-techniczeskim progressom, Naukowedieniel Informatika, 1974, Nr 12, 3-7.
5. G.M. Dobrov, J.W. Erschov, E.I. Levin, L.P. Smirnoy, Ekspertnyje ocenki wnauczno-techniczeskim prognozirowanil, Kiev 1974, 41.
6. D.M. Gvishiani, Scentralizowane kieowanie dziaalnoscia, naukowa; korzysci i problemy, "Zagadnienia Naukoznawstwa", 1973, Nr 1/33/, 74-81.
7. Y.de Hemptinne, Les structures de planification des gouvernements pour la politique scientifique, UNESCO, SC/WS/88, Paris, 3.V., 1972.
8. Z. Janiszewski, Podrecznik dia samoukow/1976/, Przedruk w: "Oeuvres cholsies", Warszawa 1949.
9. P.M.S. Jones, Lessons from the objective appraisal of programmes at the national level-implications of criteria and policy, *Research Policy*, 1971, Nr 1, 10-26.

10. J.Kaczmarek, O zasadach polityki naukowej, Seria: Analizy, projekty, opinit, AP Nr 27, 1971, KNIT, Warszawa, 31.
11. W.Kesprzak K.Pelc. Ogoine zalozenia metody prognozowania rozwoju nauki l techniki w oparciu o model potrzeb, (General Assumptions of a Method of Forecasting the Development of Science and Technology on the basis of model of Needs) "Prace Naukoznawcze", Nr 5, 1972, 4-12.
12. T.Kocowski, Systemowa koncepcja repertuaru potrzeb czowieka, Osrodek Badan prognostycznych politechniki Wrocawskiej, Komunikat, Nr 54, Wrocaw 1974.
13. H.Krauch, Priorities for research and technological development, *Research Policy*, 1971, Nr 1, 28-39.
14. M. Krzyzak, J. Mikus, K.I. Pelc, Programowanie przedsiewziec naukowo-technicznych woparciu o analize potrzeb przy wykorzystaniu zasad systemu Pattern, (Planning of Scientific and Technological Undertakings on the Basis of Needs Analysis Using the Principles of Pattern System), Osrodek Badan Prognostycznych Politechniki Wroclawskiej, Wrocaw 1974, Report Nr 5.
15. I.Malecki, Zadania i zakres studiow nad polityka naukowa, Reterat na Sesji Naukowej "Szkolnictwo wyzsze i polityka naukowa w XXX-leciu PRL", 1975, I.P. N. ISz. W, Warszawa 21.
16. K.I. Pelc, Niektore problemy prognozowania rozwoju nauki, (some problems of Forecasting of science development) Komunikat Nr. 69, 1975. Wrocaw, Osrodek Badan prognostycznych politechniki Wrocawskiej, 23.
17. E.B. Roberts, Dynamics of Research and Development, New York, 1969.
18. Science and Technology Development up to A.D. 2000 - Tokyo, 1973, Japan Techno-Economies Society, 199.
19. Studiengruppe fur Systemfors ung e.V: Priorities in Research Policy, *Research Policy*, 1973, V. 2, Nr 2, 94-126.

11

THE NEW ROLE OF LIBRARIES

Satish C. Seth

The future of libraries in India is intimately linked with the future of India itself.

A few societal features pertaining to India need to be pointed out before we can answer the question as to what we can really expect Indian libraries to be doing around 2000 AD.

These features include the basic fact that India is a large human system. It has, therefore, large human needs. We are around 630 million people now. We shall be having approximately 960 million people by 2000 AD. In fact, between the age group of 6 to 14, by the turn of the century, we shall be having 120 million children. This fact of numbers, be they children or be they adults, is a foremost factor to determine how many libraries we need, what kind of libraries should they be, and finally in what manner can we dovetail the library movement of the country to reinforce all those factors, which at the advent of the 21st century should make India a knowledge-based society.

The second important societal feature relates to the poverty condition of the country and its diversified and uneven growth. Today over 50 per cent of people (plus or minus) both in the rural and in the urban areas are below the poverty line. This means that nearly one half of India's population on a per person basis has a spending capacity only of Re. 1 per day to meet all kinds of daily needs: food needs, housing needs, education needs, health needs, transportation needs, etc. Further this sector of population suffers a double poverty. All in all, nearly 70 per cent of our population is not literate. Against this poverty condition we can easily judge that the library movement which is supposed to supplement the educational input in a society should be in a position to cater, in a special way, for this deprived half of our country and offer them free of cost, such knowledge, information, facts and figures so that the poverty stricken people may be saved the burden of education and use it instead to buy food. The leaders of library movement of this nation should ponder in what manner they can impart relevant information and knowledge to this section of society preferably near their door-steps. At least this objective could be part of a preferred future.

When one examines such aspects that characterize this society one has to *de novo* look at the institutional character of the Indian Library System which, if may hazard an opinion, today, with some exception, has an elitist character almost similar to other institutions that India has developed over the last 30 years, be it in industry, in education or elsewhere; these are preponderantly serving the well-to-do urban community. Nobody can deny that there are some libraries in the rural side too. But then our villages too have their elitist.

It is my belief that the library of the future will be the library of the people, run by the people and for the people, but guided by professionally trained librarians.

Yet another feature of India that we need to remember is that India simultaneously coexists in the state of agraria, industria and post-industria. Also, there is a strange coexistence of time in our country. Even though we are in the 20th century, we seem to dwell at the same time in several centuries. In each household there are persons whose lifestyle would correspond not to the 20th century but to different centuries; the Grandmother lives in one century, father in the second and the children in yet another. They have different value systems. Likewise, they have also different reading interests. The library movement has to respond to this Indian peculiarity also. In fact, this fact also puts additional burden on the literature content of the non-specialized libraries inasmuch as they have to become, amongst other instruments of social transformation, a potential force to promote a certain homogeneity of values, thought, information and knowledge.

One last point that is also important is that of technological plurality. India is in the bullock-cart age. India is also in the space age. India has the third largest community of scientists but to quote an eminent Indian "our scientists have science in one eye and superstition in the other."

Additionally, change is something that people in our society still want to avoid. They are too past oriented. In fact, glorification of the past is a dominant cultural trait of the Indian people. The concern for future takes a secondary place, if any. The hold of tradition also dominates and affects societal attitude governing choice of technology. The library movement too is, thus, not immune from this fact. Its growth and diversification and lack of future promotional goals and objective are judged by bureaucracies with mixed up, past oriented decisions. Even the legitimate demands of the libraries and their needs, say in terms of library equipment, etc., has continued to receive in a dithering and grudging manner, grants-in-aid which can hardly serve the cause of *status quo* rather than help the diversification of their programmes in different parts of the country. It is my belief that hereafter Library network will be deemed as integral to national educational and social literacy net-work and shall share at least 40 per cent, if not more, of the funds spent for education anywhere in the country be it at the Centre or in the States. If legislation be the answer for this preferred future, then work in this direction should commence now. After all "Future is today".

To sum up, it is against some of the above mentioned and other socioeconomic realities of the Indian life that we need to judge what the Indian libraries and the library movement shall be doing around 2000 AD particularly in a world which is increasingly becoming totally interdependent.

The scenario for the 2000 AD is one where we increase exchange of books and knowledge between the rural and the urban side. To begin with, it would be a one way traffic. Subsequently, however, the rural life shall be communicated by the rural libraries to the urban area like the folk dance or the folk music. The knowledge of the folk lore and of the rural, tribal and country life, their needs and aspirations have to be nationally shared. We need not romanticize the rural life only through hollow political slogans, instead we need to add the touch of romance to the Indian realities and local customs, traditions, the regional way of living by rousing national awareness through the use of the most sophisticated modern methods of visual and media communications. In this exercise it is my belief that the libraries will play a dominant role.

Secondly, I visualize that 75 per cent of our libraries during the beginning of the 21st century will be mobile libraries. Libraries should shed the club like character. Libraries should acquire a character of fire-brigades. Wherever knowledge is needed, a knowledge package, should begin to move in that direction.

Thirdly, it is my belief that the library movement in the early 21st century will enter some non-traditional and novel areas. For instance, internationai tourism amongst other facilities will also provide a miniature library service to the tourists. Many countries' airports and hotels, remote recreation centres, will have mini-libraries introducing the local custom, culture, history and related aspects. The similar, people oriented services could be part of hospitals, railway trains and even temples.

Fourthly, the key-note of this futuristic scenario, clearly indicate that the traditional form and role of library set-up will, hereafter, become diversified to totally unknown avenues thus requiring many new elements of training of the future libraries. The librarian of the future will not merely be a technician who knows how to classify or retrieve books. He shall also become a multidisciplinary and multipurpose professional. I visualize the future librarian as a moving store-house of immense knowledge. I see him as a guide, as a teacher, as an extension worker, a display artist and an expert who can abstract, in a very little time, the relevant information in fact, a person who can provide, of the cuff, all the need-based information.

Fifthly, if the libraries of the future in India have to perform so many functions as enumerated above, and have also to relate themselves to the societal needs, then such libraries will have to be given the best technological aids and adequate funding and even authorization to reproduce literature from complicated sources and material to an easy to read information display through pictorial or other visual-forms.

Finally, and in conclusion, I would like to restate my belief that no society in the future can hope to survive with dignity if it is not a knowledge-based society. The discrimination of knowledge to a few thousand or a couple of million people is easy. Reaching a billion people is a formidable challenge.

India's future lies in turning our population into a resource and an asset.

It is my belief that Indian educational endeavour, which

today is rigid, expensive, out-moded, elitist, and the privilege of a minority, if it has to become a developmental force and the privilege of millions of Indians then, fifty per cent of this exercise, inasmuch as it relates to disseminate information and to create conditions where learning becomes possible, will in future, be the business of the libraries of India.

INTEGRATION OF MODERN AND TRADITIONAL TECHNOLOGIES FOR DEVELOPMENT

*Arnoldo K. Ventura**

Abstract

Although the concept of improving traditional technologies by merging them with modern methods is not new[1], the upsurge of versatile technologies as a consequence of recent scientific discoveries and the prompting of Third World countries to make use of these advanced techniques[2,3] have given new impetus and meaning to this idea. However, the technological gap between the industrialized and the Third World countries is so wide that, on one hand, the feasibility of successfully accomplishing such mergers may be questioned. While, on the other, it may be argued. The poor countries cannot expect to attain a decent standard of living, or a modicum of economic independence, without participating in the new technological trends. Nevertheless, if ways were found to integrate the social and cultural advantages of traditional technologies, with the efficiency and scope of modern technologies, unquestionably much could be done to improve production in traditional communities. This paper seeks to examine some of the factors which have to be contemplated when attempts are made to graft modern technique into traditional activities.

Descriptions

Traditional and scientific technologies are ascribed a range of meanings; consequently for the purposes of this paper, they require explanation.

(a) *Traditional Technologies*

One of the chief distinguishing features of these technologies is their foundation in local traditions, mores and customs, because

* University of Miami Rickenbacker Causeway Miami, Florida, USA.

they have evolved over considerable periods of time to suit local conditions and purpose. Traditional technologies are so well fitted to local skills and available resources, that they are literally the social pivots of many populations. They have become a way of life instead of just means towards generating a living[4].

Since most of these technologies predate the scientific era, they are the empirical results of socio-cultural and environmental demands and, therefore, have transcended mere economic imperatives. Many traditional technologies are yet to be fully explained scientifically, but they are socio-culturally compatible, ecologically sound, suited to renewable forms of energy, low capital outlays and high labour content. They depend on human skills as well as home, or village, base production. The ensuing products are therefore unsophisticated and geared to serve limited and special markets.

Although the skills required are relatively simple and easily acquired, the persons these technologies engage are usually well known and respected in their communities; thereby providing a good measure of social cohesion and personal satisfaction. Essentially, traditional technologies are the foundation of agrarian economies, which still support 60 per cent of the world's population. They support rituals and agriculture, provide food, feed, clothing and shelter and maintain health in many areas.

Traditional technologies have unfortunately not evolved at a pace to satisfy the demands of ever expanding populations, progressively rigorous local conditions, changing consumer preferences and intense commercial competition from industrialized centers. Consequently, they are falling into disrepair and extinction.

(b) *Scientific Technologies*

Recent scientific developments in the physical[5] and biological[6] sciences have spawned a range of new technologies[7,8] which are revolutionizing industrial production, trade, transportation and communication. These new technologies are characterized by the fact that they are the immediate and direct consequence of forefront scientific discoveries. So pervasive are these scientific technologies that they are creating new fervor in product demand, novel manufacturing processes, modified employment possibilities, shifting trading patterns and social stability. They are rapidly forcing classical and conventional methods and productive systems into obsolescence. This new era is being compared to the agricultural and industrial revolutions in socio-economic impact.

Since these technologies are the immediate consequence of laboratory results, they have not been moulded by social or economic forces. Many are inculcated into commerce not by demand, but simply by the fact that they exist. This type of determinism has precipitated social effects, which are just being felt and understood. There are as many unsettling as there are beneficial effects being seen. Microelectronics, for example, have made many jobs on the factory floor, as well as in management, redundant, while at the same time, high speed, versatile information processing and control have opened up new service possibilities. Likewise, new bio-technologies, such as genetic engineering and tissue culture, have made it possible to produce products *in vitro*, which formerly depended on large-scale operations and much physical labour[9], while there is fear that the natural ecological balance may be severely disturbed by them.

Microelectronics, a set of scientific technologies, which arose as a consequence of applied scientific discoveries leading to the transistor and the silicon chip[10], and bio-technologies, an extensive group of technologies, emerging from genetic engineering[11] hybridomas[12] and enzyme innovations[13], among other biological developments, are the two most consequential of the scientific technologies. They are, characteristically, resource and energy conserving, relatively low capital demanding, ecologically acceptable, and suitable for decentralized operations. These characteristics they share with traditional technologies, but additionally, they allow much greater production efficiency and wider scope of operation and therefore, are highly commercially viable. Scientific technologies consequently, have the potential to replace traditional technologies as well as conventional methods which service smoke stack industries.

For expeditious creation and adoption, scientific technologies demand high level technological skills and knowledge. Unlike the static state of traditional technologies, scientific technologies are constantly changing, causing a great deal of social uneasiness and dislocation. Meanwhile, anticipation of lucrative returns from the application of these forefront methods have generated excessive competition and the restriction of technological as well as scientific information. This stands in marked contrast to the openness in which traditional technologies are practiced and the relative ease with which purely scientific information was previously obtained.

In the wake of scientific technologies, dextrous skills and age old crafts, crucial to the pursuit of traditional activities, are being lost. Instead, manufacture of products require more scientific and engineering knowledge. Pursuant to this, markets for these products are constantly changing in sophistication and requirements. In consumer oriented societies products quite quickly become outdated as greater options and new features are presented at unprecedented rates. Advertisement plays a key role in generating consumer dissatisfaction with existing products and creates a constant demand for endless change.

Situation Prevailing in Third World Countries

Although traditional technologies form the productive backbone of many poor societies, and are highly suited to such environments, they are rapidly being superseded by more efficient modern methods. In many cases they are rendered antiquated by the products of such methods, leaving many local production units idle and workers unemployed. The rate of this type of displacement appears to have increased with the advent of the flexible, and highly efficient, scientific technologies. The quality and price of products from local and foreign urban centres become more attractive to consumers than similar products manufactured in rural and other traditional settings, for example, bread, beer, furniture, clothing and household utensils. Many traditional operations just cannot compete, leading to widespread unemployment among skilled artisans and craftsmen in many communities. Consequently, there is perceptible dislocation of cultural norms and rising tides of hopelessness and frustration. Traditional technologies, which once provided food, shelter and other amenities of life, have become largely expendable in some situations and incapable of even maintaining mere subsistence in others.

The failure of traditional technologies has resulted from benign neglect over long periods of time. The attitude of insensitivity to the plight of the poor and disfranchised by the custodians and intellectuals of society, has allowed this problem to reach very damaging proportions, without any serious remedy being devised. So bad has the neglect been, that many societies, where the majority of citizens depend on traditional technologies, have not yet done a comprehensive tally of the technologies used to sustain their populations. Furthermore, many of the technologies which are known, have not yet been examined and explained in modern scientific and technological terms, and their cultural cohesiveness is sometimes appreciated only after the technologies are replaced and unpleasant consequences begin to emerge.

There is no doubt that the survival of most of the world's population will depend, at least in the short-term, on the resurrection, or maintenance, of traditional technologies[14]. This belief is based on the reasoning that large-scale introduction of new, more efficient technologies, in poor areas in the near future, is impossible because of lack of resources to accomplish this task, while abandoning traditional technologies and putting entire populations on some sort of welfare is likewise impossible. The only feasibility option remaining in the context of social justice and the complexity of socio-economic underdevelopment, is the deliberate upgrading of traditional technologies, to make them more responsive to current circumstances. This upgrading may not have been possible using components of the high capital, energy intensive, centralized and polluting, conventional technologies of yesterday, but the decentralized, low capital and energy intensive, ecological compatible scientific technologies of today, appear to offer more encouraging merging possibilities.

Possibilities for Merging Traditional and Scientific Technologies

The numerous conceivable ways in which scientific technologies may be used to enhance traditional technologies, cannot be discussed here, but a few examples to delineate the scope of scientific technologies, will suffice to show the spectrum of such possibilities.

Microelectronics, for example, can provide low cost, small-scale applications, made possible by miniaturization and economies of scale, which offer high flexibility and therefore could logically be used to improve the efficiency and scope of traditional technologies. Likewise, biotechnologies can contribute to higher yields and better processing of agricultural materials.

The opportunities which appear immediately attractive are those which impinge on the production of food and energy.

Provision of safe, biologically produced, nitrogen fertilizer could revolutionize food production in poor countries. While more efficient production of biomass, through higher yielding varieties, created by biotechnological means such as tissue culture and improved symbiotic relationships and the better harnessing of sunlight and other natural forces, by photovoltaic and microelectronic technologies, could provide more affordable energy.

Combinations of traditional with scientific technologies have taken place in a few industrialized countries. Notable is the restructuring of the traditional fermentation industry of Japan by the introduction of the most modern fermentation techniques and micro organisms[15]. This could serve as an example for immediate emulation by many Third World countries because they possess age old fermentation technologies[16]. Another example worth mentioning here, is the upgrading of the traditional textile industry in Prato, Italy, by the incorporation of automatic systems, fixing and sizing of materials by electronically controlled methods, and the use of teletext to distribute information on sectorial innovations, as improvements take place throughout the system. The importance of this example lies in the fact that the traditional decentralized activities, composing this extensive system, were not disturbed, rather they were strengthened[17]. Mini-hydro and biogas technologies are now being improved by microprocessors in some industrialized countries[18].

A few cases of successful marriages of traditional and scientific technologies in Third World countries are also reported, such as the use of new materials and microchip technology to upgrade the traditional horizontal water wheel, and the improvement of textile and metal industries by microprocessors and robotics. Simple robotics can help metal-smiths to optimize flux formations, solder and braze alloys and anodize and blue materials. Designs for metal products can be made, produced and disseminated by micro-electronics and computer aided design techniques. Similarly traditional ceramic industries may be improved by optimization of body and glaze formations, which could incorporate a greater portion of local clays and chemical earths[19].

Introduction of microprocessors and minicomputers has allowed a reversal of the trend to concentrate industries in urban areas. Since these technologies do not require large allocations of resources, nor high concentrations and close approximations of people and services, they can be transferred to rural settings, where most traditional technologies exist. Microelectronics, in principle, offer possibilities of cost reductions and increased product quality in large as well as small-scale industries.

Decentralized minifactories are now possible because of the feasibility of batch production. Microelectronics can afford better production, management, accounting and marketing. Heightened efficiency has been attained in the control and movement of materials, component parts and finished products, in shaping, designing, cutting, mixing and moulding, assembly of components, quality control, testing and inspection, as well as better analysis, design, manufacture and maintenance operations[20]. There are also successful applications in stock keeping, cost accounting and invoicing, job control and periodic data collections. This list serves to indicate the versatility of microprocessors and their ability to reduce human drudgery, improve efficiency and reduce exposure to hazardous operations.

Most Third World countries posses large agrobased economies and most have long histories of using microbes to produce vitally needed products. Also, most of the problems in these countries are biological in nature, for example over-population, soil erosion and lack of food. Logically, biotechnology offers a lot of benefits via agro-industrial development in such countries. These technologies are unfolding each day at unprecedented rates. Already they have demonstrated their superior efficiency and scope for the manufacture of products of increased value from a wide variety of renewable resources, for example, sugars, sweeteners, enzymes, food additives, fine chemicals, amino acids and many other commodities. As agriculture emerges as a significant and safe source for bulk chemicals, the importance of biotechnology to Third World countries increases. Opportunities for the application of biotechnologies in the Third World are not only many, but some are ideally suited to these countries.

Although serious changes, for example, in work habits, lifestyles, peer recognition and other social structures, are expected if traditional technologies are upgraded by modern methods, it would appear that an incremental blending procedure would be socially and psychologically more palatable than large-scale replacement of age old techniques.

Impediments to Successful Amalgamations of Traditional and Scientific Technologies

The blending of traditional and scientific technologies is expected to face predictable as well as unforeseen obstacles. The logical obstacles will stem from the technological gap between traditional and scientific oriented societies, and the less obvious ones may be more of a psycho-cultural nature. However, it is good to remember that many scientific technologies are of very recent vintage and their social impacts have not yet been fully felt, either in the South or in the North.

It is clear, considering the disparities between rich and poor countries, that traditional modes of production will have limited capacities to absorb aspects of forefront technologies[20]. Traditional producers are generally poor, producing mainly for subsistence rather than for commerce, and are hampered by illiteracy and lack of vital information. Furthermore, they live in situations with limited supplies of energy, clean water and technical infrastructure. The sophisticated skills and infrastructure required to create and use scientific technologies are largely not present in poor countries. Nevertheless, closer collaboration between scientists and traditional producers in these countries could begin the process of upliftment of traditional methods. It may well be that at first, all that can be hoped for is the replacement of facets of traditional production by tested products of scientific technologies, in such a way that not much added technological skill and inputs are required by traditional producers. This should be the beginning of a process which will gradually uplift entire populations, not only in production and efficiency, but also in attitude and willingness to innovate to solve problems.

Presently, scientific technologies instead of enhancing traditional activities, are rapidly displacing them. These technologies are also replacing conventional technologies in industrial areas as they prove to be cheaper, safer and easier to deploy, but at the same time they are causing widespread unemployment and an accelerated obsolescence of existing knowledge, skills and related values. Such effects will be devastating to traditional societies. Industrialized countries have not yet found ways to deal with these mal-effects of scientific technologies and it is difficult to see how Third World countries would cope if these features of modern technologies were indiscriminately imported in conjunction with perceived benefits.

Third World countries lack adequate local knowledge, skills, education, literacy, management, financial resources, and back-up services, which will undoubtedly make it very difficult to establish successful mergers with scientific methods, which require high levels of most, if not all, of these ingredients.

It is not so much that mergers could not be established, but whether they would exacerbate, or correct, existing problems of alienation and disfranchisement of most of the citizens in poor societies, is debatable. Memories of the green revolution are still fresh in the minds of such communities. The new varieties were of benefit mostly to those farmers, who were already well-off and had access to fertilizers, pesticides and water, necessities of the new production system.

Improvements in cost per productive unit, guaranteed by scientific technologies, is expected to increase productivity per unit of factor input as well as quality of output, in conventional, or traditional situations. But only traditional activities in the formal small, medium or large-scale sectors, with capital outlays, gumption to risk failure, access to sufficient energy, transportation, maintenance and repair facilities, are expected to benefit. Traditional activities in the informal sector will once again be left behind if well considered policies are not implemented to remedy this chronic blunder, common to all Third World countries.

The social consequences of the new technologies are not yet fully understood, but it is patently clear that a great deal of social and political adjustments will be required to reduce the dislocating effects which are anticipated. Retraining of many conventional workers appears to be one way to abate the impact of large-scale unemployment being caused by scientific technologies in the industrialized countries. In the case of the Third World, it is not a matter of retaining, but rather, the initiation of traditional workers to technical skills to ply forefront methods. The task is not only difficult but requires time, significant amounts of financial resources and patience, which are not easily found in poor societies.

Although, perpetual improvements in quality and designs may be desirable in high-income countries, poor societies, except for export purposes, are more concerned with mere availability and safety of products for internal consumption. Mergers between forefront and traditional technologies, if care is not taken, may lead to products which are excessively luxurious and irrelevant to the needs of poor countries. Which furthermore, require an inordinate reliance on outside expertise, resources and high income markets. Cost effectiveness and cultural acceptability, within small unsophisticated markets, must be serious considerations when contemplating upgrading traditional with scientific technologies.

Steps to Facilitate Successful Mergers between Traditional and Scientific Technologies

The technological gap between traditional and scientific technologies is so great that we cannot expect mergers between the two to be handled instinctively and automatically. Furthermore, scarcity of human resources, deficiencies in government planning, organization and implementation, and lack of sufficient entrepreneurship, as well as socio-psychological and cultural biases and resistance to change in traditional sectors, have prevented absorption of technologies in Third World countries. It is obvious then that dedicated planning and implementation are required to bring about acceptable successful marriages of traditional with scientific technologies. Such dedicated actions will not be possible without full government support. And such actions will not be expeditiously taken without sufficient knowledge about the circumscribed socio-economic and scientific effectiveness of traditional technologies. The tendency to belittle traditional activities in many Third World countries must logically be replaced with ideas of their centrality to the development process.

To enhance traditional technologies by blending them with forefront technologies will not only require intimate knowledge of traditional methods, but the range, scope and potential social effects of scientific technologies must be comprehended as well. Since there is rapid evolution of these technologies, there has to be an active information network to keep pace with them[21]. Likewise, the fate of mergers already in progress must be followed and analysed to establish better ways to select and predict the socio-economic viability of such marriages.

Since most of the research and development (R&D) concerning scientific technologies now take place in industrialized countries, with vastly dissimilar conditions from Third World countries, as far as is possible, the latter, either alone or in concert with others, must undertake R&D more pertinent to their circumstances. Cooperative ventures among traditional workers may also be useful in situations where inputs and production sizes are beyond the capability of individuals, or families. Also, since enhancement of traditional technologies, by the incorporation of scientific technologies, is important to industrialized countries, situations may arise where both they and Third World countries may find it mutually beneficial to tackle such problems by twinning arrangements[22].

Conclusion

It is abundantly clear that without far-reaching and urgent actions, most traditional technologies will become extinct, either by failure to satisfy local needs, or by rapid displacement with scientific technologies. Mergers between these two sets of technologies, to preserve the attractive cultural and ecological qualities of the former and to capture the efficiency and scope of the latter, are probably indispensable to the resuscitation of these age tested methods, on which most of mankind depend.

Fortunately, the versatility of scientific technologies offers a range of blending options, options which did not exist before.

The large profits, which scientific technologies promise, have spawned such intense competition, that related scientific and technical information are being increasingly restricted. Therefore, without dedicated government and international actions, many traditional societies will be cut off from the vital supply of new and emerging scientific and technological knowledge, which seems to be the only hope for their survival. Consequently, it is incumbent now, more than ever, that Third World countries become more knowledgeable about their traditional technologies and take steps to improve them through active participation in the development and use of scientific technologies.

REFERENCES

1. R.S. Sagasti, 'Reflection on the endogenization of the scientific technological revolution in underdeveloped countries" in *Technology, Planning and Self-reliant Development* (New York: Praeger Publ., 1979) pp. 163-176
2. E.U. Weizsacker, M.S. Swaminathan and A. Lemma, *New Frontiers in Technology Application. Integration of Emerging and Traditional Technologies* (Dublin: Tycooly International Publ. Ltd., 1983).
3. UNCSTD, Proceedings of workshop pioneer projects on the integration of emerging and traditional technologies (Tokyo: APIC, 1984).
4. M.S. Swaminathan, "Introduction" in *New Frontiers in Technology Application* (Dublin: Tycooly International Publ. Ltd., 1983).
5. A.King, "A new industrial revolution or just another technology" in G. Friedrichs and A. Schaff (eds) *Microelectronics and Society—For Better or for Worse* (New York: Pergamon Press, 1982) and *Microstructure Science - Engineering and Technology* (Washington DC: NAS, 1979).
6. *Scientific American* 1981, Volume 245 is entirely devoted to this question.
7. S. Jacobsson and J. Sigursdson, *Technological trends and challenges in electronics* (Lund: Research Policy Institutes, 1983).
8. "Present and future frontiers of the sciences and future of applied sciences" in *Science* Volume 209, 1980, pp. 64-122 and 123-146, as well as other chapters in this volume.
9. A.K. Ventura, "Biotechnologies and their implications for third world development", *Technology in Society* (11 : 1982), pp. 109-129.

10. "How to get a bright idea", *Economist* (December 27 : 1980) pp. 59-66.
11. S.A. Narang, *Genetic Engineering: The Technology and its Applications.* A report from consultations in the implications of advances in genetic engineering for developing countries (Vienna: UNIDO, 1981).
12. "Making pure antibodies", *Economist*, (February 7 : 1981) p. 95, and H.J. Phaff, "Industrial micro organisms", *Scientific American*, (245 : 1981) pp. 77-89.
13. D.E. Eveleigh, "The microbiological production of industrial chemicals", *Scientific American*, (245 : 1981) pp. 155-179.
14. E. Goldsmith, "Traditional Agriculture in Sri Lanka", *The Ecologist* (12 : 1982) pp. 209-212.
15. A. Bull and J. Bulock, "The living micro-revolution", *New Scientists* (82 : 1979) pp. 808-810, and personal communications with several Japanese technologists and scientists.
16. A.K. Ventura,. "Marriage of traditional and modern technologies for the amelioration of underdevelopment" in *New Frontiers* (1983).
17. *Blending of New and Traditional Technologies*, A portfolio of experiments and projects (Geneva : ILO, 1984).
18. U. Colombo, Keynote speech at the International Workshop. Pioneer projects on the integration of emerging and traditional technologies (Tokyo: UNCSTD/ APIC, 1984).
19. E.S. Ayensu, "Technological Innovations and the Third World Nations" in *New Frontiers* (1983).
20. A.S. Bhalla and J. James, "An approach towards integration of emerging and traditional technologies" (Geneva : ILO, 1983).
21. A.K. Ventura, "Jamaica's Bauxite Battle", in *Intelligence for Development* (Paris: OECD, 1984).
22. A.K. Ventura, "Criteria for establishing twinning arrangements" (Stockholm: World Association of Industrial Technological Research Organisations, 1983).

TOWARDS A MORE COMPREHENSIVE SOCIO-ECONOMIC ANALYSIS

Mario Kamenetzky

Introduction

Our capacity to feel, to think about, and to act upon the problems arising in our lives develops in three distinct steps. In the first of these steps, we gain an ability to perceive problems and needs but we do not go on to analyze them. This describes the situation we have seen among poor, despondent peasants who perceive their poverty, their suffering, their illness, but do not understand the reason this is happening to them or what they might do about it. It is also the situation of the early navigators who perceived themselves to be sick after long periods of sailing but could not relate this sickness to their lack of fresh food.

In the second step of our development, we acquire an ability to analyze and experiment. Now we can divide each problem into its parts and deal with these separately. This is what some community development movements are teaching to peasants, who then inquire into the causes of their poverty and discover that they possess the power to assume control over their destiny through overcoming the problems of poverty. Scientists followed a similar pattern of analysis when they discovered that the illness of sailors, contracted on long travels, was a consequence of lack of vitamin C in their diet. Having analyzed the problem, they were then able to recommend addition of citrus fruits to the sailors diet, and later on to even synthesize vitamin C.

As humans, we tend to arrest our development at this second step, failing to press on to the third in which we would acquire an ability to take a holistic view of ourselves and our situation in life. Thus, while we appreciate the power of analytical thinking and the ability it gives us to see cause and effect relationships, we fail

* (The author is currently with the World Bank).

to see the interconnections among these relationships, to see how things are put together and work together, to deal with the whole system and not only with its parts. Only by pressing on into this third step do we gain wisdom. In the development of poor communities this wisdom is reached when peasants learn to connect their personal problems at the village level with the political context of the country and the world, when they begin to act locally but to think globally.

Unfortunately, most of the sciences have not yet reached this third step. Although they have developed powerful analytical tools and use these with great effect, they fail to carry on their efforts within the framework of holistic wisdom. For example, a person who has been living on a deficient diet may contract heart disease and die of it, but doctors will very likely diagnose the cause of death only as heart disease and ignore the malnutrition. Indeed, the chances are that the doctor will have been treating the person only for heart disease.

In this paper, we propose to submit the socio-economic system to an analysis that is more comprehensive than that of current practice, examining both, the factors required by the functioning of the system as well as the elements resulting from that functioning. This complex analytical scheme will enable us to suggest some of the elements for the design of new socio-economic paradigms. We shall then conclude this paper by calling for research on the degree and nature of the relationships among the different elements of such a paradigm. We indicate that greater knowledge is required to perfect the analysis and to increase the feasibility of a holistic design.

The Increased Complexity of Socio-economic Systems

The relationship between inputs and outputs of a given socio-economic system is becoming more and more complex. It is no longer possible to make the simple assertion that capital, labour and natural resources are mobilized to generate products, services, and sometimes a surplus of capital; or to argue that as long as the money introduced into the market to pay for the mobilized capital, labour and resources is backed by the appropriate amount of goods and services, the society will be economically stable. If we want to have a clear picture of present problems and try new-ways of solving them, we must refine our analysis. New elements will appear and some of the old, all-embracing representations will need to be divided into simpler and more distinctive components in order to better understand their separate and individual roles.

Each division and addition introduces greater complexity to our analysis; these complexities are presented below, not in the historical sequence of their scholarly acceptance, but in the order that we recognized them as we tried to integrate them into a single holistic relationship. All but one of the complexities proposed below have been studied in the literature on sociology, economics and technology. The introduction of libidinal energy and gratuitous satisfactors is an original proposal of our own.

In what follows, we shall use the term "market" to mean any set of actual or potential buyers, sellers, users, consumers, producers and manufacturers of satisfactors who are engaged in transactions of one kind or another. Following this definition, we may say that products and services are marketed in both capitalistic and socialist economies.

First Complexity: The Production of Waste

Whenever capital, labour and resources are mobilized in the production of goods, they are accompanied by the wastage of a given amount of energy and materials. As there is no marketable item generated as a counterpart to the cost of the capital, labour and resources consumed in producing this "waste," the process of production inescapably creates a certain amount of inflation. (Rifkin, S., 1980). Some of the goods and services produced, particularly arms and armies, are themselves waste because they are produced to be kept outside the consumer or capital goods markets. Hence, the huge amounts of money — about $450 billion in 1981 alone—spent for military purposes have a much stronger inflationary effect than the waste resulting from the normal productive activities of a society. Accordingly, waste and armaments should be studied as a distinctive kind of output of a socio-economic system. They are neither marketable goods and services nor are they satisfactors.

Second Complexity: Renewable and Non-renewable Resources

We need also to distinguish between resources that are renewable through nature's short and medium-term cycles and those that are the product of long-term or one-time evolutions. As the latter become depleted, their very scarcity causes their price to increase. This is a source of additional inflationary pressure.

Third Complexity: Knowledge

Production today goes beyond mere mobilization of capital, labour and resources to require the application of knowledge. A country with oil reserves and even abundant labour and money will find these rèserves remaining underground as potential resources which do not increase the country's product unless it is able to command the technological knowledge required to organize the exploration, extraction, and processing of the oil, and the distribution of the refined products.

It is only recently that technology, defined as the organized set of empirical and scientific knowledge required to produce goods and services has begun to be considered as an additional production factor. In the past, the knowledge required for production was mostly empirical and embodied in the workers, managers, and entrepreneurs. Hence, paying salaries to workers and managers and directing dividend benefits to entrepreneurs was considered to remunerate the use of knowledge. Ninety-five per cent of the energy used for production was supplied by human muscle.

Today the situation is just the opposite. Only five per cent of the total amount of energy used in production now comes from human muscle while knowledge of the use of other forms of energy of the control of tools and of production processes has become increasingly scientific. This knowledge, embodied in books, diagrams, computer programs and the like, must now be remunerated apart from labour. Moreover, the process of using technology for production also creates more knowledge. It is the traditional process of learning-by-doing which on many occasions, accounts for a sensible increase in productivity. (Dahlman, C. and Westphal, L., 1981). But we may also purposely mobilize capital, labour and existing knowledge for research which produces new scientific knowledge and new technologies. Knowledge is always an input to production, but it may also be an output from either productive or research work.

Fourth Complexity: Libidinal Energy

Labour traditionally has been considered as a form of human energy spent in productive activities and remunerated through wages and salaries, but human energy can also be spent for the direct satisfaction of individual needs through what we propose to call "libidinal activities" (Kamenetzky, M., 1981). We can satisfy needs through the use of our own body, through elements that are freely available in nature, or through products and services that we may purchase. Libidinal activities that make use only of the body or of free elements in nature are termed "gratuitous libidinal activities". Those that consume products or draw on services can be called "wealth consuming libidinal activities". Through gratuitous libidinal activities we experience the enjoyment of being, while through wealth-consuming libidinal activities we know the satisfaction of possessing. Productive activities provide the means for possessing and, within certain limits, they also add joy to being.

We should hence make a distinction between the two inputs to the activities performed in any economic system; one such input is human energy spent in productive activities and remunerated as labour and the other is human energy spent in libidinal activities and rewarded through the consumption of goods and services or through gratuitous satisfactors.

Fifth Complexity: Self-Help and Mutual Help Activities

Each of us has a given and limited supply of energy, a quantum, to be spent in our daily routine. Hence an inverse relationship exists between energy spent in productive activities and energy spent in libidinal activities ; also between the amount spent in libidinal activities that are wealth-consuming and the amount spent on such activities that are gratuitous.

Under primitive conditions, when the energy used for production was almost exclusively human energy, libidinal manifestations were limited to satisfying the barest biological needs for survival (nutrition, sleep, excretion, clothing, shelter and reproduction). Beyond these needs for survival, most of the remaining energy was devoted to productive purposes. Technological change then began to make possible the release of constantly increasing amounts of human energy from survival and work. This newly liberated energy could have been channelled towards gratuitous libidinal activities, particularly those of a sensual, recreational and relational nature. Instead, however, it was diverted to the consumption of goods and services. Services for the care and protection of the body and for learning, which were formerly provided gratuitously among individuals through self-help, mutual concern, and use of the quasi-free natural elements, became increasingly organized and centralized in the form of sophisticated marketable services to be purchased at increasingly high costs. The libidinal activities of a sensual nature, which could also be satisfied through gratuitous satisfactors, were kept under tight repressive control. Hence, even erotism became a field for big business.

There are indications now of a new trend towards re-evaluating self-help and mutual help activities. Forty-one million Americans already spend several hundred million hours each year on do-it-yourself home renovations. In 1980, such efforts had a $ 28 billion retail value Thirty-four million American families have vegetable gardens where they spend, on an average, nearly fifty hours each summer seeding and hoeing. These gardens produce fruit and vegetables worth an estimated $ 15 billion. Ten million people now belong to mental and physical mutual-help health-care groups, ranging from Weightwatchers Anonymous to Psychotics Anonymous. Their activities were valued in 1980 at $ 60 billion. (Stokes, 1982).

Consequently, we should consider the goods and services originating in self-help and mutual help activities as additional outputs in any socio-economic system, additional to the marketable goods and services and the gratuitous satisfactors.

Sixth Complexity: Population Growth

Population growth is the result of the only libidinal activity that can be (re) productive as well as gratuitous (relational and recreational sex) or wealth-consuming (prostitution and birth control). When lack of information and means or the weight of taboo and belief prevents reproductive sex from being clearly and distinctively separated from relational and recreational sex, population increases explosively. This is especially so when technological development extends life expectancy at birth from 32 years as average for all developing countries in 1935 to 49 years in 1970 (Morawetz, 1977).

The President of the World Bank recently stated that "in Africa there has been considerable progress in education, and in human resource development generally, though much yet remains to be done." But, he added, "there is one area—the continued growth of population—that still received inadequate attention. This matter requires urgent consideration if even modest prospects for growth in the near term are not to be overwhelmed by the demands of burgeoning populations." (Clausen, A.W., 1982)

With population growth rates in the order of two to three per cent per year, scarce resources are rapidly exhausted and the environment polluted beyond its self-cleaning capacity. Newborns should hence be included among the outputs in the analysis of any socio-economic system. We should account for the capital, human energy, natural resources and knowledge that will be required in order to feed, clothe, lodge, educate and provide healthcare services to these newborn—until they become productive.

Seventh Complexity: Forms of Capital Ownership

A holistic socio-economic analysis should go beyond the traditional distinction between public and private capital. Experience shows that, within these two forms of appropriation, two other forms have evolved: centralized and community-owned capital.

Centralized capital appears in market and centrally planned economies when production and distribution is performed by large corporations. These are highly hierarchical organizations that do not allow participation by the workers, and even less so the consumers, in establishing their objectives and in controlling their accomplishments. Community-owned capital is a form of ownership which is increasingly developing in the western industrialized societies and in some developing countries. Its mode of production is highly decentralized and its products or services are distributed in rather small markets. Both workers and consumers share the capital formation and participate in the design and control of the undertaking. All these forms of capital ownership should be taken into account if we want to build therapeutical, and non-utopian, paradigms.

Eighth Complexity: Foreign Exchange

Foreign exchange is a different form of capital. The word "capital" may be reserved to designate the result of internal accumulation while the term "foreign exchange" would refer to the product of external transactions. Production may require input from foreign exchange in addition to local capital. In some cases, wealth consuming libidinal activities also use foreign exchange in order to import satisfactors that are not produced locally. Some production on the other hand is export oriented and generates foreign exchange.

Summary

Initially, socio-economic analysis was based in a rather simple relationship between production factors and outputs, expressed as follows:

Capital + Labour + Natural Resources
Yield
Goods + Services + Capital

Slowly, under the pressure of technological change and the depletion of certain resources, it became necessary to give explicit consideration to some other previously neglected aspects. The relationship then appeared as follows:

Capital + Labour + Renewable and Non-Renewable
Resources + Knowledge
Yield
Goods + Services + Capital + Waste + Knowledge

At present, then the design of new paradigms requires a much more finely tuned analysis. For this analysis, the relationship among the inputs and outputs of a given socio-economic system may be written as follows:

> Centralized and Community-Owned Capital + Foreign Exchange + Human Energy Used for Productive Activities + Human Energy Used in Libidinal Wealth-Consuming Activities + Human Energy Used in Libidinal Gratuitous Activities + Renewable and Non-Renewable Resources + Knowledge
>
> *Yield*
>
> Goods and Services for Local Markets + Goods and Services from Self-Help and Mutual-Help Activities + Gratuitous Satisfactors + Capital + Foreign Exchange + Knowledge + Waste + Population Growth + Arms and Armies

Suggestions for the Design of a New Paradigm

When this above set of variable factors is used to design sociological paradigms, the following observations on markets and their organization should be taken into account:

(i) Consumption should refer not only to goods and services that are supplied to the markets by production units, but also to gratuitous satisfactors and products and services resulting from self-help and mutual-help activities.

(ii) The distribution of marketable goods and services will continue to be based on the consumer's ability to pay, while the latter will still be a function of current income, accumulated wealth, or both. Hence an equitable distribution of income should increase the ability of the poorest sectors of an economy to pay for marketable goods and services.

(iii) On the other hand, the distribution of gratuitous satisfactors and of goods and services resulting from self-help and mutual help activities will be based on the skills and talents of individuals to satisfy their needs by themselves or by cooperating with others. Education should develop these skills and talents at all levels of the society.

(iv) Large corporations, both public and private, will still play a role in infrastructural services, i.e. long distance transportation and communication systems and data banks, and in production of some raw materials and certain basic commodities like metals, fossil fuels, plastics, elastomers, and basic and fine chemicals. Efficiency in the production and distribution of these goods and services is of key importance in assuring the infrastructure that other smaller, local community-based enterprises need in order to flourish. The latter would aim at satisfying the needs that can be met by using decentralized services and consuming goods produced locally either by transformation of agricultural outputs or from raw materials and basic commodities distributed by the large corporations.

(v) The production of certain goods and services on a large-scale leads to a concentration of economic power in a few hands. The excessive potential power which results from this is often unresponsive to social wants. Hence, there is need for some form of social control on prices and practices of large public and private corporations, a form of control that can permit initiative and creativity even while prohibiting the manipulation of markets and people and a destructive use of Nature.

(vi) The public sector should facilitate the entry of small community-owned enterprises into their particular markets by providing financial support and organizing efficient market-oriented technical support services, i.e., information, trouble shooting, quality control. Governments should also promote and support research work to improve existing technologies for small-scale production or create new technologies when necessary and feasible. Public support to this type of research is required because small-scale community-owned enterprises producing for local markets lack incentive of the extra benefits which may derive from larger share of the markets that can be achieved through product differentiation.

(vii) It is increasingly difficult for the invisible hand (or voice) of the market to provide all the answers to the questions of what, how and for whom goods and services shall be produced. Some form of flexible planning is needed and it should be a planning that promotes decentralization. It should be based on the satisfaction of universal and unvarying needs (Kamenetzky, M., 1981), on the careful choice and design of technology under the particular constraints and opportunities of each investment project (Kamenetzky, M., 1982) and on the design of organizations that will help people to voice their desires, expand their productive and creative potential and take control over their own development.

(viii) Special educational programs are needed to awaken administrators of public enterprises and managers of large private corporations to an awareness of their rights to a full exercise of libidinal gratuitous activities. This could lead them to prefer an enlargement of their existence over seeking more possession and the expansion of their enterprises. This would have a highly positive effect on other levels of the society. Because they are the most visible and influential figures in our current socio-economic system, they are in an excellent position to promote the new legal and political frame-work that would allow the fearless and guilt-free exercise of gratuitous libidinal activities by all in their societies.

(ix) In the small towns and villages where small-scale undertakings should be developed, repression of gratuitous libidinal activities is often more severe than in the large cities. Such rules will need to be changed in order to produce the environment required for full human development within a small community and for effective and efficient small-scale production. Only under those conditions will small be felt as beautiful and a better balance between urban and rural areas be achieved.

(x) The distinction between foreign exchange and capital will be important in the design of paradigms if we want to go beyond the inward-looking and the export-oriented models of growth. We should be able to integrate these two models into an approach that will promote decentralized production for local markets and stimulate local demand without neglecting opportunities for exports based on real comparative advantages. A holistic vision should keep its distance from the misleading perception that there are unlimited external markets for products of competitive quality and price. Equally deceptive is the perception that it is possible to stop external flows to and from a given socio-economic system.

Proposals for Future Research

Some past experiments on social change have touched—with varying success—on such issues as the relocation of the locus of ownership of capital, the regulation of consumption, the reduction of the amount of human energy spent in productive activities, the balance between foreign exchange earned and spent, the protection of Nature, and a more efficient use and production of knowledge. None of those experiments attempted firm and durable steps towards facilitating the expression of gratuitous libidinal activities. Issues on individual gratification and interpersonal relationships are seldom brought to the political arena. And legal systems are slow in reacting to changes in the patterns of expression of gratuitous libidinal activities.

Societies which are delivering large amounts of marketable goods and services may be poor in allowing for gratuitous satisfactors and for goods and services derived from self-help and mutual-help activities. Their overall benefit/cost ratio may hence be lower than it could have been. The ratio may even increase when there is a decrease in marketable goods and services, if at the same time the social environment interposes no obstacles in the way of gratuitous activities and promotes self-help and mutual-help activities. This would happen either because of an increase in total output or because self-help and mutual-help activities often use less capital than that required for the commercial production of similar goods and services. The benefit/cost ratio would certainly increase with a decrease in the production of waste, in the number of arms, and in the size of armies.

In order to assess carefully the overall benefit/cost ratio of a given system in social terms, we should develop ways of accounting for the social value of the gratuitous satisfactors. For instance, singing and dancing could be valued by considering how much one would pay in order to be a spectator at a similar theatrical presentation. Prayer and meditation—with nothing more than the mind and the body as instruments to go beyond time and space into the realm of Mystery, the Sacred, and Infinity—could be valued at the average cost of religious services in a given community. The inputs of human energy for these and other gratuitous libidinal activities could be valued in terms of their average hourly consumption of calories. The valuation of other outputs of a system such as arms and armies may present similar challenges for their pricing in social terms. Arms could be negatively valued by taking into account the human life, wealth and resources that can be destroyed by their use. Analogously, armies could be negatively valued as the amount of labour lost in the form of soldiers who are outside the productive sector.

All these questions need to be addressed in future-oriented social research. Another appealing subject for future-oriented research is a determination of the optimal combination of the different elements required for or resulting from the activities performed in any socio-economic system.

PART TWO

Pyramids and Parameters of Public Policy

FUTURES STUDIES AND DEVELOPMENT STUDIES

*Johann Galtung**

Introduction

When we compare the situation today, in the middle of the 1970s with the social and economic situation ten years ago when the future studies movement in a sense emerged, there are some very important differences that probably may account for some of the changes in the future studies in recent years.

Thus, seen in retrospect, those were years of stability in the rich, industrialized countries in the West where future studies as a movement first appeared, at least under that name. There were certainly ups and downs, the Vietnam War caused severe and important doubts in many people, but by and large economic growth looked like something to be relied upon. And this had one important consequence, what would society be like if economic growth continued unabated?

In a sense future studies could be seen as an effort to answer this question: what to do in a society of affluence, with abundance of material means of satisfying human needs, and with abundance of free time. But there were nagging doubts. There was certainly a feeling among many that we could see the end of the road. Thus meaning that a very high proportion of the population was in the tertiary sector of economic activity, with primary and secondary sectors automated, highly productive and employing something like five per cent of the working force each and with GNP approaching orders of magnitude unheard of earlier in human history. The doubts were probably inspired by the feeling that we were already far along that road, far enough to doubt that further quantitative changes would lead to a qualitative jump that would bring in an era of happiness and self-fulfilment.

Thus, future studies in a world perspective became studies of how to solve leisure-time problems of the world's upper classes

---

* The author was the President, World Future Studies Federation.

—in a way so as to provide societies quickly running out of developmental programmes with new goals. But, and this is where the second doubt entered: there was a world outside the rich western world and the social and political dependence on this world made itself very clearly felt through the Vietnam War, ultimately ending with the fall of Saigon, 30th April 1975 — just as the economic and even military dependence on the Third World had become very clear through the oil action fall 1973.

One might probably say that this led to a new phase in future studies, a globalization of the futuristic concern leading to the era of the world models. In the world models the Third World was certainly brought in. But it was not brought in on their terms, in terms of unfulfilled aspirations, material and immaterial, of two billion or so people — most of them longing for autonomy. Rather, the dominant approach, as seen in the reports to the Club of Rome, was coloured by perceptions held by elites in the First World. There was the feeling of crisis. Hence, a report had to express, indeed give a basis for a crisis understanding, while at the same time producing the type of approach that made crisis management from western centres in the world not only possible but necessary.

It is well known that the way this was done was through the introduction of ecological variables; the idea of the finite world of global scarcity. Whereas earlier one could say that the more stable the period the more future studies were carried out, but it now looked as if the more crises the western - dominated system was exposed to the more future studies would be produced with a public appeal because they delivered crisis images, but seen as resource crises, in terms of local scarcities that were then presented as global scarcities rather than as structural crises.

Gone were the days when the major concern was leisure-time activities and how to manage a society of affluence; the days of crises and the question of how to manage scarcity had come. In characteristic western fashion, the transition from one to the other was a quick one. And it had one additional impact on future studies: it probably made them more present-oriented than future-oriented. Social dynamism became too high rather than too low, activities now and here seemed more relevant, more valid than thinking and experimenting about an abstract future. Nowhere is this so clearly seen as in the change of focus of interest that one of the futurist "think-tanks" seems to have gone through: we are thinking of the Hudson Institute with its concern with the year 2000 richly advertised, with trends relevant to business practise today.

A Plea for Future Studies

However, this is not a salutary trend. In the world models produced recently, the tendency towards world managerialism, the idea of managing the hungry periphery from western centres, is more than clear enough. But the idea of contemplating more desirable futures for the western centre is more or less absent. And this comes at a time when future studies should become more relevant than ever. The need for alternatives, for visions, for ideas and not only as an intellectual and scientific game or as artistic performance but as dire necessity is higher than ever, particularly to help avoid regressive, even fascist responses to the situation in which the world finds itself.

That situation is often referred to as "limits to growth". There may be agreement that there is a limit to production, but no agreement as to why this is so. To some, as mentioned, it is seen as a question of limited resources. To others, it is seen as a problem of limited markets and limited resources, not because of natural constraints but because the world periphery is claiming control over their own resources, and use their means of production for their own markets. In other words, it is perhaps a problem of periphery consciousness formation, mobilization confrontation and striving for a new international order, rather than a problem of natural constraints. Needless to say, the latter presents premises in a form more acceptable to the centre since the system can still be treated as a "black box" with no need for analysis of the self-defeating characteristics of the dominant economic structure.

However this may be, the conclusions may not differ too much: economic growth cannot continue unabated. And that leads immediately to a new task for future studies: not that of designing leisure-time activities for an affluent world elite, but of designing futures for countries used to a high and increasing level of material output and then suddenly finding themselves in a situation where not only the rate of growth may decrease but even become negative.

One basic thesis, then would be that the more such studies are produced and the larger the proportions of the populations involved, the less will the probability of fascist regression be when the "limits to growth" become more apparent. For, imagine that more manifestations of the under lying structure of the crisis in the world economy come to bear on the rich world, and not necessarily in the form of commodity scarcity. What would happen to the health services in some of the richest countries in the world if all the physicians and nurses from developing countries suddenly went home? A country totally unprepared in terms of alternative futures will try its best to reproduce the *status quo*, by direct or indirect intervention in Third World countries that are seen as the evil causes of the crises, and by strict internal control to repress domestic groupings sceptical or highly critical of *status quo*. If it now can be shown, and we think this is the case, that *status quo* simply cannot be maintained, that it is both politically and morally (not the least in terms of avowed western values) untenable, then the search for alternative future visions should become a major concern of our countries.

The Development of Development Studies

At the same time development studies have undergone a profound change. Gone are the days of the 1950s and 1960s when development was identified with economic growth and economic growth with processing and distribution including foreign trade, so that development more or less came to mean increasing GNP (per capita) and increasing trade. It is now relatively clear that this conceptualization of development not only left out the problem of satisfying the basic needs of those most in need in the population, but also was in the interest of the rich countries because it stimulated the type of efforts in developing countries complementary and indeed necessary to the growth of the rich, industrialized western economies. The idea of "closing the gap" was formulated, and increasingly rejected not only because it is seen as impossible (the more one tries to close it the more will the richer countries be stimulated through exactly these efforts and hence move ahead so that the gap widens even further), but also undesirable (one would have to use some of the same methods as today's rich countries have used, including imperialistic practices- and in addition to this, those very same countries are very quickly losing their character as model countries, showing their cracks, a process to which former President Nixon contributed conspicuously and profoundly through his important contribution to the Watergate debacle).

Thus, development seems increasingly to be defined in terms of satisfying basic human needs, material and immaterial. At the same time, those who have claimed that development is not so much a problem of differences between rich countries and poor but as a problem of the relations between them, have gradually gained the upper-hand in development studies and steered them away from the concerns with local traditions and customs, cultural and climatic factors towards global models. But this time global models are seen not in terms of world managerialism but in terms of exploitation and imperialism, indicating what the periphery countries would have to gain, by changing the parameters of the structure profoundly, even opting out of the system, at least for a while. Like the world models produced by and for the world centres, these world models probably also promise too much: the former exaggerate the degree to which the world is manageable from the centre and the latter exaggerate the degree to which an exploitative structure accounts for all evils of mankind.

But the important thing in this direction is that convergences are found between future and development studies.

Firstly, whereas before both development and future studies had a tendency to focus only on the production of things, the distribution within social systems and the transformation of social structures, there now seems to be much more interest in human beings. Development being increasingly defined as the "development of human" beings, there has to be some more specific ideas as to how human beings develop, also beyond satisfaction of basic material needs. The interesting point is that the moment the list goes beyond the basic material needs, it becomes evident that in addition to misery pockets in rich countries, it is also an open question to what extent people in rich countries really are developed — for instance, do they enjoy such intangibles as creativity, a sense of identity with themselves and others, a sense of meaning in their lives, etc.? Needless to say, one important consequence of not extending the list beyond material needs is precisely to avoid a classification of rich countries as "less developed countries", thus maintaining Western superiority.

Secondly, what has just been said also applies to nature. Both development studies and moreso future studies, pay much more attention to the natural habitat of man in general and ecological balance in particular, than before as the concern with human development is so pressing in developing countries. Sooner or later, however, developing countries will also have to come around to realize that there may be important constraints put by nature on their production and consumption wants and particularly so, if they go in for more self-reliant practices and henceforth economic cycles with less possibility of pushing environmental imbalances into other corners of the world.

Thirdly, a further convergence, as mentioned above, lies in the circumstance that both are increasingly global in their concern. Whereas only a few year ago future studies were about rich countries, and development studies about poor countries, both groups seem to realize that the future of either is directly related and for that reason have to be set in a global context. At the very least the other part of the world is an important "text" even in the sense that conditions of the internal development of one is a condition for developing images of the future of the other.

Fourthly, there is some convergence even in the organization of the two types of studies. Whereas until a decade ago, future studies were only for the rich countries and also developed by them and development studies were for the poor countries but also developed by the rich countries, today future studies seem to be spreading to more poor countries and development studies seem to be finding their way into rich countries, perhaps disguised in the form of district development. So far, future studies are probably only found in the richer countries, and perhaps mainly in highly elitest groups (but this is also true to development studies in those countries), and only few rich countries will be willing to admit they have a "development problem". But we are quickly coming to the end of the period in human history when development problems were studied and taught only by white western people in institutes in their countries to people from Third World countries. Although it is not very likely in the foreseeable future that the future development of todays rich countries will be a subject taught and studied by the people of Third World countries to students lucky enough to obtain scholarships from the old countries in todays centres so that they can study in those centres of learning; more symmetric arrangements seem to be emerging.

And it is these symmetrical arrangements that interest us. Increasingly these two views on development studies will now have to merge and produce a less schizophrenic approach to the human conditions. For this to happen, the poor countries will also have to study the rich, great progress will be made the day when researchers from the periphery countries start studying as systematically as the rich studied them the developmental/future problems of central countries, such as identity, alienation, fragmentation and segmentation of individuals, marginalization of the very old into old-age homes and the very young into kindergartens, and so on. Today people in poor countries have accepted the basic image held by people in the rich countries, viz, that world problems are created in their countries, not ours. In short, futurist and development institutes all over the world, more symmetrically composed and tightly related, open to the problems of human beings in a finite nature everywhere with priority given to the problems over the local setting!

The Under-development/Over-development Dialectics

A symmetric view of the world is facilitated considerably the moment one accepts the idea that all, or almost all countries are mal-developed simply because they fail to satisfy human needs; the difference being that, some are under-developed and others are over-developed. There may be various ways of defining these concepts. Thus, one way of approaching the probiem would be to say that "under-development" applies to the lack of satisfaction of material needs (food, clothes, shelter, health and eduction) whereas, over-development is more focused on the lack of satisfaction of immaterial needs—the idea being that the material needs have been satisfied, and even beyond the optimum point.

Another approach might take the distinction between means and ends as a point of departure, stating that the end is to satisfy human beings, materially as well as immaterially. Under-development is what obtains in a country, or in a part of a country, when the means available are insufficient; over-development, is what obtains when the means available are more than sufficient to the point of being counter-productive (people eat too much and become over-fed, people are over-exposed to information and become apathetic as a consequence, and so on). We shall prefer the latter approach since it makes use of material and immaterial needs in a more symmetric manner. As a consequence of that, development can be seen as a general problem, no longer as a Third World problem alone. The perspective would be that we are all mal-developed, only located on different sides of a social optimum; hence that we need each other!

But the relation between under-development and over-development is not merely a verbal one, a tie constituted by semantic links. There may be over-development in one group of countries as materially linked to the under-development of another group through the ways the dominant economic cycles have been operating during the last centuries. The availability of cheap oil in western industrial countries has not only tapped the oil producing countries of resources at a very low price and led to systematic distortions in their economies, but has also made energy available in the rich countries at a price that has led to a degree of mechanization and automation of societies that cannot help but have some severe impact on human beings. It is not a question here of distributing guilt, saying that Saudi Arabia is as responsible for the over-development of the United States as vice versa — it is more a question of being sensitive to the dialectic between the two basic themes of under-development and over-development. To the extent that development studies deal with the former and future studies with the latter (not necessarily a bad definition, incidentally), one might say that the two are dealing with different sides of the same coin which would be one more reason for systematic cooperation, even confusion.

This is particularly evident when one considers what seems today to be the basic solution to the problems of under-development and over-development: increased use of self-reliance as a strategy. Basically self-reliance, as practised for instance in China as a whole, and indeed by the 70,000 Chinese peoples communes, will probably come from the periphery of today's system the Third World. Economically it will increasingly take the form mentioned above: the use of natural resources for their own purposes, more inward oriented, less oriented to trade with the First and Second World. But this will affect the rich and industrialized world profoundly and produce conditions under which a struggle against over-development will become more meaningful, possibly also forcing a higher level of self-reliance, whether at the local, national or regional levels as a strategy for rich countries as for poor, because it is a way of trying to satisfy immaterial needs, while at the same time keeping a reasonable level of material needs satisfaction. Hence the principle does not imply self-sufficiency, it does not exclude some type of exchange, it can be combined with the twin ideas of establishing a social minimum or floor in the poorer parts of the world and a social maximum or ceiling in the rich part.

And this is nothing but another formulation of the problem of under-and-over-development: the floor is the level below which one should not go, the ceiling is the level above which one should not get either—and not only because eating too much meat is dangerous to individual health, but also because it is too taxing on natural resources, because it leads to inequalities and injustices between groups of people and because under the current practices, use resources which should be used to feed the poor in order to over feed the rich.

And that brings us to the final point: future studies should be reoriented so as to have a centre of gravity in the study of alternative lifestyles in rich countries less counsumptive of scarce material resources, lifestyles that are more sensitive to immaterial needs of all of us. Thus, the idea is not necessarily that future studies should become development studies or vice versa. The division of labour making future studies to some extent specialize in rich countries and development studies in the poor is not necessarily a bad one as long as they are in good contact. For instance, take the global context and the nature context into consideration, and that the dialectic relations are clearly seen. Under these conditions we have all reasons to see a rich future for both of them, for development studies and for future studies, singly and combined.

As a final point: it should also be emphasized that it is our task to contribute to images of future worlds by taking as a point of departure, human beings and their needs, leading to conclusions as to how systems and structures have to be changed, not how a system left to itself will generate anti-human or at best non-human patterns, ultimately leading to some type of catastrophy. Ours is not the task to contribute to the easiest and cheapest of all intellectual exercises, well- reasoned pessimism; but ours is the task of adding to the human condition of today, a case for optimism.

THE HIGHER PUBLIC SERVICE IN INDIA

Satish C. Seth

One of the most important problems facing the Indian administration is how to build a strong, efficient and healthy bureaucracy. Our tradition to deliver the goods of welfare to the people, through the agency of thousands of civil servants, is familiar to one and all. Some people have been critical of our bureaucracy, while others have found it as one of the most efficient and dedicated body of public servants. Notwithstanding, the merit and demerit of the Indian bureaucracy, the fact remains that the Indian administration in the context of Future does face a problem, like other administrations, elsewhere in the world, that of getting the right man for the right job.

The Existing System

Our personnel policy has three essential features. Firstly, the recruitment to higher public services is open to all graduates, who are subjected to a combined competitive examination, by which, they can qualify themselves for further selection into one of the twelve Class I, or six Class II services, depending, of course, on their rank in the merit list; their medical fitness; their option; and the number of vacancies available in each of the aforesaid services at a given time.

Secondly, in our system like the British system, "the administrators are thought of as best trained by apprenticeship, and administration is thought of something only to be learned by doing it — like riding a bicycle".[1] As such, the selected candidates are first subjected to a short spell of in-service training, which can be both of a general and a functional character but mainly they are left to learn the art of administration 'by actually doing it.'

And, the third key characteristic of the Indian administration is the policy of exchange of civil servants between the Centre and the State Governments, which it is expected, ensures a healthy administrative partnership, between the various units which constitute the Indian Federation. This is largely confined to a segment of the higher Public Service, namely, the members of the IAS and the IPS.

Generalist Versus Specialized Approach

Clearly, the basic philosophy behind the Indian personnel policy comes much closer to the British assumption, that a 'graduate' is good enough a material who can be moulded into the right sort of administrator; and that this can be best achieved, through a process of training and experience gained on the job; and such a finished product can be asked to shoulder any kind of administrative responsibility. Not only does this 'graduate' after a lapse of a number of years' service, make an outstanding administrator but could also be trusted, to handle all kinds of technical tasks. The logic behind this assumption is that a 'generalist administrator' may not himself know or possess the technical skills, but, would be quite capable of handling, advising and controlling the technicians, the scientists, the engineers and others.

Quite opposed to this practice of running the administration with the help of 'intelligent amateurs', is the system which strongly advocates that, any administrative job is also a technical job, and so it should be handled by only such administrators, who possess the required technical skills. In other words, modern administration is not considered as a grand exercise, to be undertaken with the aid of 'generalist-virtues' only, but instead, it is thought of as a predominantly technical business, in which an extra emphasis on the specialized skills is considered essential. Consequently, a personnel policy, which would be governed by the kind of thinking would require: that the selection of personnel, should be done not merely to choose lay administrators, through a bald and non-purposive academic examination; instead, it should be achieved through a deliberate process in which only such are chosen, who possess the 'skills', which the multifarious activities of the Government need for the efficient and speedy execution of the public policy at a given period.

This kind of conflict between the generalist approach of building a bureaucracy and a more technical approach to do the same has, both in theory and practice of Public Administration, almost come to occupy the place of an unending warfare between the protagonists of either system. In fact, it is a fruitless war. There are merits and demerits in both the systems. But, if we look at the Indian socio-educational set-up, the administrative equipment and requirements of today and of tomorrow, and then, if we objectively try to reckon, what ails our bureaucracy today, then it would be not easier to determine, which of the above system would offer itself as the right course to determine our future personnel policy for building the higher public services.

Drawbacks of the Existing System

The broad features of our bureaucracy as outlined above have been subjected to a variety of criticism, some of which can be briefly recaptured here. First, category of criticism is directed at the king-pin of our Recruitment system, who happens to be the 'Indian-graduate'. We need here to find out, exactly, what does our graduate represent, in terms of his education? What kind of technical skills does he possess? What kind of administrative know-how does his education impart to him? To what extent, has he been exposed to the academics of Public Administration, law, and general knowledge of the Indian and the world affairs. How good is he at the Sciences and how well-versed is he in the Humanities? How good is his sense of judgement upon which would be raised the super-structure of the Indian bureaucracy?

The answer to these questions is relatively simple and obvious. It is well-known and as well as an acknowledged fact, that the Indian graduate as compared with his international counterpart, is a substandard product. He is neither good at the general knowledge, nor does he possess any know-how of the Indian administration, leave aside the knowledge of other administrative system prevailing in the world. In fact, with a few exceptions, he is also weak, both in the written and spoken language. The truth of the matter is that the educational system, which produces him, is in itself feeble, both in terms of the syllabus used, and, the methods of teaching adopted at the Indian schools and colleges.

The Indian universities, today produce as many as several thousand graduates every year; of this number the competing range has been from approximately sixty thousand graduates or post-graduates, who usually take the aforesaid competitive examination meant for the higher services each year. The successful candidates then compete for the three to four hundred places available annually, for their posting to the various vacancies in the All-India and Central services of the government. The test to which these graduates are subjected to, does not attempt to judge, their capacity to take decisions, or to handle any administrative task like planning, organizing or supervising the administrative functions of the Ministries and Departments at the Centre, or, those of the States. Such an examination simply duplicates the examination process through which these candidates have already passed while they were at their college, or, the university. In fact, just as in the Indian educational system, a great deal of emphasis is laid on the role of 'memory', rather than on 'intelligence' and one's ability to exercise and display 'judgement', likewise, the combined competitive examination also attempts to test a 'graduate's faculty of 'memory' much more, than anything else. And the astonishing thing is that this 'memory', from Sanskrit literature to higher Physics, might be in any field. Such an examination, therefore, fails to test a candidate for the 'skills' that he, as an administrator, should possess to do specific jobs.

Another group of criticism, arises out of the egalitarian motives and is mainly directed towards the structure of the bureaucracy. Here it is argued that the present system of recruitment is neither democratic, nor, is it representative enough. It is, therefore, argued that the present mode of recruitment should be replaced by one which has a single point of entry to the public service, in order to keep bureaucracy free from the 'castes' and 'classes' of high and low officials. There are others, who even go a step further. The non-acceptability of such a system, would obviously be due to the fact that this method would not be able to procure the right kind of personnel needed by a modern Government, which *inter alia*, calls for the services of all kinds of advanced 'skills', which have to be bought and brought in at different levels and from varied sources. To this, however, the critics reply that under the existing practice of manning of our bureaucracy, we ignore the 'claims' of the non-graduates, and other skilled and semi-skilled sections of our population. Even if they could today enter the public services at the lower levels, they shall have little opportunity, if any, for them to compete for their entry into the higher echelons of the public services. If good administrators, the critics persist, can be raised by doing a job in the Districts, then, why wait till a man has become a 'graduate'. Can't they be caught 'young' and, grilled into the administrative chores, by rigorous in-service administrative education? Also, they can be sent at Government expense, sometimes later on during their career, to obtain the so-called higher skills. Moreover, the protagonists of making bureaucracy increasingly representative and responsive, than it is today, have, in main, supported the cause of 'lateral entry'. What they oppose most is the invidious distinction that emerges, by making the 'graduates' the sole claimant for a place in the higher services, as against the non-graduates.

A third set of criticism has been directed against the practice of sharing the bureaucrats, between the Centre and the States. It is somewhat of a mixed criticism, since the critics do agree in principle that, in a federation, an exchange of officers is both desirable and essential. But, on account of the disparity of the conditions of service between the public servants of various services working in the States and at the Centre, the system tends to build awkward and unsound bureaucratic traditions. And so, they argue, that this partnership operates in a mode of unease. Those who are working in the States constantly keep an eye on getting a job in the Centre, and those, who are working at the Centre soon become least interested in returning to their States. The sharing of bureaucrats, to achieve a uniformity of administrative standards, the limited manner in which it is being worked today, therefore, does not help either in strengthening the States' bureaucracy, nor does it help the Centre much. In this connection, it is worth quoting here the view of an independent observer of the Indian government and politics, who says:

> "The factors which determine the career movement of an IAS man between Centre and State are several, and evidence regarding their relative strength is not easy to assemble. Some force attaches to the old notions of mobility, still guarded by the services division of the Home Ministry:

spells at the Centre should be followed by a return to the State to whose cadre he belongs, the rounded officer of an all-India service being one who carries with him always the viewpoint of district and State as well as of New Delhi. But sometimes it seems that the establishment chiefs can only preside over a real tug-of-war between Central government departments and State governments, each wanting the best men. It is alleged that the movement is frustrated, in that, many who go to the Centre stay there, while others remain always within their states. Personal and quasi-political factors are also believed to play an important part. States ministers are said to develop favourites among the senior civil servants; there is a suggestion that weaker ministers prefer local men or men of their own community or political viewpoint, while stronger ministers like to have men from outside the state as impartial top administrators. The wishes of powerful state premiers carry some weight even against central ministries and service opinion. Federalism is a reality even in the management of the all-India services."[2]

The essence of such a federal 'partnership' in an administration geared to planned development, lies in building up the managerial qualities and experience of officers, irrespective of officers 'locale'. A Centre-State exchange of personnel is but one method to accelerate this process by widening and diversifying a man's 'area' of administrative activity. But such a system can become more meaningful only if the officials working in the States are also given an opportunity to broaden their vision through an exposure at the higher policy formulating levels outside his state, and not ignored to this training-privilege just because they have not been recruited on an all-India basis. Secondly, such an exchange would also be useful if most civil-servants working at the Centre can also get increasing opportunities, to gather first hand knowledge of the local conditions, of such tasks and areas, for which they are responsible officially. And thus, it is suggested that to achieve the above two objectives, the Centre-State mobility should not become the preserve only of IAS and IPS alone; instead, it should be open for all kinds of civil servants. An all India experience is relevant for all ranks and services, and should be a part of public servants' normal acquisition of skills and training, and should not degenerate to some kind of administrative escape for a few, for the limited purposes, such as the lure of petty pecuniary gains. Thus, an exchange purporting to develop an 'All-India outlook' could be 'selective' but it should be broad-based.

New Needs of Bureaucracy

Notwithstanding, the manner in which the aforesaid bureaucracy is organized and worked, the Indian Public Services draws its main strength from the Weberian bureaucratic values of permanence, responsibility, career structure, and a contributory pension. In the bureaucracies of the Western countries, these drawing points do not any longer hold the same attractive power, that they once possessed. In India, these values still continue to attract a "queue of qualified applicants," since the Indian Public Service Commission is not yet, "required to enter a market and sell our goods like any one else", — a state of affairs which may, perhaps, not last very long.

Under the present circumstances, therefore, our recruiting methods, our classification principles have not shown any remarkable development from the time of the Victorian Civil Service. Nevertheless, there is a silent inner realization both within the Government and outside it, that the needs of the Civil service, ought to be looked into, in a more rational, objective, direct and prejudice-free manner, in order to find out how best can our civil service system be reorganized, not only for the needs of today, but also for, more difficult responsibilities that are going to arise during the next few decades.

As against this realization of our national objectives the need for administrative reform to rebuild a healthy bureaucracy, would in turn call for, the search of a practical Indian answer to the familiar problems of Public Administration, which amongst other things requires for the balancing of the role of the lay-administrator *vis-a-vis* the specialists; the elimination of unhealthy influence of service structure on the career values: replacement of the faulty trends in our recruitment of the administrators, scientists, and professional civil servants; and the need of introducing adequate manpower planning and a liaison service (which is conspicuously absent, today), with the various schools, colleges, technical institutions and the universities. A solution to these problems is not needed for a mere academic satisfaction; instead, whatever answer we shall arrive at would become the *sin qua non* of the weakness or strength of our bureaucracy's capacity, to cope with the far-reaching changes, and new burdens, that this country will face in the future. Bureaucratic reorganization should, therefore, be seen in the context of widely changing, and, an ever increasing role of the modern Governments, which has somehow made modern Public Administration far different and a far more specialized business. This is a realization which has been universally felt. The Estimates Committee of the House of Commons, in its 6th Report on "The Recruitment of Civil Service" voiced somewhat similar thoughts. It observed: "The tasks facing the Civil Service are undergoing far-reaching changes. The range of experience and the specialist skills required by the Government are continually widening and changing and the interests of Ministers and Members of Parliament are changing with them".

"Just as the job of the Civil Service is developing, so is the field from which the service is recruited. The acceptance in the last few years of the right to tertiary education of all who can benefit from it, and the measures set in train to implement this, are opening up to many occupations, a new and considerably wider and more varied field from which to recruit. This is also changing the character of many aspects of the wider community of which the Civil Service is a part."

"Both these trends have been accentuated in the last decade. Though changes have been made, there has been no adaptation of the structure of the service to meet either the demands of the first or the opportunities of the second".

"There are three areas in particular where detailed examination might be expected to lead to proposals for change. The first is the extent of mobility, both within the Civil Service, and between the Service and other occupations. With this should be considered other means of acquiring wider experience and keeping the Service in touch with the development community.

The second is the need for professional training and the means available for acquiring a knowledge of specialist techniques at the beginning and in the course of a career. Thirdly there is an urgent need to examine the supply of qualified manpower on which the Civil Service is to draw. It is fallacy to suppose that, in the long-term, the supply of qualified people is in any way fixed; the recruiting policies of the Government themselves have an impact on the total supply".[3]

A New Plan for Staffing Higher Public Service

If the above mentioned ideas are valid enough for the Whitehall, which is a citadel of conservatism, and where 'changes' are not easily accepted, then, it can reasonably be considered a timely index to the fact, that a stage has come, when we in India, should also give to our bureaucracy a new basis and should now, think and devise, modern methods of classification, recruitment and training, so that a specialized point of view may find its right place in our Government? And, this can be best attained only, if we make our system less rigid. Flexibility may not be the right kind of 'virtue' to be sought after, in the seats of Government, yet good administration is one which is continuously responding to the expectations, urges and needs of a society. Rigidity makes administration wooden and administrators 'out-of-tune' with the 'need' of the hour. Flexibility, within a broad-though-rigid-framework of Governmental activity, could make, an administration, responsive and, therefore, dynamic and progressive. Consequently, an objective reappraisal of the different elements of our personnel system would reveal that our bureaucracy is today seething with limitless discontent which arises from several directions. This has to be studied and necessary 'departures' have to be made from the *status quo*.

In this context, the new philosophy of personnel should also take into account and rectify the dominant feeling of a depressed status arising out of a comparison with each other's service condition as to which one does belong, which is so characteristically the disturbing feature of the Indian bureaucratic organization today.

Moreover, no personnel system worth its salt, can accept

wastage of manpower. There is, therefore, need also of the location and eradication of the varied forms of the manpower wastage as it exists today. In the public services, in order to correct the impression (which happens to be another unhappy aspect of our civil service organisation) that, "in many cases square pegs are being secured into round holes".

If one accepts the principle that today's administration is a specialized business and that a 'general graduate'[4] is not the only right material to be used to build a bureaucracy, and if the civil service structure should really be a reservoir of skills, and not a life-long imprisonment of an inferior or of a superior kind, then we have the right basis to build an alternative system of career development. The reorganized bureaucracy for today and tomorrow in our system then, will have to undergo few changes, some of which are as enumerated below. In this new personnel plan, an attempt has been made to make a judicious combination of the best features of both, the generalist system which is rule oriented and, the specialist system, which is 'position' and 'skill' oriented; at the same time, in this plan an attempt has also been made to avoid the existing, known demerits, of either of the systems. The various features of the new Plan of Bureaucratic Reorganization have been summarised in the following paragraphs.

1. The present day recruitment to higher Public Services, is open to a 'general graduate' between the age of 21-24, and he has to qualify at a combined competitive examination held by the Union Public Service Commission of India. In the new system, the first important change would be that this examination, as was also recommended by the Planning Commission, in its First Year Report[5], should be open for all candidates who are between the age group 21-28. The minimum educational qualification being, either a University degree or its other professional equivalent.

Secondly, the form of this examination will have to be greatly recasted. After all, today, as this examination is being conducted, it aims, simply in doing two things : (i) it is intended to narrow down the field of selection and (ii) secondly, it is trying to feed the vacancies of certain well-established services. This examination, in the nature of things, is merely achieving the above objectives, through a 'repeat exercise' of an academic examination, to which most of these candidates, have already been subjected to, while they were at their college or University. Moreover, this test, is sometimes examining the candidates for such academic subjects too, on which, they have tried to focus their attention, only temporarily, say, during the few months preceding the examination, in order to comply with the rules and regulations regarding the numerous subjects in which a candidate has to take examination, in order to become eligible for the consideration of his candidature to some of the services. In the reorganized plan, such an examination will not only be both written and oral but would be directed more towards the judging of a candidate's real intelligence and his administrative ability, if any, instead of merely 'testing' his academic 'memory' in totally odd and unconnected combinations of subjects that candidates, have to offer; voluntarily, such as : Higher Physics with the British History; or, a combination of a paper on Political Theory from Hobbes to the present day, or one on Sanskrit or Mathematics or, the Organic Chemistry and so on... A testing in neither of the subjects can help us to evaluate the potentiality nor the quantum of a candidate's administrative intelligence. Hence, we should resort to different intelligence tests, which will also establish uniformity of evaluation, if these examinations are going to be held in all the constitutionally recognized regional languages of this country.

The success in this examination does not give a candidate any claim, or, right to an appointment or, a particular post, or service; instead, it would simply make them eligible for entry to an appropriate place in the higher Public Service provided to them by various other tests, as well.

2. In the new scheme the candidates selected through the preliminary testing would be immediately put to, a six months foundations training course, which would initiate the eligibles to the various aspects of Public Administration and *inter alia* acquaint them to: what a Government is; what are its various functions, responsibilities, what are the different 'skills' it has to employ, in order to realize the goals of the Public Policy, as laid down from time to time. This short training will conclude itself after all the candidates, have taken two more tests, which would be conducted not by the Training Academy, but by the Union Public Service

Commission. The first of these tests would try and measure in detail the depth of the administrative potentiality that a candidate may possess, by virtue of his qualifications, and academic background, and as acquired at the foundational training, now imparted to him. The second test would be the aptitude test. This would try to draw out the interest and aptitude of a candidate, as to the kind of work in the Government, he would like to do most, and the work which, as the test should reveal he, could best do. In this test, amongst other things, the examiners will, of course, take into account the views reported on a candidate by the Training Academy.

Once, the above tests have been carried out, the marks obtained in these two tests, would then be added to the marks obtained in the written and the oral tests taken earlier at the time of the preliminary selection, and then a merit list prepared. On the basis of this finalized merit list, candidates would then be assigned to the various functional pools, which would replace, what is today known as the 'services'. Whereas, in the system prevailing today, candidate, after the declaration of the results to some extent do come to know in advance, which service he is likely to enter; in the new plan, this would not be the case. A candidate will be placed where, he should give his best. In so far as the scramble to enter into the Indian Administrative or the Indian Foreign Service, etc., is concerned, that would no more be the order of the day; the candidates will go only to such functional pools for which they can show real intelligence and aptitude. And in this plan, thus, the new entrants do not join the Government, for a particular service because such and such 'service' carries more 'prestige' or attractive 'pay scale'. Instead, they would be called upon to do, the hitherto-prestigious-kind-of-work, provided they are found, suitable. In the reorganized bureaucracy, all sort of work shall carry the same hazards and the same prestige. Entry to all pools in term of career prospects thus, would be equally attractive or unattractive. Since we are a Federation, these 'pools of skills', would be as much meant for the benefit of the Centre, as for that of the States. They shall all have an all-India complexion about them. These pools would be the repositories of the 'skills'; for example, we can have pools for the executive jobs; pools for the technical and scientific jobs; pools for diplomatic jobs; pools for the financial and economic jobs; pools for educational and welfare jobs; pools for district work; agricultural work; pools for research and teaching jobs; pools for the special public utility jobs; such as the Railways, the Post and Telegraphs, and other industrial, or commercial activities, etc. There could thus be a number of pools to cover the vast range of occupational groups, which a modern Government is required to possess, in order to render the various services, that a society demands of it.

4. All members, irrespective of the pools, they have opted for, will carry similar conditions of service. There is no high, no low, involved in the new scheme. Let us not forget that, one of the ills of our present day bureaucratic organization, arises due to the gaps between grades or classes in terms of pay, conditions and status. It is an unhappy reality which has been taken note of by foreign observers, as well. Referring to this, Prof. Morris Jones, has remarked that, "These gaps have been considerable in India. In part a legacy from the days when the top administration was British—both between some service significantly termed 'superior' and others and between classes, within services, such as the Central Secretariat Service. India is a country in which most men speak enthusiastically of equality but, in spite and because of this, cultivate distinctions with loving care and nowhere more assiduously than inside the civil service. If we add to this the difficulty of man-to-man imaginative sympathy in India — to say nothing of superior-inferior relationships — we can see a situation readily damaging to good morale".[6]

5. Consequently, the new plan seeks to eradicate such anomalies. Once a person has entered a given pool, unlike the pattern that prevails today in our 'services', a new entrant to the higher public service in the new scheme, after becoming the member of a pool, will, thereafter, be left at his own. He would now risk at his own merit and not be considered favourably for deputations, promotions, etc., simply because he belongs to a particular 'elite' or 'nonelite' service, as is the case today. Besides, the fact of 'equality' between the various pools, will reduce the gaps between the conditions of services and emolument, etc., which seem to worry the incumbents of different services, today.

Moreover, these pools are not static or stagnant in nature. There would be scope for a free flow of officers from one pool to another, provided: (i) officer desiring a change has served for a period of at least five years in one pool; and (ii) provided, before he asks for a change, he has been sufficiently exposed to a short-term training programme oriented towards the 'skills' of the new 'pool', he wishes to go to, and, also if, (iii) he has been given a test of 'fitness', for this kind of transfer, by the Academy of Training which will conduct an orientation course as also test him. This migration will be limited to two or three chances in an officer's career.

It is obvious, that the aforesaid different functional pools, exist on the same footing, and shall be created at the same level in a horizontal plane. Every officer within these pools is then governed by a single vertical ladder, which is offering them similar career values with respect to their pay scale and other conditions of service, no matter, whether they are dealing with : Information, Accounts, Income-Tax, law and order, Magistracy, Railways, Diplomacy, Post and Telegraphs, Police, Secretariat sections, or Lands and Cantonments, etc. As stated earlier, a person's mobility vertically; would now be entirely dependent on (a) his personal ability and meritorious record, revealed by his Annual Rating, (b) his capacity to show initiative and good administrative judgement, (c) an able use of his skills as shown by his success in the various supervisory, and promotion tests, to which he will be subjected to from time to time. Thus, only a fit person would now rise above, since, he would not, hereafter, be supported by extraneous factors.

6. However, in order to man the top policy posts, we need, yet another Policy and Managerial pool. Each officer, who has already put in ten to fifteen years service in the various functional pools, will, hereafter, be eligible to enter this pool, subject, of course, to his success in certain tests to which, the eligible officers, would be subjected, before they can be placed in the Managerial pool of the policy makers. Members of this pool would go to fill the various positions at the level of a Commissioner, a Joint Secretary, and above. The role of these officers, is primarily that of a policy maker, and a coordinator, and the people who will man these senior positions can now be safely styled as the 'elite civil

servants'. They are not 'elite civil servants' simply because they have belonged to any elite civil service as, was the case with the Indian Civil Service of the IAS & IA & AS. Instead, the members of this pool would be treated as the 'elite', since, they would have arrived at the higher echelons, only by virtue of their sound administrative background, as assessed from time to time, and as revealed by the various promotional tests, which would be several, in this new system and at the same time rigorous ones, as well. Here, it may be interesting to quote, one of the recommendations of the Royal Commission of Inquiry, set-up by the Government of New Zealand. This Commission in their Report entitled "The State Services in New Zealand" submitted in the year 1962 made the following observations, while recommending, what in their judgement, should be the right character and composition of an elite group of civil servants, those who in the Whitehall, administration, are known as belonging to the so-called 'administrative class'. The Commission, observed:

"We have proposed that the Services should be classified into a number of distinct occupational classes with their own conditions of service, and their own work to do in various departments. But, it is obvious that there are other public servants who coordinate and control the work of the various occupational classes with departments, and who give the work central direction. They fill a managerial and administrative role which needs to be distinguished from the more specialist role of a member of an occupational class. Members of this group in a department will be drawn from the various occupational classes though some classes will no doubt tend to produce more administrators than will others'.[7]

In our system, therefore, a similar principal could be applied to staff the top positions in the civil service by using a method of selection, which is based solely on merit, and in which we are choosing our 'elite' public servant from as wide an area as possible.

7. It may, however, be mentioned here that sometimes it is argued that one cannot combine technical policy makers with the general-administrative-policy makers. If so, we can have two pools of policy makers : one consisting of the technicians and scientists, and the other of those, whose work has been predominantly of a

non-technical character. But our new plan, emphatically rejects the age old thesis, that the 'experts', should be kept at the 'tap' and not on the 'top'. In administration, the 'top' lies with the political chief of a Department or Ministry. It should, therefore, be left to a Minister, whether, he would like to be advised by a scientist or a generalist. While making his choice, he will, of course, pick his top adviser, in most cases from those who belong to the Managerial and policy pool, provided they satisfy the norms of 'seniority' and 'merit'. Such a system alone would help to build healthy Civil Servant-Minister relationship, on the one hand and on the other, would make the concept of ministerial responsibility more meaningful and realistic. Hereafter, no Minister could possibly pass the buck in the lap of his senior administrators and advisers, for purely ministerial failures of policy and leadership.

Conclusion

The bureaucratic reorganization in India has not so far been subjected to a systematic analysis and a rational treatment. Changes that have taken place have been the result of piecemeal administrative engineering. There has been some kind of limitation of outlook, with the result, that, as Professor A.H. Hanson observes: "Even today most discussions of Indian administrative' problems are excessively IAS oriented".[8] We have to accept the fact that the restructuring of the administrative system cannot be confined to support only a microscopic administrative aristocracy of the Indian bureaucracy. After all, "The Indian maid-of-all-work", the district officer who is an IAS cannot be a be-all and end-all of Indian administrative thinking-purporting to civil service reform. It is an erroneous view, that a few years work in the district imparts to a person all those 'skills', which will make him competent to handle any kind of job at the federal headquarters of administration. In personnel matters, we must think afresh, and try to do better. Because, what was valid for the administrative needs of yesterday may not be relevant for the India of tomorrow. We have to consider changes in our classification principles and recruitment techniques in order to scrap what Paul Appleby alluded to as the "feudalistic heritage" in our personnel policies. It is not, as if, we are not aware of our shortcomings. Also, there is no dearth of imaginative people who, if they have an opportunity, can rationalize the personnel system. But, the fact remains, that there is some kind of an inbuilt resistance in our system towards change. Little evidence is available if ever a coherent view of present day personnel needs has been taken. Whenever suggestions have been made, they have remained mostly on the papers, on which they were written. A good example of this is evidenced by the non-fulfilment of the recommendations of the Reports of the Estimates Committee and the Five year plans on administrative matters. Referring to such recommendations for administrative change, in the Second Five Year Plan Report, and commenting on its non-compliance, Professor Hanson observes: "It is difficult to say what all this amounted to... There must have been some genuine improvement, but no fundamental changes occurred either in organization or in attitude. Painstaking subordinates, working slowly and unimaginatively within a framework of rather obsolete routines, continued to carry out the orders of a handful of highly intelligent but fantastically over-worked top-level generalists, inadequately advised by an insufficient number of technical specialists. New approaches to training made only the slightest dent in this situation. The barriers to inter-service promotion remained high and the 'Pooh Bah' status of the IAS, obliquely criticised in the Second Plan report, remained unshaken. Morale, particularly at the middle and lower levels of the services, was undermined by favouritism in promotion (in which caste politics often played a part), and by the continued erosion of inadequate salaries by inflation. Corruption certainly did not diminish, although the IAS and services of equivalent status seem to have remained and indeed still do remain-relatively immune from it".[9]

He further adds : ' Independent India, in fact had taken over an imperialist' administrative machine with all its old virtues and vices, to which were added a few new ones. The new virtues were mainly at the top, in the shape of a fresh generation of administrators who, although inferior to their predecessors in educational background and general 'culture', surpassed them in development mindedness. The many vices clustered around the lower levels of the hierarchy, where literal-mindedness and petty corruption continued almost unchecked."[10]

In conclusion, he says, "Perhaps the most extraordinary thing, to the observer unfamiliar with Indian conditions, was the retention, with only peripheral changes, of the old codes of civil service regulations, reasonably well adapted to the need of a night-watchman state run by an expatriate administrative aristocracy, but ill adopted to those of a planned and economically developing society.[11]

Analysing the various reasons which have frustrated reform of administration and bureaucracy in India, in a radical and rational manner, Professor Hanson observes that "The reason would appear to lie partly in a failure of nerve, partly in politics, and partly in sheer administrative inertia. Nervousness finds expression in a reluctance to tamper with a going concern — even though it may be going far too slowly — for fear that the result may be a complete breakdown. 'Politics' comes into the matter in three ways. Firstly, the Indian bureaucracy itself constitutes a politically influential segment of society with certain habits and expectations which it is reluctant to see disturbed. From its point of view, radical reform would at least involve the learning of tricks by old dogs and might conceivably mean the wholesale dismissal of a mass of superfluous personnel which could not find alternative employment. For these reasons, there is a strong vested interest in retaining the familiar and employment creating complexities of the system. Secondly, few politicians are interested in administrative reform as such, and are dependent on the bureaucrats themselves for such advice on the subject as they receive. Thirdly, the attitudes of the politicians are in many cases positively unhelpful. Politicians are no less interested than the bureaucrats themselves in 'making work'; they persistently interfere, for self-interested reasons, with administrative processes which should be insulted from their direct influence; they seldom realize that their power over the administration is one to be used with tact and discretion; they resent advice from the administrator which cuts across their prejudices and predilections; and they are a major source of the prevalent corruption. These political factors, which obviously favour the maintenance of the *status quo*, are reinforced by an inertia which comes from the genuine respect which the less imaginative of the bureaucrats feel for the established system, and the difficulty they experience in conceiving of any alternative set of arrangements which would be workable".[12]

Be it as it may, there can not be two opinions that today we are certainly a reform-oriented administration and would like to take a few steps towards the re-building of our bureaucracy. And would be willing to innovate as realistically as is possible. No innovation can, of course, be hundred per cent foolproof. And thus, notwithstanding, the shortcomings that any personnel policy we may have, it is expected, however that the new plan for bureaucratic reorganization as outlined above, if adopted could, perhaps, be the first bold step in the right direction, and it is bound to make the Indian Higher Public Service a truly representative, responsive, specialized, efficient and a happy working force.

REFERENCES

1. C.H. Sisson, *The Spirit of British Administration and Some European Comparisons* (London), 2nd Ed. 1959, p. 29.
2. W.H. Morris-Jones, *The Government and Politics of India* (London) 1964, p. 125.
3. See E.C. (H.O.C.), The Recruitment of Civil Service, 6th Report, (Session 1964-64), pp. XXXII-XXXIII.
4. A term coined by Prof. W.J.M. Mackenzie (See ibid., p. XXV).
5. See First Five Year Plan Report, p. 120. (The upper age limit recommended by them here was 30).
6. Morris Jones, op. cit., pp. 126-29.
7. Report of the Royal Commission of Inquiry. The State Services in New Zealand Wellington (1962), pp. 209-10.
   Also See The future structure of the Civil Service;
   A Note by Her Majesty's Treasury. A paper submitted to Fulton Committee on the Civil Service (May 1966). Summarised in *Public Administration*. Winter 1966, Vol. 44, pp. 473-82.
8. A.H. Hanson, *The Process of Planning: A Study of Indian Five Year Plans* 1950-64 (London), 1966, p. 272.
9. *Ibid.*, p. 289.
10. *Ibid.*, p. 290.
11. *Ibid.*, p. 290.
12. *Ibid.*, p. 290-91.

THE CLASSIFICATION OF BUREAUCRACY

Satish C. Seth

The Classification System Process and Anomalies

Classification is "a process of grouping objects alike in one or more characteristics in classes", example, classification of foods in grocery stores, books in libraries, chemical terms, plant families, etc., in the sciences.

There can, however, be several basis for classification. Since things are alike or different in more than one respect; they lend themselves to classification on more than one basis to which this classification can be put to. World over, the services have been classified by two well-known methods. The first is the traditional way, in which public servants are classified according to their rank just as in the army. The classification of the British "Treasury Classes", to which the classification of the Indian Public Service offers a close parallel, are good illustrations of classification by rank system. Here, we have a classification system which has, "established the principle of a broad division of work not on the American basis of recruiting persons for individual positions — but on the basis of dividing the work of government into large blocks for which persons taken for particular stages of the national education system were judged to be best suitable." However, we have to remember that even in Britain, the "Treasury Classes" constitute only a microscopic minority compared to the bulk of civil servants who belong to various other classes, such as the professional, scientific and the "departmental classes".[1] And in the Indian system of bureaucratic classification, the concept of 'education' is not a fool-proof and identical index of the class-categorization of Whitehall.

The other method is a more modern method by which the positions and posts in the Government are classified according to the rules of Position Classification, wherein "a position is a group of current duties and competent authority, requiring the full-time or part-time employment of one person." The system of position classification first devised in Chicago in the USA is now being used in almost every country in the world, including Britain, Canada, Australia; New Zealand, Philippines, Thailand, and Japan.

The Canadian experience should interest us in India since the administration of both these countries have had a common British background. The interesting question is why Canada abandoned the rank classification and instead took to Position Classification? And what are its essential features.

In Canada, "The Civil Service classification system had its origin in the study by Arthur Young and Company of Chicago, who reported to the Canadian Parliament in 1919.[2] It was a time when there was a strong public sentiment in favour of bridling patronage. The "merit system", which was intended to relate appointments and promotions to qualifications for the work to be performed rather than to political favour required a system of classification which would accurately define each position.

Since its inception in 1919, the system of classification has been administered by the Canadian Civil Service Commission. It may be pertinent to briefly refer here to principles that the Civil Service Commission approved for the use of those who were engaged in the classification programme in Canada. These statements of principles are as follows: -

1. That the duties and responsibilities pertaining to a position should be the criteria for determining the classification of the position because these attributes the fundamental characteristics that distinguish the position from other positions and because all of the purposes of classification will be served by a grouping that will bring together positions involving substantially the same duties and responsibilities.

2. That position involving substantially the same duties and responsibilities call for practically the same qualifications as to education, experience, knowledge, and skill in their incumbents and that for this reason, such qualifications requirements dependent as they are on the work to be performed, constitute on auxiliary basis for determining the proper classification of a given position.

3. That neither the degree of efficiency with which the duties of a position are being carried out by the persons who may be filling it, nor the qualifications such persons may possess or lack, nor the pay they receive, nor any other fact dependent solely on

his individuality, shall be considered as having any bearing on the classification of the position in question.

4. That the simplest practical grouping of positions should be adopted that will serve the purpose for which the classification is needed: that in conformity with this principle the unit of classification would be a group (called a "class") embracing all those positions in the service, regardless of departmental lines, that involve duties and responsibilities which are substantially the same.

Clearly, under the new system, the Canadian Government tried to seek an accurate job description to achieve organizational clarity and to develop equal standards for duties, responsibilities, education and skills. This type of classification operated across the departmental borders, and concerned itself with duties and positions and not persons.

The modern position classification, based on duties analysis, thus, refers to the organizing of position into groups or classes on the basis of their duties and qualifications requirements. The position concept evidenced in public service classification plan is a relatively modern approach to personnel administration although one cannot say still if it is a very precise instrument. The major steps in development and installation of a classification plan have over the years, become widely accepted and standardized; though many variations are possible in the specific cases. It does not accept the administrative notion that general educational ability makes a person qualified enough to handle every kind of job in the Government. It is thus a science of "administrative specification" - and recommends that, "only specific skills and knowledge" be used and developed at each 'level', 'post' or 'position' in the Public Service. In other words, position classification is also a system of identifying and describing the, different kind of work in an organization, and then of grouping the similar positions together under common job titles. Generally, speaking therefore, an administrative system which has adopted the position classification plan is bound to take the following four basic steps:

1. Analysing and referring to the duties and other distinctive characteristics of the positions to be classified (job analysis and description).

2. Grouping the positions into classes upon the basis of their similarity in terms of duties, difficulties and responsibilities.

3. Writing such standards or specifications for each class of position as will indicate its characteristic, definition, its boundaries and serve as a guide in allocating individual position to the classes and in recruitment and examinations, that is to say, the same jobs to be filled by persons possessing the same qualifications, skills, and experiences and subjected to the same tests of ability.

4. Installation by allocating individual position to the classes thus described.

5. Reinforcing the position classification plan, by a pay plan which ensures, "equal pay for equal work."

The main slogan of position classification system, therefore, is: "The job is the thing."[3] As a contrast, in our system the slogan is; "Your service, your rank and your seniority is the thing" — but your knowledge, education, skills, aptitude, ability — are all secondary." Position classification thus tries to classify public services on the basis of a uniform job language.

It is not as if standardized job-code can't be evolved for classifying public servants in any other way. For example, the military rank system does so, but it does not do so, in all cases, on the basis of 'skills' and 'duties'. It is here that there lies the difference. Since, in position classification system the main objective is, "to lay foundation for equitable treatment for public employees by the accurate definition, orderly arrangement, and fair evaluation of positions in the public services."

Position Classification as a Tool of Management

The main uses and advantages of a position plan can be judged in two respects: First, is its use as a "tool of management" and second, is the fulfilment of the objectives set for it "to achieve the purpose of facilitating all phases of personnel administration."[4]

The position classification as a tool of management aids the following three activities of Management, namely:

(i) Planning the ways and means by which the job shall be done — Organization Planning.

(ii) Controlling operations to see that the job is done efficiently — budgeting.

(iii) Selecting and developing the people who will do the job — personnel administration.

The manner in which position classification aids each of these activities is described below:

1. *Organization Planning*

(a) A classification plan permits the easy translation of broad organizational plans with the assignment of duties and responsibilities to individual positions.

(b) In the course of day-to-day classification activities, poorly defined authority, responsibility, and overlapping and duplication of effort often come to light; these can be referred to organizational planners for appropriate action.

2. *Budget*

(a) Position classification furnishes standard nomenclature which can be used to complete a meaningful statement of position within an organization.

(b) Classification provides logical functional groupings upon which compensation schedules can be based.

(c) Combination of these two furnishes — budget the major tools which it uses in obtaining funds and justifying their expenditure.

3. *Personnel Administration*

(a) Position classification furnishes standards on which can be based qualification requirements for recruiting, testing, selection and placement.

(b) Permits equal pay for equal work.

(c) Permits the establishment of positive promotion, transfer, and separation programme.

(d) Facilitates performance rating and in-service-training programmes." Finally, position classification becomes a common bond which, properly utilized, ties the various elements of the management job into a unified, concerted force.

In meeting the various objectives, etc., for position classification to achieve the purpose of facilitating all phases of personnel administration, it helps in the following six directions:

1. *Establishes Uniform Occupational Terminology*
   (i) Prevents the setting up of fictitious titles as a basis for attempts to mislead personnel or fiscal authorities.
   (ii) Enables Civil Service Administrators, department officers, budget officials, the legislative body, interested citizens, and tax payers to get an inventory view of the Government service to find out how it is organized as to kinds of personnel, what numbers and kinds of positions exist, how the various appropriations are distributed as to jobs, and similar items of information on a reliable fact basis.
2. *Establishes Equal Pay for Equal Work*

Establishes a sound basis for providing equitable pay for the work to be done and for providing that pay in an equitable manner.

   (i) In order to put into effect the principles of 'equal pay for substantially equal work' position classification plan determines what work, is, in fact, equal.
   (ii) Under the same employment conditions, our pay scale can be established for a class of positions with the assurance that if it is right for the whole class of positions, it is right for each individual positions within the class.
   (iii) Ranking sequence of classes permits the association of higher work, and lower pay scales with less exacting work.
3. *Makes for Informative Budgets*
   (i) Means of control can be established to ensure that the will of the appropriating body in authorizing positions of certain kinds will be carried out and that the salaries appropriated will be paid for the kinds of service contemplated.
   (ii) Because of uniform, defined terminology the classification plan can be used by administrative officials as a definite tool for presenting requests for funds for personal services in comprehensive form.
   (iii) Executive and legislative agencies concerned with recommending or passing upon requests of administrative heads for appropriations are enabled to get a clear picture of the organization and position-content of the different operating units as a basis for action.

4. *Basis for Recruiting, Testing and Certification*
   - (i) Position classification serves the Central personnel agency as an orderly arrangement of facts about the duties, responsibilities, and qualification standards of positions.
   - (ii) These facts form the basis for:
     - (a) Planning and preparing tests.
     - (b) Informing prospective applicants or other interested persons about the duties of positions to be filled and, the basic qualifications to be tested and rated.
     - (c) Preparing eligible lists.
     - (d) Controlling use of such lists in the filling of requisitions for the certification of eligibles.
   - (iii) In testing process itself position classification plan is a tool, that saves time, money, and confusion.
     - (a) Personnel agency does not have to travel the same ground over and over again in order to determine duties to be performed and qualifications to be tested everytime a vacancy occurs, a new employee is to be hired, or an examination is needed.
     - (b) Personnel agency can hold one test covering all positions in a single class.
     - (c) Decreases numbers of different kinds of tests held, and number of eligible lists maintained to meet the needs of operating departments.

5. *Basis for Promotion and Transfer*
   - (i) Formulation and administration of such plans, equitable regulations, and definite requirements governing promotions and transfer of employees are constant challenges to public personnel agencies.
   - (ii) The arrangements of classes of position in position classification plan, supported by position classification standards identifies position in their proper relationships for promotion and transfer purposes.
   - (iii) Such a plan is prerequisite for the classification of promotion and transfer programmes and transactions.

6. *Employee Training Programmes*

(i) Analysis and position classification standards of a position classification plan are a starting point in the development of employee training programmes.

(ii) Before employees can be trained, the work for which they are to be trained must be described and analysed, the necessary knowledge and abilities deducted, and selection from among them made, to serve as a basis for the training programme.

To summarize these various uses and advantages, the adoption of position classification helps in:

1. *Facilitating other Personal Objectives*

(a) It provides a rational crit :rion for control of pay levels, by making it possible to equate whole classes of positions with common salary ranges.

(b) It reduces a variety of occupations and positions to manageable proportions, so that recruitment, qualification requirements, examination, and selection can be made for whole classes of position at a time.

(c) It defines in objective terms the contents of jobs or what is expected against which the performance of incumbents — how well it is done — can be measured.

(d) It furnishes job information upon which the content of orientation and other in-service-training can be based.

(e) Although it does not in itself guarantee a good promotion and placement policy, it supplies a systematic picture of opportunities and position relationships, which is essential to an orderly promotion and placement procedure.

(f) It provides a foundation for common understanding between supervisor and employees as to the job and pay, which facilitates employee-management relations.

2. *General Aids to an Organization*

(a) By use of standards class titles, it establishes uniform job terminology.

(b) It clarifies, by requiring definition and description of duties, the placing of responsibility in each position.

(c) It provides an orderly basis for translating needs for

positions into fiscal terms, thus facilitating budgetary procedures.

(d) It provides information on job content that aids in the analysis, or organization problems and of procedures, by bringing out points of duplication, inconsistency, and the like, in the work process.

3. *Particular Values in the Public Service*

The foregoing points apply to all organizations, public or private, whereas the following two points are relevant and have special significance to Public Administration:

(a) It assures the citizen and tax payer that there is some logical relationship between expenditures for personnel services and the services rendered.

(b) It offers as good a protection as has been found against political or personal preferment in determination of public salaries.

Characteristic of a System which Does not follow a Position-Classification Plan

If an administrative system does not follow the Position-classification Plan it shows some peculiarities of its own. Of these easily noticeable are the anomalies of rank and pay. Such a system would be studded with too many rules and regulations; in fact, with much larger number of amendments, corrections and interpretations. Here there will be more emphasis on procedures rather than on substance. It will be too dilatory and time consuming with low production and output. It will also show that employees under such a system are not getting adequate rewards and compensations, and little job satisfaction, if any. There chances of promotions would be few; and the general loss of morale very high.

In such a system there will be no scope for specialized use of skills: everyone would be thought of as good enough for any kind of duty, difficulty, and responsibility. Its training programme would also be of a general and non-specific nature. Its officials will have vague titles; and their performance is bound to be far from satisfactory. In fact, such a system can never develop an adequate tool of measuring performance.

Some such examples, can also help us to understand the merit of Position-classification Plan, since in them one cannot miss certain peculiar features where, consciously, an exception has been made here or there, to the intelligent and rational grouping of duties, positions, and Pay Plan. In such a system, we will find following cases:

(a) where there is no correlation between a person's educational qualifications to the job he is performing;
(b) where he would bear some title which would not give any meaningful idea as to the actual work he is doing; and
(c) where people would get paid differently for doing the same work. Following illustrations bear out these points.

Example I: In County X, truck drivers in the Road Department are called Labourers and paid $10 a day. Truck drivers in the Sanitation Department are called Sanitation Foremen and paid a monthly salary of $286. An employee with the title, Building Manager, is actually working as Private Secretary to a member of the Board of Supervisors. There are seven entirely different positions called Clerk with salaries ranging from $180 to $540 a month. County X does not have a functioning position-classification plan.

Example II: In Department Y there are three officers all designated as Deputy Secretary and, they are doing the same kind of job. But they have been brought on deputation from three different services: say Indian Administrative Service, Indian Accounts and Audit Service and Indian Revenue Service. Each one of them is drawing a salary which is different from the other, although they have put in the same number of years in the Government, since other things being equal, length of service goes to determine their rank and pay. Clearly the designation Deputy Secretary does not indicate the functional aspect of their work, and, since they are drawing dissimilar pays, the Department Y does not have a position-classification plan.[5]

Example III: The Government of India employs nearly 2,000 section officers which is the first supervisory level at the Central Secretariat. Whereas each person in this group has been given the same qualifications and experience, they are recruited by the same test of ability.

Further, even if officers designated as superintendents (which section officers are) are performing identical supervisory duties, they would not hold a similar gazetted status, if they were working in an attached office, for example, AGCR or, in any of the provincial secretariat. Clearly, the class title of superintendent or, a section officer, is misleading, and does not include all officials who should normally be classified on the basis of an equitable assessment of similar duties, difficulties and functional characters of a 'position'. Such a classification, cannot help us, in developing for such officers, a meaningful training programme, either. Clearly, therefore, under such a personnel system we are not functioning with a position-classification plan.

Example IV: In the Government of India there are Research Officers working in the Planning Commission, in the Legal and Treaty Division and in the External Affairs in the Legislative Department and in the Defence Ministry. These officers do have a functional title. It is clear that their professional job is to carry out research. It is also clear that they would, perhaps, possess similar educational background in their respective disciplines. But these officers do not enjoy the same service privileges, and, clearly, this mode of classifying the skill of research does not follow the principles of principles-classification. See Table 1 below.

TABLE - 1
UNEQUAL PAY SCALES OF RESEARCH OFFICERS IN GOVERNMENT OF INDIA

Designation	*Department/Ministry*	*Pay Scale*	*Class*
Sr. Research Officer	External Affairs	Rs. 1150 - 1250	I
Research Officer	Planning Commission	Rs. 400 - 950	I
Research Officer	Legislative Department (OLLC)	Rs. 700 - 900	I
Sr. Research Officer	Defence	Rs. 700 - 1250	I
Research Officer	External Affairs	Rs. 350 - 800	II

Example V: In Railways the designation Booking Clerk is suggestive enough of the duties of its incumbent. But a Booking Clerk placed in Class III has three different pay scales, e.g.,

Note: All scales given in this chapter pertain to sixties, i.e., before the Third Pay Commission.

Rs. 150-5-170-8-240; Rs. 150-5-175-6-205-EB-7-240; Rs. 110-4-150-EB-4-170-5-180-EB-5-200. This is a negation of the principles of position-classification, since, to have a rational personnel system we should either have a different designation corresponding to each pay scale or, we should have specific classification of the incumbent's position.

Example VI: It has been noticed that a change in the organization of work can also bring about a change in the conditions of service and pay scales, even if the officers, bear same occupational title and discharge similar responsibilities and duties. For example, a stenographer bearing the same educational background and technical competence will be paid at higher rates if he works in a Ministry, but would be paid at a lower rate, if he happens to work in an attached office of the same Ministry. Not only this, even in the same Ministry or a Department the pay scales of the posts of a Stenographer differs with the officers with whom the Stenographer is working. If they are placed in dissimilar pay scales; clearly, the classification of this category is unsound; it lacks clarity and is inconsistent with the criterion of equal pay for equal work. Also, this dissimilarity would create difficulties in the matter of an orderly career development, resulting in job classification and loss of morale.

'X' attached with a Deputy Secretary, moves in a vacancy with a Joint Secretary, he will draw pay on a higher scale. Here his classification is not because he has acquired higher skills or qualifications, but because he is working with the officer of a higher status. Such a system is, therefore, not following a position-classification plan.

Be it as it may, the chief objective of having a rational classification plan — which position-classification plan indeed is — is to organize personnel system on the basis of skills and expertise on the one hand, and to ensure a just, equitable and uniform treatment for employees in terms of their conditions of service, particularly, in terms of "equal compensation for equal work", and it is also a system which provides for "fair and ample" opportunities for the career growth of employees of all ranks.

Example VII: The following is a peculiar example of a somewhat complex regulation which helps in the process of pay fixation. It reads as follows:

> "It has been decided in the consultation with the Comptroller and Auditor General that where a person goes from post 'A' in his parent department to a post 'B' elsewhere and reverts to post 'C' in his parent department and post 'C' is higher than post 'A' but not higher than 'B' the pay in post 'C' should be fixed under FR 22-C with reference to the pay in post 'A', if the pay so fixed is more advantageous than the pay fixed, under the normal Rules, with reference to his pay in the post 'B' ".

In a Position-classification Plan, there would not be any such complications for pay fixation rules, here the rules will not be governed by such complex formulae. A man moves to the position for which there is already an assigned salary. It takes little time and it can be easily understood by both the employer and employee.

The main issue under consideration here is not whether the aforesaid examples are typical and correct to the third place of decimal. Instead the important thing here is to find out the answer to the following few questions. What is the genesis of the classification plan of the Government of India? What are its goals? What are the various personnel purposes it serves? Does it in the same way as the Position-classification plan help towards:

(i) Organization Planning: that is: Planning the ways and means by which the job shall be done.

(ii) Personnel administration: that is: Selecting and developing the people who will do the job.

(iii) Budgeting: that is: Controlling costs and operations to see that the job is done efficiently?

Also what are its other merits, if any? What is its main contribution in facilitating other personnel matters, such as: Programme Staffing, Staff Training, Performance Rating, Promotion and Placement Policy and better Career development?

Does it or does it not, help in the growth of specialization and specialized skills in the administration? Does it help in seeing the right man occupying the right job and see that he is punished if he goes wrong and is rewarded if he works well.

Does or does not our classification system help in establishing a rational of an equitable system for Paying Civil Servants? Does it, in doing so, provide the following five objectives of a Pay System:

(1) to pay more money for more difficult and more responsible jobs;
(2) to provide comparable pay in all ministries for comparable work;
(3) to motivate employees to work effectively and productively;
(4) to reward employees according to their proficiency and to advance them to more higher posts according to their abilities to undertake more responsible work; and
(5) to provide pay which will attract and retain many capable persons?

We have already seen in some details that the two most important values of position-classification are that it enables managers to (1) establish qualifications for posts which are based on their duties and responsibilities and (2) establish a rational system for pay that permits comparable pay for comparable work. In addition, the system facilitates the development of career patterns in which employees are rewarded for the development of greater technical skills. This provides motivation for the development of depth of knowledge about the work they must perform.

Position classification focuses the attention of the employee and the manager on the work to be done. Now, the main question to be answered here is, does our classification system also bring to the Indian administration and its employees, the aforesaid, key advantages?

And finally, therefore, we have also to find what are the various disadvantages that this system has. How purposive it is? How purposeless it is? What are the various administrative complications, if any, it causes? Should it be continued or partially amended or totally effaced? And if so, what should be the new system that should replace it?

The Classification System in the Central Government

The Indian classification of the public services is a grand exercise on the theme of high and low ranks. It is highly status oriented and does not follow an occupational terminology and as the Second Pay Commission in its report remarked:

> "With the possible exception of two or three neighbouring countries, this kind of classification is peculiar to India."[6]

The genesis of this kind of classification can be traced deep down in the history of the British Raj in India. Until the Islington Commission (1912 - 15), the Government offices came to belong to superior, subordinate and inferior services. The Islington Commission, however, made the first departure by a recommendation that where there was a large body of work not sufficiently important to be entrusted to officers of the Imperial Services, but yet of a kind which could not be performed by a subordinate agency, there should, be over and above the subordinate services, two services, or two classes of one service to be described as Class I and Class II. But the nomenclature Class I and Class II came into force only in 1926. This position continued until India got Independence.

The first post-independence development in the field of classification came from the recommendations of the first Central Pay Commission of 1946-47 which is popularly known as the Varadachariar Commission. This commission which was India's first pay commission introduced the terms Class Ill and Class IV as substitutes of the then existing description of the lower services as subordinate and inferior. This Commission was not sure if such a four-fold classification was the correct manner in which public services should be classified. However, it advised its retention with the following interesting comment:

> "Even under any new constitution that may come into existence, it is not unlikely that appointment to the higher posts will be made by subordinate authorities under some kind of delegated power. This differentiation cannot, therefore, be regarded as something objectionable in itself. In the statutory rules as they now stand linked up with differences in privileges in respect of disciplinary action, right of appeal, etc., and it will not be worth-while disturbing the scheme by altering the classification unless—and except to the extent to which a—change seems necessary."[7]

Curiously enough, today, the India's public servant gets classified in four different ways, namely: (i) service-wise grouping; (ii) classification in four classes, (iii) the gazetted and non-gazetted ranking, and (iv) classification as determined by the range of pay which a particular service/post carried with it. Broadly speaking, the class in which a service or post is to be placed is determined by the rate of pay it carries, and the general pattern is as shown in Table 2.

TABLE - 2
CLASS OF PUBLIC SERVANT VIS-A-VIS RATE OF PAY

Central Adminis-tration in India	*Under British Rule Service Stratifi-cation*	*Post-Inde-pendence Service-wise Grouping*	*Class-wise Classifi-cation*	*Max. of Pay Scale (Rs.) and Class Placement Today*	*Ranking*
	Secretary of State and Imperial Services	All India Services & Central Services	Class I Services and Posts	950 and above Class I	Gazetted
Officers	Subordinate Services		Class II Services and Posts	576 to 949 Class II	Gazetted but some Class II posts are non-gazetted
			Class III Services and Posts	111 to 575 Class III	Non-gazetted
	Inferior Services		Class IV Services and Posts	Not exce-eding 110 Class IV	Non-gazetted But some cate-gories belong to Class III

Curiously enough, little evidence is available of what good Indian classification plan does. Unlike, the position classification system, it concentrates little on the "work" aspect of the Personnel administration. But it does serve to preserve and complicate the anomalies of Pay and Promotion, as they arise of the class differences. There is, however, ample adverse official comment on the seamy side of our classification system. Most vocal authentic of all, and pertinent of such views, of course, is of the Second Pay Commission. For instance, explaining the peculiarities of the classification pattern by which the class in which a service or post is to be placed in terms of the rate of pay it carries, the Second Pay

Commission observed. "That even this pattern is not free from inconsistencies". Illustrating this point it observed:

> "Exceptions are permissible, but only with the concurrence of the Ministries of Home Affairs and Finance; and some exceptions have actually been made. While they may have given some satisfaction to the services which have been placed in a Class above that to which their pay entitles them, the exceptions have caused heart-burning among those in the same pay range who have not been so elevated. Some of the exceptions are Section Officer (Grade II) and Assistants in the Central Secretariat, who though on the scales Rs. 530 - 800 and Rs. 160 - 10 - 300 - 15 - 450 have been placed in Class I and II respectively; some other examples are Postmen and Linemen in the Posts and Telegraphs Department, and Notice Servers in the Income-Tax Department, who though on the scale Rs. 35-1-50 have been placed in Class III."[8]

The Indian classification system is thus the instrument that upholds differences between one kind of civil servant and another in the most aggressive and irritating possible manner. This fact has been noticed time and again but has seldom been put to any remedial measure, even though these differences belie a proper understanding of the Government of India's personnel policy; and most of the time make management of personnel administration and career development impossible. Sometimes, it even leads to litigation. The intervention of the Indian Courts, have many a time helped the employees to bring justice to such civil servants to whom the classification system had brought nothing but grief in their administrative career.

The Second Pay Commission, it must be said, did show the courage of exposing some of these glaring class differences although they conceded that, it was beyond their terms of reference to judge. "Whether these differences are justified". Referring to how the Indian Classification promotes "class consciousness" they observed that:

> 'Until a few years ago, there were differences between one class and another in respect of several conditions of service, and the difference as between Class IV and the other classes

were particularly marked - extending to rates of pension and gratuity, qualifying service for pension, medical benefits and leave entitlements. With progressive liberalization of conditions of service of the lower classes of employees, the differences in regard to leave, retirement, benefits, etc., have virtually disappeared and a few minor differences still exist; they are not all favourable to the higher classes: for instance Class IV staff has more generous leave travel concessions, and a considerable proportion of them have a higher age superannuation. In respect of certain other conditions of service, and of recruitment, differences still exist, and they are mentioned below:

(i) While all first appointees to Class I Services/ posts are made by the President, lower authorities are empowered to make such appointments in other cases;

(ii) All posts in Class I, and the bulk of the posts in Class II, are "gazetted", but others are not;

(iii) The President is the disciplinary authority for Class I and the appellate authority for Class II; the disciplinary and appellate authorities for Class III and Class IV are mostly heads of Departments or officers working, under them; and

(iv) While direct recruitment to all Class I and Class II Service/posts is made in consultation with the Union Public Service (unless any are specifically excluded), there is no such general rule in regard to Class III and Class IV Services.[9]

To briefly recapture, the broad features of the Indian Classification System are, as follows:

1. The classification system is rank oriented (Class I, II, III, IV).
2. The classification system overlaps the services classification.
3. The classification system pre-suppose the efficacy of grouping officers into "loose general classes".
4. The classification system spells out appointment authorities and disciplinary authorities which are different for officers of different classes.

5. The classification system is not connected with the pay plan policy. It does not help in giving equal compensation for equal work.
6. This classification system does not serve as a useful tool, in handling the various chores of personnel management; such as selecting and developing the persons who can do a job well.
7. The classification system and the in-service training programme of the Government are more or less independent of each other. Since this classification system does not furnish such job information upon which the content of orientation and other in-service-training can be based.
8. This classification system does not define in details the contents of a job. It also does not spell out in the qualitative or quantitative terms what is expected to be done, against which the performance of an incumbent — how well it had done — can be measured. Thus, it gives no aid to adequately meet the requirements of performance rating.
9. This classification plan does permit the easy translation of broad organization plans in terms of the assessment of duties and responsibilities of individual positions. Since its motto is: "Any-position-anywhere to-meet your rank."
10. This classification does not help in building up scientific standards on which adequate selection, placement, promotion, transfer or career development may be organized; In fact, it aborts adequate career growth.
11. This classification neither does desk audit nor does any job analysis and, this prevents the emergence of a uniform occupational terminology.
12. This classification has been used to determine the mundane, administrative tasks such as, the calculations of: travelling allowance, leave admissibility superannuation allowance and similar extraneous matters, which can easily be handled despite such a classification scheme.

Clearly, therefore, such a classification system, is not only unscientific and unnecessary in itself, but also presents serious difficulties in the way of administration in sorting out its personnel matters in a rational manner. It does little good, if any, but can do incalculable harm with respect to an officer's career growth. Such an opinion against this classification, was also observed by the Second Pay Commission:

> "The weight of evidence, however, is in favour of this classification, the main ground mentioned being that it serves no practical purpose which cannot be served without it, and that, on the other hand, it has an unhealthy psychological effect. We are in agreement with this view."[10]

Wholeheartedly, rejecting the Indian classification system which is not a tool of personnel management but instead of a caste system which may satisfy some vanities, but serves no public purpose, the Second Pay Commission made a very bold pronouncement when it observed:

> "We attach importance to the need for developing among civil servants a feeling that they will belong to a common public service; and any system of classification or nomenclature, or for the matter of that, any feature of public personnel administration, which is likely to hamper the growth of such a feeling, however small a measure it may be, should, in our view, go unless it serves a definite practical end which cannot be served adequately otherwise. Other countries, including those with a large and complex civil service organization, have apparently, not found it necessary to superimpose upon their civil grades and occupational groups a broad horizontal classification like ours; and we do not think any serious inconvenience will be caused to the administration in India if the classification under consideration is given up. All that would be necessary are some amendments of Central Civil Services (Classification, Control and Appeal) Rules, 1957, and of certain other rules and orders. We, therefore, recommend the abolition of the present classification. We have had to refer to the existing classification throughout our Report and it is possible that

on the abolition of the classification some of our recommendations may require to be suitably adapted. We, do not, however, expect this to present any difficulty."

Introducing Position Classification in India: Doubts and Possibilities

There are some general premises from which one can now look more clearly at the classification needs of a modern Government. Today public administration at the Center and in States is a highly technical and specialized business. In any of these organizations, there is a great need for the use of extensive skills and knowledge for each position or post, however, small or high. Although the Indian personnel system has undergone some changes it is still basically similar to that established prior to our Independence. It is designed to produce a staff more concerned with process than with substance. Today an officer should be capable of dealing effectively with both. This thus calls for a new approach in the field of personnel management. It means that for each administrative agency, hereafter, we should study the duties, difficulties, and responsibilities of every post in order to determine the knowledge, skills and abilities required in them. It also means that there would be need for intensive job analysis at all levels — from Secretary to an L.D.C.— and a specific set of work norms evolved to enable a qualitative evaluation of job performance. All this would also mean than employees, hereafter could be placed only in such positions for which they are well qualified and best suited. And once we use position classification as an every day tool of good management then we will run the administration in terms of specific needs, specific qualifications and specific achievements. There is an immediate need to abandon the general and broad categorization of personnel which is of little help in managing the personnel administration in a specific manner. In this, connection one of the important question that is usually asked is: what is the harm if broad and general categories are retained? In fact, the advocates of the rank system have suggested that in the Indian administration we do make use of the principles of position classification while making a selection of the scientific personnel. They also point out that in this particular segment of bureaucracy, it is not possible to adopt rigid classification categories and class titles. Instead, one has to take recourse to more flexible titles and broad general categories such as Scientists, Engineers, Technical Officers. And if these general class titles are good enough to describe the technical personnel, then, what is wrong with the broad general administrative categories and: titles, as they are being used today under the rank system? Cannot they be retained also?

The nature of any classification plan is largely determined by the use which one wants to make of it. If its basic purpose is to spell out many salary differences among positions, we may have to have a very detailed plan involving narrow classes. If the purpose is to provide for recruitment and selection of individuals with broad basic abilities who are to receive extensive in-service training on the job, then, we would use broad classes. If the need is to select persons with highly specialized knowledge and skills and if there is little or no training to be given to employees subsequent to their appointment, then we must have more narrow classes.

Broad classes mean fewer classes and, therefore, fewer examinations to provide eligible lists. In addition, tests can be general instead of highly specialized subject matter. It is usually easier to recruit for general rather than highly specialized skills. On the other hand, the employee selected from an eligible list for a broad class will probably require considerable training before he can fully perform a specialized assignment, but he may be able to work very well in a more general assignment. If a formal certification of names from a list is limited to one name, the broad class may be ineffective. Even with three names there may be problems if the class is too broad. This becomes a particularly serious matter under a system of competitive promotion by examination and must be considered in deciding the breadth of classes to be used. What is then needed in India that could be provided under a Position Classification Plan? First, most work in the entrance level posts and in lower level posts is specialized. The higher the level of the job, the more general it, usually, is. An Indian Position classification Plan should provide many specific classes in lower grades rather broad classes in the highest grades.

In so far as the use of class titles are concerned, a good title has three characteristics: (1) it should be descriptive of the type of work; (2) it should indicate relative class level of rank; and (3) it should be as short as possible. The logical grouping of similar positions under meaningful job titles provides a common language for everyone concerned with planning and budgeting. Without meaningful titles, the legislative body cannot really know what it is appropriating money for. With meaningful titles, taxpayers, employees, and administrators can have a meeting of minds on these matters. Classification surveys in other countries have often revealed titles which had no relation to the duties performed. In some cases, "high-sounding" titles have been used for routine work, resulting in excessive salaries and waste of public funds. Sometimes employees with "unimportant-sounding" titles have important but un-recognized responsibilities and unfairly low pay.

Broad general titles like Deputy Secretary, Under -Secretary, Section Officer, etc., do not help management in arranging a meaningful development of the employees-training programme for special skills that they need, nor does it realize fully a career development plan. After all the main object of position classification is to make clear to the administration and to the various incumbents the necessary "depth of-skills" This objective is usually lost in having large and loose groups with non-specific general titles commonly used to describe personnel in the rank oriented system.

Decision making in Government is a corporate activity and, therefore, it is necessary that we keep both the staff and the line continuously activated towards specialization. Just as the white light can be broken into seven colours, we need to adopt a prismatic approach also to break a general class and diversify it by recruiting highly skilled persons, who are needed within each broad general category, such as section-officers, assistants or clerks, etc. The continuation of broad general categories would not help our administration to perfect our staff selection or testing training, placement and promotion programmes. In any case, the complexity of 21st century governance does not need an obsolete, feudalistic system.

Another doubt usually expressed is: will not the introduction of position classification mean that we shall have to set up some ancillary machinery and evolve more scientific methods of handling personnel matters. Would not this, therefore, mean that we will have to employ skilled people even for handling the personnel matters also? And under such a system will our selection agencies have more work because they shall now be testing the new entrants by different tests for different skills? All this means more work and more money. And therefore, it is asked if in terms of cost benefit ratio will it be a wise step to adopt position classification?

The answer to this question lies in the fact that: initially the setting up the position classification plan does involve extra expenditure, in that, we shall have to have trained personnel analysts, who alone can and who alone should, handle the personnel matters. We shall, therefore, have to invest some money in training them. But once installed, the system is cheaper to maintain. So far as the selection agencies are concerned, there won't be any increase of work load or expenditure on them, since even now they are examining the candidates. And they would continue to do so under the new plan also. In fact, if we adopt the position classification plan, we shall then, make use of less cumbersome methods of examination. The increasing use of simple psychological tests would mean that, hereafter, less time would be developed in selecting people, which would also ensure greater objectivity in testing and much less expenditure in terms of examiner's fees and expense on answer books and papers. In strict cost benefit terms, it is common knowledge that specialized approach, has it own advantages. Specialization leads to savings in a very different way. It means greater efficiency. It means a qualitative performance of work. If means more productivity. It also means that a system is now geared to a benefit accruing system. In short, specialization is just another word for good administration. And thus, any money spent in replacing the existing loose and non-purposive classification plan by a more scientific and rational classification system and its concomitant personnel practices is worth spending in. Whereas, in today's system we think that any responsibility and difficulty is something, which can be handled by employing the officers of a particular service or rank; in the position classification plan, what matters is the qualifications of the employee, and the quality of his work. And such a policy holds good for the incumbents at every position from the lowest to the highest level.

It is also pointed out that in today's system in the Central Ministries and departments, employees are getting stuck at various levels for a number of years.[11] For example, in the Central Secretariat, at an average, the LDC spends nearly 13 years before he can become a UDC. A UDC spends 10 years or so, before he can become an assistant. An assistant spends 15 - 20 years before he can become a section officer. And, similarly, a section officer has to spend 12 - 15 years before he can become an under secretary and so on. In fact, officers, even in the privileged services like the IAS and IFS and IAAS also get stuck at various junior or senior levels of pay scales. And, therefore, it is asked, can position classification accelerate promotion probabilities? Will not the promotion depend on the availability of vacancies in both the rank and position classification system? How then is the position classification a better alternative than the rank system? This is easily answered. Since it is a widely recognized fact, that in an administrative system which had adopted the position classifications system, promotion goes to the best qualified person rather than to the most senior person. Besides, under the position classification plan one can easily adopt a two-track system for promotion which means that if there is a single administrative line of promotion in an organization, then, one can also, create a line of promotion for experts, and, thus in the scalar - promotional ladders in an agency, one can accelerate the frequency of promotion. In fact, there are several examples of this expert line being created in the Central administrative set-up in India, for example, the Educational advisory service, the legal advisory service following Seth's Law of Hierarchical Parallels, etc. The main difficulty in the service-approach has been that even these advisory services, instead of offering an avenue of promotion, have become close corridors of their own. And over and above this, their main objective has been merely to establish parallels and relativities of rank and salary with respect to the administrative hierarchy of their respective departments and Ministries. The same outlet under position classification plan would have been handled in a much more flexible and meaningful manner so that people do not have to wait always, for openings, and vacancies. Instead, there own positions could be reassessed and classified, if there are sufficient grounds, to give a rise to an incumbent, to the extent that funds are available, employees may be advanced to higher-level posts as soon as they meet the qualification requirements for the more responsible work.[12] In the American system, as funds become available for a promotion, all qualified employees compete and the best man is promoted. Judging of who is best is done in some instance by establishment officers and in others by committees of officers of rank equal to or above the level of the post to be filled. It is, therefore, a mistaken notion that in the position classification system, career sequences are bestrewen with road-blocks, which are insurmountable by many. In fact, the position classification plan cuts across seniority. In this system what matters is not the minimum number of years put in before a promotion can be granted, as is the case in the Indian system: instead the important thing is: what kind of work, you do and the system always pays due regards to the ability and qualifications of the incumbent. Thus, promotion is linked with one's skills, one's talent, one's performance, and one's meritorious record. It is the individual and his work that matters not his service, or the number of vacancies, or, some peculiar formula, which can handle more promotions. Besides, in this system, there never should be cases of unequal compensation for similar qualifications and quality of work.

Finally, one of the most interesting questions that is usually asked is, whether in India position classification can be introduced without making any fundamental change in the pay Plan.

This is an important question and deserves a careful scrutiny. It is true that one can certainly introduce position classification plan without making any fundamental change in the existing salary scales but what is the advantage? The great advantage of the introduction of position classification is to rationalize the pay plan. Besides, we should not forget the big motto and the big advantage that position classification plan has to offer to all: "equal pay for equal work". If we are introducing the position classification plan, then, it would be worth our while to streamline and rationalize our salary administration also. Here we might examine the basic object of a Pay Plan and its relationship to the position classification system, drawing illustrations in these two fields from the Federal service practices in the United States of America, who can easily claim to possess the most rationalized position-classification and Pay Plan system, in use in any Government anywhere else in the world.

The chief objective of a Pay Plan, in the United States, Civil Service Commission, is to establish a pay plan which will attract an adequate number of competent applicants and retain the best of the qualified employees. Today, with an increasing number of private enterprises getting set-up in India, it is likely that these two objectives will apply here also within the next five or ten years period. For instance, with Current Governmental pay-scales, one is not getting the best computer experts.

A second objective of the American Pay Plan is to provide employees with "incentives to ever greater productivity, and incentives to seek positions of high responsibility." The American pay plan lay special emphasis on the point that those who have greater responsibilities and more difficult duties should be paid more. Thus, a senior engineer will be paid more than a junior engineer. However, a junior engineer will be paid more than the Superintendent of an office. We also do the same in India but our pay fixation is governed by several limitations like one's service and class, which sometimes thwart higher compensations to be made for the discharge of higher responsibilities.

The ultimate objective of salary-policy everywhere is that pay plans be both reasonable and rational. In other words, it must be fair to the employees and understood by them and their union representative as well. It need not be reiterated that in India we have had more than 5000 pay scales in operation in the Public Administration sector. How can this be considered as a rational salary plan?

In United States a pay plan is closely attached to a position classification system. Every job is described in writing. All related jobs are brought together into class series. An example of a class is Junior Engineer. In this class would be assigned employees who have engineering degrees but no experience. In the engineering class series, one would find such classes as junior engineer, senior engineer and principal engineer. The pay plan will provide different rates for each class. The use of a position classification scheme makes it possible to compare government jobs with those in industry. We hardly do this kind of comparison in India. But we may have to do it in the near future.

A few words may also be added here regarding the structure of a pay plan and how the position classification helps in achieving it. A pay plan is always the expression of Government's policy. For the most important decision usually is: "What is the lowest pay to be given? In most Governments there are many more employees in the lower-grade classes than there are in the top-grades. For example, in the Government of India in 1963, over half of the employees received Rs 150 or less, while less than 2 per cent received Rs. 1,000 or more. An increase in the pay affects immediately the Government budget. In that term, an increase of Rs 5 per month for those getting Rs 150 or less would have cost over Rs 8 million a month whereas an increase of Rs. 500 per month for the top grades would have cost only Rs 27 million. In United States workers at lower levels are often members of unions which bring strong pressure on government to pay more and more. It is the feeling in the United States that the lowest pay should permit the government employee to live comfortably and to feed his family. The lowest pay would also reflect the objectives of the pay plan as stated above.

In the United States the Government does not seek to be the employer that pays the most to the lowest employees. Commonly, Government seeks to pay somewhat higher than the average rate of all industrial units.

The higher salary to be paid to the highest level officers is also an important, political decision. In the United States, "Government seeks to pay a high grade employee a salary which will permit him to live among persons of high status in a good neighbourhood". So far, Government has not paid Heads of Departments as much as Heads of large industries. In the Federal Government, the salary paid to senators has become an effective ceiling for most government officials. It is difficult to collect here the various reasons that go to determine the higher salaries in India. Although there are two popular views about it: one is that, it is a poor country and so the servants of the people should not draw a disproportionately high pay. The other view is that; just as there is no dynasty of philosophers, there is no dynasty of civil servants either. But, if some people have been chosen as civil servants and it they have difficult and responsible obligations, then they be paid as well as those for similar work outside the government. However, we are not interested in this debate here; our main object is to determine which system of classification can help the rationalization of an Indian pay plan. Apparently, if we are to get rid of the anomalies referred to earlier, the position classification plan, can help us better in this respect. It can also help in establishing an adequate salary range, which means:

(i) a minimum rate; which is the entrance rate of the Class, below which no employee occupying position in the Class can be paid, so long as his work is sufficiently satisfactory to warrant his retention in that position;

(ii) several intermediate rates for the purpose of rewarding degrees of increased usefulness and efficiency; and

(iii) a maximum rate beyond which no employee may be paid while occupying a position of that Class, no matter how efficient he may be on that particular work.

In USA, as in India, a pay range is established rather than a single rate. For example, if a Junior Engineer in the United States is paid $5330 to start, then he will receive annual pay increases. At the present time 10 pay steps are provided, the maximum being $6915. The USA has 18 levels of pay, fifteen of the levels have 10 pay steps each. The top three grades have a smaller number of pay steps.[13]

It is this intermediary gradation of salary-stages which needs an early introduction in India in order to achieve a better pay policy. Today an increment is received by every person in a given class provided, of course, he is not subject to any disciplinary charge. Efficiency of a person is recorded negatively; that is he should not get a bad confidential report, which is again an annual feature. Employees lead their official lives under a vague hope — a mirage like experience — of one day occupying the highest post in the hierarchy. The truth, as studies on staffing have revealed is that at an average a person does not rise more than two levels higher to the level of his first entry. Exceptional people may go upto or beyond the third rung in the administrative ladder — until and unless their cadre has pre-structured promotional levels.

Apparently, therefore, in order to remove deception and frustration from the minds of the civil servants at all levels, it is better to give them a salary-satisfaction —subject, of course, to their satisfactory and efficient discharge of their duties — rather than an obscure and empty hope of promotion to higher echelons.

The next question is: what should be the difference between the first step and the highest step and what should be the difference between each step. In United States the objective has been to provide an annual pay increase which will be significant to the employee. There are different opinions on this matter. One view is that each increase should be at least 5 per cent. For example, if a person receives Rs. 1,000 the pay plan should provide an increase of at least Rs. 50 each year. The same consultant recommends that the highest step be 20 to 40 per cent above the first step. That would provide this kind of a scale: Rs. 1,000 - 50 - 1,400. Let us apply this to a series of related classes of Civil Engineers. A rational pay scheme tied to position classification might have three pay scales as follows:

Junior Engineer	Rs. 350 - 20 - 430
Intermediate Engineer	Rs. 450 - 20 - 530
Senior Engineer	Rs. 550 - 30 - 700
Supervisory Engineer	Rs. 750 - 40 - 950
Chief Engineer	Rs. 1600 - 60 - 1800

If this pay scheme were adopted it would apply to all engineers, not just civil engineers.

A rational basis would, therefore, be to evolve a pay plan adopting the American pay plan as Model. (See Table 3). It is interesting to see how in such a small space, one can bring together the total pay picture in a concise and meaningful manner, describing the salary-scales of all civil servants; from a lift operator to an Ambassador, without any complication of pay fixation, as can be caused because of one's service, or, grade, or, status as is usually the case in India.

In order to evolve a better pay plan also a recourse to the position classification system would seem logical and desirable. Besides, it is also necessary that Government of India as well as

TABLE - 3

FEDERAL RATES WITHIN GRADE IN USA AS AVAILABLE DURING SIXTIES

GS	1	2	3	4	5	6	7	8	9	10
1	$3,609	$3,731	$3,853	$3,975	$4,097	$4,219	$4,341	$4,463	$4,585	$4,707
2	3,925	4,058	4,191	4,324	4,457	4,590	4,723	4,856	4,989	5,122
3	4,269	4,413	4,557	4,701	5,845	4,989	5,133	5,277	5,421	5,565
4	4,776	4,936	5,096	5,256	5,415	5,576	5,736	5,896	6,056	6,216
5	5,331	5,507	5,683	5,859	6,335	6,211	6,387	9,563	6,739	6,915
6	5,867	6,065	6,263	6,461	6,659	6,857	7,055	7,253	7,451	7,649
7	6,451	6,664	6,877	7,090	7,303	7,516	7,729	7,942	8,155	8,368
8	7,068	7,303	7,538	7,773	8,008	8,243	8,478	8,713	8,948	9,183
9	7,696	7,957	8,218	8,479	8,740	9,001	9,262	9,523	9,714	10,045
10	8,421	8,709	8,997	9,285	9,573	9,861	10,149	10,437	10,725	11,013
11	9,221	9,536	9,851	10,166	10,481	10,796	11,111	11,426	11,741	12,056
12	10,927	11,306	11,685	12,064	12,443	12,822	13,201	13,588	13,595	14,338
13	12,873	13,321	13,769	14,217	14,665	15,113	15,561	16,009	16,457	16,905
14	15,106	15,629	16,152	16,675	17,198	17,721	18,244	18,767	19,290	19,813
15	17,550	18,157	18,764	19,371	19,978	20,585	21,192	21,799	22,406	23,013
16	20,075	20,745	21,415	22,085	22,755	23,425	24,095	24,765	25,435	
17	22,760	23,520	24,280	25,040	25,800					
18	25,890									

the State Governments establish a permanent Pay-Research unit which may exercise necessary vigil on the Pay Policy and Pay-structure.

Conclusion

Main Recommendations:

1. Position classification is one of the modern tools of personnel management. Under this system its important elements have been defined as follows:

Position: A collection of duties and responsibilities the attention of a person full time normally or part time.

Class: A collection of positions of a similar type calling for work of about the same level of duties and responsibilities.

Class series: A group of classes arranged in the order of their importance from the least difficult class.

Position Classification: A process by which posts are studied, classes and class series are established and posts assigned to classes.

As stated earlier, the adoption of a Position Classification Plan, in our system, would mean that, in our Public Services all positions of similar nature would be included in a single type or "class".

"A class of positions" in this context would be a "a group of positions sufficiently similar in respect to the essential character of their duties and responsibilities, and consequent qualification requirements, so much so, that with respect to a given class of positions, it would be possible that the:

(i) same descriptive title can appropriately be used;
(ii) same qualifications of holding a post can reasonably be required;
(iii) same test of fitness can appropriately be used; and
(iv) same scale of compensation can be applied with equity.

Reduced to its simplest terms the 'Classification of position would mean that we initiate a process to find out by obtaining the facts and analysing them, that different kinds, or, 'classes' of positions, call for different treatment in personnel process, there are in the service; it further includes, that we make a systematic record of the classes found and of the particular positions found to belong to each Class.

The duties and responsibilities of the positions are thus the basis upon which classes are determined and the individual positions assigned or allocated to their appropriate classes.

The first question that we would be called upon to answer here is: in what manner can position classification be brought about: office-wise; class-wise, service-wise, or, skill-wise?

The answer to this question is that we can start with any of the above alternatives. Of course, considering the Indian service complexities, the best approach would be to introduce position classification in a phased programme. The various steps to be taken in this connection are as described below: -

1. All positions and posts which are today designated as falling in the Class II (Gazetted and non-Gazetted) Classes III and IV, category should first of all be covered by a position classification plan. This plan would cover all the Class II services; as well as other clerical or technical services up to and including this level. As soon as the position classification is adopted, the present classification nomenclatures of Class II, III and IV or Group B, C and D would be abandoned. We should thus first give to the infrastructure of our Ministries and Departments a rationalized classification basis.

2. Secondly, all the services, and posts to be designated as Class I Service or Class 1 posts. The Group A should be covered according to the strict principles of classification plan in the phased programme which can commence, after a period of five years beginning from the time the classes below these services and posts have been covered by the Position Classification Plan. This would complete the abandonment of the present four-fold classification nomenclatures Class I, II, III and IV? or as group A, B, C, D. However, until we commence bringing the posts and positions falling in Class I, under the fold of Position Classification Plan it would be desirable, that in respect to the filling of the vacancies of the so-called ex-cader and other openings of Class I posts and position of the Central Services of the Government of India, the establishment officer would show due consideration to the following factors, before making a final placement.

These are:

(i) The qualifications required by the posts.

(ii) The aptitude and training experience and specialization, if any of the candidates who are likely to fill these posts.

(iii) An entrance orientation training programme to give the generalist (i) the technical and other special aspects of the language of job trade (ii) of general administrative skills, which may, help in developing decision making ability.

3. The next question to be answered here is what are the basic steps we have to take to implement the Position Classification Plan. Using the model, of a small administrative agency, in which we have about 500 to 1,000 posts, the basic steps would be as laid out below. The process would, of course, apply to large organizations like a Ministry as well. These steps are: -

(a) *Survey*

The first step is to obtain information about the work that is being done. In a small survey, an analyst may visit each employee and officer and prepare job descriptions from his interviews and observations.[14] In surveys covering over 500 to 1,000 posts, an analyst will distribute questionnaires to employees and officers asking them to describe what they do. He then will visit only a small number of persons in order to clarify questions that arise as he reviews the questionnaire.[15]

(b) *Analysis*

The job descriptions are reviewed and separated by the type of work being done. For example, all job descriptions which involve correspondence preparation would be in one box, all those which involve stenography in another and so on.

(c) *Drafting Grade Descriptions*

With knowledge of the work being performed, the analyst then drafts grade descriptions for example:

Grade 1: Positions involving very simple work such as that done by a sweeper and *farash*. This grade would also include other functionaries in technical organizations, who would wash bottles, more laboratory equipments or do other similar work.

This grade will also include positions involving simple work which requires a minimum reading ability such as that done by a peon, gardener, etc.

Grade 2: Positions involving the carrying out of office routines such as stitching files, assembling files, or locating old files, typically requiring a middle school education. It also includes positions which require mechanical ability in such fields as carpentry, technical repair, or other skilled trades. Typical posts include machine operator, wireman, carpenter, blacksmith and *daftri*.

Grade 3: Positions involving simple office work such as maintaining diary, typing, despatching, making movements of papers, indexing papers and files, simple accounting duties such as preparing pay, travel, and contingency bills, in the educational requirements of matriculation level. It would also include positions which require some knowledge about the purchase and maintenance of office requirements and of buildings, and of skilled trades. Typical posts include: lower division clerk, upper division clerk, mechanics, cabinet makers, sub-inspectors, sub-overseers and computer operators.

Grade 4: Positions involving analysis, of cases, processing fresh receipts, noting and drafting application of well established rules, etc., which typically requires the services of persons possessing a bachelor's degree. Also posts included are positions which require knowledge of professions or sciences sufficient to perform subordinate duties in technical fields. Typical posts included are: assistants, technical assistants, Hindi assistants, research assistants in the Secretariat, or computer operators.

It also includes posts which require ability to supervise skilled trades or similar work. Typical posts included are: engineering supervisor, overseers and others. To sum, up this Grade thus includes all classes of positions the duties of which are: (1) to perform, under general supervision, difficult and responsible work in office, business, or fiscal administration, or comparable subordinate technical work in a professional, scientific or technical field, requiring in either case: (a) considerable training and supervisory or other experience, (b) broad working knowledge of a special and complex subject matter, procedure, or practice, or of the principles of the profession, art, or science involved, and (c) to a considerable extent the exercise of independent judgment; or (2) to perform other work of equal important, difficulty, and responsibility both in the office and in the field and requiring comparable qualifications.

Grade 5: Positions involving supervision of office work, inspection and scrutiny of offices, scrutinizing, of notes and sending of them, and under immediate and general supervision, to perform routine work. It also includes posts which require the ability to perform an intermediate level of professional or scientific work. Typical posts included are: section officer, junior engineer, and junior research officer, accounts officer, junior chemist, etc. To sum up, this Grade includes all classes of positions the duties of which are (1) to perform; under general supervision, work of considerable difficulty and responsibility along, special technical or supervisory lines in office, business, or fiscal administration, or comparable subordinate technical work in a professional scientific, or technical field, requiring in either case (a) considerable specialized or supervisory training and experience, (b) comprehensive working knowledge of a special and complex subject-matter, procedure, or practice, or of the principles of the profession, art, or science, involved, and (c) to a considerable extent, the exercise of independent judgement; (2) under immediate or general supervision, to perform somewhat difficult work requiring: (a) professional, scientific, or technical training and (b) to a limited extent, the exercise of independent technical judgement; or (3) to perform other work of equal importance, difficulty and responsibility both in the office and in the district and requiring comparable qualifications.

(d) *Drafting Class Definitions*

Having grade descriptions, the analyst then takes each type of job (Statistical Assistant), for example, and sorts them by grade levels. This sorting brings together a group of jobs which are called a "class". For each class he assigns a specific title. For instance, we have officers designated as assistant, technical assistant, and they may be doing, statistical work. In the new scheme such officers would be known as statistical assistants. This means that instead of saying (as we do so today) that so and so is an assistant or a technical assistant, Class II, non-gazetted, under the new plan his class designation would be:

Class Title: Statistical Assistant. Grade 5.

Class Definition: To this class will be assigned pools in which a graduate in statistics or mathematics will learn how to apply his theoretical knowledge to surveys, economic models, or planning problems. He will perform multiple calculations, determine standard definition, correct for carvilineer variances and perform other similar calculations. He may design simple questionnaires and process data, preparing tabulations and accompanying narrative descriptions.

Class Title: Typist, Grade 3.

Class Definition: Types letters, memoranda, reports and other materials from hand written or typed source documents, or from dictating machine. Receives and routes correspondence coming into the office, prepares correspondence to other offices. Receives and places telephone calls. Files materials in accordance with departmental filling instructions. Maintains calender of appointments for supervisors; acts as receptionist for office visitors.

(e) *Assigning Position to Class*

Using the class definitions, the analyst now assigns each questionnaire (or interview report) to a class, writing the title and grade on the sheet.

(f) *Establishing Class Series*

In Section (c) above, we have mentioned how grade descriptions are written, such grades cut across all occupations and ministries. For a number of reasons, related classes are usually brought together and designated as a class series. For example, in a stenographer class series would be placed at two levels, junior stenographers and senior stenographers. Other series may have more levels, for example, a physicist series might have 5 levels; Executive physicist; Principal physicist; Senior physicist; Assistant physicist; and Junior physicist.

But it is upto us to retain such higher or junior job titles or reject them. A simpler, elegant and popularly acceptable title would instead be Physicist Grade I or II or III, etc.

When establishing classes, the analyst makes sure that the differences in the duties and responsibilities and in the qualifications required are significant and indeed warrant difference in the pay attached to the higher grade.

The 'Series' are commonly limited to a single occupation, as for example, physicist, geologist, and economist. Some series may branch out in lower levels. For example, an administrative and clerical series may look like this:

Administrative Officer V
Administrative Assistant IV

Correspondence Clerk II	Purchasing Clerk II
Correspondence Clerk II	Purchasing Clerk II

Series are established to assist the analyst in distinguishing between different levels in the same occupations. However, they also indicate common lines of promotion. Here is an example of a series made up of a group of related occupations that are brought together to provide a logical promotion pattern. However, the merit of a series concept as against the 'service' concept lies mainly in that, whereas a series helps to show an incumbent a line of career growth, it does not create any hindrance in an incumbent's desire or chance of movement in any other series or professional line. In other words, today, the service concepts limits a person's mobility both upward and side-ways because of the restrictions imposed by the recruitment rules, cadre formula, etc. The series concept on the other hand, would not limit a man to some posts alone. A man belonging to a series could be his own free agent also. His career growth would not get thwarted in terms of promotion or pay fixation, as is the case today with the incumbent of any 'service' in the Central administration. A service and a class series resemble each other closely but differ in some major respects as shown in Table 4.

Thus, speaking in the terms of career patterns, the position classification for Government of India, would make services unnecessary. (I am conscious of the fact that such a change may not take place ever.)

TABLE - 4
DIFFERENCES BETWEEN SERVICE AND CLASS SERIES

Class Series	*Service, GOI*
Always tied to duties, and occupation	May be tied to an occupation as Accounts (police) or not (as IAS).
Any qualified employee can move from Series to another	Posts reserved for A one service is usually, closed to the other.
Persons doing similar work have same title description of their duties	Persons having same titles may do very different work.
Qualifications are derived from duties	Qualifications are very general.
An employee in a lower grade is a logical candidate for advancement in a series	An employee at a lower pay scale is usually arbitrarily limited in his advancement to posts reserved for his service.

(g) *Combined Concept: Grade and Class Series:* Let's now look at the combined concepts of grade, and class series. A grade is like a horizontal divides in a bookshelf and a series is like a vertical division. One grade and one series cross each other like this:

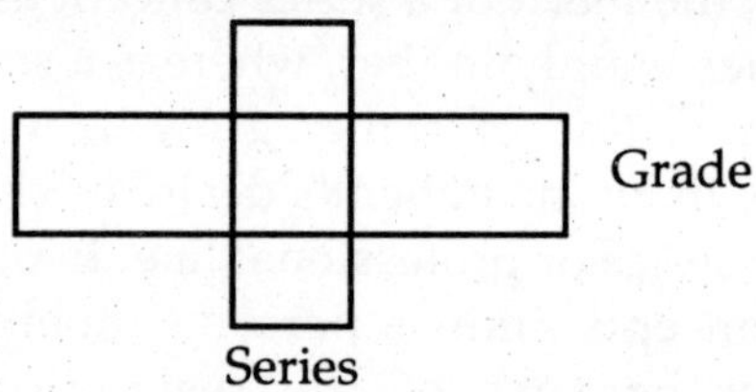

Therefore, a number of series and grades would produce a pattern like this:

Grade				
	×	×		.
5	×	×		×
4	×	×	×	×
3	×	×	×	×
2	×	×	×	
1				
	General Clerical	*Corres-pon-dence*	*Typist Steno-grapher*	*Purchas-ing, etc.*

(h) *Pay Plan:* All these steps have to be finally related to a Pay Plan. For example, for all positions in Government, this might produce a single pay scale for most or all posts that might look like this:

Rs. 1,500—60—1,800
Rs. 750—40— 960
Rs. 550—30— 700
Rs. 440—20— 540
Rs. 330—20— 430
Rs. 275—10— 325
Rs. 200—10— 250

(Note: The scales are only illustrative in nature)

This differs from the present Indian practice in which many different pay scales today cover this range of pay. But let's go further. How would some of the Government of India positions fit into such a scheme ?

First, we bring together as described above, posts, which belong together in a class. Then we bring together related classes into a class series.

Then, we assign class/services to appropriate pay schedules.

Let's relate three class series to the above pay schedule, stenographer series, civil engineer series, and physicist series. As stenographers are less skilled, they should receive lower pay than the other two, as both civil engineers and physicists must obtain 4-6 years of college work. They should get the same starting salary. If the most experienced physicists do more difficult work than civil engineers, then their pay schedule should be much higher. Thus, our pay scale might look as shown in Table 5 (A).

TABLE - 5 (A)
THREE CLASS SERIES OF ANY SCHEDULES OF STENOS, CIVIL ENGINEERS AND PHYSICISTS

Grade	*Pay*	*Stenographer Series*	*Civil Engineer Series*	*Physicist Series*
7	1500—60—1800			×
6	750—40— 960			×
5	550—30— 700		×	×
4	440—20— 540		×	×
3	330—20— 430		×	×
2	275—10— 325	×		
1	200—10— 250	×		

A pay schedule like this can be easily summarized as shown in Table 5(B).

TABLE - 5(B)
SUMMARY OF PAY SCHEDULE

7	1500	1560	1620	1680	1740	1800
6	750	790	830	870	910	960
5	550	580	610	640	670	700
4	440	460	480	500	520	540
3	330	350	370	390	410	430
2	275	285	295	305	315	325
1	200	210	220	230	240	250

To summarize, it is recommended that the Centre and States install a position classification plan which will cover as rapidly as possible officers and employees in Classes II, III, and IV, and apply, such a plan 5 years after the completion of the basic steps, to officers in Class I. Meanwhile, in Class 1 postings, greater attention be paid to specialization through training and imaginative placement policy. The purpose of this action would be:

(1) to develop a staff of employees and officers who not only efficiently follow refined policies and procedures, but who, also develop needed knowledge and skills in the qualitative transaction of their work;
(2) to provide equal pay for equal work;
(3) to provide an orderly pattern of career advancement;
(4) to motivate production and reward productivity;
(5) put to give the public administrative apparatus a modern base so that the administration may easily cope with the needs of the 21st century.

ANNEXURE A
JOB AUDIT CHECK LIST

1. Review written job description.
2. Check post descriptions or audit reports on same or related jobs.
3. Review class specification.
4. Obtain background information on agency, organization, occupation involved, etc.
5. Clear appointment for employee interview with department head and supervisor.
6. Interview employee - check:
   - (a) what is done?
   - (b) methods used;
   - (c) tools or other aids used;
   - (d) responsibilities for results;
   - (e) consequences of actions;
   - (f) guidelines provided;
   - (g) supervision exercised and received;
   - (h) personal relationships required;
   - (i) any other pertinent factors.
7. Confirm findings of fact with employee and his supervisor.
8. Upon return to office, evaluate findings and prepare report with conclusions.
9. Notify employee and department head.
10. If appeal received, reinterview and prepare new report and recommendations.
11. Notify employee and department head of decision on appeal.
12. Enter action on allocation list or other official record.

ANNEXURE B
INSTRUCTIONS FOR COMPLETING JOB DESCRIPTION FORM

This Form is used to obtain basic information about your job with Description Form.

This form is used to obtain basic information about your job which will be used to determine the classification of your job or to determine your pay. Therefore, you should be as clear and accurate as possible and fill out the form completely.

First, prepare your answers in rough draft on a separate sheet of paper. When you are sure that your answers are complete and accurate, copy them on one of the Job Description Forms and hand it to your supervisor, who will have additional copies typed and returned to you for your signature. Your handwritten copy will be returned to you for your personal file. If you need additional space, extra pages may be attached but should be identified by your name and department.

As this form is intended for general use, some of the questions may not apply to your job. If so, skip them. If the questions do apply, fill out completely, be specific, and illustrate your statements with examples.

This form is to be completed by you in your own words. Your supervisor and department head will review your job description to determine the completeness and accuracy of the statements and to clarify or give additional information concerning your duties and responsibilities. Under no circumstances, however, should the supervisor or the department head change the answers as given and certified by you. In the space provided, they may make whatever statements they think are necessary before signing the report.

Item 7: Indicate any allowances you receive, such as rent-free housing, free meals, laundry services, transport, etc. Indicate any cash received in lieu of such allowances or the approximate cash value of such allowances if known to you.

Item 9a: Answer this item only if you are actually responsible for directing the work of others. Inspecting, checking, or proof-reading the work of others does not in itself constitute supervision.

These types of indirect (functional) supervision should be described in your answer to Question 12.

Item 9b: Include employees (by number only) whom you direct through subordinate supervisors. For example, a Supervising Clerk who supervises a section composed of two units, each supervised by a Senior Clerk, would answer this question thus: "Archana Sharma, Senior Clerk; Alka, Senior Clerk; seven Intermediate Clerks; three Junior Clerks."

Item 12: The answer to this item requires an exact account of what you do. Describe your "whole job" or year-round duties, not just those which might be performed during rush or peak periods of activity or when you are substituting for other persons. Start with your most important duties and describe your occasional or infrequent duties last. Use a separate paragraph for each major duty.

In the left-hand column indicate the proportion of time devoted to each major duty. Use percentages, or, if it is easier, an estimated number of hours per day or days per week or, weeks per month or year. Any time break-down which adequately explains your job will be acceptable.

Item 13: This question asks how long you have been performing your present job in this jurisdiction rather than how long you have been employed by this jurisdiction.

Item 14: Indicate here the parts of your job which demand the greatest care and thought or the most skill or understanding. Which duties would be the most difficult for another person taking your place to learn? Tell us what makes these duties difficult and give one or two specific examples.

Item 15: In this space explain what guidepost helps are given to you in your work and what kind of instructions, written or oral, are given to you. For example, "I follow a prescribed procedure set forth in the accounting manual" or "I am shown how to operate the equipment and then work on each job as it is given to me to do" or "I am given a project with instructions as to results expected and general methods but details are left to me" or "I work according to the requirements of my professional field and am guided only by general administrative policies set down by my supervisor."

Item 16: This item should be used to explain whether your work is reviewed in detail or only on overall results. Is your work reviewed for the way you do it as well aś for what you accomplish? Is it a personal review by observation of your work or a review of a written report? How frequently is your work reviewed, as for example, every day, once a week, at periodic intervals, or only on completion of a total project?

ANNEXURE TABLE - 1
EXAMPLES OF GOOD AND POOR DUTIES STATEMENT

Poor Statement	*Good Statement*
Assist in handling correspondence.	Receive, open, time stamp, and route in coming mail.
Maintain grounds and landscaped areas.	Mow lawn with power mover and hand mowers. Rake and weed grounds. Trim trees from ground and from ladder, using power saws, Lubricate mowers or another gadget.
I do finish concrete work.	Place forms, mix, pour and finish concrete walks and curbing.
Keep claim registers.	Prepare registers of all claims showing allocation of budget expenditure and total amount of expenditure for month in which claims are made.
Do general kitchen work.	Clean and cut fruits and vegetables. Make salad dressings. Serve at steam table. Wash pots and dishes and store away utensils and foods. Once or twice a month, bake cookies and tarts.
One unit is responsible for keeping all purchasing records.	I compare invoices with purchase orders. Review requisitions submitted, by the different departments for accuracy, then give them to the Purchasing Agency for his O. K.

Note: All this is an illustrative description of how to structure a questionnaire for eliciting job description data feed-back.

ANNEXURE C
POSITION CLASSIFICATION QUESTIONNAIRE

1. Mr. Last Name First Middle Initial
   Mrs.
   Miss
2. Official Title of Position
3. Regular Schedule of Hours of Work

	From	To	
			Total Hrs. per Week____
Mon	______	______	Explain rotation of shifts, if any:
Tues	______	______	
Wed	______	______	____________________
Thur	______	______	____________________
Fri	______	______	
Sat	______	______	Hrs. of ".On-Call" Time
Sun	______	______	per Wk. __________

   Length of Lunch Period __________
4. Commission, Board, or Department
5. Division or Institution
6. Section or Order Unit of Division or Institution
7. Place of work or Headquarters
8. Is your work ______ Full Time? _____ Part-Time _____ Year Round?
   ______ Seasonal? ______ Temporary?
   If work is seasonal temporary, or part-time, indicate part of year or proportion of ____________________________________
9. Do you receive any maintenance (room, meals, laundry, etc.) in addition to your cash salary ?
   Yes __________ No __________
10. Describe below in detail the work you do. Use your own words, and make your description so clear that persons unfamiliar with your work can understand exactly what you do. Attach additional sheets if necessary.

Time	*Work Performed*	*Leave Blank*

11. Name and Title of Your Immediate Supervisor.

12. Give the names and payroll titles of employees you supervise if five or fewer. If you supervise more than five employees, give the number under each title. If you supervise no employees, write "none".

---

13. Machines or equipment used regularly in your work. Give per cent of time spent in operation of each:

%	%
%	%
%	%

14. What is the nature and extent of instructions you receive regarding your work?

15. What is the nature and extent of the work or review of your work?

16. Describe your contracts with departments other than your own, with outside organizations, and with the general public.

CERTIFICATION

I certify that the above answers are my own and are accurate and complete.

Date_________ Employee's Signature_________

STATEMENT OF IMMEDIATE SUPERVISOR

17. Comment on statements of employees. Indicate any exceptions or additions.

---

18. What do you consider the most important duties of this position?

---

19. Does this position involve typing?
    No
    Yes—Give % of time spent on typing.

20. Does this position involve shorthand?
    No
    Yes—Give % of time spent in taking shorthand.

21. Indicate the qualification which you think should be required in filling a future vacancy in this position. Keep the position itself in mind rather than the qualifications of the individual who now occupies it.

	Basic Qualifications	*Additional Desirable Qualifications*
Education, general:		
Education, special or professional:		
Experience, length in years and kind:		
Licenses, certificates, or registration:		
Age, sex, physical requirements, or other factors:		

Date _______ Immediate Supervisor's Signature _______

STATEMENT OF DEPARTMENT HEAD OR OTHER ADMINISTRATIVE OFFICER

22. Comment on the above statements of the employee and the supervisor. Indicate any inaccuracies or statement with which you disagree. Please comment on the qualifications suggested by the supervisor.

Date _______ Department Head's Signature _______

Your signature on the certificate on the front of the form indicates that the answers are your own and to the best of your knowledge are complete and correct. Do not sign your name until you have re-read your statement.

INSTRUCTIONS FOR SUPERVISORY STAFF

If you are a supervisor reviewing this form, you should remember that your certification means you accept responsibility that the statements made constitute a true description of the duties and responsibilities of the job. If the description does not meet with your idea of the job, it is your responsibility to see that statements made are qualified or elaborated in your comments. Under no circumstances, however, are the employees' statements to be changed.

It will be your responsibility to arrange to have copies of the employees' Job Description Form typed, and returned to the employee for his signature. You should review the completed and signed forms for correctness, completeness, and accuracy of statements, then add any comments which you believe are necessary, sign the forms and forward them through regular channels.

ANNEXURE D
JOB DESCRIPTION FORM

Leave this space blank

____

Information on this form will be used to help classify or set the pay for your job. Please be as clear and accurate as possible. Fill up completely.

1. Mr. Mrs. Miss ______________________ (*Cross out two*)
2. Department ______________________
3. Pay Roll Title ______________________
4. Address of Employment ______________________
5. Rate of pay $ ______________________
6. Hours of Work
   (a) Total per week ______________________
   (b) Shift schedule (days and hours) ______________________
7. Allowances for quarters, uniforms, meals, Laundry, etc. ________
8. Who is your immediate supervisor? ______________________
   Name Title
9. If you supervise others, list their names and titles ((list number and titles only). (if through subordinate supervisors)
   (a) *I Supervise directly:* (b) *I Supervise through subordinates*
   Name Title Number Title

---

10. List any machines, equipment, or motor vehicles you are required to use. Indicate percentage of working time spent in operating each.

    ____

11. For office positions only *Not Required* *Words Per Minute Required*

	Not Required	*Words Per Minute Required*
Typing	( )	( )
Stenography	( )	( )

CERTIFICATE OF EMPLOYEE

I hereby certify that the answers to the foregoing questions are my own and that to the best of my knowledge they are complete and correct.

Date________19___ (Signed) _______

CERTIFICATE OF IMMEDIATE SUPERVISOR AND DEPARTMENT HEAD

I hereby certify the answers given by this employee to questions 1 through 16 on this form are correct and complete as to the facts within my knowledge except as noted here (or in attached memo).

Supervisor Department head

____

____

Date________ 19____	Date________ 19____
(Signed)____________	(Signed)____________
(Title)____________	(Title)____________

12. Description of your job. This is the most important item on this form. In your own words, explain your duties. List the most important first. Estimate the amount of your working time spent on each duty. Use percentage or number of hours or days, or a similar breakdown.
    % or amount of time ____________________
13. How long have you been doing duties for this jurisdiction ?
14. What parts of your job are the most difficult to do or the most complex?
    Why? Give examples.
    ____
15. Explain the kind and amount of work guidance you receive from supervisors, manuals, or established procedures. ____________
    ____
16. Explain in what way and how often your work is reviewed by your supervisor. ____________
    ____

REFERENCES

1. See Baruch Isınar. Position Classification in the Public Service. A report submitted to the Civil Service Assembly, by the Committee on position classification and pay plans in the Public Service. [Chicago. Civil Service Assembly of the United States and Canada 1941]. Vth Print (1948).

2. See Civil Service Commission of Canada, Report of Transmission to Accompany the Civil Service of Canada. Prepared by Arthur Young & Co. (Ottawa, 1919).
3. See O. Glenn Stahl. Public Personnel Administration. (New York) Harper & Brothers, 4th Ed. (1950), p. 183.
4. See U.S. Civil Service Commission. Basic Training Course in Position Classification - Part 3 Administration and operations (Personnel Methods Series No. II - Part 3), pp. 46, 48.
5. There is another interesting rule [Office memorandum issued by the Ministry of Finance (Department of Expenditure) *vide* F. No. 3 (26) Est. III/57 dated the 4th September 1957] according to which, "in the case of an officer of the Central Services, Class I, the special pay should be so regulated that the total of pay plus special pay that would be admissible in the same post to an officer of the Indian Administrative Service with corresponding seniority/length of service. In reckoning seniority/length of service for this purpose, any period of past service in Class I including the service in the Emergency Cadre in Class I should be taken into account. Past Service of any kind should also be taken into account to the extent that credit is given for it in the parent service concerned for seniority.
6. See Report of the Commission of Enquiry on Emoluments and condition of service of Central Government Employees (1957-59). Chapter on classification of Services' Ministry of Finance Government of India, p. 560.
7. See Varadachariar Commission Paragraph 20 (1946-47), p. 15.
8. Second Pay Commission Report (1957-59), pp. 500-61.
9. Ibid., p. 561.
10. Ibid., p. 562.
11. See Seth, S.C., "Position Classification as an Aid to Staffing." An enquiry into its nature and scope of application in the Central Administrative Organisation in India Mineographed 1953. Indian Institute of Public Administration, New Delhi.
12. This is now being done for Scientists working in Laboratories, Science Department of the GOI under the flexible complementing scheme.
13. These figures are not what actually is paid currently. These are only illustrative in nature.
14. See Annexures A and B.
15. See Annexures C and D.

A PLAN TO INSTALL AN ALL-INDIA FEDERAL CIVIL SERVICE

Satish C. Seth

The concept of an all-India service dates back to the East India Company. This idea, which got institutionalized in the form of an Indian Civil Service has persisted all along and is still a live administrative notion.

An all-India service presupposes the following three factors, namely:

(i) It is a service to which recruitment is made, from the Indian citizens irrespective of their area of domicile.

(ii) The officers recruited encadred in an all-India service are eligible to be posted anywhere on behalf of India at any time and place.

(iii) Finally, in such a service arrangement the total and final control of cadre management should be with the Center, including the authority to review and rate the performance of the members of such a Central service.

In the context of Independent India, the creation of the Indian Administrative Service (IAS) as the successor to the Indian Civil Service of the British time (ICS) was taken by the interim Government of India in the year 1946. The conference of the Provinces confirmed the idea in October 1946. The constitution of India *vide* Article 312 (1) accorded the constitutional recognition to the formation of two all-India services, namely, the Indian Administrative Service, and the Indian Police Service.

The broad reasons for the creation of such a service was the need in what Sardar Patel described, "A Central Service". In his speech delivered in the Premiers' Conference, Sardar Patel, who was the Home Minister at that time, observed:

> "You all know that recruitment was stopped during the period of the war and the Secretary of State has already announced that no more recruitment to the Services will be made due to the constitutional changes that are taking place

> in this country and that power has to be transferred from the British to Indian hands. So India has to make its own arrangements for its efficient administration and for that purpose the question to be decided by us is whether we want a Central Administrative Service."
>
> He further added:
>
> "As I have told you, we are all agreed that it is advisable to have such a Service. Except for the control of the Secretary of State, which can be replaced by the control of another Indian agency, and for the difference in the scale of pay, there should be equally good guarantee of security; the question of discipline and other incidental matters will be considered in such a way that the service might feel happy and contented and may not be at the mercy of changing parties or changing conditions in the country; the service must not have to participate in the activities of any political party or other party.".

Referring to the nature of experience that the personnel of such a central service should possess, Sardar Patel, observed that it is essential that the officers of this Central Administrative Service should possess different administrative experience and a wider outlook in a larger sphere in the provinces. He said:

> "A combination of these two experiences should make the Service more efficient. They will also serve as a liaison between the Provinces and the Government and introduce certain amount of freshness and vigour in the administration both of the Centre and the provinces. Therefore, my advice is that we should have a Central Service."

In the aforesaid context of the concept of all-India services — administrative, constitutional and management aspects — the use of all-India service label for the IAS and IPS is a misnomer since these services are actually State services.

The Indian Civil Service which was an all-India service was such, because of the Indian politics — Constitutional set-up at that time, provided for Unitary system of government. The only all-India services, today, are those which have been wrongly named as the Central services such as: Income-tax, Railways, etc.

The concept of developmental administration in India has to be worked through the Parliamentary system of democracy; and we need to understand the role of the President at the Union headquarters and that of the Governors and Lt. Governors in the States and the Union Territories. The Constitution of India makes these dignitaries as the repositories of the chief executive power, but they are to act at the advice of the Council of Ministers. The growth of different political parties brings the need of Central, i.e., the national responsibility into forefront. The chief Federal agent, namely the Governor, hereafter, can not afford to be a passive onlooker of the slow and tardy progress in his State. His government will have to be assisted by competent senior civil servants of a truly all-India character.

In the future it would be necessary that the federal government should possess long arms of the executive control so that the Indian administration is able to:

- (i) oversee the progress in the field of plan schemes and developmental administration;
- (ii) coordinate the regional development;
- (iii) establish a cadre of experienced elite civil servants who are a group of both the generalists with specialization and the specialists with administrative know-how, some of whom can play the role of an Inspector-General;
- (iv) give to the country experienced men of action, true and loyal to the cause of India's progress and unity.
- (v) foster a spirit of emotional integration in the country.

In the present day context, the State Civil Service including such officers of the Indian Administrative Service who work in the States are not able to manifest their total Administrative personality and they fail to deliver the goods in a wholesome manner. The IAS officer, who is mainly the chief administrative authority in a district remains to a very large extent, a ceremonial officer of the district, although he does act both as the law and order officer as well as a co-ordinating authority of development. But his work, his contribution, is both narrowly limited and narrowly local in character.

The Governors in the States are not able to exercise much control over the progress of administration and plan schemes.

Also they cannot even protect the IAS officers, if they are ill-treated and transferred at the whim and fancies of the local politicians.

The State politicians sometimes even consider the Governor an outsider and, therefore, they do not always listen to his advice. Both, the Federal element in Governors, and, the so-called all-India officers, today live at the mercy of the local political pressures.

There is, therefore, a real need today to establish an all-India federal service which can truly serve the regional concept of a Central administrative service as enunciated by Sardar Patel.

This all-India federal service would consist of the elite civil servants who would be chosen from all functional pools, as described in the chapter on 'Higher services', provided they have a meritorious record and have been found fit in the selection test. The managerial and policy maker's pool, would consist of officers of a Joint Secretary, a Commissioner or an equivalent level, drawn from both the technical and non-technical pools and services. They will go to constitute the bulk strength of the Indian federal public service. There could also be some lateral entry from outside professional groups.

Thus, the all-India federal services would consist of the following:

(1) 75 per cent recruitment by promotion from both the technical and non-technical functional pools or services after a due test.

(2) 25 per cent direct recruitment from the open market in the age group 40 and above. This will also bring in the senior specialists in the bureaucracy.

The formation of an all-India service would have to be scuttled and converted into the Administrative Service of each State. This would also be a logical development, since, hereafter, as the examination of the UPSC and other Commissions, the candidates are likely to take examination in the regional languages; such candidates would have only a regional personality, suitable for their own State.

The proposed all-India federal service would be an 'elite' service and the 'elite' will be born in the Indian bureaucracy at a time when alone they should emerge as an 'elite' that is, after they have shown their administrative ability and competence consistently over a period of 10 to 15 years service. Its composition, it should be remembered, need not undermine democratic decentralization or devolution of authority. What we need is a qualitative Federal action for developmental work.

The President and the Governors would, hereafter, be given staff agencies, consisting of senior members of the Indian federal service, who would be their advisers both in times of peace and in times of administrative and constitutional emergency. These officers would also from time to time act as the national overseers, federal watch-dogs, and counsellors of the States, districts and the local administration. To achieve this we need a national consensus followed by constitutional amendment.

Conclusion

The Indian bureaucracy in the light of the imperatives of the Future could thus be staffed in the following manner:

Mode of Entry	*Level of Employment in Administrative Hierarchy*	*Chief Characteristic*
75% Promotion 25% lateral entry	The Policy and Managerial Pool	All-India Federal Civil Service.
	↑	
50% Direct entry: consisting of Graduate entrants who are recruited on the basis of intelligence tests, aptitude tests and who enter several functional pools plus 50% by promotion from below 100% entry on the basis of Position Classification.	The Middle Management and The Supervisory Group	All pools to have equal status, same pay scale. Promotions to take place on merit and success in Promotion-Tests.
	↑	
	The Infrastructure	Consisting of technicians, clerks, mechanics, etc., chosen: (a) from open market, or (b) recruited as administrative cadets at a young age and trained in the diverse skills by the Government.

MANAGEMENT OVERHAUL FOR AND TOWARDS FUTURE

Satish C. Seth

One of the concerns for future is to build a new society. Management is the key to this developmental task. The shifting scene of managerial practices both in the Government, in the private sector and in the public sector suggests, that we are moving in the right direction. If we look at the 50's and then at the 70's, we can see that the emerging scenario of the year 2000 is one of hope as well as ample fulfilment. This is not to say that we do not face any crisis points. Management of India's resources, the management of man and material and the development of science and technological inputs hold the secret to our future prosperity. We are today 800 million people. We may be around 960 million or more in the year 2000 AD. This vast humanity can be our asset. The capacity to organize ourselves and to manage our affairs well can guarantee and provide the right strategies for survival and to ensure a certain quality of life. It is in this context that a new plan for rebuilding our bureaucracy has been made in the earlier chapters.

If we look at our Organizational structures, personnel policies, programme content, use of new technologies and tools of management critically, notwithstanding its structural flows in building up the scenarios for the year 2000, one cannot escape the temptation to say that the Indian managerial force has the necessary vigour, capability and expertize to prepare for a secure future which can guarantee a state of affairs where the right man is working, at the right job, with the right techniques, to ensure conditions in the country where food is available for everyone; and our people possess appropriate skills; can get employment as they are and where they are; can generate wealth in its numerous forms; and with the discrete use of known technologies both indigenous and those which characterise a post-industrial society, to possess the ability to instal the right management systems to deliver the goods of welfare in time.

When we look at the emerging management profile of India, three things become clear. Firstly, the new managers, the manager of today and tomorrow, would have to be one who is intellectually well informed not only in the national context but who is also familiar with the international data in the area in which he specializes, be it the field of exports, marketing, production, or resource or planning. Such a knowledge on his or her part would be needed in addition to the general knowledge and creative ability. At the minimum, they (i.e. our bureaucrats) shall have to possess the ability and means to acquire international data and information. Secondly, the responsibility of the Indian management is primarily one of managing "a large human system" be it in the field of education, transportation, health or whatever else one may think of. The Indian "need" element, as it gets accentuated and aggravated by ever increasing population, would make tremendous demands on our management capability, accountability and timely delivery of the services in numerous areas. Thirdly, in the context of these emerging responsibilities and the qualitative demands that shall get put on the management, any management, public or private, the paramount need of tomorrow and for that matter, even today, is that of resource management. No matter how much we advance, there could always be a live crisis that our resources could fall short of what we need to offer to the people — a bare minimum standard of life, not without a certain touch of quality. This would then be an additional task, a heightened challenge and indeed the paramount duty of each manager to think of those innovative social systems whereby even with minimum level of resources we may be able to ensure `maximum happiness to the maximum people'. All this would demand a management system which is less alienated from the Indian social milieu, a management system and managerial style where concern for others and the concern to deliver goods speedily should take precedence over traditional norms of procedures, rules and regulations and the formality of the `process' prescribed for due accountability. This could be the case with every management function, be it prevention of disaster or be it pre-or-post-disaster servicing.

The emergence of a mature self-governing, self-sustaining,

self-relevant society calls for a new management style. The ability to analyse facts, formulate alternatives, take a decision, implement it to its minutest details, the essence of modern management which is information based and at the same time indicative of a creative and futuristic outlook. Such should be, indeed, bureaucracy if it has to serve the 21st Century India.

The paucity of resources, trained personnel and insufficient community participation are three obvious crisis points that characterize Indian Management scene. We need to take every conceivable step to overcome the same. Community participation with the management and an Indian version of 'social self-management' in the form of citizen participation with administration, in the form of industrial democracy, in the form of participative decision making process for whatever also be the form in which the community action could be organized, would one is compelled to consider, hold *inter alia* the key to new organizational forms and decision making process for the emergence of the future management system and an effective bureaucracy.

The time has come when feudalistic structures have to yield to a participative management culture. And an intense state of active competition shall prevail hereafter, when in our bureaucracies shall have not only to get hold of and employ a well-informed manager, but all organizations will have to struggle hard to retain his or her services. In order to produce a good manager — a creative and bold decision making executive — we shall have to begin his training earlier than is the case today. We shall have to make management an educational discipline to which our children have to be exposed from the very beginning of their learning experience, right from the school age. Management is indeed a great educational responsibility making the Human resource development as the most important task for a nation as vast and great as India is. Management is one important input in this entire process. Management for 2000 AD clearly indicates that our immediate task today is to do everything possible so that our developmental plans and policies could turn our population into a 'resource'.

The scenarios presented here are based on a methodology

which has included the use of discussion, brainstorming sessions, questionnaire, the Delphi and intensive face to face interviews with top management executives and administrators of this country. One need not add that, a study of the secondary source material, preceeded the testing of the futuristic formulations of the trend and the preferred scenarios for Indian Management for 2000 AD. Briefly, our research data indicates that the management for and towards future will be one which is less alienated in character.

The need for modern management is not that of the large organizations alone. The small industries and the small farming operations equally need the advantages that can accrue from sophistication. In fact, management-wise, they still are a neglected sector. We need to spell out concrete areas in which massive work should commence, be it organizational development or the emergence of non-hierarchical, data innovative and task force oriented administrative action. Mere advancements in technology would not make the society more modern until and unless the men and women who handle the new technologies are well-trained and are basically result oriented managers. Without a participative management culture which permits freedom for initiative and innovation to all functionaries, big or small, we would not be able to go very far. As indicated earlier, the management culture needs to be freed from the 'feudalistic-cum-clerical' negativism. The question is, even after forty years of independence, are we ready for it?

The management of the future indicates the need for the emergence of a participative culture which is creative and at the same time has that innate strength which turns the seeming catastrophe into a great opportunity. A creative problem solving outlook. Indian Management and its bureaucrats, one fervently hopes, will swiftly move in this direction.

In India, the poliferation of State's functions and the S&T sophistication of industrial activities have given rise to numerous management patterns, organizational forms and managerial styles. Today, we do notice that the impact of the Western administrative and managerial systems does continue to dominate the thinking and practice both in the private and the public sector. The role of multinationals is equally visible in influencing management culture, at least of the larger companies. Even the management education has been so far highly Western oriented and, by and large, it has been elitist in character. An equally important development has been the growing emphasis on training and administrative and managerial reform. As a contrast, this must however be admitted that the impact of modernization has not been experienced, accepted or implemented by all the institutions within the public or the private organized sector, at all levels. The small industry being a case in point. Also the local administration in India too still displays a management style, more typical of the 19th Century. All this has to change.

The real task of management in India is basically the task of managing a "large human system". Some of the questions amongst others that we have to ask ourselves are as follows:

(1) Is our management system suited to the task of managing a large human system? (800 + million people in 1988 and 960 + million people in 2000 AD).
(2) Is our management system, in the fourth decade of the 20th Century, amply tuned to cope with the challenges of the 21st Century?
(3) What should constitute the dynamics of management change?

In an attempt to look at the future one can offer numerous scenarios which could be developed on one or the other following approaches:

(i) Scenario based on a model of 'business as usual';
(ii) Scenario for several expected futures; and
(iii) Scenario for a preferred future.

These scenarios have to be seen in terms of the societal and human needs on the one hand, and the national capabilities on the other. And thus, the management for the future, or the management towards the future can be glimpsed by using a set of selective indicators, both in terms of the trend scenario as well as a preferred future Scenario.

The concept of a preferred future in any field tends to be subjective. The national needs, however, do help to focus attention on certain values, programmes and institutional arrangements which deserve attention and eventual acceptance. In terms of the national policy therefore, one can outline an 'accelerated' implementation scenario of a preferred future scenario.

The preferred future for the Indian Management, a bureaucratic rebuilding would be one which amongst other things, would try to achieve the following few goals:

1. Availability of increased management know-how to all management structures (tiny units, medium-scale enterprises, large organizations);
2. Information system to include both national and international data base for decision making process;
3. Increased recourse to long-range planning. (Commodity profile, sales profile, marketing profile, technology assessment, etc.);
4. Emergence of bureaucratic recognition on non-hierarchical forms (different power structures); at all levels of management;
5. Emergence of participative management (accountability to workers); again at all levels;
6. New managerial lifestyle and attitudinal changes on the part of managers and administrators. (Less alienation to environment, people, users of services);
7. Rural orientation (increased decentralization);
8. Innovative administration (De-routinization) and bureaucratic freedom to think afresh.

In terms of the concern for future even though it is usually targeted to a distant date (2000 AD or 2020 AD) our conclusions (several alternates) must lead to new current decisions. The priority area of management concern for the 21st Century is essentially one where current decisions for management change should commence immediately both to eliminate crisis situations (known and not so known), such as: (a) Scarce resource management; and (b) Just Personnel Policy (right man for right job and equal growth opportunities, etc.) and augmentation of our efforts in favour of new bureaucratic preferences. Some of these priority areas would then be as follows:

1. Increased delegations;
2. Emphasis on initiative;

3. Programme orientation;
4. Installing of new Personnel plan as described earlier;
5. Resource management, introduction of increased managerial inputs in the field of water, agriculture and energy management;
6. Modernization of management in neglected areas, such as, the small industries, the village and the agricultural farmer;
7. Enlargement of national and local information base;
8. Increased professionalism in bureaucracy at all levels;
9. Role of management in service sector; increased emphasis in fields like Transportation, Communication, Hospitals, etc.;
10. Reorganisation of S&T Institutions; problems of management and running of laboratories (R&D management in general);
11. New approaches in sectoral administration; to be made non-hierarchical;
12. Emphasis on "ad-hoc-cracy" versus "bureaucracy";
13. Emergence of non-hierarchical organizational structures at all levels upto Panchayats (Village level self-government);
14. Free mobility of personnel from Government to Education, from Education to Industry, from Industry to Government, and so on;
15. Overhauling of Defence management; Need for long-range Technology Forecasting;
16. Adoption of post-industrial technology leading to diversified management styles;
17. Emergence of new management systems relevant to Indian conditions involving community participation;
18. Introduction of management education in school curriculum;
19. New Trends in Managerial lifestyle to avoid public versus private sector contrasts; and
20. Higher institutional emphasis on forecasting, Anticipatory Management or Perspective Planning.

To sum up, in the context of Futurological bureaucratic

reorganization demands, we need to study the new technologies and relevant social goals. We need to make a scientific assessment of the Indian physical and human resources and of the way they should be managed and utilized so that we can assure a reasonable success for the Indian people and the Indian society which has indeed a great future. In this process we cannot overlook the familiar "crisis points" in different walks of life. Our concerns are not merely for newer ideas but we have also to look at such methods whereby our bureaucracy can be trained to eliminate wastages in all walks of life. We need to make judicious use of our resources. As managers and administrators we are vitally concerned with the impact of management technology on life; and with the right choice of managerial tools and style of work relevant to our needs, our people and our society. For all this, we should take into account a long-range viewpoint based on which the current decisions taken to re-build our bureaucracy relevant to serve should be the managerial needs of the 21st Century.

THE TREND SCENARIO : MANAGEMENT : 2000 A.D.
MANAGEMENT IN GOVERNMENT: PUBLIC SECTOR VIS-A-VIS PRIVATE SECTOR

Parameters examined	*50's*	*70-80's*	*2000 A.D.*
1. Nature of Bureaucracy 2. Work Methodology	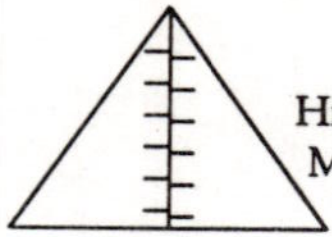 Too Hierarchical Monolithic	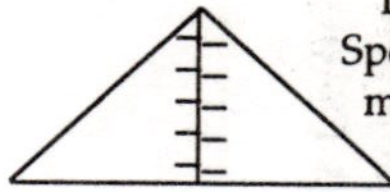 Increased Specialisation more participation	Participative Team work less Hierarchical 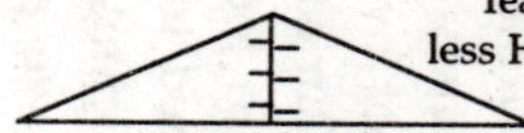 Broad-based
3. Organisational Structures.	1. Characteristic Weberian typology (W.T.); establishes rational legal bureaucratic order	1. Weberian typology gets enfeebled (W.T.) as State functions multiply.	1. Gradual crumbling of adminis-trative pyramid leading to shrinking of policy levels and concomitant programme executing organisations.
4. Personnel Management.		2. Administration still tope heavy; limited extension of delegation of powers.	2. The character of decision making alters with the increased delegation of authority and due to in work-style.
5. Training Function	2. *Impact of British Administrative System*	3. Decision making process hierarchical and still precedent oriented. Consultative aspect dominates.	3. New administrative ethos lays emphasis on targets; time bound programmes; greater facility in implementation policies.
6. Reforms Function	(1) Executive part and parcel of legislature.	4. Poliferation of Governmental responsibility gives birth to new formations.	4. Flow of personnel from industry to Government and vice-versa.
7. Decision making process	(2) Doctrine of Ministerial responsibility. (3) Politically neutral civil service. 3. *Limited Functions* (1) Law and order (2) Limited development functions.	5. Influx of specialised personnel.	5. Increased lateral entry.

(3) Slow moving workstyle.	6. Training function increase as well as reform function gains momentum.	6. Likely crisis in personnel management due to proliferation and diversity in the conditions of service of different types of personnel.
(4) Highly pyramidical structures monolithic top heavy.	7. Work study, operation research new technics begin to receive attention.	7. Likely emergence of partly in personnel policy as amongst different functionaries/services etc.
(5) Personnel selection: traditions prevails: competitive examinations continue. 4. Training Function Limited in character	8. The continuation of planning and process alters the decision making process in various organisations.	8. Emergence of S&T institutions leading to new approaches to programme fulfilment.
(6) Selection process non-related to candidate's specification	9. Project management and role of consultancy increases.	9. Emphasis on task forces/groups/ teams as against vertical hierarchical decision makers.
5. Reforms Function Beginning of O&M exercise. Early emphasis on statistical study of work-load.	10. Hierarchical attitudes approach continue to dominate the secretarial work.	10. Strengthening of management and cooperative sector.
	11. Growth of S&T organisation & emergence of short range & long range S&T Planning.	11. Emergence of new styles of rural development and District administration.
6. Decision making process. Hierarchical: limited delega-tion of authority; over-whelming concern for precedents; decision making highly consultative and therefore time consuming; highly backward looking too: Historical orientation dominates. 7. Commencement of planning		12. Emergence of new administrative culture accompanied with attitudinal change.

BUSINESS MANAGEMENT

Parameters Examined	*50's*	*70-80's*	*2000 AD*
1. Organisational style	Closed Sector	More Open & Exposed to Professionalism	
	1. Family owned concern.	1. Emergence of professionally qualified people.	1. Increased participation in management.
2. Personnel policy.	2. Role of managing agencies.	2. Managing agencies abolished.	2. Better industry Government relation.
	3. Foreign collaboration and emergence of multinationals.	3. Strengthened emergence of multinationals.	3. Increased role of multi national.
3. Programmes	4. Lack of management training.	4. Increase in professionally qualified personnel.	4. Increased emergence of the joint sector.
	5. Personnel management highly personal and subjective.	5. Claim of social purpose made.	5. Increased R&D effort.
	6. Lack of social purpose.	6. Increased management education and training effort.	6. Increased meritocracy.
		7. Diversification of industrial activities.	7. Crisis situations arise from resource scarcity.
		8. In-house R&D, O&M, Operations research and adoption of new management technics.	
		9. Emergence of joint endeavours with public sectors.	
		10. Better industrial relations.	
		11. Emergence of professionals in sales, marketing, public relations, etc. & allied managerial tasks.	
		12. Increased delegations of authority and decision making ability to lower functionaries.	

PUBLIC SECTOR VIS-A-VIS PRIVATE SECTOR

Parameters Examined	*50's*	*70-80's*	*2000 AD*
		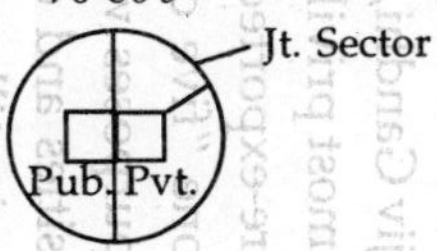	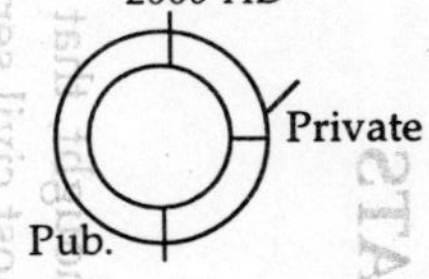
1. Management Style 2. Personnel Policy. 3. Training functions.	1. Narrow public sector base.	1. Increased proliferation of public sector undertakings.	1. Public sector and private sector cooperation increases to 60% greater collaboration, exchange of personnel and joint activities.
	2. Rigid demarcations between private and public sectors.	2. Phase of revaluation of work strategies personnel policies industrial relations in public sector.	2. Training and management sophistication increase.
4. Decision making style.	3. Emergence of new definitions concerning the role of public sector.	3. Emergence of joint sector.	3. Time bound programme take upper hand.
5. Impact of engineering and allied S&T discipline.	4. Third plan decides public sector should make profit.	4. Creater intercourse between private and public sector both professional and commercial.	4. Great increase in research development and design activities with the emergence of several in-house R&D units.
	5. Implementation of Industrial Policy resolutions leading to increase in the public sector activities.	5. Project Management evaluation technics strengthened.	5. Free flow of ideas and trained managers from one sector to another.
	6. Work style still hierarchical.	6. Increased emphasis on R&D.	
	7. Slow impact of professionalism in the field of project management marketing of R&D etc.		

TRAINING BUREAUCRATS

Satish C. Seth

Only a year or two ago, who would have ever thought, that even the Cabinet Secretary of India who is the top most civil servant, could be compelled to go, atleast, for a day, for training. Well, times are changing fast even in the steel frame of the top echelon of India bureaucracy. The Cabinet Secretary, a few months ago was at Poona for a full five days enjoying an enforced stay of training with several other younger colleagues of his ilk—the Indian Administrative Service. Prime Minister Rajiv Gandhi, thus did enforce the movement of a few thousand and most privileged bureaucrats of the Indian Civil Service for getting re-exported to a class-room setting in two parallel programmes one "five days" and another of a months duration for training purposes which were organized by different Institutions, Universities and other Management training outfits of India. The process is still on.

I do have, over the years, got some close familiarity with the credentials and of a few missing aspects of Training and Public Administration in India, of our Training outfits and the contents of their programmes, by having addressed two such programmes, on in Jaipur and the other in Trivandrum. Besides, having been a founder Member of the Indian Society of Training and Development (ISTD) the Indian Council of Management and Future (ICMF) and the Centre for Anticipatory Management (CAM). Added to it, the experience of having served, earlier in the Administrative Reforms Commission of India 1968-70, the Institute of Public Administration in New Delhi (1963) and have been a regular speaker in India and overseas in the field of Anticipatory Management and Future-scan as an aid to Policy formulation, thus, in any formulation of new guidelines of training for our bureaucrats, I can say with some confidence that the first point that we need to closely look at is the difference between (a) the skill generation training effort and (b) the broadening of the mental horizon of the trainees. These are two entirely different institutional training obligations for providing the right kind of training inputs.

The "skill-formation" input of training is akin to teaching people, say, "How to ride a Bicycle" whereas, the "broadening of mental horizon mode of training inputs" are there to make trainees to learn, to reflect on: "How to design, improve or reinvent not only a new Bicycle" but also how to go into the morphology, sociology and engineering associated with mobility". Besides, this can in the second mode learn to associate their "reflections" to the current policies in a quest to seek, new "ways and means" of realizing "new possibilities". Such reflections can help trainees to identify the loop-holes and the inadequacy of current policies on the one hand and can further help them to generate numerous alternates and ideas for seeking relevant "policy-shifts" - to build a new kind of future in the area of their interest of enquiry.

Apparently, "the skill formation mode" is a process of transmitting, the body of knowledge accumulated in the past, whereas the "broadening of mental horizon" is a distinct and deliberate posture to explore the "future" — the future possibilities or the ways and means of doing things a new. In short, the later aspect, deals with an enquiry into several facets of "change". At this stage we shall not enter into a debate as to which is more important "the past" or the "future" trainers of our bureaucrats ought to realize that they better face some prime questions that arise here, such as:

(1) Whose (which institution's) job it is, to train "Awareness in skills".

(2) To what level of officer and in which kind of programmes, the emphasis should be on "skill" awareness, and where, for whom, the emphasis should be on "Re-awakening, analysis, enquiry probe into change and creativity"?

(3) And, above all, the key question would be: In the present context, when each sector and system is being exhorted to move with a fresh vigour towards the 21st Century in both modes, what exactly should constitute the right "product-mix" of a given training programme and for whom? - to be administered by whom?

If the training programmes, could be reduced to the: (i) Awareness and familiarization aspects (How to do it-learning process and the (ii) Reflective creative process - (where one probes deep into a problem as a Philosopher and as a designer like an engineer or a technocrat). Then one would have no difficulty to see through the trap in which our Training Institutions stand caught presently. By their very constitution-genetically speaking - they are overloaded with the skill - formation functions in order to cater to a rigidly prescribed mandate, as fixed of Ministers who fund the given training institution be it for Railways, Income Tax, Police or Telecommunications. The core - staff of these Institutions are those experts, who are outstanding repository of the skills; and they do good job to run through the year, their equally rigid syllabi within a time-frame acquainting their clients with the "process" - (the rules, regulations and prescribed Governmental procedures). And the functional training indeed is a grand exercise of imparting "How-to-do-or-not-do Knowledge"-extremely necessary-and is the essence of "Skill-Awareness" training. But let us not miss the point that in such training programme the questions of change, creativity and reform or redesign do not, infact, and cannot possibly figure.

In order to keep up with the current trends and in order to display Institute's awareness to the new developments, concerning the Theories of Management education and new managerial theories and new practices, these institutes, do bring in outside speakers to give a few odd lectures on Organisational Development (OD) or Behavioural inputs, or the Sensitivity Training or the Transactional Analysis, etc. All these lectures constitute, firstly a mere, added "Awareness"- contributing little to the second component of "Training" where, one should expect to train people to open up trainee's "mind" and inspire them to learn how to "look beyond ones nose", in order to reflect to search the creative and innovative ideas concerning, the process and purposes of one's organization and work.

It ought to be noted as well that the exposure to non-prescriptive syllabus, through lectures, whether by an insider or by an outside speaker contributes very little to the skill armoury of the trainees, since none of these new ideas that the trainees can get to know would be well enough to enable them to take back for use on their desks or in their work situation. Our official training

Institute can hardly feel sorry for that: They have a well specified task somewhat a rigid job, a fixed time-frame, besides a limited budget. The question of deviation does not necessarily arise.

The Indian Institutes in the Indian Public Administrative domain have mostly highly qualified trainers of the "known". Such trainers are not concerned with the reflections about the "unknown", "change", "innovation" or creativity. All such elements are indeed integral to the realm of the "unknown", the "tomorrow" – infact, the future,– the so called 21st Century. Since these concerns are not part of the "mandate", or, the syllabus of the official Training institutes; one can not blame them for ignoring the concerns of future and creativity. The question that ought to be posed to the Training- policy makers, squarely is, should it be so? One can further ask: Is probe into future not the prime job of an established training institute? Then, where should our bureaucrats be sent to probe and explore the nature and characteristics of the "unknown"? Do we need a new training academy for disseminating the knowledge of the unknown (future) ? Can the setting up of such a body be justified? Or, do we "futurize" the existing institutions? One need not emphasize the point that it is only such nations, who care to know the "unknown" which have added to the body of knowledge now available in the field of Forecasting and Creativity and these inputs to help development of human resource as with Science and Technology; so mankind's new findings, are part of the story of an endless quest (a) to know the unknown and (b) to constantly ask: What Next?

One need not therefore, wonder if it is recommended that in our training, Non-conformism and going beyond the given boundary – conditions, ought to be pursued to search excellence, rationality in the functioning of bureaucracy and in bureaucracies handling of the official performance which *inter-alia* does constitute the hallmark of a new managerial culture which can help shape and influence "change", "development" and "Future".

In the present context, the key fact of teaching about "unknown" if it is to expressed in terms of the familiar, then, obviously the first would be that the "Research activity" which is an organized exploration of the "unknown". The key is that Ninety Nine per cent of the Indian Training Institutions (those that operate in the Public Administrative System in India, do not have, with one or two exceptions, any auxiliary "Research mechanism associated or incorporated within the Training Bodies. Consequently the training knowledge does not quite flow from the "probe" in to "live data" but comes more from the dated books and Manuals, of course these are regularly supplemented by the foreign text- 'books. Our libraries are full of varied knowledge contained in the journals belonging to the Harvard, the Rochester the Columbia and the Wharton School or that of the Ox-Bridge systems – but little if any indigenous research enquiry has been codified for use on training our administrators and managers; the Tatas, Birlas and others manage things to generate so much wealth without there having ever go to any of the training Academies – whether Indian or Foreign.

Moreover, even in terms of the indigenous literature and themes, we do have a plethora of unprocessed and unedited indigenous reservoir of reports and allied literature available, but they are seldom used as a training aid.

We need, therefore, to reflect why do not our Training Institutions create Research posts and whatever else goes with it? We need further to reflect why we keep using the foreign text-books for acquainting ourselves only with an alien Management Theory, Principle and Practise. It is always good to know how others manage things. But it is even more important to understand what are the key elements and components, its failings, and its strengths in our own situation.

One other aspect also worth noting is that for a given organization having multiple levels of authority in its hierarchy the training function, as far as possible should not be divisive in character. For the past fifteen years, I have been advocating the need to impart training to composite groups. Thus, the best part of recent move, with respect to the training of the officers of the Indian Administrative Service, lies in having them as a composite group of officers in a single programme in spite of differing seniority. This approach ought to be extended to all other services and officers working at different levels in our ministries and departments and subordinate offices.

In India, unlike in some other countries, the training has also been treated, as if it is a special way of giving the trainee an administrative reward. In India, this feeling is much more so than in other countries – the Indian or Overseas training opportunities, have been used by the establishment as an instrument to show both resentment or pleasure by not sending or, sending an officer on training. I even remember a case where during training, an officer was, constantly being sent out to one training programme or the other since his superiors felt, that he is less of a nuisance to the Department when he is out.

Be it as it may, I would like to highlight three more aspects of training: Firstly let us avoid wastage in training. Often we train personnel for "X" speciality but, on return we transfer them to such desks and responsibilities which do not require the kind of training he or she was sent for. This certainly is an avoidable wastage.

Secondly let us not give an impression that training brings us closer to promotion or raise hopes of getting it amongst officers who were sent to be trained. The trained officers, often carry a chip on their shoulders and treat it as a premium or a gate-pass for promotion. Training should instead be treated as an on-going learning process.

Thirdly any training whether for skill-generation or for mental awakening could yield richer dividends – if it is linked also to organizational change be it of the structure or of developing a new managerial attitude and culture. Currently this is not at all happening in the Indian public administration at least not because of training.

To sum up therefore, if we have to turn our bureaucrats into fine managers of today and tomorrow then we have to realize the fundamental fact that the training functions are only a reinforcing input. The prime thing we need to go for is the search of a new administrative philosophy and a new work ethics. An organization is the structural aspect of a Philosophy while administration is the implementation of that Philosophy. Here too, the purpose of "Management" and Training is neither to tend nor to tame men and women; Its purpose is to release the power of "men" and "women"?

20

CONCLUSION

Satish C. Seth

The task of rebuilding bureaucracy for the 21st Century, it is apparent, is a multifasceted task of administrative reform concerning several aspects, such as the recruitment, the classification, the placement, the carrier development, the training, the work-culture, etc.

Connected with the above aspects, before deciding on any bureaucratic reform we must also look at the task of programme implementation at the grass-root level, the State level and the Central level. Moreover, connected with it will be a special recognition of the emphasis on planning, on monitoring and on the required operational styles of the bureaucracy; we can add to it the way bureaucracy, can take people into confidence for a 'bureaucratic – people', joint endeavour towards socio-economic development so that it may become a meaningful, responsible and responsive exercise.

Some of these policy and structural changes need rethinking; for example, we usually keep less qualified people to work at the grass-root level. If we really wish to achieve effective decentralization then, we need to bring administrators of 15 to 20 years experience to work at the block level administration, who should be senior enough like a joint secretary of the Central bureaucracy or a Commissioner of the state; and who should further be supported by experts and programme specialists. We need further to set-up special Federal task forces who should act as "fascilators" and "programme implementators" working together with the state level bureaucratic cadres.

Apparently, therefore, we may have to go for several radical changes. We need more to step up our training activity both for the "Skill formations" as well as for the "Long range perspective planning". This should embrace all the personnel working at the planning desks at the centre, the states and the district levels. Today, our Collectors, the administrative heads of our districts, have no long range forecasters or planning experts to assist them.

What with the new emphasis on the District level planning, the addition of such an expertise could bring a certain qualitative change in the operations of the Grass-root level bureaucracy.

In any bureaucratic rebuilding exercise, it is now absolutely clear, that the recruitment of the generalist cadres shall have to be kept at the minimum or gradually reduced over the years. Instead, we do need to step-up the recruitment of the scientific, and technical personnel. Such functionaries, whether they are the computer programmers or the information or the agricultural scientists – all of these, will need to be trained specially, either through Governmental training institutions or, through our universities.

A quantum jump is also needed in other allied administrative areas, be it for introducing automation in the offices, or, be it for the sectoral operations, pertaining to the socio-economic development at the village level.

Finally, the perspective planning work too needs to be made obligatory, both on the part of the public sector, as well as the private sector. Until and unless we develop, in critical areas, some joint perspectives which have a national flavour, we can not either make proper resource utilization or determine the right national priorities or, achieve inter- sectoral (private/public sector) coordination. Else, how can we create a suitable climate for long range goal setting and investments by either of these sectors and go for a higher level of productivity; or how else can we go for the early adaptation of the technologies of tomorrow.

Notwithstanding many imponderables, the answer to achieve this "task" surely does lie only with the Public Administration experts who also happen to be "Futurologists". And thus, with the emergence of a new vibrant India, it does seem a certainty to one and all, that it will largely depend on how we rebuild our bureaucracy, working at different levels. We need a band of people who can work for and towards the 21st Century and those who do not believe only in conformity but also can pay attention to creative non-conformity, which in fact, is now widely reorganized as the essence of the new management in Government.

PART THREE

Instruments of Social Transformation

THE ADMINISTRATIVE HIERARCHY IN THE CENTRAL GOVERNMENT IN INDIA

Satish C. Seth

Wherever for the transaction of certain specified functions, one man sits over the other, the system of hierarchy takes its birth. The term hierarchy has been variously defined. In its simplest meaning it stands for, "classification in graded sub-divisions[1]. In the qualitative sense, however, it has been defined as, "an ordered structure of inferior and a superior being in an ascending scale."[2] In both the senses, the term hierarchy when applied to administrative organizations implies the presence of the following three elements:

(i) The need of a formal ordering or arrangements;
(ii) The existence of different levels of authority, function and importance, and;
(iii) The existence of a relationship in command and obedience in a vertical setting.

These conditions are, in fact, basic to any administrative structure, irrespective of its place or constitutional background.

The Indian Pattern

The administrative hierarchy of the pre-independence Central government as well as that of free India equally displays the above mentioned characteristics. During the colonial administration, its hierarchical pyramid justified the need of a definite ordering; it possessed different levels of functional responsibility, prestige and power; there was a clear-cut relationship between the superior and subordinate members of the civil service. In the welfare administration of today, the action of administrative hierarchy still continues to be, "a symbol of relationships believed to be desirable, in which some impose themselves upon others in a serried order. The god chief rides his solitary peak and his subordinates fall away below him on either side, with faces turned to the radiance of authority which they themselves cannot generate, but can only reflect".[3]

The different echelons of the administrative hierarchy in India correspond to the internal organization of a Ministry. A Ministry consists ordinarily of a single department and is headed by a Minister in most cases of a cabinet rank. It could, however, consist of two or more departments[4]. Such departments would then be under the charge of a minister of state or a deputy minister who are subordinate to a minister of the cabinet rank. The Ministry in India which is comparable to any large department in other Commonwealth countries is held "responsible for the formulation of the policy of government within its sphere of responsibility as well as for the execution and review of that policy".[5]

All ministries in India share a common administrative hierarchy which consists of several grades of officers belonging to different service groups, classes and status. This hierarchy, including the political part of it, runs as follows:

Minister of the Cabinet rank—Minister of State—Deputy Minister—Secretary—Additional Secretary—Joint Secretary—Deputy Secretary—Under Secretary—Section Officer—Assistant—Upper Division Clerk—Lower Division Clerk—Peon.

The nature of the functional responsibility status in the administrative context of this hierarchy, runs as under.

Minister-in-charge—Minister of State/Deputy Minister

Theoretically speaking in, "a parliamentary democracy, the minister is politically responsible for all decisions taken in regard to matters falling within his portfolio, although it is neither necessary nor possible for him personally to consider all such matters". What cases in practice should come upto the level of a minister, came to be examined by the Public Accounts Committee in India.[6] On its recommendation, the Ministry of Home Affairs issued an office memorandum giving the list of illustrative cases which should be submitted to ministerial level before the issue of orders except where action has to be taken urgently and it is not possible to take the minister's orders. In the subsequent years the O & M Division followed up its implementation in all ministries[7]. "Apart from the political responsibility" it was explained, "there is also an administrative responsibility resting with an officer by whom any particular decision is taken, and the manner in which such administrative responsibility is discharged remains subject to parliamentary review through bodies such as the Public Accounts Committee and the Estimates Committee." It is, therefore, of considerable importance that the officers concerned should have a reasonably clear idea of the matters in which administrative authority may be exercised by them without reference to the minister and the matters, which except in an emergency, should be submitted for personal consideration at minister's level before issue of orders".[8] Since every cabinet minister in almost every ministry had the assistance of one or more ministers of state or deputy ministers, it was felt desirable, "in the interest of efficient and smooth working of the machinery of government, to arrange for standing orders, setting out the allocation of work among the ministers so that where ever orders are required at the minister's level, the officer concerned may not be in any doubt as to the particular minister, to whom or through whom, the case is to be submitted".[9]

The illustrative list issued by the Home Ministry, thus shows those cases in which the "administrative hierarchy" under special circumstances shares its, "powers of disposal" of cases with the "political hierarchy" in a ministry. These amongst others, included cases which require submissions to the President, Cabinet or Cabinet committees; those involving legislation, parliamentary business, for example, questions, resolution, etc.; cases, involving or likely to lead to dispute or difficulty with the Parliament, State governments, press; cases involving major questions of new policy or change of existing policy; cases where it is proposed to reject the recommendation of the Comptroller and Auditor General, UPSC, Election Commission or other statutory authorities; cases involving rejection of recommendation emanating from a Minister in some other ministry, a State government or even a Head of Department relating to a major matter; cases relating to appointments, transfers, major disciplinary action against Class I officers; appeals and memorials in disciplinary cases where an order in the name of President is to be issued; cases involving substantial financial implications; statements of cases disposed of (other than routine cases) and any other case or class of cases which the minister wants to be submitted to him.[10]

Secretary—Additional Secretary

The first and foremost members of a ministry who form the apex of the civil service part of the hierarchy are designated the rank of 'Secretary' in India. This was so even under the British rule. Their position corresponds to the permanent secretary/ Departmental Head in the UK, the Deputy minister in Canada, the Permanent Head of a Ministry/Department in the Commonwealth of Australia and New Zealand.

Like their Commonwealth counterparts, Secretaries in the Indian hierarchy, are the principal advisers of the minister (the political head of a ministry/department) in all matters of policy and administration within their ministry and their responsibility is complete and undivided.

In certain ministries, for example, the Ministries of Finance and External Affairs, where there is more than one secretary, the seniormost amongst them, is designated as the principal secretary one of them used to be known as the additional secretary whose rank and pay is usually lower to that of a special secretary or the secretary. The position of an additional secretary came to be severely criticized time and again. The Gopalaswami Ayyaggar's Report on Reorganization of the Machinery of Government (1949) was the first to recommend its abolition. It was taken up again by the Estimates Committee presented to the Parliament during 1950-51. However, the post of the 'Additional Secretary' still continues to exist in more than two or three ministries.

Joint Secretary

Whenever a ministry has to cope with great volume of work which exceeds the manageable charge of a secretary, the Indian practice today is to establish one or more wings with a joint secretary in charge of each wing. He enjoys the, "maximum measure of independent functioning and responsibility in respect of all business falling within his wing, subject, however, to the general responsibility of the secretary for the administration of the ministry as a whole".

Even this post came under severe criticism by the Second Estimates Committee of the First Lok Sabha who felt that, "many of these senior officers are being wasted on comparatively minor jobs of lesser responsibility." "The position has now almost become such," the Committee added, "that what the Deputy Secretary used to do in pre-war days, is now being handled by a joint secretary and even in some cases by the secretary. The committee considers that a deputy-secretary should take all the responsibilities in respect of the work done in the branches or divisions under his control. The aspirations in the secretariat regarding promotions seems to have gone high. Previously, an officer had to render certain number of years of service before being promoted to a higher post. Now it is not uncommon to promote an officer as soon as he has completed a year or so in a particular post because the creation of higher posts is unrestricted. The committee, therefore, urge that the whole matter should be thoroughly investigated and firm policy laid in regard to the creation of posts of joint secretaries of equivalent rank and above".[11]

Today, practically every ministry has one or two joint secretaries working in it. In fact, a joint secretary, has now become an important administrative link between the secretary and the hierarchy below him. He is no more a glorified deputy-secretary, as was considered sometimes. Even though, the secretary is the highest officer to whom the subordinate officers are authorised to 'level-jump', but in actual practice, it is the joint secretary who is the highest and the easiest approachable officer for the rank and file.

Deputy-Secretary

A deputy-secretary in the Indian administrative hierarchy is an officer who acts on behalf of the secretary. He is in charge of a secretariat division, in a ministry and is mainly responsible for the disposal of government business dealt with under his charge. He is a high powered officer and shall ordinarily, "be able to dispose off the majority of cases coming up to him on his own responsibility". In matters which would go to his senior officers much would depend on his discretion. He may take orders from joint-secretary/secretary on the more important cases whether orally or by submission of papers.

The deputy-secretary who is commonly known as the 'divisional head' is indeed the most important officer in the entire chain of officers in the hierarchy. He is the actual man on whose personal qualities of leadership, initiative, managerial skill, capacity of organization, drive, personal disposition towards his subordinates and working relations with his seniors, much of the success of the governmental work depends.

The divisional head is normally in charge of two or more branches, each branch in turn consisting of more than one section. He has thus working under him, practically the main bulk of the secretariat staff whose output, welfare and service prospects would vary from the quality of one head or another. It is common knowledge that in the central secretariat, officers below the deputy secretary's level have been seen choosing their postings and transfers on the basis of their personal liking for one divisional head or another. The divisional heads in the Indian system can and do play a highly important part in minimizing social distances as amongst the superior and the subordinate officers. In fact, the way they tackle the administrative processes and public servant's morale, goes a long way to give the secretariat its true character.

Under-Secretary

An under-secretary is in-charge of a branch in a ministry and in respect thereto, 'exercises control both in regard to the despatch of business and the maintenance of discipline'. As branch officer, the manual of office procedure says, 'he will dispose of as many cases as possible on his own responsibility, but will take the orders of the deputy-secretary or higher officers on cases of important nature or those involving questions of policy.' He is required to endeavour to reduce the number of cases to be submitted formally to the deputy-secretary by taking his verbal directions.

Section Officer

The official incharge of a section is known as the section officer. Until recently, there were two kinds of them viz. Assistant Superintendents and Superintendents. The distinction between the two kinds of section officers is also recent. Before the Constitution of the central secretariat service, there was only one grade of superintendents; a new grade was introduced to enable some direct recruitment at the level. The original idea was that, "there would be equal number of posts in the two grades of section officer, and those in the lower grade would hold charge of smaller and less important sections. Further, for direct recruits, the new grade was to be a training grade".[12] In both cases, that is, for the Assistant Superintendent and the Superintendent there are not much qualitative or quantitative differences in their duties. The Assistant superintendent begins his career by learning the supervision of work of the staff in his section which the superintendent has also been doing. In either case, a section officer, apart from the supervisory responsibilities, is also considered responsible, for, "the handling of important and intricate cases himself". The two grades have since been amalgamated.

Assistant

The Assistant occupies a very important position in the Indian hierarchy. He works under the orders of the Head of the Section and is responsible for the office duties entrusted to him. These duties in the main involve:

1. Examination of fresh receipts; and in this initial examination, the assistant, puts up a suitable note and a draft for approval giving proper referencing, quoting precedence, etc., if any.
2. Proper opening of new files, their maintenance, due follow-up when the files are in movement, and final closing of the file for recording, once the cases they carry have been disposed off finally.
3. Maintenance of the Assistant's diary (since abolished), standing guard files and other necessary record.
4. Any special item entrusted, for example, coordination work amongst the different sections in a given division.

Upper Division Clerk (UDC)

An upper division clerk comes below the assistants in the administrative hierarchy. However, in most ministries they usually perform secretarial functions similar to those of an assistant.

Ordinarily, important cases would not be entrusted to an UDC though, in several instances, drafts put up by him could reach as high as the secretary.

Lower Division Clerk and Typist

They are of the same status. In fact, most LDC's are typists in a section. The Manual of office procedure lays down that lower division clerks are, "ordinarily entrusted with work of routine and mechanical nature such as the maintenance of the section diary, the file register, indexing and recording of files, preparation of arrear-statements, supervision of corrections to the reference books, proof correction, typing, comparing and despatch etc.".

In a report of an O & M study group, LDC's functions came under the scrutiny of the group. Referring to the functions detailed in the Manual of Office Procedure, the study group observed:

> "This list is by no means exhaustive. The `etc' is rather significant. The LDC happens to be the odd-job-man who is expected to turn his hand to any type of work which the assistant is reluctant to do or may not have time to attend to. The LDC is the hardy pleb of the secretariat organization who can and does at a pinch the normal work of the patrician assistant also".

The functions performed by the LDC have increased a great deal. Unlike the pre-independence days, today, an LDC sometimes even deals with simple case-work. In this respect, however, there is no uniform practice in the various ministries.

Peons

They are the Class IV workers of the Government of India and are entrusted with routine messengerial services. Technically speaking, they are not an administrative rung of the hierarchical ladder.

To sum up, therefore, the Indian administrative hierarchy at the central government in India consists of eight main positions. These positions carry such functions and administrative responsibilities as constitutes the internal organization of a ministry or department. This relationship can be stated as in Table 1.

TABLE - 1
HIERARCHICAL POSITIONS WITH CORRESPONDING AREA OF AUTHORITY

Designation of the Administrative Position in a Ministerial Hierarchy	*Corresponding Administrative Unit in the Ministry*
Secretary (Note: Special Secretary/Additional Secretary (are) exceptional entrants)	Head of the Ministry/Department
Joint-Secretary	Head of a Wing
Deputy-Secretary	Head of a Division
Under-Secretary	Head of a Branch
Section officer	Head of a Section
Assistant	
UDC	Part of a Section
LDC	

Hierarchy in Operation

The answer to the question: How does the hierarchy work in India? could be examined in two ways. One way to look at this problem is in terms of the structure. The second way is to understand it lies through the people who fill that structure. Without going into the various theories regarding each of these aspects, we shall first deal with the actual work-process at the center.

All work in government arises either from within or without. The implementation of a policy in any field is the normal process by which an item of work originates within a ministry. When an item of work comes from outside, it is usually in the form of an enquiry from the public or it could be a matter concerning a scheme that had earlier originated from within.

A policy matter which originates from 'within' is handed down by the political chief to the administrative head of the department. How much lower in the hierarchy will such a communication, which is in the nature of a command travel, would entirely depend on the nature of the work and the decision of the secretary. A communication which arises from outside the ministry, from the moment it is received in the central registry, till the relevant file is first submitted to the section-chief, usually, passes through the following three stages:—

1. The Central Registry stage: i.e. the stage from the receipt of a communication by the central registry till it is passed over to the section.
2. Diarising and allocation stage, i.e., action taken in the section till the communication is transferred to the Assistant concerned; and
3. Examination and submission stage, i.e., further action taken up until the time of the first submission of the case to the head of the section.

The Manual of office procedure, which is a valuable gift of Mr S.R. Bapat, the then Establishment Officer of the Government of India, as also the Director of O & M division, had evolved a method of classifying all receipts, irrespective of their origin. It was mainly designed for "the purpose of measuring the time taken in the disposal of individual items of work". All communications were accordingly placed by the Manual into two broad groups, namely:

(i) 'Primary' or to use a brief symbol 'P' receipts, i.e., receipts which provide a starting point for new action. (The interval between the date of receipt of such communication and the date of completion of final action thereon represented the time taken in its disposal).

(ii) 'Subsidiary' or 'S' receipts which do not by themselves raise any distinct or new matter for action or consideration but which arise out of work already in train on a 'Primary' receipt. Such receipts arise during the process of consultation with other ministries, state governments, etc., in order to get comments or information in relation to matters raised on a 'Primary' receipt. They have no significance of their own and the date of receipt or despatch of such correspondence was considered of no consequence for the purpose of measuring the speed of disposal.

(iii) A third category was obtained by the 'subdivision' or 'primary receipts' into P and PX. "Some primary receipts", it was explained in the Manual of office procedure, "will not ordinarily take very long but others, particularly those which may need elaborate examination or prolonged consultation with other ministries, state governments, etc., may take more than a month to dispose off. The receipts of the latter type are to be distinguished from other, 'Primary' receipts by using the symbol 'PX'. The others, i.e., receipts which are not likely to take more than a month in their disposal will be marked 'P'. A control mechanism in terms of statistical charts was also devised to measure the quantitative disposal of work labelled as P, S and PX. This system was worked for a while and was later on considered as unsatisfactory and was abandoned.

An objective examination of the Communication cycle in a ministry on the aforesaid basis has to take notice of the following three aspects:—

(i) Source Aspect: Here it has to be seen as to where a communication comes from and is to be examined in terms of the nature of its contents (it could be a policy matter or a routine matter; a command or an enquiry).

(ii) Disposal aspect: is to be seen in terms of the powers of initiation, submission and disposal.

(iii) Time aspect: It is to be seen in terms of the speed of disposal. (It matters little what symbols are used to classify it; it could be P, S and PX or something else).

In the Indian system, these three aspects are mainly governed by the prescribed, "channel for submission of cases". We have already seen the functions that the various officers perform in the administrative hierarchy. Now these officers in their day to day working, while they are dealing with a command from the top which may or may not be a `P' function or an outside, `enquiry' which again could be a `P', `S' or `PX' function, are required to deal with them at different levels. But before an action is complete, each action needs to receive the approval of a final authority which in fact becomes the actual disposal level. It can be easily established that mere functional distribution of work, without due assessment of the power aspect, would not, and did not lead to correct assessment of the `time aspect.' Whatever be the merits or demerits of the Bapat Scheme it did put the Secretariat staff on the alert but failed to add to the quality of disposal on the one hand and left the Power-element of the hierarchy practically untouched. In a secretarial hierarchy or for that matter in any organization the cycle of disposal must include more than one authority. A secretary could be an authority of initiation; he could as well be the authority of disposal. Nevertheless, he cannot be both at the same time. There is an inevitable time lag between the two actions. Before he disposes of an action initiated by him, it passes through other hands. Likewise, irrespective of the nature of the communication, even if the authority of initiation is a lower-division clerk (which is seldom the case), before the communication has finally been disposed off it must go through one or two or all the levels of authority in a given hierarchy. It must pass through the inevitable time-lag.

In a hierarchy, therefore, the work-flow is intimately linked with the levels of authority each of which may be either an authority of initiation or an authority of disposal. It is also important to note that the power element that works at each such level starts diminishing as we descend from the top to the bottom. In other words, in a given hierarchy, below a certain level, one will find an authority of disposal. It is a fallacy to believe that even if he is not an authority of disposal, he is an authority of initiation. For example, the central administrative hierarchy in India as indicated above has eight distinct levels. The last authority in the hierarchy who at its own could initiate and dispose off certain items of work is a section officer who is a counterpart of an Assistant Principal in White Hall in the UK. Even though most cases are processed and work initiation on a file is done by the assistants, upper division clerks, or in routine matters by the lower division clerks; they are not an authority of initiation. They are the levels of submission.

The level of submission is again a feature which in a given hierarchy starts upwards from the base, and in an ascending order, diminishes gradually at each level of authority. The power of disposal shared by an authority is thus related to the power of submission in an inverse proportion. The two go to determine the total delegation of power in a hierarchy.

The relationship between the powers of disposal (represented by symbol 'd') and the powers of submission (represented by symbol 's') in a given hierarchy could be represented in terms of the law of delegation of power Mathematically expressed:

$$\text{Power of disposal} \propto \frac{1}{\text{Power of submission}}$$

$$d \propto \frac{1}{s}$$

or $$d = \frac{D}{s} \text{ or } D = d.s. \qquad .....(i)$$

where, D is a constant representing the total administrative power of a given hierarchy.

The operative aspect of this law implies that in a given administrative hierarchy, the various incumbents exercise two kinds of powers; the powers of disposal and the powers of submission. It has been pointed out that there are two more elements involved in the process of power delegation. These are:

(i) The power of initiation.

(ii) The submerged section, who do not exercise any of the above three powers.

The power of initiation clearly applies in two directions:

(a) In one sense — power of initiation is equivalent to the issue of directive. For instance, when the various receipts come they are examined (rather quickly) say, by the deputy secretary of a division. He gives the directive what should be done. This is the initiation through direction.

(b) In the second sense — the power of initiation amounts to the implementation of the directive. After a directive has been issued either verbally or orally, the actual examination of the 'communication'/receipt would commence from a level below the one that issued the directive. This is initiation through implementation.

We have explained it earlier that the initiation in the first sense, i.e., through the 'issue of directive' could come only from such an authority who also possesses the power of disposal for the said item of work under consideration. If it were not so, and if a directive had to come from the secretary, of the concerned matter or work, which could have easily been undertaken by a subordinate, then, it only indicates both a mal-distribution of 'power' as also its mal-utilization.

The point we are stating is simply this; Power of initiation (represented by symbol 'I') is not an independent 'power-element'. But it is inherent partly in the powers of disposal and submission. Since the man who, 'initiates for implementation' does enjoy powers of 'submission'. In both senses, power of initiation, either as—

I (d) (i.e.) = Initiation through directive, or as:

I (i) (i.e.) = Initiation through implementation, is simply an attribute of d and s, that is, of the power of disposal and of the power of submission, which an incumbent possesses at his given level. Restated, therefore, d and s of Equation (i) above would be:

d = (sum of powers of pure disposal and initiation through directive);

s = (sum of powers of pure submission and initiation through implementation); or,

d = (Xd + Id)

s = (Ds + Ii) (where X is an unknown but identifiable variable)

The Law of delegation of Power as expressed in equation (i) above would thus be represented as follows:

$$D = (Xd + Id)\ (Xs + Ii)$$

This analysis leads us to the following three conclusions:

Firstly, that even though D in the above equation may seem to be the disposal power of one level but it actually represents the total power that the administrative hierarchy could exercise. It could, in fact represent the legal power of the ministry. As an illustration, if an administrative ministry in India is authorised by the Finance Ministry to spend without any prior consultation, a certain amount, say rupees five lakhs, then in this sense, D= 5 lakhs. The decision to spend this amount has been exercised by one person or through the power combination of one or more than one level.

Secondly, the submerged section who do not exercise either d, s or I powers, includes the administrative adjuncts like the steno-typists, or the statisticians, etc. In certain organizations, even the specialists are thrown in the departmental pyramid as administrative adjuncts. Clearly, the submerged section is seldom a part and parcel of the administrative hierarchy; that is why, we may notice that their organizational demands would invoke Seth's 'law of hierarchical parallels'[13]. Since, such administrative adjuncts also wish to have the d, s and I powers they would try to get a hierarchy of their own. The submerged section, therefore, does not affect the law of delegation of powers, in a given hierarchy. It easily indicates in a relative sense, how much authority of disposal, initiation and submission is being shared at any level in a given hierarchy.

Finally, it is important to point out that the time aspect of the work-flow in a hierarchy is equally related to the power-aspect which energizes its communication system. The time-factor would therefore, be as much governed by the levels that intervene between the levels of initiation and the level of disposal, depending on the powers of the disposal and submission that is shared on these extremities. Clearly, therefore, without a prior specified knowledge of Power Aspect, any quantification or assessment of the time aspect of work flow would not give us any accurate measure of the same. We now turn to examine the various other implications of these relationships in the historical and administrative context of the Indian Organizational set-up.

Hierarchical Levels and Work Efficiency

The method of disposal of work of the central government in India came under severe criticism many a time. In fact, even during the British rule, several attempts were made to improve upon the secretarial procedure, in order to ensure greater work efficiency: Llewyen Smith's Report, Wheeler Committee Report and the Maxwell Committee Report were notable efforts in this direction. However, when the Estimates Committee (1950-51) constituted under the Republican Constitution presented its Second Report, it found that the system of disposing off of files and papers by officers was highly unsatisfactory. The Committee observed that the method of disposal of work in the secretariat at present follows the rule: "Send the paper or file to the lower man;

he would examine it and then put it up". "It is obvious", wrote the Committee, "that this system is so archaic, procrastinating and extravagant that it is àltogether unsuitable to our present day conditions." "The Committee, therefore, recommended that each receipt should be tackled at an appropriate level by one or two officers" and, "each officer in the chain should dispose off as much work as possible himself and not merely supervise or approve of the work of his juniors".[14]

The real change in this set-up, as stated earlier commenced with the setting up of the O & M division in 1954. It immediately undertook the drafting of the Manual of Office Procedure. An attempt was made to rationalize secretarial procedure with a view to speed up the disposal process. In its first Annual Report, it was stated that the division is giving its due attention to such ways as would help, "to save the time unnecessarily consumed in the upward and downward movement of papers". It was customary for a file moving through the hierarchy to go back to the section officer and the Diarist at every stage to keep a note of its movement and whereabouts. "Steps have been taken" the report added," to eliminate several trips by making files travel direct to the recipients from Deputy-Secretary upwards, a record of their movement being kept by the stenographers of the officers concerned". We have already referred to the classification system of the receipts which, it was hoped would improve the time aspect of the work and would assist in keeping a watch on the progress of and speed of disposal.

The Manual also considered questions of the delegation of, 'power of disposals' and that of raising of the 'level submission'. In this connection, it is interesting to note that the section officer was the lowest officer in the hierarchy to whom alone certain 'powers of disposal' in routing matters came to be delegated.[15] The Manual also laid down the 'channel of submission of all case work'.

The arrangements devised by the Manual, it soon became clear, did not bring substantial changes. In fact, its defects became obvious enough to make O & M Division rethink of its scheme. The O & M Director, in a letter addressed to all secretaries, discussed the matter at length.[16] The issue raised therein was thoroughly considered in the Third Annual Report (1950-51) of the O & M division and a reform scheme known as, "jumping levels" was introduced. It advocated maximum delegation of power down the line and some deliberate level jumping in suitable cases. It was suggested that steps should be taken, "to ensure that individual case reaching the level of Joint-secretary/Secretary should pass through only one officer (either under-secretary or deputy-secretary) but not both. This liberalization took another step when in order to reduce the time taken in the consideration of a case at different levels, the central economy board directed that it should be made a rule that, "not more than two officers within a ministry should note on a case".

As a further step in the same direction, ministries were also advised to allow assistants with more than five years service to submit cases direct to their branch officers/deputy secretaries. This arrangement, it was felt will have "twin advantages" of training and developing senior assistants into potential section officers and enabling existing section officers to devote more time to original work and to their supervisory duties.

The elimination of intermediate stages in the consideration of a case, as between initiating level and the level of final disposal leads only to the increase of powers of submission of the subordinate staff. It does not add to their 'power of disposal'. Clearly, therefore, these changes do not minimize the power aspect of the hierarchy. The central administrative hierarchy still continues to be divided into various power levels amongst whom there exists considerable disparity of power. It is still top heavy hierarchy as it was during the colonial administration. It is true that, in any hierarchy, the share of power as amongst successive levels decreases, as we descend down the scale. Nevertheless, a rationalized hierarchy would not have vast gaps as between the powers of disposal and powers of submission at different levels; until it is so, the top level bureaucrat may continue to be too authoritarian, in his ways. Power in any hierarchy ought to create its own balance. A democratically scaled hierarchy as opposed to a feudal hierarchy will have less difference between the powers exercised at different levels.

The process of democratization of an administrative

hierarchy could be achieved in two ways. First it could be done through greater delegation of power of disposal and consequent decrease of 'power of submission'. Secondly, it can also be achieved by having a smaller number of echelons in a hierarchy, as illustrated from the Indian system, two positions in this hierarchy could be easily eliminated. These could be the post of either a section officer or an under-secretary and that of either the LDC or the UDC. This would bring down the hierarchy from the eight to six levels of authority. Naturally, this would automatically result in the redistribution of the functions, administrative responsibility and authority. The level jumping does not democratize the hierarchy; the reduction of levels easily does so. This in turn affects the time-aspect of work flow and work disposal.

It is important to point out that a rationalized and democratic hierarchy is more conducive to efficiency than a hierarchy which is divided into several levels of authorities most of whom are divided by vast differences of power. It could be demonstrated mathematically. We know well that in a given organization its input is equal to the strength of the service (S) and the total time (T) spent on a specified work. In other words:

$$\text{Input} = \text{Time} \times \text{Strength of Service}$$
$$= T \times S$$

The work efficiency for this given system will be:

$$\text{Efficiency} = \frac{\text{Output}}{\text{Input}} = \frac{\text{Output}}{T \times S}$$

$$\text{or, Output} = \text{Efficiency} \times T \times S$$

$$\text{or, } O = E \times T \times S \qquad \text{....(i)}$$

where, E represents work-efficiency and
O represents output.

We have already noticed that efficiency in any hierarchy gets impaired if there is a tremendous time-lag between the level of initiation of an item of work and that of its disposal. In other words, in a given hierarchical set-up, work efficiency would be inversely proportionate to the time taken at each level and the number of hierarchical divisions/levels. That is to say:

$$\text{Efficiency} \propto \frac{1}{\text{Time taken per level number of levels}} \quad \text{...(ii)}$$

It needs no emphasis that the time taken at each level, amongst other factors, has a direct relationship to the incentive that an employee has for his work. Lesser the Incentive more will be the time taken. In other words:—

$$\text{Time taken per level} \propto \frac{1}{\text{Incentive}}$$

$$\text{or} \quad \frac{1}{m}$$

where, m represents the element of incentive.

Substituting this value in equation (ii) above :—

$$\text{Efficiency} \propto \frac{1}{1/m \times L} \qquad \text{or, } E \propto \frac{m}{L}$$

where, L represents the number of levels

$$\text{Therefore, Efficiency} = \frac{km}{L}$$

where, km represents the promotion probability, hereafter represented by symbol λ

$$\text{Therefore, Efficiency} = \frac{\lambda}{L} \quad \text{...(iii)}$$

Substituting the value of efficiency in the equation (i) above

$$\text{Output} = E \times TS$$

$$= \frac{\lambda \times TS}{L}$$

$$O = \frac{\lambda \times TS}{L}$$

The above equation clearly points out the following important points:

(i) That the output in a given organization would be more if, the hierarchies engaged in it have the minimum number of levels of authority. In other words, both the output and work efficiency, could be increased by minimizing the hierarchical levels. The above formula has also the possibility of application in measuring output through a system of controlled experimentation.

(ii) Secondly, a hierarchy with the minimum tiers of authority will be a rationalized and democratic hierarchy. It stands in a clear contrast to a feudal hierarchy with all powers at the top and all submission at the lower levels. Since it will be more evenly powered, it is bound to raise the incentive for work at each level.

(iii) Finally, the less number of hierarchical divisions also increases the organizational efficiency as also the chances of promotion. Consequently, in a rationalized hierarchy the promotion probability (λ) will be the greatest. Theoretically, it is true that in a given organization whatever be the hierarchical arrangements, the chances of becoming the boss, other things being equal, will always be 1/(S–I), where, S is the total strength of the service in the organization.

But how often are other things equal? Even the furniture that is supplied to officers working in the Indian Secretariat, and for that matter elsewhere, varies from the incumbent of one level to the other. Proximity to the top is all that 'human beings' crave for! If it could be brought about, would it not be an inexpensive way of satisfying humàn ego which is so little fed in the world of civil service - at least in the case of those who began the professional lives at and are destined to retire from the same level of submission.

NOTES AND REFERENCES

1. *Chamber's Twentieth Century Dictionary.*
2. "Hierarchy and Hieratics by Earl Latham "quoted from his article in *Ideas and issues in Public administration.* A book of readings (edited) by Dwight Waldo. McGraw Hill Book Company (1953), p. 105.
3. Ibid.
4. Central Secretariat Manual of Office Procedure, Para 6.
5. Ibid.
6. See Public Accounts Committee (16th Report.)
7. O & M Division. O.M. No. 2/25/60-O & M dated the 28th June, 1956.

8. D.O. No. 2/25/56-O & M (Cabinet Secretariat) 6th July, 1957.
9. Ibid.
10. See Ministry of Home Affairs O & M No. 23/27/53 RE. dated the 21st April, 1954.
11. Estimates Committee: Second Report (1953-51) Reorganisation of the Secretariat and departments of the Government of India. Parliament Secretariat, New Delhi (Feb. 1951). (The chairman of this committee was Hon'ble M. Ananthasayanam Ayyanagar, the then Deputy Speaker of the Indian Parliament) p. 2.
12. Report of the Commission of Enquiry on Emoluments and Conditions of Service of Central Government Employees (1957-59), p. 113.
13. See 'Central Administration in India' (Asia Publishing House, Strand, London).
14. Estimates Committee (Second Report) 1950-51), p. 10.
15. See para 26 of The Manual of Office Procedure. Also see D.O. No. 6/7/54 O & M dt. 13.1.55 circulating a statement showing the powers delegated to section officers by certain ministries "which go a little beyond what the Manual prescribes".
16. D.O. No. 2/16/57-O & M Cabinet Secretariat (O & M Division) March 18, 1957.

A COMPARATIVE STUDY OF INDIAN AND AMERICAN EXECUTIVES' LEADERSHIP STYLES

***G. Rangaswamy and Donald Helmich**

The purpose of this research is to study the leadership styles of executives in India and America, as well as to make executives aware of their role as leaders in business by enabling them to ponder on certain questions involving leadership practices. Because few studies exist which compare the differences of the executives in these two countries, the research presented will help managers of developing countries contribute to the growth and knowledge of administrative practices.

The study focuses on an attempt to reveal whether the executives, as a group, in these two countries are generally task oriented, employee oriented, or somewhere between these extremes. These aspects and others relating to organization size, education level and origin of degree (if any) obtained will be surveyed.

Background

The recent interest and the accompanying problems in leadership literature have been summarized aptly by Browne and Cohen:

Leadership has been recognized to an increasingly greater extent as one of the significant aspects of human activity. As a result there is now a great mass of "leadership literature" which, if it were to be assembled in one place, would fill many libraries. The great part of this mass, however, would have little organization; it would evidence widely in theoretical and methodological approaches, to a great extent, therefore, leadership literature is a

* Govindrajulu Rangaswamy MBA was the Director, Coimbatore Pioneer Mills, Tamil Nadu, India and Dr Donald Helmich was in the University of San Diego, San Diego, California at the time of writing this article.

mass of content without any coagulating substance to bring it together or to produce coordination and point out inter-relationships.[1]

Fiedler further points out that leadership is 'probably the most important single factor influencing group and organizational performance.[2] Yet, there are very few scientifically established facts about leadership and the dynamics of groups. The number of well substantiated theories in the area is even fewer. While laymen have spoken confidently about leadership traits, and while practically every manager and industrialist prides himself on his ability to pick the good leaders on the basis of a five-minute interviews, psychologists have not been successful in their search for leadership traits. And yet, we also know of military leaders who have achieved outstanding successes and various circumstances, in combat as well as in peacetime operations, on the battlefield as well as in administrative jobs. Similarly, there are business executives who have been consistently successful in rebuilding "sick" organizations and in revitalizing demoralized departments, while there are other men who could not organize a game of "ring-around-the rosie".[3]

Psychologists have been concerned with two major questions in their research on leadership: "How does a man become a leader?" and "What kind of personality traits or behaviour makes a person an effective leader?[4] People who become leaders tend to be somewhat more intelligent, bigger, more assertive, more talkative than other members of their group. What most frequently distinguishes the leader from his co-workers is that he knows more about the group task or that he can do it better. A bowling team is likely to choose its captain from good rather than poor bowlers, and the foreman of a machine shop is more likely to be a good machinist than a poor one.

Becoming a leader, then, depends on personality only to a limited extent. A person can become a leader simply by being in the right place at the right time, or because of such various factors as age, education, experience, family background and wealth. It is commonly observed that personality and circumstances interact to determine whether a person will become a leader. There are limited number of ways in which one person can influence others to work towards a common goal. He can coerce them or he can coax them. He can tell people what to do and how to do it, or he can share the decision making and concentrate on his relationship with his men rather than on the execution of the job. Most research by pyschologists on leadership has focused on two clusters of behaviour and attitudes, one labelled autocratic, authoritarian and task oriented, and the other as democratic, equalitarian, permissive and group oriented.

The authoritarian, task-oriented leader takes all responsibility for making decisions and directing the group members. His rationale is simple: "I do the thinking and you carry out the orders." The second type of leadership is typical of the "New Look" method of management advocated by men like Douglas McGregor and Rensis Likert. This leader provides general rather than close supervision and his concern is the effective use of human resources through participation. Experiments comparing the performance of both types of leaders have shown that each is successful in some situations and unsuccessful in others.

As noted, a man's basic style of leadership depends in part upon his personality. Changing his style to a certain extent means trying to change his personality. A leader's personality is not likely to change as a result of attending a few lectures or even after a few weeks of intensive training. However, training programmes could be designed to provide the opportunity for a leader to learn in which situations he can perform well and in which he is likely to fail. For example, Fiedler's theory of leadership effectiveness predicts that a leader's performance can be improved by engineering or fitting the job to the leader.[5] A man who is able to avoid situations in which he is likely to fail, and to seek out situations that fit his leadership style, will probably become a highly successful and effective leader. However, one must remember that good leadership performance depends as much upon the organization, as it does upon the leader. This means that one must learn not only how to train men to be leaders, but how to build organizations in which specific types of leaders can perform well.

There are, of course, several types of power styles: autocratic, participative and free-rein. For example, the autocratic or authoritarian manager centralizes power and decision making in himself, whereas participative management decentralizes managerial authority and the manager's decisions are not unilateral because they arise from consultation with followers and participation by them. The free-rein manager avoids power. He depends largely upon the group to establish its own goals and work out its own problems.

Early Research

Early research on leadership style was done at the University of Michigan and Ohio State University. In many types of organizations such as truck manufacturing, railroad construction, and insurance offices, the strongly employee-oriented manager achieved higher morale and productivity. Subsequent studies confirm this tendency and report desirable side effects such as lower grievance rates, lower turnover, and reduced stress within the group.[6] So it appears that the most successful managers are those who combine high employee and task orientations, giving somewhat more emphasis to employee orientation.[7]

To support the three types of power styles previously mentioned (autocratic, participative and free-rein), Cock and French worked with sewing machine operators, introducing changes in three different ways in matched groups.[8] The results, obtained showed that within a given time, the most number of units were produced by the group under free-rein management and the lowest number of units were produced by the group under autocratic management.

For example, Negandhi and Prasad[9] conducted further research study of 17 American subsidiaries in Indian-owned companies, with regard to: (1) whether or not the chief executive of the company formulated the company-wide policy alone and (2) to what extent functional managers participated in the policy making process, insofaras their functional departments were concerned. The results showed that in more than half of the Indian-owned companies, the chief executive formulated company-wide policies by himself, while in six of the US companies, chief executive policies were similar. In the remainder 11 US companies and 4 Indian companies) the committee form of policy formulation was evident. This shows that the majority of the Indian-owned firms are autocratic and the majority of US firms are democratic.

Likert, in his book *New Patterns of Management*, has written that task-centered supervision is providing supervision to see that workers perform their designated tasks, using a specified procedure at an acceptable rate, as determined by such procedures as timing the job.[10] Employee-centered supervision includes, where ever feasible, using incentives in the form of individual or group piece rates. Supervisors with the former orientation will be called "task centered."

Hypotheses and Methodology

The research findings and literature review cited above shows that high-producing managers, much more often than low-producing managers, have built the personnel in their units or departments into highly effective organizations. These operations are characterized by favourable, cooperative attitudes and high levels of job satisfaction on the part of the members of the organization. Consequently, in view of this material viewing leadership styles (task versus employee oriented), organizational situation and educational aspects of administrative leaders, the following hypotheses are explored in the forthcoming study of Indian and American business executives.

Hypothesis 1: There is a significant difference between leadership styles of Indian executives, as a group, in manufacturing firms and their counterparts in America.

Hypothesis 2: There is a significant difference between leadership styles of Indian executives, as a group, in manufacturing firms and their counterparts in America, when size of the company is held constant.

Hypothesis 3: There is a significant relationship between the age of Indian executives and their leadership style.

Hypothesis 4: There is a significant relationship between the size of the company of Indian executives and their leadership style.

Hypothesis 5: Their is a significant relationship between education level of Indian executive and their leadership style.

Hypothesis 6: There is a significant relationship between origin (Indian university or foreign university) of the degree obtained by Indian executives and their leadership style.

In conducting the study the researchers made use of some selected aspects used in prior research by Helmich,[11] who had collected 110 questionnaires from US executives: The present questionnaire used to measure variables relating to size of firm (assets), age of respondent, and level of education, subsequently were sent to 150 business executives and managers in India, whose names and addresses appear in *The Times of India Book of Who's Who* for 1973,[12] with the answers obtained from them, a comparison study was done to arrive at the conclusions and recommendations. A cut-off date for receiving the questionnaires for analysis was set at August 5, 1974, so that questionnaires received after that date were not included in the research and analysis of this study.

From the profile of the Indian executives (see figure 2 below) it can be noticed that a good percentage of the respondents belonged to medium and large sized companies and over 75 per cent of them had a college education. The titles of the respondents varied from manager to vice-president, president and managing director. A total number of 56 questionnaires were received between June 2, 1974 and the cut-off date of August 5, 1974.

Respondent Profiles

Industry	
Chemical Manufacturing Firms	12.50%
Textile Manufacturing Firms	39.20%
Petroleum Manufacturing Firms	7.10%
Tool Manufacturing Firms	41.20%
Formal Education	
High School	25.0%
Bachelor's Degree	44.6%
Master's Degree	8.9%
Foreign Bachelor's Degree	10.7 %
Foreign Master's Degree	10.7%
Age	
Under 30 years	33.9%
33 - 39 years	32.1%
40 - 49 years	14.2%
Over 50 years	19.6%
Size of Firm	
Small	14.2%
Medium	51.7%
Large	33.9%

To determine whether a leader maintains a task-or employee-centered style, executives were asked to describe the person with whom he can manage best. Each of these two persons may be someone the leader has managed with in the past or is managing with presently. A comparison of these two descriptions yields the ASO score. The computation of ASO score is quite simple. 'Consider' two descriptions, both by respondent "M". The first is a description of his least preferred co-worker (LPC), using O's.

The second is the description of his most preferred co-worker (MPC), using x's. Each of the four scales range from the most favourable point of 7 to the least favourable point of 1, thus:

Very pleasant /7: x/6: /5: /4: 0/3: /2: /1: Very unpleasant
Friendly /7: /6: x/5: /4: 0/3: /2: /1: Unfriendly
Warm /7: /6: /5: x/4: /3: /2: 0/1: Cold
Helpful /7: /6: /5: x/4: 0/3: /2: /1: Unhelpful

SCORES OF M

Scale Items	*LPC*	*MPC*	*Diff.*	*Diff. sq.*
1. Pleasant-Unpleasant	3	6	3	9
2. Friendly-Unfriendly	3	5	2	4
3. Warm-Cold	1	4	3	9
4. Helpful-Unhelpful	3	4	1	1
	D = 4.78			23 = D^2

A high difference (D) score, relative to other respondents in the survey sheets, indicates a low ASO, whereas a low D score suggests a high ASO. It should be noted at this stage that the leadership questionnaire sent to India is a modification of and borrowed from Fiedler's[13] 16-item Semantic differential. Also the internal consistency and stability of this type of personality inventory is fairly high.

Another variable used in this study is the Least Preferred Co-worker Score (LPC), which is obtained from the respondents (O's) on the questionnaire. This is known as the leader's "esteem for his least preferred co-worker" (LPC) score. To obtain this score, the leader rates his LPC on bipolar adjective scales (e.g., warm......cold) in the questionnaire and the sum of these ratings is treated as his LPC score. In general, this score has been viewed as an effective measure of leadership style with the high LPC leader seen as being human-relations oriented, and the low LPC leader seen as task oriented.

Results

The LPC and ASO score measures which were obtained for the Indian executives were compared with American executives' LPC and ASO scores. The Indian and American executives' responses were analyzed through two tests: the student T-test and the z-test. The data for the American executives were obtained from Helmich's[14] previous research in which only the LPC, ASO and size (large, small) of the company variables were tested. Once the results were obtained for the Indian executives, their style measures were related through correlation coefficients to the other variables in this study, such as size of the company, age, level of education achieved and where degree was obtained (within India or in a foreign country).

TABLE 1
HYPOTHESIS 1: STYLE COMPARISON FOR INDIAN AND AMERICAN EXECUTIVES

	Means	*Standard Deviation*	*Statistic*	*P<*
LPC 1	47.6	12.81	3.88	.0005
LPC A	39.3	13.6		
ASO 1	9.4	3.92	–2.21	.025
ASO A	10.8	3.46		

From Table 1 the comparison and the test of the mean leadership scores of Indian and US executives indicates a difference in leadership style significant to at least the 90 per cent confidence level and provides evidence supporting the advanced hypothesis. From these results, it is seen that Indian executives are more permissive in their firms than their American counterparts. A permissive leader of course, is one who depends largely upon the group to establish its own goals and work out its own problems. This conclusion interestingly does not support the earlier cited work of Negandhi and Prasad.[15]

One possible reason why the Indians are found in this research to be more employee oriented is the overwhelming influence of people oriented Hindu religion. The religion preaches helpfulness and peaceful cooperation. A second reason for the findings may be explained by the Indian culture's extended family structure, where responsibility is always delegated to younger members of the family. Here this process of subordinate participation may reinforce a more employee approach to management by the chief executives of Indian concerns relative to their American counterparts. A final reason that might be advanced to explain the unexpected findings with the style-industrialization hypothesis concerns the influence of large bureaucratized communication channels that prevail within many conglomerated companies of America. Early studies by Max Weber[16] have documented that large organizations breed increasing formalities in communication amongst the executive ranks. This would partly explain the tendency for American executives as a whole to be relatively more task-oriented in their leadership style than Indian executives operating within smaller sized organizations. Unfortunately, this particular reason is somewhat invalidated by the findings of Hypothesis 2 and 4 — as discussed below.

TABLE 2
HYPOTHESIS 2 : STYLE COMPARISON, HOLDING CONSTANT ORGANIZATION SIZE

		Means	*Standard Deviation*	*t Statistic*	*P<*
Small	LPC 1	42.6	12.0	0.8	.25
	LPC A	38.2	14.8		
	ASO 1	11.7	3.9	0.2	—
	ASO A	11.4	3.8		
Large	LPC 1	49.8	11.1	0.8	.25
	LPC A	40.4	12.3		
	ASO 1	8.6	4.1	–0.65	.25
	ASO A	10.4	3.3		

Although the results are not statistically significant, the tendencies in Table 2 support the same trend found in Table 1.

Because of the decreased significance levels, however, one now suspects that organizational size is indeed a variable that confounds the first hypothesized relationship. Upon a further examination of this table one could suggest that as organizations become larger, there is a tendency for the leaders to become more employee oriented. It appears now that organizational growth with its pressures for professional management encourage an employee-oriented style. This one-man management approach to leadership appears more prevalent in the small organization, where the chief executive leader has ultimate control.

TABLE 3
HYPOTHESIS 3: STYLE VERSUS AGE OF INDIAN EXECUTIVES

	Correlations With Age	*Z statistic*	*P <*
LPC	0.018	0.0132	.49
ASO	0.127	–0.95	.1711

From Table 3 there appears no significant difference in Hypothesis 3 as management training is just beginning to be offered in Indian universities.

As such, there is no real reason why age should make a difference in managerial style. Indian executives appear to be set in their leadership style.

TABLE 4
HYPOTHESIS 4: STYLE VERSUS ORGANIZATION SIZE FOR INDIAN EXECUTIVES

	Correlations With Size	*Z statistic*	*P <*
LPC	0.173	1.29	.0985
ASO	–0.236	–1.78	.0375

The results for Hypothesis 4 now confirm that their is a significant relationship between size of the company of the surveyed Indian executives and their leadership style. The data show that as the size of the Indian company becomes larger, the leader tends to get more employee oriented than task oriented. This seems logical because as the firm expands in size, the leader is no longer in a position to manage and control everything. He has to put trust and faith in some of his subordinates and give them a certain amount of responsibility and authority to carry out the functions of the company. Due to this process the leader has to become more employee oriented. Only then can he expect his subordinates to carry out the functions effectively and efficiently.

TABLE 5

HYPOTHESIS 5: STYLE VERSUS EDUCATION LEVEL OF INDIAN EXECUTIVES

	Correlations With Education	*Z statistic*	*P* <
LPC	–0.129	–0.8	.2119
ASO	0.096	0.06	.4761

TABLE 6

HYPOTHESIS 6: STYLE VERSUS EDUCATIONAL ORIGIN OF INDIAN EXECUTIVES

	Correlations With Education Origin	*Z statistic*	*P* <
LPC	–0.139	1.00	.1587
ASO	0.065	0.04	.4840

One would think that the liberal arts degree (to include business administration as a social science) might induce an employee oriented approach to management because of educational acquaintance with human relations and participative management approaches to problem solving. One further, would assume that degrees obtained from very industrialized countries (foreign educational origin) with established educational programmes in organizational development might yield a tendency towards an employee approach to management. In Tables 5 and 6, however, this reasoning appears not to be the case. Several explanations are offered. One, perhaps there are too many confounding variables intervening between educational measures (level and origin) and leadership styles of Indian executives. For example, there are such factors as national origin and religious beliefs. Two, often educational experiences in the classroom with participative management techniques are not sufficiently lasting to influence leadership behaviour on the job. And, third, the style of centralized management existing within family owned firms —

predominating in India — tends to set the organizational climate for subordinate executives to follow. In any event, these conclusions should not indicate that management education and the practice of leadership are not unrelated nor unimportant for the future of developing nations. Certainly more research and experience is required to further explore the style education relationship.

Conclusions

The research presented in this inquiry has found that Indian executives in general are somewhat more employee-oriented in their style of leadership than their American counterparts. Although this finding is somewhat unexpected, it may be explained in part by the Indian culture and religious influences towards helpfulness and peaceful cooperation. Additional results indicate that leadership styles of Indian executives tend to become more employee-oriented as the company increases in asset size. Justification for this relationship may be explained by the process of management delegation which often places pressure on key administrators to develop subordinate trust in decision making.

Because of the growth of American enterprises relative to other nations of the world, one can suggest that a job or task oriented style is effective in the right organizational setting. Leadership in all countries would be improved if executives could be flexible by developing task as well as employee-oriented behaviour. In order to try to make Indian managers more aware of a task oriented style on a practical sense, the most probable solution in the short run would be to: (1) improve the establishments of professional societies, and (2) develop opportunity for business managers to attend modern management classes on a part time basis (e.g., adult night schools). In terms of long-term solutions, the following programmes could be instituted: (1) a revamping of the educational perspective which is practiced in Indian institutions of higher education, and (2) an inviting of the Indian government to authors and lecturers of modern management, possibly through international professional societies.

In conclusion, the researchers feel that this study has been of significance to the understanding of people and their motivations. If any of the recommendations which have been made turn out to be successful, then the nation and business culture of India, as well as developing nations, will benefit to a great degree. India, like other developing nations, is plagued by problems of a growing population and thus, possible starvation. The growth of the Indian economy whether it be by finding of gold, nuclear energy, or by the application of better management techniques may turn out to be one and the same.

NOTES AND REFERENCES

1. Clarence Browne and Thomas Cohen, *The Study of Leadership*, Danville, Illinois: Interstate Printers, 1958, P. i.
2. Fred E. Fiedler, *Group Dynamics: Research and Theory*. New York: Horper & Row, 1963.
3. Ibid., p. 31.
4. Ibid, p. 39.
5. Fred Fiedler, *A Theory of Leadership Effectiveness*. New York: McGraw-Hill and Co., 1967, pp. 1-100.
6. James B. Mullan, *Personality and Productivity in Management*: New York: Columbia University Press, 1966.
7. At Ohio State, employee orientation was called "consideration," and task orientation was "structure." E.A Fleishman, *Leadership Climate and Supervisory Behaviour*. Columbus, Ohio; Personnel Research Board, Ohio State University Press, 1951.
8. Lester Cock and. John R.P. French, Jr., "Overcoming Resistance to Change," *Human Relations*, I, No. 4 (1948), pp. 512-532.
9. Anant R. Negandhi and S. Benjamin Prasad, *Comparative Management*. New York: Appleton-Century Crofts, 1971, pp. 68-69.
10. Rensis Likert, *New Patterns of Management*, New York: McGraw-Hill Book Co., Inc.
11. Donald Helmich, "Successor Type and Organizational Change. In the *Enterprise, Administrative Science Quarterly*, Vol. 17, No. 3, pp. 371-81, and "Corporate Succession: An Examination." *Academy of Management Journal*, Vol. 19, No. 3, pp. 429-41.
12. *The Times of India Book of Who's Who For 1973.*
13. Fiedler, *A Theory of Leadership Effectiveness*, op. cit.
14. See footnote 11.
15. Negandhi and Prasad, op. cit.
16. Weber, M. *The Theory of Social and Economic Organizations*. trans, T. Parsons. Glenroe, Illinois: The Free Press, 1947.

THOUGHTS ON ADMINISTRATIVE INNOVATIONS

Nitish De

In an intellectual quiz if thoughtful Indians are asked to name two items of national significance since the dawn of independence, it is most likely, on hindsight, they will name population planning and administrative innovations. The common thread between the two is that both have been neglected for over three decades at all the critical levels, national policy makers, higher echelons of administrative and managerial hierarchy, and the informed public. The only difference between the two seems to be that in recent years, concern over the fast growing population is on the increase although lack of innovative policies backed by thoughtful action in this matter is also conspicuous by unclarity and ambiguity.

The term "innovation" does not imply an earthshaking new idea or action. It may very well be something which is an improvement on an old practice or existing policy or a system or a device. Gains may be great or incremental. What matters, however, is the ever-growing spirit of innovation in an organization, be that a government agency or a commercial complex or a manufacturing outfit. Gardner (1965), a distinguished academician, who also held the position of the Secretary of Health, Education and Welfare in the US Administration, gave a considerable part of his time and energy to the issue of self-renewal of an organization system. His deep concern was with the need for generating a culture of innovation. In human systems of various kinds in the contemporary world it is also relevant to point out that a culture of innovation cannot be conceived as a quality or virtue confined to a few functionaries of an enterprise. The culture needs wide dispersal, so much so, that members of an enterprise at various levels are able to inculcate the spirit of change, improvement and innovation in their respective sphere of work as well as in their collective sphere of fulfilling the overall purpose of an enterprise.

It may be worthwhile here to refer to Gardner who mentioned a set of five rules:—

(a) An organization must have an effective programme for recruitment and development of talent;

(b) It must have a hospitable environment for an individual to realize his potential;

(c) It must have built-in provisions for self-criticisms (in our view, as distinct from the confession);

(d) It must have flexibility in the internal work structure; and

(e) It must have some means of combating the process by which persons become prisoners of the procedures.

Should we consider these five criteria and seek to judge, at random, any organization, private or public, we may come out with an interesting profile which will show how many of these five items are in vogue and to what extent.

One obvious comment that perceptive observers will make is that in our government system Principle No. (e) where a person is not a prisoner of the procedures is considerably, if not totally, absent. The most frustrating, if not alarming, aspect of the government system which is all pervading in any developing country with India as no exception, is that many senior level public servants known for their insight, integrity and committed application to work do firmly believe that innovative spirit is alien to government system and its static work culture. This attitude is particularly unfortunate because other types of enterprises seek to emulate the government system, public enterprises for example. A spirit of resignation that in the absence of inspired leadership in taking the government style of functioning out of the morass, they will be unable to change their own organization systems effectively asserts itself. It seems that, this malaise has to be recognized as a reality before one proceeds any further in the matter of administrative innovations.

Administrative innovation can be comprehended in terms of the principle of deviation amplification. This principle has been articulated by Maruyama (1963) in a insightful paper. One part of the principle is fairly well-known. If there is a small crack in a wall which is accessible to the vagaries of nature such as rainfall, then the chances are that the crack will become bigger and bigger. This example can be applied to many other situations. Basically, it means that if there is a flaw of any kind in a system and it remains unattended or ignored, probability is very strong that the flaw will become a major defect. Applied to our public affairs, we can see that in many aspects of our national affairs, this negative phenomenon is visible, primarily because no productive counter-measure was adopted in time.

But there is another side of it too. If someone or a group of determined persons bring about a deviation in the pathology of day-to-day practice in the working of an enterprise by introducing a positive change, however minor it may be, and determinedly pursue it, then the deviation which is positive in nature, will also grow and in the process, there will be the amplification effect on the whole system. In other words, like the psychological principle of self-fulfilling prophecy, deviation amplification principle can result in positive or negative consequence.

Let us provide an example of the positive side here. Anil Kumar Lakhina, an administrator whose name is familiar to many by now, initiated a series of minor to not-so-minor planned changes in the Collectorate of Ahmednagar, which was originally set up by the British in 1817, with a view to improving the public-government clerk-work relationship, demystifying office procedures, making the required documents accessible to the staff and the public and creating a better congenial work environment for the staff of the Collectorate. After a period of four years' change programme this particular office can now claim to be a model one in the country. These observations come from a number of sound administrators. The lessons derived from this administrative innovation are being experimented upon in 26 other districts in India, some with equal measure of success. The reason for quoting this example is that the cynics among the government officials and members of the public may wish to understand how these changes can be brought about in an old institution like District Collectorate, which many would like to believe to be the last administrative bastion for any meaningful change. But this has become a reality.

Keeping the above mentioned observations in view, we may now spell out some of the basics and action steps that are required in bringing about a revolution of innovation in our work organizations. We shall mention these in positive and negative statements with requisite elaboration.

In the first place, elitist approach to administrative innovation is a non starter. A wise owl laying down the golden rules, whether in the matter of punctuality in attendance or the movement of files or the quality of notings or the canons of conduct towards the public, will fail miserably simply because his wisdom is not a shared perception of his subordinate colleagues. Organization innovation cannot rest upon one person's shoulder, however, broad and strong it might be. What is needed is a new paradigm in that one person or more can take initiative in developing a shared culture, throughout the organization, that administrative innovations can emanate from any level and that it is highly desirable keeping in view the concrete interests of the members of the organization itself. In other words, there is no substitute to participation on a large-scale as the beginning norm of desirable administrative change.

Secondly, it is necessary to accept the principle, as a corollary from the first one as mentioned, that planning and doing are an integrated process. Nothing can be more deterrent than the belief that thinking is the close preserve of a select few and translating these thoughts into action with the same spirit as energize the thought-givers by others, who in most cases happen to be of subordinate levels in an organizational hierarchy. It is easy to mention this requirement but not so easy to practise. We recall that when a group of senior engineers in the first phase of the installation of the Bhilai Steel Plant was sent to Soviet Union for orientation programme, they were asked to plan their work which was a comfortable exercise but with equal emphasis they were made to use their hands and muscle to do the work and many of them felt resentful. When we interviewed some of them in Bhilai occupying senior positions they mentioned that their initial resentment against the order to carry out the work otherwise meant for the workers was misplaced and that they were grateful for helping them to learn work not only through the medium of thinking, but also through type of integration as a potential force in generating a culture of innovation. Most experimental scientists will accept this principle as natural and will not question its validity. The trouble is with those who are accustomed to giving orders and instructions. The very process of direction and guidance creates a hiatus between work planning and work implementation.

Thirdly, there is scientific evidence that human beings are capable of generating constructive ideas and implementing them with vigour. The basis for such assertion is our increasing knowledge about the design of human brains. Neurophysiologists and Anthropologists have collected evidence that the human brain changes in tune with the changes in human consciousness. As consciousness of our social reality and its dimensions changes, the brain that processes new information and transforms it into knowledge also changes. The more we know, the more we are capable of knowing (De, 1984-A). The need is to create appropriate levels of challenges for human beings in work situations to use their brains and in the process of using the same to augment its capacity.

Fourthly, we come, as a deduction from the earlier principle, to the vital issue of designing organization system. The major contribution towards the development of an appropriate climate for generating innovations in an organization will come from the designs of work organizations. It is interesting to note that bulk of studies and research leading to definitive role of work system design in energizing employees towards creative venture have been carried out by mid-1960s (De, 1979). Thomas J. Peters, et al., (1982) have popularized these ideas and in a way have simplified these principles in the book, *In Search of Excellence*. This book has caught the imagination of industrial managers. Public servants have yet to respond to this book with enthusiasm. Be that as it may, the basic principles can be summarized in a few terse ideas:

— Development of a climate of trust among employees through concrete efforts;

— Developmental type of leadership which will combine the basic elements of a sound head and stout heart;

— Task oriented flexible work system which will facilitate communication, encourage persons to take risks and learn from the results;

— Ability to work towards goals which have long-term

implications and create a work situation where career goals and large goals of the organization can exist in harmony.

Nonetheless, there exists a challenge in designing work system in such a way that it provides for adequate diversity in the organization so that creative ideas can be conceived and proposed and at the same time the diversity should not be so wide that it will call for intricate bargaining mechanism to get a constructive idea accepted and implemented. That is why earlier a point was made that planning and doing should be looked upon as a systemic integrity.

That this is possible at the grass-roots level in various types of organizations has not only been confirmed by Lakhina's work in Ahmednagar District, as already mentioned, but in a variety of work situations, governmental as well as industrial (De, 1984-88). It has always been observed that while taking a fresh look at the work system in a concrete manner, the concerned employees have never lagged behind in generating practical ideas and that it has also been possible to implement these ideas successfully. It has further been established that even in unionized enterprises, trade unions have not stood in the way of such innovations being implemented.

Lastly, it is necessary to mention, based on empirical data, that organizational innovation tends to emphasize one component much more than another component. (Damanpour & Evan, 1984). Let us elaborate the point. Organizational innovation refers to implementation of an internally generated or a borrowed idea, whether pertaining to a product, device, system, process policy, programme or service, which is new to the organization at the time of adoption. Associated with this concept is another concept which we may call organizational lag. This idea refers to the discrepancy in the rate at which new technical and administrative ideas are implemented in an organization. Let us highlight the phrase, the discrepancy or more specifically, the component of delay in implementation and sometimes more than delay, the distortion in implementation.

We have made a reference to the emphasis on one component compared to another. This implies that there are two components in organizational innovation. One is technical innovation which occurs in the technical system of an organization and is directly related to the primary work activities of the same. Technical innovation may refer to the implementation of an idea for a new product or a new service or production processes or operational activities. Basically, it refers to improvements in the performance of the technical system of an organization. The use of laser in complicated surgical operation is an example of technical innovation. Same is the case with microprocessors. An improvement in the method of storing information and weeding out unnecessary papers and files is yet another example of technical innovation. One may go on multiplying such examples. Administrative innovation is the other component. It occurs in the social system of an organization. The reference is to the relationship among persons who interact to accomplish a particular goal or tasks. It also includes rules, roles, procedures and structures that are related to communication and interaction among members of an organization and between the members and the relevant environment. Distribution of power, flow of information, existence or otherwise of trust among persons are some of the components of administrative innovation.

The President of Honda, a well known Japanese enterprise, once declared that the Corporation over which he presides did not have a formal organization structure. Instead, he went on to say that what existed were multiple task groups with relevant number of members who would work towards an objective and as soon as the same objective was reached, the members would regroup themselves to take up another task or objective. At one level it speaks of the enormous flexibility that has been built into the system with the provision that the flexibility so built-in does not generate a state of chaos or disorder. This is a simple example of administrative innovation where the freedom enjoyed by employees has not degenerated into licence. What has happened really is that quality of work relationship has improved, so much so, that the employees do not hesitate to bring to their activity the very best that they are capable of.

The highlight of empirical evidence is that technical innovation is usually given more predominance and administration innovation is usually relegated to a secondary position. Task-oriented administrators and managers, more often than not, are comfortable with ideas around technical innovation taking the administrative set-up as given. That this "holy cow" approach to administrative system as something sacrosanct is most unfortunate, to say the least. There is incontrovertible evidence that, should an enterprise develop a strong and sustained culture of administration then it becomes a guarantor of technical innovation. Simply stated, it implies that administrative innovation which basically refers to the quality of relationship among the members of an enterprise, is the foundation on which the superstructure of technical innovation can be built. Although this is a simple statement, its implication is not so simple. In order to get the best out of a computer installed in an office, it may be advisable to look at the human culture of that office. We are aware of a large office where Rs 12 lakhs were spent to instal a computer to get certain vital information in a critical area of government operation. The social organization of the office remained as it was. The computer is lying idle in a locked room for over two years now. The example may sound dramatic but we presume that in a manner this type of reality might be in existence in many enterprises and offices.

It is conceivable that if the felt-need of the employees is to create a better work environment, in physical sense of the term, then a beginning will be made to redesign the work place in a manner which is acceptable to them with as much economy of effort and resource as possible. This will surely fall within the area of technical innovation. The significant point is that, active involvement in technical innovation will start transforming the social relationship among the employees and that is how the seed of administrative innovation will be sown.

We have provided this example to illustrate the point that even if one begins with technical innovation, the crux of the issue is that administrative innovation is essential. The absence of that will create conditions which will weaken the base of technical improvements.

That human beings are the most precious capital asset of an organization is not a banal statement. It is a serious matter and worthy of thoughtful reflection. Young and Sloman (1982) have authored a book entitled, *No, Minister*, whose sub-title is "An inquiry into the Civil Service". The message of the book is that the civil servants in the UK have structured themselves in such a way that in the day-to-day working, a higher level civil servant may mean "no" although his verbal expression is "yes". This dramatically reflects the quality of poor relationship between the political masters and the permanent public servants. Continuity of such a relationship will not allow in the long run even technical innovation to take roots in a system. Currently, in India a new wave has gathered momentum in favour of administrative reforms. It is heartening that the lead has been provided from the top.

This is all the more a reason why there is need for caution. The tempo has to be maintained, not by generating eloquent notes or persuasive arguments but by undertaking administrative innovations in such mundane affairs as management of records, demystifying rules and procedures, bringing about an improvement in receipt and despatch sections of offices, improvement in quality of notings. If at all notings are necessary, and many such matters which, taken in isolation, have no great consequence but considered in the aggregate would contribute a great deal. Attention to such matters which are not glamorous is the basic challenge to administrative innovation. We may benefit from what the authors of *No, Minister* have to say, by way of concluding comments:

> Only when ministers are determined to pursue new and perhaps radical, policies challenging the arguments of reality and continuity in the process-will the politicians exercise real power and be effectively on top. The promotion of policy change is the principal challenge of politics. We want good civil servants to identify the factors of reality, and to make clear any disadvantages of discontinuity; but, even more we want good politicians who will be determined, clever, and if necessary, cunning enough to harness the intellect, energy and imagination of civil servants to the task of overcoming the obstacles, which too cautious a view of reality, or too great an emphasis on continuity, can sometimes place obstacles in the path of the government. For both minister and civil servants politics remains the art of the possible. But

the beginning of wisdom for the politicians is the discovery that the greatest success in politics depends on transforming into the possible what seems to be impossible. For that an attitude of mind confined to "No, Minister" on the part of their civil servants can never be enough.

REFERENCES

Alternative Design of Human Organizations, New Delhi, Beverly Hills, London, Sage Publications Limited, 1984-B.

Damanpour, F. and Evan. W.M., 'Organizational Innovation and Performance: The Problem of Organizational Lag", *Administrative Science Quarterly*, September, 1984.

De, Nitish, "Bureaucracy; Obsolescence and Innovations", In Dube, S.C. (Ed.), *Public Services and Social Responsibility*, New Delhi, Vikas, 1979.

Gardner, John W., *How to Prevent Organizations Dry Rot*, Harper, October, 1955.

Lakhina, A. K., "Reforms in the Collectorate of Ahmednagar (Maharashtra)—A Report", *The Indian Journal of Public Administration*, Vol. XXX, No. 2, April-June, 1984.

Maruyame, Megoroh, "The Second Cybernetics" *American Scientist*, June, 1963.

Overcoming Under-Development, Shillong, North-Eastern Hill University, 1984-A.

Peters, Thomas J., et al, *In Search of Excellence*, New York, Harper and Row, 1982.

Young, Hugo and Sloman, Anne, *No, Minister*, London, British Broadcasting Corporation, 1982.

EDUCATION: THE PREFERRED FUTURE

Satish C. Seth

The concept of a preferred future in any field tends to be subjective. The national need, however, does help to focus attention on certain values, programmes and institutional arrangements which deserve attention and eventual acceptance.

In terms of the national policy, therefore, one can outline an "accelerated" implementation scenario.

Education for the future and education towards the year 2000 AD, in the Indian context, should aim at certain futuristic targets. The adoption of such targets as an integral part of the six five-year plans that separate the year 1976 from the year 2000 AD would influence the course of current decisions in educational planning.

By the year 2000 AD we shall be around 960 million people. If education is conceived as a life long exercise then, we would have to aim at establishing an infrastructure for education which could meet the varying types of educational needs of this vast and diverse population. In India today, we have created institutions which, to some extent correspond to the best in other parts of the world. We have our Harvard, our Oxford and our Eton. But the experience gained from the functioning of such centres of 'learning' patterned on alien models have introduced gross distortions in our education-system which is reflected in the injustices and inequalities of our present day society. Among the criticisms-levelled against the present system are:

(a) It caters largely for the needs of elitist groups in our society.

(b) Because of the formal nature of the system, the time element (10+2+3), the cost and the highly selective nature of the preparation required for entry into these institutions renders them beyond the reach of 85 per cent of India's population.

(c) It suffers from acute 'knowledge obsolescence' which is visible both in the calibre of the majority of the community of teachers and professors as well as in the design of curricula. There is no system by which knowledge updating and knowledge renewal can be ensured.

(d) It is not geared to suit the real needs of our society. For instance professionals such as nurses, doctors, engineers, etc., undergo stereotyped learning for four and five years at high cost to the society and high personal cost in time and money. They are made to forcibly fit into job situations that do not require such elaborate training. What is being neglected by our present system is the training of middle level professionals who would be available more quickly to society (through short-term courses, etc.,) and who could, if need be, go back to their institutions for further training and acquisition of more sophisticated skills.

If the above premises be correct then the preferred future for Indian educational system would be one which, among other things, should embrace the following goals:

(1) Achievement of 100 per cent literary (I will not here go into the polemics surrounding the definition of literacy).
(2) Education to be free up to secondary level; for higher levels and professional education, gradual reduction of costs over the years.
(3) 'Cafeteria' system of education where one has a greater freedom in choosing areas of ones interest and time schedules that do not require rigid sequential stages of school and college attendance with fixed hours in the day time for 'acquiring' knowledge.
(4) Flexible syllabus and course to ensure greater creativity and less curricula burden on the pupils.
(5) Assessment to be made in terms of performance credits and not necessarily written examinations.
(6) Degrees to be valid over a limited time-frame. To overcome knowledge obsolescence, degrees shall have to be 'renewed'.
(7) Mode of education, "Study-work-study" in all fields with increased emphasis on 'creativity' at all levels.
(8) Educational content to have relevance to life, society, ethics, socio-economic imperatives and culture.

(9) Compulsory teaching of history of science, history of civilization, world geography, international institutions and comparative religion.

(10) Compulsory work experience in rural development and military training.

(11) An increasing larger portion of the total outlay for education to be devoted to building the infrastructure and the software needed for nonformal education.

(12) Conventional higher educational opportunities to be provided only for highly meritorious students in the normal run; and, specialized training in narrow specialities to be open to one and all.

(13) Technical education to have a much larger "practical" component.

(14) Industry to be called upon to bear a share of the cost of technical education since they are the biggest beneficiaries of the products of technical education.

(15) Delinking of degree requirements from jobs and linking jobs to work experience and work credits.

(16) Increased use of new educational technologies: Audio-visual aides. SITE; correspondence courses and open universities.

(17) Vocational stream to commence from class VIII onwards.

(18) Special emphasis on education of interest group such as: women, handicapped persons, tribal and hill people and nomads, etc.

(19) New educational structures: greater autonomy for academic institutions.

(20) Increased student participation in determining the course content and running of educational administration.

(21) Gradual emergence of common school system.

In conclusion, an additional emphasis needs to be laid on the fact that it is necessary to be done should be done to promote egalitarianism, rationalism and creativity through our educational system. We cannot ignore the fact that education does remain that potential instrument which alongwith other factors promotes inequality in society. It should be our hope, that over the years this would not be the case.

PART FOUR

Key Building Blocks of Future

ELECTRONICS IN INDIA: THE EMERGING SCENARIO

G. N. Acharya

Perhaps the most spectacular and significant discovery having far-reaching applications in transforming the life of man on earth in the present century is that of the tiniest negatively charged particle called the "Electron" which was discovered by a Cavendish Professor, Sir J.J. Thompson in 1897. This important discovery followed by further investigations into the nature of the behaviour of electrons and the application of the science of electronics has led to a revolution in the 20th century civilization, which not only dominates our lives substantially, but is also going to determine our future. This new revolution, aptly called the "Electronics Revolution", plays an important role in all activities of human endeavour starting from simple consumer items of daily use like the radio, television and digital watches, to extremely complex electronic systems such as, computers and microprocessor based systems for a variety of applications in transportation, Industrial Process Control, Defence and Aerospace and Communications.

Electronics has also been rightly considered as the nerve centre of modern industry. This rapidly developing technology with many facets covering Microelectronics to Power Electronics and simple hand-held calculating machines to large Electronic Systems, has found wide acceptance in every field of engineering and production, be it chemical, electrical, mechanical, hydraulics, transportation, medical, or petrochemicals and fertilizers; or production of consumer items such as sugar, paper, drugs and textiles. Recently it has been playing an important role in efficient energy systems also. It can play a dominant role in agro-industries covering a wide range of applications starting from soil testing, micronutrient and water feed control for proper plant growth, to problems covering grain procurement, storage and preservation.

---

* Dr. Acharya was Director, Central Electronics Engineering Research Institute Pilani (Rajasthan).

Knowledge of the rapid advancements in this vital field of electronics and intensive research leading to its application in modernizing our lives, therefore assume special significance.

In this short presentation, it is proposed to give a very brief overview of the field of electronics with special reference to current and future developments and the significant role it can play in all aspects of our national development.

The Present Scenario

The early applications of electronics, during the first half of the 20th Century were restricted to entertainment items such as radio and television, and a few professional applications like Broadcast Transmitters, high power industrial controls and Radar Systems for Defence, all using heavy and bulky vacuum tubes which needed a heated metal source for generating electrons and large vacuum cavities. In fact, the first electronic digital computer ENIAC commissioned in 1946, used as many as 18,000 vacuum tubes, weighed about 60,000 pounds, occupied a large area of 1600 sq. ft. and generated enormous heat.

However, the picture changed radically with the invention of a new device called the transistor in 1947, which was based on the motion of electrons and holes in a semi-conducting solid such as germanium or silicon. This was soon followed by the developments leading to integrated circuits in which as many as a few thousands, to a few million devices can be accommodated on a tiny chip of silicon. It is this miracle chip which has transformed the electronics revolution into a microelectronics revolution of our times.

Today the microelectronics technology, which has a promising future, has already enabled us to have a series of new electronic items for a 'variety of' applications.

In the consumer electronics area, we now have pocket size and match box size radio receivers, television sets, video cassette recorders and players, digital watches including fountainpen watches, high fidelity stereo amplifiers, pocket calculators working on paper thin batteries or solar cells and a variety of personal microcomputers.

Although development of integrated circuits in the mid

sixties led to further miniaturization in which entire functional board of transistor circuits could be replaced by a single silicon chip carrying a few lakh transistors and associated components like resistors and capacitors in a very small area of a few mm^2, the real breakthrough came in 1971, with the invention of programmable integrated circuits by a young engineer, Hoff, from Intel Corporation in USA, which led to an entirely new generation of integrated circuits called microprocessors. The microprocessors ushered a new era in the field of Electronics and opened up an entirely new vista of applications in which the circuit functions could be modified at will to suit a variety of jobs by programming them through simple key boards and similar devices. The microprocessor is basically a very large-scale integrated circuit on a single chip of silicon containing a large number of electronic components wired as a central processing unit of a computer and it performs various arithmetic, logic and control functions. Together with other integrated circuit chips, it performs the function of a microcomputer. Any microcomputer from the simplest one used for controlling temperature to the most sophisticated multi-tasking process controller consists of (a) a Central Processing Unit (CPU) performing arithmetic, logic and control functions, (b) Memory chips which can be of the "READ/ WRITE" type also called Random Access Memory (RAM) or "READ ONLY" type called (ROM) and (c) INPUT/OUTPUT interface for peripheral control.

Microprocessor based systems are now finding many applications in industrial production transportation, home appliances, office automation as well as Satellite Communications. These systems have transformed the second industrial revolution by replacing manual control in Industry with Electronic Control which would not only help in increasing the productivity of essential commodities many times bringing down the cost, but it would also ensure uniformity of quality and reliability of consumer durables. It is growing at such a fast rate that by the year 2000, it is expected that 5 to 10 billion microprocessors and microcomputers will be in service throughout the world. Which means that there will be approximately one microprocessor per living person on the earth by the turn of the present century.

While the search for new microelectronic devices was going on, another breakthrough came up with the development of very powerful semi-conductor devices such as Thyristor and Gate-Turn-off devices (GTOs). Although the thyristor family devices were discovered in the sixties, their commercial availability and real applications came up in the seventies and eighties. Today these powerful devices are extensively used in many applications involving high-efficiency energy conversion such as DC, DC Converters, HVDC, DC-AC Inverters, variable speed DC and AC motor. Drives involving choppers, PWM Inverters and cyloconverters for Transportation and Industrial applications.

The electronic devices can be divided broadly into following two major categories.

(i) Low Power Microelectronics Devices working on very small voltages of the order of 3 to 5 volts in the form of integrated circuits having dimensions of connection lines and devices of the order of a few micro-metres, performing the "brain and nerve" functions; and

(ii) Power Electronics Devices with Comparatively large dimensions which can operate at several hundred volts and can carry several hundred amps of current performing the "muscle and bone" function of modern electronic systems. In between are other devices in the medium power range such as hybrid microcircuits, discrete low power transistors and SCR's which can perform other functions.

However, in the very high frequency, high power range such as those required for Radars, Microwave Communications, Microwave ovens, etc., special purpose high power microwave tubes, which can generate and amplify frequencies in the gigahertz range and which can generate powers of the order of few kilowatts to few megawatts, are the only ones which will continue to be used.

Some Application Areas

Apart from consumer items mentioned earlier, modern Electronic Systems are used progressively in many other applications as mentioned below:

(i) *Industrial Process Control* for increased productivity and improved quality of essential commodities such as food processing industries including sugar, tea and bakery items, textiles, paper, cement, fertilizers, drugs and pharmaceuticals and whole range of chemicals. These cover a wide range of applications starting from measurement and control of process parameters such as temperature, pressure, flow, liquid level, viscosity, etc., to very advanced electronic systems required for consistency control, automatic pH control, chemical reagent control and controls for overall efficiency as well as improvement in quality coupled with highest possible productivity through overall plant controls. In the past, such functions were being performed by a single computer which was controlling the whole plant, whereas the modern philosophy is to use dedicated process controls for individual processes through intelligent electronic systems based on Microprocessors and to connect them through a Data Highway use in Distributed.

Digital Process Control configuration. Such systems are aided by Colour Graphic Display systems similar to that of Colour Television Receivers used in homes, which enable the operator to look at the screen and see what is happening inside the plant and take corrective action by simply using keyboard similar to that used in the ordinary typewriter.

(ii) *Electronic Systems for Transportation* such as those used for Railway Locomotives and electronic controls for Energy Saving used in Diesel and Petrol driven vehicles as well as in electric vehicles of various types including trolley buses and Battery Powered Road vehicles.

(iii) *Microwave Systems* for strategic applications such as those used in Defence and Aerospace and Digital Data Handling Systems for Satellite Communications.

(iv) *Electronic Systems for Office Automation* involving simple Electronic Typewriters and Word-processors to more complex applications including Data Base Management, Corporate Management and Financial Management required at individual offices as well as in large-scale systems such as countrywide computer networks. In this field Personal Computers ultimately leading to "offices at home" are likely to play a dominant role for quite sometime.

(v) *Electronic Aids for Education* ranging from simple automatic slide projection systems to more complex video display systems suitable for presentation of specialized training programmes, recorded on video tapes, displayed on Colour Television Receivers as well as on more advanced projection systems in auditoria. This is an important application which needs to be fully exploited in our country, starting from basic literacy programme to advanced educational programmes.

Future Trends

Electronics is growing at such a tremendously rapid rate that it would be difficult to predict what might happen even during the next 6 to 10 years. However, the trends indicate that further developments are likely to take place in the area of Microelectronics in which few million devices would be available on a chip of the size of a thumb nail. Today a large number of firms have started entering the area of 1 to 1.5 micron CMOS microchips and the race will continue for establishing 1 micron and possibly submicron technology. Apart from the development of submicron geometry devices, there may be introduction of new techniques, such as the use of supperlattices which would be composites incorporating alternating layers of various compounds like Gallium-arsenide, Aluminium arsenide and Gallium-aluminium arsenide. Investigations for submicron geometry integrated circuits on Silicon microchips would also continue and new techniques in the areas of electron and ion beam lithography leading to nano-lithography would be evolved for commercial production of these highly complex microcircuits.

In the fifth generation computers, one can expect the use of new technologies such as Josephson junctions working at liquid Helium temperatures and High Electron Mobility Transistors (HEMTS) which can have extremely high switching speeds of the order of 13 to 17 trillionths of a second. This will help in further developments in all areas of application, particularly in the new scientific discipline called "Artificial Intelligence" that crosses the boundary between computer and the human brain. Thus, we can expect a new generation of "thinking computers" in the next few years. Rapid developments of new microelectronics techniques would lead to the 32 bit microcomputer on a single chip of silicon with low cost, thus giving a boost to the computer market and enable the mankind to enter rapidly the new age of informatics.

Flat Screen Television picture tubes may lead to pocket size television sets and extremely small size computers.

Other breakthroughs could be due to the development of "photonic logic" leading to high speed optical computers, optomagnetic discs which can record 100 times more data than the floppy discs used in today's microcomputers.

Application of Microelectronics to Transportation would lead to new concepts and systems and microcomputer control of electric road vehicles using brushless A.G. motor drives will make them more efficient resulting in increased range because of the reduced battery drain. Microprocessor controlled variable frequency A.C. Drive Systems coupled with novel design of high efficiency motors such as switched Reluctance machines with speed may dominate the transportation scene.

Another area of far-reaching importance to industrial production is that of electrical transducers which transform parameters like temperature, pressure, flow, liquid level, etc., into a digital electronic signal compatible with the computers. Integrated Digital Transducers with signal processing interfaces for microprocessors would be progressively available on a single silicon chip. Fibre optic sensors also are likely to play a dominant role in this field.

In the field of communications, Digital Signal Processing techniques will continue to predominate and Digital Data Links using fine optical fibres which are ultrathin glass fibres, thinner than human hair, will be progressively used. This would enhance the signal handling capacities to Gigabit rates and will also enhance the channel handling capacity manifold. Speech synthesis and analysis microchips shall add a new dimension.

In conclusion, it can be said that by the end of this century, there will hardly be any human activity which is not influenced by the role of electronics technology in various forms, whether it is for entertainment, high quality production of consumer goods, transportation systems, or for management applications. The rapidly growing field of biotechnology is also likely to be influenced by these rapid advances in the field of electronics.

Scenario in India

Recently there has been general awareness and good appreciation of the need for taking full advantage of the emerging technology of microprocessor based systems and to some extent ASICS for various application areas with special emphasis on modernization and upgrading of our core sector industries. Although this is a good trend, simultaneously there is an increasing trend for import of items of microprocessor/microcomputer based equipment, quite often without examining the relevance, compatibility and adaptability of such systems to the conditions prevailing in our country. Availability of a multitude of various types of 8 bit, 16 bit and 32 bit systems with different bus structures on the world market has complicated the picture still further. With intensified effort on software training programmes, it is hoped that the picture may change and there would be more effort on systems engineering and development of applications software which, in turn, will not only boost this activity, but also give rise to designs of new ASICS in some application areas. Choice and standardization of system architectures and bus structures should be simultaneously examined and finalized to give the industry a good start.

Level of Technology

As far as VLSI is concerned, current level of device technology in India is restricted to 8-bit microprocessors and 3 micron geometry LSI/VLSI circuits which can also be conveniently used for Application Specific Integrated Circuits. In production units like SCL and BEL as well as in R & D laboratories like CEERI, 5 and 3 micron technologies have been fairly well tried out and work has been initiated for 2 micron CMOS technology. Plans are also being considered for getting foreign collaboration for CMOS technology, upto about 1.5 micron level, but such steps have to be taken with great care, keeping in mind the necessity to define more clearly national policies regarding the specific role which microelectronics is expected to play in our developmental activities. Simultaneously bipolar IC's which are required for strategic applications are also to be manufactured with foreign collaborators in India. Proposals for R & D in submicron technology are also under way.

As far as application areas are concerned fairly advanced

Microprocessor based Electronic Systems for various applications have already been either developed or are in an advanced stage of developments in R & D Labs., but there is a large gap between what is available on commercial scale and what is actually required for many applications including modernization of our traditional industries.

The problem of overall national development based on such high technology areas is closely linked with many factors such as availability of R & D facilities and industrial infrastructure, trained manpower and the political will to support such programmes.

Analysis of the Present Scenario in India

There may be half a dozen different reasons for low levels of the activity in the field of VLSI technology, some of which might have been brought out in the VLSI Task force which had been actively working for almost two years (1983-85). However one of the main reasons can be considered as lack of a national goal which can bring the R & D organization and Industrial Undertakings to share the tasks and work hand-in-hand towards a common objective. The R & D is at a low key and worthwhile plans are not receiving enough support which are quite often rejected on the basis of 'large investments' which the country cannot afford, or on the basis of 'lack of linkages' with the industrial undertakings. On the other hand, industrial undertakings are preparing and finalizing proposals independently for collaboration and choice of technology is clearly dependent on what is the best offer available in the world market for transfer of technology. Whenever there is a change in technology, attempts are made for still another collaboration, without examining the potentialities available in the country. In fact, there is a large communication gap between the Industrial undertakings and R & D units. There is no formal organizational linkage between R & D units, and Public Sector Undertakings which can bind them together and make it mandatory to share the expertise and facilities without going through long drawn procedures.

Even in cases where some preliminary dialogue and short-term collaborative programmes have started emerging, the designs and developments have to be based on the design rules available to the Industry from our collaborators. There is not enough scope for innovative VLSI designs because of the lack of foundries and other industrial infrastructure required to give them a fair trial.

Under such circumstances, an impression has been created that only a large industrial infrastructure for large-scale production and quality control requiring several crores of Rupees (Rs 200 to Rs 300 crores) is required for VLSI technology, where there can be some scope for evolving new VLSI architectures.

It is, therefore, first of all necessary to examine whether a medium scale facility based on a versatile Electron Beam Machine, capable of Director Writing facility, coupled with processing facility for trying out VLSI chips on a small-scale can be considered for ASICS so that innovative designs get their fair share in the Indian market.

Weakness and Proposed Remedial Measures

Remedial measures for transforming this situation can suggest themselves if we make an objective analysis of the past achievements and the role of R & D in the same.

When we talk of large-scale commercial productions of various items in this country, we find that only a small percentage of the same is based on our own R & D, because we have never realised that large-scale outputs need commensurate inputs in transforming the results of Research into production through extensive pilot production studies and through development of production technology to make such commercial production economically viable. As far as microelectronics area is concerned, microprocessor based system development based on our own design and application software has succeeded to some extent, because of lower levels of investments required for the same, while the VLSI design and production of microchips based on our own designs have still a fairly long way to go.

Another problem is that of the availability of trained manpower. Analysis of the out-turn of the scientific and technical personnel in India and its effect on the utilization of the results of indigenous R & D indicates that: Whereas the number of graduates qualifying in pure science subjects in India is comparatively larger than in other countries, the number qualifying in applied science is only 30 in India, as compared to 950 in Japan, 2154 in Canada, 200 in Brazil, Italy and USA, 150 in France and more than 100 in UK. This low percentage of students qualifying in applied sciences in India shows a critical gap in our technology thrust, lower industrial activity with much smaller applied scientists working in Industry. This lack of involvement of engineering talent has an adverse impact on the rapid utilization of our R & D. This is one of the important factors which has led to failure of our R & D in making a visible impact on our national development.

Analysis of total R & D expenditure as percentage of GNP in selected countries indicates that India spends approximately 0.6 per cent of GNP, which is much lower than that in advanced countries where it is more than 2 per cent (between 2 and 4.5 per cent). This is comparable to other developing countries where it is of the order of 1 per cent of GNP. Expenditure on R & D in Electronics, however, forms a very small percentage of the total R & D expenditure, the amount available for specific result oriented tasks being only a small fraction of the same.

However, a large percentage of this amount comes from the Central Government and unlike the developing countries, the percentage allocation by the industrial sector for their in-house R & D in real terms is negligibly small. This is in direct contrast to the countries like Japan and USA.

Today Japanese are leading in the Electronics industry, though the initial developments were in USA, because Japanese manufacturers spend almost one-third of their turnover on reinvestment plus R & D, which they have kept up even when recession struck the industry with the rise in energy price. This enabled them to obtain 70 per cent of the world market for 46K Dynamic Random Access (DRAM) memories in 1981. For example, Fujitsu set aside 10 per cent of their gross sales for intensive R & D effort, which enabled them to edge out IBM from its paramount position in computers in the Japanese market.

Today Hitachi in Japan has more than 900 Research Scientists working on approximate 200 research projects in their Central Research Laboratory, but altogether in the different groups of Hitachi there are 11,000 employees engaged in R & D and expenditure on R & D in 1984 exceeded 210 Billion Yen (approximately Rs 850 Crores), amounting to about Rs 8 lakhs per employee. This is the record of just one Japanese company whose net sales have crossed 4,3000 billion Yens, i.e., about 17,400 crores including 1200 billion Yen (i.e. about Rs. 4800 Crores) sales in the overseas market.

As we are yet to start on the technology development on our own, it would be good to keep this example before us and increase our investment in appropriate automation, microprocessor based electronic controls and associated ASICS substantially to enable the country to reach a reasonable position in this "high tech," era.

It is necessary to appreciate that, although our technology can also be based on our own Scientific discoveries, it really thrives in an industrial atmosphere that meets the industry's requirements of product refinement, quality upgrading, cost reduction and consumer satisfaction.

This demands engineering skills, multidisciplinary knowledge and proper market orientation. Through the new electronics policy of the Government of India, it can be hoped that an industrial infrastructure can be created soon in which electronics research can possibly thrive better and there would be a shift from conventional R & D to forward looking result oriented innovative work which can enable us to catch up on the 21st century.

Fortunately electronics offers many interesting opportunities at relatively lower levels of investment compared to highly capital intensive industries in which we have been committing large resources.

Electronics has an inherent potentiality to employ as many as 300 persons for every crore of rupees invested and can lead to labour productivity of the order of 1.6 lakhs per person. It consumes minimum energy and an annual turnover of Rs 10,000 crores envisaged by the end of the Seventh Plan. The power requirement is only 400 MW. Value added to the final electronic equipment varies from 2 to 8 times of the cost of raw materials and the transportation requirement is also small and there is a good possibility of dispersal of industrial units to rural and far-flung areas throughout the country. Reasonable investment in this important area starting with Application areas with a result oriented approach, is, therefore, absolutely essential.

Outline of some areas in which Electronic systems based on Microprocessors and ASICS can be Introduced in India

Introduction

Some of the priority areas in which applications of electronic systems would play a major role have to some extent been identified. The main objective of introducing such systems in the country would be to improve the productivity, increase production and also to establish export market through improvement of quality of some of the commodities.

In the first phase, highest priority would have to be naturally given to essential commodities of mass consumption, which must be made available to the common masses at reasonable cost without sacrificing the quality. The 7th Plan envisages a twofold increase in the production of a number of commodities which, at present, are being manufactured by traditional methods. Most of these are based on our own raw-materials but the production methods adopted for them are outdated and need modernization through introduction of electronic systems for improving their productivity. Full utilization of the installed capacity is another aspect to be considered in some of the commodities. Since large investment in capital have been committed in setting up production units for these items, the strategy should be to introduce modern electronic systems based on microprocessors or microcomputers for modernizing the existing plants.

A few areas in which modernization using microprocessor based systems and Applications Specific Integrated Circuits (ASICS) can be introduced are presented here. Agencies and nodal laboratories/organizations have also been identified wherever possible.

Agriculture

1. Soil testing equipment using microprocessor based systems to give direct reading of soil moisture, temperature and pH values and process these parameters to give indication of suitability of the soil for a particular crop.
2. Microprocessor based equipment for drip irrigation for controlled feed of water, based on measurement of leaf temperature and soil moisture.

Specially designed microprocessor controlled drip irrigation equipment for sugarcane growth based on continuous monitoring of leaf temperature, birth control and soil moisture, pH and soil micro-nutrients such as phosphates which are useful for non sugar removal in sugar factories.

3. Grain storage problems and problems of temperature control in large cold-storages with a microprocessor based monitoring system required for storage of items like potatoes, apples, oranges, etc.
4. Electronic systems for rodent control and bird scaring units for reducing the loss of grain during harvesting and storage.

Food Processing Industries (Including Sugar)

1. *Bakery Items:* Process Control for making bakery items like bread, biscuits, etc. Details are available with CFTRI, Mysore where pilot production plants have been set-up.
2. *Sugar:* This has been identified as one of the high priority industries for modernization because of the tremendous potential available in the country for sugar and sugar by-products. India produces 25 per cent of the world's cane but contributes less than 10 per cent to world sugar production. Although India had exported sugar worth as much as Rs 460 crores during 1978-79, by now India is importing sugar from other countries to the tune of Rs 180 to Rs 200 crores.

   Whereas some of the microprocessor based equipment developed in the first phase is already in production, a very large number of microprocessor based controls for different processes starting from juice extraction, and juice clarification to pan boiling, crystallisation and final weighing of sugar bags have been well identified and work on this is in an advanced stage at CEERl (Pilani) under a scheme partially funded by DOE ASICS for this have also been identified.
3. *Edible Oils:* Microprocessor controlled equipments for solvent extraction process using hexane for improving oil extraction efficiency and introduction of advanced temperature, and pH control systems for oil refining (Edible oil is an item involving large imports causing FE drain of Rs 1200 crores per year).

Details of controls required are available with Regional Research Laboratory, Hyderabad (AP).

Moisture control equipment for oil-seeds production in the field particularly for groundnut production using special polymers such as 'Jalshakti' developed by National Chemical Laboratory (NCL), Pune.

4. *Electronic Systems for Food Preservation:* Fermentation control equipments for testing canned food-products during production such as consistency measurement of items like tomato juice, and automatic inspection systems for canned food products for assessing their shelf life as well as for finding quality for export.

Paper Industry

(Involves large imports of raw-material as well as finished paper).

Present capacity of 10 lakh tonnes per annum has to be boosted to 30 lakh tonnes per annum by the end of the plan. The microprocessor based quality control equipment such as on-line measurement of basis weight, moisture and calipre and process control equipment for digital control involving chlorinity control, flow control, pH control, etc., are required particularly for manufacture of paper base: on Indian raw-materials like straw and bagasse available from sugar industry. Work on quality control instrumentation is under field trials and Microprocessor based controls and ASICS are being identified for further work in this area. (Contact Laboratory: CEERI, Pilani and Madras).

Leather Industry

Needs immediate modernization because of export market. This industry has been neglected in the past. Starting from leather processing controls for controlled dehairing, to final manufacture of leather garments and shoes based on advance computer aided design (CAD), Indian leather and leather goods have a tremendous market abroad and without modernization it is not likely to catch up with the Chinese or Korean industry. (Contact Laboratory: CLRI, Madras).

Building Materials

Increased productivity of bricks using advanced technologies such as those based on sand and limestone or flyash, bagasse ash, or rice husk ash, as raw-materials incorporating high pressure processing methods for production.

Robotics based on advanced microprocessor based systems can be used effectively to double or triple the rate of manufacture reaching production capacity to reach 2000 to 3000 bricks/hour, thus reducing cost of production of high quality bricks. Microprocessor based controls are required in the Cement industry also. (Contact Laboratories: CBRI, Roorkee, Cement Research Institute, Cement Corporation of India, New Delhi).

Textiles

Apart from controls for cotton thread manufacturing, introduction of microprocessor controlled garment manufacture, and for improving the productivity of high quality garments for export is another unexplored area needing attention. (Here opportunities for boosting the present level of exports from Rs 800 crores to Rs 1200-1600 crores are very good). Contact organisation: ATIRA (Ahmedabad), SITRA (Madras), BITRA (Bombay).

Transportation

Here there are tremendous opportunities for introducing modern electric vehicles, particularly the commercial vehicles like buses and trucks which need to be modernized using advanced microprocessor based AC Motor Drives which have inherent advantages over DC motor drives.

Considerable amount of initial work on these has been done at CEERI and a 40 KVA AC motor Drive using Thyristor invertor has been successfully tried out on a mining locomotive. Experimental trials and detailed tests on this vehicle clearly indicate reduced battery drain and effective use of regenerative braking.

Controls for Electric Locomotives for mainline and shunting locomotives for Indian Railways are immediate needs of the country for which some Electronic Control Systems and ASICS have been identified.

Considering that these systems have to work in harsh environment, large number of CMOS, IC's and Hybrid microcircuits would be required in this area, some of which have already been identified. Some ASICS compatible with VME bust system have already been designed under UNDP programme at CEERI for PWM AC Motor Drives for Electric Vehicles. (Contact Laboratory: CEERI, Pilani and BHEL (TSG) Bhopal).

Industrial-Boilers (Using FBC)

Opportunities and identified needs in this area are in those connected with fluidized Bed Combustion Technique which can be used with a multiplicity of fuels such as coal with high ash content and materials like industrial and municipal wastes and bagasse in sugar factories.

Microprocessor based systems for monitoring and optimizing the parameters such as fluidizing velocity, air/fuel ratio. ID/FD fan controls, CO and Oxygen content in fluidgas and number of ASICS can be identified. (CEERI, CFRI, CMERI and BHEL).

1. Saving of raw-materials like bagasse through more efficient combustion for paper factories or for cogeneration of electricity is the main objective for introducing Fluidized Bed Combustion Technique in the sugar factories where there is an urgent need (separate detailed reports on this are available with CEERl, Pilani, in which Microprocessor based controls have been mentioned but some ASICS have to be still identified).

Herbal Medicines

This is an unexplored area which can offer tremendous potentialities for introducing standardization and quality controls and production of products with uniform quality through introduction of microprocessor based control systems for process control for controlling various processes such as fermentation control based on temperature and pH.

A large number of herbal medicines based on Ayurvedic and Yunani preparations, such as syrups, Asavas, etc., which are produced in few thousand to a million tones per year, can be introduced in the world market. There is already good market for these in the country, but productivity and quality need to be improved.

(CIMAP Lucknow, RRL Trivandrum and Ayurvedic Medicine Manufacturing Centres).

Telecommunications

Immediate need is for electronic exchanges and introduction of microchips and Hybrid Microcircuits for various modules required in equipments being manufactured by C-DOT in India. (A microchip replacing 28 general purpose IC's in a 32 line exchange has been designed and fabricated by CEERI, Pilani). But a lot more work needs to be done including 64-line and other exchanges compatible with 6502 microprocessor being manufactured by SCL in India.

Outdated communication system is one of the weakest links in the developmental activities of India and it is impeding the growth of industries in the country.

(ITRC and C-DOT, New Delhi).

Mining Electronics

A separate committee of DOE has identified many electronic systems for modernization in this area. Immediate need in the introduction of microprocessor based systems for safety in the mines (e.g. methane monitoring, roof fall warnings, mine-winder monitoring controls, etc., microprocessor based mine winder control has already been developed) CMRS Dhanbad and CMPDI, Ranchi).

Drinking Water and Water Management Problems

Availability of drinking water to all citizens is a national mission. Introduction of Solid State Switches for automatic protection and soft starters for AC motors for water pumps, tubewells, etc., and introduction of electronic systems for water treatment control are some of the areas. Solar Cell operated pumps is a good possibility requiring considerable amount of work for introduction of large desalination plants with electronic systems for controlling the transformation of salt water into drinkable water using controlled flow through spiralled cellulose acetate membranes developed in the country is an urgent requirement.

(CSMCRI, Bhavnagar, NCL, Pune and NGRI, Hyderabad).

Wood Based Industries

Apart from paper, other wood based industries that need modernization are, match box industry, rubber industry and plywood industry. Electronic systems for these industries have been identified and all of them are based on microprocessor based systems or programmable ASICS, some of which have been identified.

Generalized Temperature Data Acquisition, Monitoring and Control Systems for Various Applications

Temperature is the most important variable in all manufacturing units since it is related to energy as well as process control. Such systems have a direct bearing on the energy management problems in most of the industries. Iron and Steel Industry, Oil Refineries, Paper and Sugar Industry, Cement Industry, Fertilizers & Pesticide Industries and Distilleries are only a few examples in which temperature measurement, monitoring and control during processing would be essential.

In addition some of the areas in which temperature measurement and control is necessary are those connected with energy generating systems such as industrial boilers of various types and solar thermal systems which have a good potentiality for introduction in this country.

Concluding Remarks

As is obvious from the above discussions, introduction of microelectronic technology in the form of Microprocessor based Systems and Application Specific Integrated Circuits (Custom/ Semicustom microchips) has a tremendous potential for future growth and modernization of our industries as well as other activities leading to higher productivity, quality and reduction in the cost of production of many essential commodities. This can, therefore, be used as a powerful tool in transforming the rural scene and ultimately for changing the lifestyle of our people.

Any efforts in harnessing these potential advantages are likely to pay rich dividends.

SMALL ENERGY SOURCES

Some Management Considerations Towards Installing an Integrated Energy System for Rural and Urban Poor

Satish C. Seth

The energy question, both globally, and locally, has been discussed, debated and now written about fairly extensively. Hence sometimes one wonders if any further comment or appreciation is not a repetitious exercise.

The oil crisis and its implications for different countries is as much a familiar story as is the knowledge about the alternative energy sources and technologies. What still, perhaps, remains to be studied and discussed in the whole question of 'management' of energy of both the conventional and non-conventional, new, small sources of energies. On this aspect, usually one comes across two kinds of arguments: Firstly, energy management has necessarily to be the capital-cum-high-technology-business. Secondly, in the context of the developing societies, the set of traditional technologies which people have evolved over centuries, in spite of their inadequacy, can, with a radical reorientation of science and technology, be still pertinent and usable for the good of community. In short, the "small" effort is also a relevant effort.

The truth, perhaps, lies somewhere in between these two views. The choice of technology to meet energy needs is not the choice for a single alternative. It is not an either/or question. The right choice eventually is, perhaps, a judicious combination of various sources of energy. The developing world seems to have overindulged in a meaningless debate entitled, "large is bountiful" versus "small is beautiful". Large has its own place and so does the small. In the field of Energy Management, likewise, criteria of choice of technology does not lie whether it is "low" or "high". Amongst other considerations, this choice would rest on the appropriateness of a technology to a certain environment. It has to respond to 'a concept of development' which can ensure the satisfaction of the basic needs of the poorest of the lot. If this necessitates application of a high or advanced technology (a network, a device or a system) then it too would be the appropriate technology. If, however, the need element necessitates a low or primitive technology (device or system) then, in the context of development of a region and a given set of people, such an option too would be appropriate.

Whereas the energy solutions, based on high technology and conventional known sources or likely future breakthroughs in the nuclear or hydrogen energy sources, etc., would continue to find their due and prominent place in solving the global energy problems, there still is, it is acknowledged, every definite place for tapping the "small energy sources also", be they renewable or non-renewable.

On this aspect too there is no dearth of literature. We still, however, need to seek more innovative ideas concerning the institutional, managerial and other socio-technical systems through which the small sources of energy can be tapped, managed and delivered to the 'needy'.

The management of small energy sources again, somehow, falls into a similar trap as to what shall constitute appropriate management system. Should the management be an advanced, cost intensive, highly skilled and trained managerial operation? Or, can it be a labour intensive, less costly, social-oriented State-cum-community operation? The geography and the state of development and the capital availability has much to say about this. If a "small source of energy' were, for instance, to be tapped in Ohio, the utilities or the institutional mechanism which will go to work on it there will essentially be a management of a kind which even if it were relevant to be tapped in a remote Indian village with the small energy source there, may not quite lend itself to easy duplication in another soil, given the state of indigenous resources and status of contemporary development. However, the principles and the basic management tenets and elements used in Ohio, if not the technologies and tools, would retain its universal relevance.

The management literature can furnish the variety of management-modules from which one can pick and choose. The important lesson is that no single set of principles or single organizational mode is sufficient. A 'management product-mix' which can help the installation of an appropriate techno-managerial system that ensures an optimum, economic and efficient delivery system of low cost energy supply is what one should search for and it shall be region and culture specific.

Finally, the people's viewpoint, particularly of those, who live under the so-called poverty line in several Third World countries invariably gets forgotten in our search of alternate source of energy. Every source of energy has costs. And these costs cannot be paid for by millions of people in the Third World by both rural and urban poor, who, for centuries have been meeting their domestic energy needs almost free, though not on a zero-cost basis to their respective societies. Thus, in any tapping of the small sources of energies a unique management challenge lies in finding ways and means to provide a "low cost" or a near "zero-private-cost" energy source for millions of the rural and the urban poor. This is indeed still a critical problem to which an adequate solution has yet to be found.

This study makes a plea for creating conditions where an attempt be made to examine various aspects of management, installing an integrated energy system, keeping in view the preferred objective: to serve the rural and the urban poor of the Third World countries for whom, till they become economically strong, one should ensure, at least, a very low cost energy to meet their diverse energy needs.

Whatever else lies in the realm of conjuncture and probability one thing, however, is definitely clear. The application of science and technology has conquered the problem of hunger in many Third World countries. But if the modern world fails to provide an adequate supply of domestic-cooking-fuel to the vulnerable sections of the Third World, then, it may lead to conditions of social tension and unrest and may even give cause for the occurrence of social 'riots' for fuel. Wisdom demands that we learn to manage our scarce resources well and learn to optimize and augment them to devise and ensure a just social-energy-distribution system.

Small Sources of Energy have a great deal to offer, provided we manage them well to safeguard and ensure a better future for the millions of the rural and the urban poor in the Third World countries. This also constitutes a new context and starting point for international cooperation. One should hope that collective wisdom shall once again triumph over our numerous handicaps.

Energy Planning

The planning process has *inter alia* to accept two basic facts. Firstly, the need of the developing countries of the Third World to augment their conventional sources of energy and to search for the alternative sources of energy in order to sustain their economic development is paramount and an inescapable necessity. The small energy sources also provide sufficient economic feasibility and, therefore, they have to be exploited with the same urgency as the conventional energy sources.

Secondly, it is all the more necessary to set right the existing imbalance of the energy utilization in the world where 30 per cent of world's population consumes 85 per cent of the world's conventional energy supply, while the vast population of the Third World countries survive on the balance.

A planned effort in the above respect, therefore, is the first management step that needs to be taken. Here, it must be pointed out that short-term planning yields only short-term results. Secondly, in looking at a 3 to 5 years supply/demand picture, the economists sometimes tend to overlook the possibility of deploying tomorrow's technologies in the current plan allocations. Thus, the short-term planning eliminates advantages that can accrue if, a long-range perspective, was instead kept in view. Investments once made do constitute an irreversible decision. There are numerous reasons why, the Third World societies, which are less developed and some of whom have a very high population growth rate should, in all current day policy decisions, try and accommodate 15 to 20 years likely future challenges and demands. For instance, in the case of India, in 1981, its population is around 680 million (plus or minus) people. In less than 7,000 days i.e., by the turn of the century, this population can be anywhere in the region of 960 million to 1 billion (plus or minus). Naturally, therefore, it is necessary that in the current day decisions and energy planning, such alternates, options and even R&D investments are taken into account for funding, which can, hopefully, accommodate the needs of a larger population of the Future.

It is, therefore, recommended that while planning a policy to tap 'small energy sources, in place of short-range planning, we should take recourse to anticipatory process and take note of long-range considerations in choosing physical and fiscal targets and investments.

We shall not go into a detailed analysis of planning except to recapitulate here three essential steps.

Firstly, we need to make an intensive survey as to the location of small energy source on the one hand and as to their Techno-economic feasibility of a particular source becoming critically viable. Scientific studies can also go to help determine the choice of an energy alternate relevant to a region.* For instance, trapping the solar energy in regions where sun-shine is not adequate could be avoided, in the same way, as we should avoid installing wind mills in regions where the wind velocity and average wind density is sub-critical.

Likewise, a geological survey report would be valid for identifying other small energy sources, such as shale or tar. And in a particular region, it may prove to be a more relevant-source to other alternates. Such decisions cannot be taken without intensive surveying.

Survey information and data collection about the small energy sources is, therefore, the first requisite to any energy plan. It is a well-known fact that not all Third World countries have adequate survey data. Although in some of the developing countries, excellent scientific surveys both by the conventional surveying techniques, and now through remote sensing techniques, sufficient data and information is being readily made available.

Here it is strongly recommended that for surveying there is a good scope for establishing regional cooperation or of bilateral—

---

* In an energy study (1976) pertaining to the economic viability of Energy Plantation as an alternative source of energy mainly for the economically weaker section in the State of Gujarat, India, the following cost pattern provides an interesting case of competitive source of energy:

Comparison of cost of fuel per million BTU for:

Coal	Rs 9.80	(At current price of coal as Rs 130 per tonne as available to Power Stations in Gujarat).
Oil	Rs 17.50	(At International price @ Rs 700 per tonne).
Fuel Plantation	Rs 11.15	(If 50 tonnes of fuel wood is available per hectare).

country to country cooperation—amongst the Third World countries. They can borrow each other's expertise for surveying. Additionally, even the developed countries can provide excellent technical surveying aid to such countries.

The second step in terms of planning would be techno-economic-feasibility-status-report of a particular small source. This calls for a certain kind of expertise which, while using the known methods of project evaluation can give a clue as to selection of the right energy alternate. It is surprising how such calculations can amply help discard the fact, occasionally advanced, in that the small energy sources do not have any economic edge whatsoever.

Finally, at the planning stage itself, apart from current allocations to a project for tapping a new or small source, there is need to provide for significant allocations towards research and development (R& D) work pertaining to the technology perfection or to achieve technology self-reliance.

Except in the case of the rural need for plenty of energy input for agricultural activities, insofaras the essential areas of planning are concerned, one can concentrate on the following four common needs of the rural and urban poor:

(1) Domestic lighting and cooking fuel needs (Fuel Power);
(2) Transportation needs (mobility);
(3) Small industry needs (mechanical power); and
(4) Civic and community amenities needs (street lighting, drinking water, etc.).

Two additional points with respect to scientific "need based energy planning" will be in order. Firstly, for long-range Need/Research, forecasting exercise, is an important prerequisite to generate several alternatives before an energy plan can be formulated. Secondly, in the rural context, in particular, as a UN Report pointed out, "much greater emphasis will have to be given to self-sufficient systems involving the maximum use of solar, wind, water and biological energy than to trickle down benefits of centralized systems", such as the Rural Electrification Scheme or the idea of setting up of the Nuplex (Nuclear Agro-Industrial complex). It means that in a given Energy Plan a great deal of resources will have to be released "to implement more quickly maturing decentralized schemes." Essentially, the suggestion offered here only says that the 'planning for rural energy supplies need not be separated from national energy planning; rather than rural energy supply should not be contingent on centralized energy system but should be separately planned for and integrated, whenever possible, with centralized system'. This principle re-establishes the important contribution that small energy sources can make, besides meriting a detailed discussion of the organizational and institutional aspects, to which we now turn.

Institutional and Organizational Aspects

No matter how we look at the choice of a correct organizational form for the exploitation and harnessing of the small energy sources integral to the national energy policy of a country, one thing is absolutely clear that, as far as possible, multiplicity of organization dealing with energy be eliminated or at any rate minimized.

A single line of command ensures speed and coordination between the centralized structure and the decentralized centres or units.

There are views for and against a monolithic centralized organization. It has been argued that—if you are dealing with atomic energy, there is a justification for a centralized organisation. But when you deal with small and renewable sources of energy, a decentralized system is better. No clear-cut academic or administrative principle is involved here. The expediency demands that energy policy and planning has to be a well-coördinated centralized function. In fact, in my view, even R & D activity, pertaining to small energy sources equally deserves to be a centralized operation. Let us explain it further.

In the Third World context where, the lead to evolve a National Energy Plan and its implementation rests with the State, we need to have at an apex level, a National or a "Federal Small Energy Sources Commission" and at the grass root level or the field level, according to the peculiarity and the conditions of a country, we need to have a number of Rural/Urban Small Energy Centres. An interesting illustration of such a combination can be seen in the recently established Commission for Additional Sources of Energy by the Government of India.

This Commission is responsible for:

(1) formulating policies and programmes for the development of new and renewable sources of energy;

(2) coordinating and intensifying R&D activities;

(3) taking conscious steps for commercialization, exploitation of the technologies already developed or being developed; and

(4) for ensuring implementation of Government's policies in regard to all matters concerning all types of new and renewable sources of energy.

This Commission is also required to function as a Data Bank on all aspects of new and renewable sources of energy; be responsible for international cooperation, and for operation of industrial import licensing policies and procedures in this area; advise the Government on import of technology, and recommend various intensive measures for production and utilization of new and renewable energy products, devices and systems.

This centralized Commission will have under it a variety of centres, such as, the Solar-Thermal Energy Centre, the National Solar Photovoltaic Energy Administration Centre, the Wind Energy Centres, the Biomass Energy Centres, and the Technical Advisory Committee to direct activities in the area of ocean energies. It shall also have a number of task forces for R & D programmes, or in specialized context, for exploitation of hydrogen energy, etc.

Whereas the above cited Centres have a special focus on R&D and design engineering but when we talk of the needs of the rural and urban poor, we have to set-up Small Energy Centres too, preferably in their neighbourhood. Such Small Energy Sources Centres would *inter alia* be responsible for the following functions:

(1) exploitation, generation and production of small energy sources;

(2) developing an energy distribution system;

(3) installation of a maintenance system; and

(4) acting as a Centre for spreading energy awareness and for demonstration.

Additionally, the centres can also provide to 'the apex body and other concerned specialized R&D centres feedback data on items such as:

(1) costs;
(2) problems of social acceptance;
(3) utilization of the local raw material;
(4) report on the success or failure of a given system or application;
(5) data on organizational and maintenance aspects; and
(6) other technical details concerning the permutation and combinations of different energy sources that can be combined to meet diverse local energy needs.

It is necessary to reiterate that, the advanced and developed countries have several infrastructural advantages, even advantages of media or advanced communication systems and, therefore, the enlightened user of energy and people having near homogenized socio-cultural ethos in such countries, are not living in the kind of poverty ridden rural/urban poor of the Third World we are focussing on. Such nations have the capability to instal capital intensive energy delivery systems.

In the context of the less developed Third World countries, adoption of technology has to be a slow and phased activity due to lack of infrastructural facilities, finance and sometimes due to problems of language or even illiteracy. In his paper entitled, "The Design of Rural Energy Centres", Dr. A.K.N. Reddy has made the following pertinent observation:

"Notwithstanding the technical attractiveness of establishing a complete rural energy centre as a 'one-shot affair', there is an important sociological reason why technological innovations must be introduced a few at a time and not all at once. Each innovation constitutes a perturbation imposed upon the village system which is forced to go into a transient response before settling down to a new state of equilibrium. It is the finite relaxation time of the village system which demands that new innovations be introduced only after the system has recovered from the previous ones. In other words, because the technology subsystem must fit into the larger socio-economic and cultural system of the village, it follows that a rural energy centre must grow in a phased manner; it must not be externally imposed as one massive perturbation which throws the village system into an instability from which it can save itself only by rejecting altogether the technological 'fix'. The phased growth of a rural energy-centre also facilitates the mid-phase and inter-phase modifications of total system design which are certain to become necessary because of inadequate a *priori* understanding of villages and/or complex energy systems.

To sum up, therefore, while designing an institutional frame for smell energy sources we need, at the apex level, a National Small Energy Sources Commission. This should be supported by appropriate specialized Research and Development Centres for different small sources of energy. Such a centralized system should, in turn, be dovetailed to a field network of several Rural/Urban Small Energy Centres.

Four additional management points, however, are important and should be kept in mind. First point relates itself to the organization and funding of R & D Back-up System for Small Energy Sources. It has been noticed that, in most Third World countries, initiative for R&D unlike the Western countries where private industry took a lead, has come from the State, who have encouraged the setting up of either a chain of National Laboratories, or, are in the process of sponsoring and funding research in the Engineering and Technical Institutes and Universities, etc. Such diffused funding of R & D in a given area, say solar research, to a number of individuals and institutions may sometimes not lead to well-coordinated critical results. Such amorphous and disjointed and individualistic research may prove subcritical. It is, therefore, important that in order to accelerate the pace of R&D and in order to minimize costs, organizationally speaking, we need a single umbrella organization, of all those engineers, technologists, planners and designers, who should be brought together to work in a coordinated manner. In this context we are not suggesting any dilution of the academic autonomy for scientific and technical research. Instead, the key point lies in the fact that if, a nation is serious about making an early technological breakthrough then, for better results, the piecemeal distribution of funds is potently bad management. What is needed is that, under a single umbrella, all experts available in the country should be asked to work against a time bound and well-coordinated R&D objective. A classical management example is provided by the NASA where, for a single objective, 33,000 narrow specialities were dovetailed and coordinated to yield time bound successful results.

The decentralized Rural/Urban, Small Energy Centres, even if they are predominantly engineering and technological units and staffed by such technical experts, they need to establish good coordination interface relationship with the appropriate local administrative functionaries operating in the region where the Energy Centre is located. It is purely a problem of seeking cooperation. This second point concerns itself with the management of the interface questions amongst organizations operating at the grass-root level.

If a Small Energy Sources Centre, is thus, being set-up in a particular district or a Commune or a Prefect, it is essential that such a Centre has a good rapport and coordination with the local district authorities since such a Centre cannot operate in its own grand isolation. Besides, without the local authorities' cooperation, it will fail in its mission of reaching people and community to satisfy and meet their energy needs involving setting up of a distribution and socially viable delivery system. It will be more so in societies which are poor and, socially, highly fragmented.

Thirdly, an inherent limitation in the administrative style of the Third World countries is that any new programme pertaining to socio-economic development, or, even that of science and technological development is saddled with, and suffers from pre-dominantly, by bureaucratic red-tape. Since the leadership comes from the Government, the State functionaries, who are members of the elite bureaucratic core, also play the role of a social change-and-developmental-agent. Whereas at the policy making level bureaucrats, supported by technically qualified advisory groups, will have a major say, yet, at the operational level we need to have a major say of the scientists, technologists, engineers and other energy experts.

Operational institutions and centres with a grass-root network should have more experts and technologists than members of the die-hard bureaucracy at the "Energy Policy" level.

It is to be understood that in order to let the small energy sources make a tangible contribution towards meeting the community's energy needs the same *modus operandi*, which was once used by companies, who introduced electricity, in different countries decades ago, necessarily, be copied in one way or the other.

Finally, whatever be the institutional or organizational form, in the current day developmental efforts, it is also necessary that-at the grass-root level, we consciously involve consumers and people. The community participation in programmes extending developmental services of which energy constitutes a very major segment is an inescapable necessity. We would not attempt to describe here the various ways in which community participation can be ensured. One can simply emphasize that community participation, in the context of Third World nations, is extremely important not merely to obtain a wider-spread of benefits but also to make operations of a network, administratively effective and socially successful (See the Chart).

Technological, R&D, Commercialization and Informational Aspects

The technology status and technology availability depends on many factors such as, capital, import capability, status of Science and Technology, manpower, and that of Research, Development and Design activities in a country.

Secondly, today in many sectors, technology is like a 'toy'. Either a nation has the inherent capability to "build" it or to buy it.

Thirdly, all technologies travel in the geographical sense across the national and the regional borders; except that it takes "time".

Fourthly, all technologies, initially have a high cost but over the time it usually goes down.

Finally, the real application of technological success requires a certain degree of knowledge, skill and creative back-up and in Engineering and Manufacturing context—continuous maintenance back-up.

In the case of small energy sources, a great deal of effort, in using appropriate technology, rests with a healthy research and development network. Research, development and design engineering holds the key to instal an efficient and economical energy delivery system.

The maximum use of local raw materials and a mechanism where maintenance support system and maintenance training can be set-up would, by and large be intergral to the effective R&D establishments.

We have already hinted that R &D can have both, centralized as well as decentralized, network. This would be determined by the R&D task in hand. The success of such a network can be ensured through adequate linkages whereby, up and down communication, is possible. Additionally, we need suitable conduits and allied mechanisms to help diffuse R&D efforts towards commercialization and horizontal transfer of such relevant technologies.

It must be repeated that resources need not be wasted amongst too many marginal R&D efforts. It only will lead to lack of criticality in the development of any single technology. It has also been observed that, in the Third World countries, there is usually reluctance to support large-scale field trials of more promising technologies. It is necessary that R&D activities when they have attained a pilot stage are handed over for commercialization. It is quite possible that in the field of energy some States would like to make this activity an exclusive affair of the Government. However, in order to have such commercialization, which may help reduce technological cost, it is necessary that the private manufacturer or manufacturers, who are a public sector undertaking, are associated in some manner with the progress of R&D work from as early a stage as possible. It may be worthwhile to mentioning here that, sometimes, many private entrepreneurs have unproven indigenous capability. It will be a useful idea, as is the case with the National Research Development Corporation of India, that the State could participate in building up the initial R&D capability towards commercialization stage and subsidize, by 50 per cent, the cost of such development. Other similar incentives are discussed elsewhere.

Creating Energy Awareness: Informational Aspects

The creation of energy consciousness and awareness is another important feature whereby, one can make an impact on people's lifestyle, firstly, to accept a new form of energy and, secondly, to reduce the wasteful and high energy consuming social and other practices. The very fact that the rural poor predominately depend on firewood—which is leading to forest depletion and likely near future occurrence of the fuel famines—making them change over to other forms of energy alternate, is by no means an easy task. This calls for first, the development of alternate small energy source, and secondly, that of its popularization and general use, be it a solar, bio-mass, wind or any other alternative. This being an additional challenge of generating, demonstrating and popularizing appropriate skills.

Instead of depletion of forest, the use of village wood lots and energy plantations, is not merely (i) an R&D exercise; (ii) it is also a commercialization proposition, and (iii) it is a communication function to persuade people to change their old habits and lifestyle.

The introduction of micro hydro-generators in hills and areas where fast moving small rivulets are running is, likewise, (i) an R&D function, (ii) a communication function and (iii) a horizontal diffusion of technological function.

It can be seen that as a commercial activity, any small source demands application of the most subtle high level design engineering and manufacturing qualities.

It is necessary to make such alternate technologies take root, they are popularized, and given an adequate, demonstration, and informational spread. The key question still remains how can we cut down the cost of such new sources for millions. Let's face it that the real contribution of small energy sources in any society would rest on how the State can handle its financial and commercial aspects.

A positive recommendation that one can make here is that for "R&D, Technology and Commercialization" International cooperation can come if, like World Bank, the UN also sets up, a "Technology Bank" from which the Third countries can supplement and reinforce their own R&D and Technological and Commercialization efforts.

A final word may be added in the context of Technology Assessment (TA). As is the case with most technologies, we have, while choosing a Technology, or a particular small energy source, also to take care to avert social and environmental adverse effects.

An interesting sociological facet can be glimpsed from the fact that in some parts of India where community bio-gas (based on cowdung and vegetable wastes) was introduced, it affected the livelihood of such people, whose main source of income, was free collection of cow dung, as a source of fuel, and also, as a source of income, for selling of the dung cake.

Apparently, introduction of a new technology, namely, bio-gas—which is a small source of energy—had severe social implications for the vulnerable sections of the society. It is not being suggested here that same would be true in other cases also. But the fact remains that, until and unless, we examine the social impact of a technology, particularly, its long-range consequences, third order consequences, it would be unwise to opt for a particular technology in a big way—even if it be for a "small source of energy".

The Financial Aspects

The financing of the "small energy sources" in order to make them available free or available at near "zero-cost-energy" would entail, at least, in the Third World country context, heavy subsidizing. Tax incentives and subsidies have also to be extended to such manufacturers, who go into the manufacture of technologies relevant to the small source energy.

The Indian example, in this respect, is worth mentioning. For instance, in order to (i) provide promotional incentives and (ii) keep the initial cost structure of the devices and systems for small source energy and (iii) achieve better market penetration on a large-scale and its widespread adoption in commercial and industrial use, the Government of India has decided to introduce several schemes of incentives so that the barriers to rapid commercialization of small energy sources and equipment can be overcome.

Amongst others, it includes (i) enhanced depreciation allowance of 30 per cent on machinery or plant installed for manufacturing renewable energy devices and systems; and (ii) a similar enhanced depreciation allowance on renewable energy devices or systems used for business or profession.

The Government has also exempted from the excise duty, the devices and systems designed to use solar, biomass and wind energy.

Indian financial institutions have agreed to treat the institutional credit for the manufacture and installation of renewable energy systems on the same terms and conditions as are applicable to the priority sector.

Those eligible under the Differential Rate of Interest Scheme can also avail of the facility of institutional finance for using renewable energy appliances for productive purposes.

This ensures that financial institutions will provide loans on suitable terms both for manufacturers and for users, who wish to instal such equipment.

Further, like any other industry, this industry will also be eligible under the existing deferred payment schemes of the financial institutions.

It is apparent that the association of banks with the small energy source operations, in all its forms—from the site of survey to R&D, to technological operations and manufacture to dissemination, distribution and the setting up of the programmes for deliveries and supplies, including information dissemination—at all these stages, banking and other financial institutions will have to be involved, as they play an important role in every development programme.

Conclusion

Briefly the plea that we make here is that the small energy sources deserve the application of both high level management and a systems-approach of the same order, as any other source of energy would need it.

Secondly, so far as the fiscal aspects are concerned, in the initial stages, sufficient financial inputs will have to be provided by the State in order to make these energy sources widely available.

And, finally, the aim should be to dovetail Small Energy Sources towards the energy supply of at least near 'zero-private-cost energy' to the poorest, neediest and the vulnerable poor masses of various Third World nations, at least, for cooking fuel.

All this can be possible only if, the Third World countries set up an accelerated R&D efforts and seek fiscal, technological and manpower support through North-South dialogue. This can be done through international and regional cooperation and country-to-country bilateral science and technology agreements.

UN should, perhaps, seriously consider the setting up of a "UN Technology Bank for Small Energy Sources".

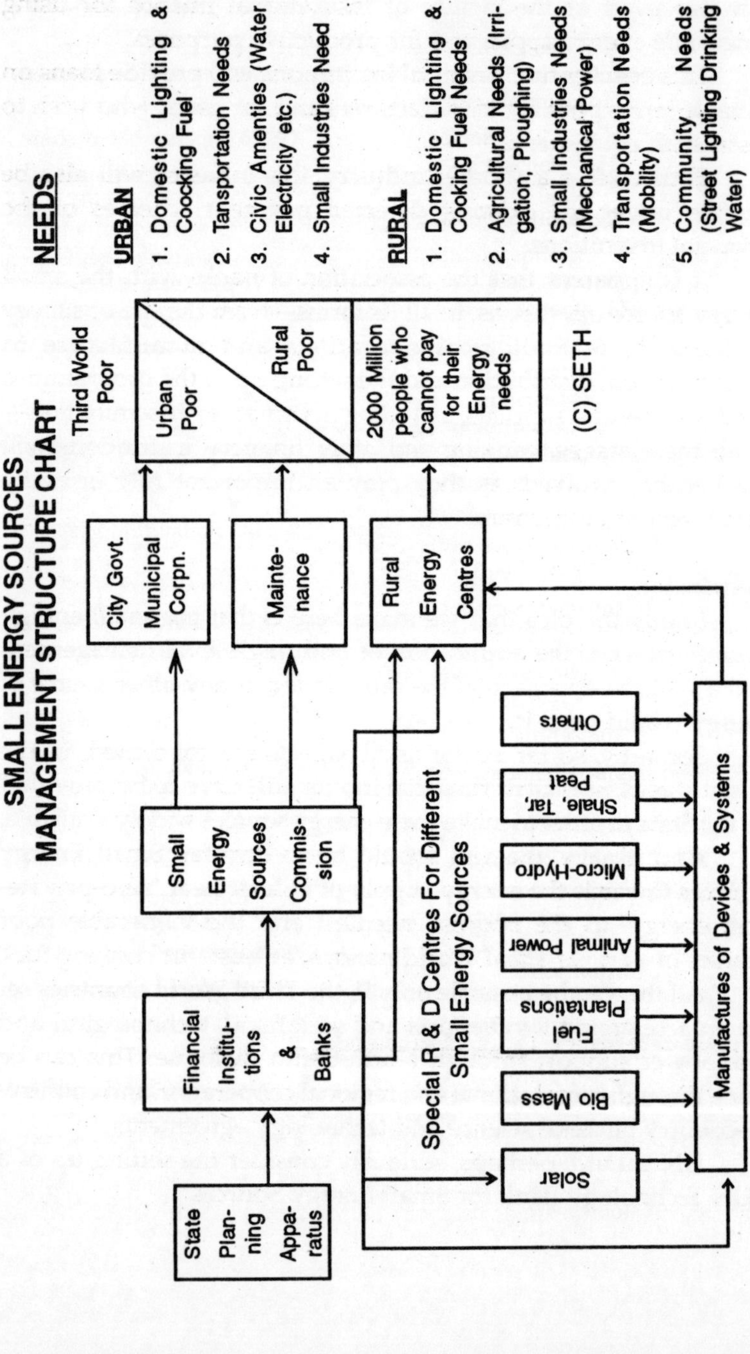
SMALL ENERGY SOURCES
MANAGEMENT STRUCTURE CHART
State Plan-ning Appa-ratus
Financial Institu-tions & Banks
Small Energy Sources Commis-sion
City Govt. Municipal Corpn.
Mainte-nance
Rural Energy Centres
Third World Poor
Urban Poor
Rural Poor
2000 Million people who cannot pay for their Energy needs
(C) SETH
Special R & D Centres For Different Small Energy Sources
Solar
Bio Mass
Fuel Plantations
Animal Power
Micro-Hydro
Shale, Tar, Peat
Others
Manufactures of Devices & Systems
NEEDS
URBAN
1. Domestic Lighting & Coocking Fuel
2. Tansportation Needs
3. Civic Amenties (Water Electricity etc.)
4. Small Industries Need
RURAL
1. Domestic Lighting & Cooking Fuel Needs
2. Agricultural Needs (Irri-gation, Ploughing)
3. Small Industries Needs (Mechanical Power)
4. Transportation Needs (Mobility)
5. Community Needs (Street Lighting Drinking Water)

THE INFORMATION AGE

*W. Harman**

It has become commonplace to hear the "next era" of industrial society described as "the information age" or some equivalent appellation. The phrase has somewhat the ring of self-evident truth about it. Both because of increased educational levels and because of the development of information-handling technology prodigious in its capabilities, manipulation of information, will, no doubt be more evident compared to manipulation of physical materials and things.

Yet, it is equally clear that when phrases like "the information age" are used, often people have very different images in their mind. I would like to contrast three such images of "the information age" to remind you of their differences, and to hazard a guess as to which way we might be headed for (or in process of choosing). So that we can deal with these more conveniently, I'll give them different names: the "information society", the "knowledge society", and the "learning society". We will be talking about three different emphasis, recognizing, of course, that any real society is going to involve a mixture of emphasis and so such designation is going to be fully accurate.

The Information Society

A familiar argument for the "information society" goes like this: Originally, every industrial country was agrarian, with the largest number of workers on the land. After the industrial revolution, the fraction of workers involved in industrial production increased steadily, and the fraction of agricultural workers decreased. Then, more recently, the fraction counted in the "services" increased and came to predominate over the production fraction. Now we are moving into a period when the largest fraction of workers will be classed as "information workers".

* Outline of the "keynote luncheon" remarks by Dr. Willis Harman, (SRI International) at the First Global Conference on the Future, held at Toronto, July 22, 1980.

Thus, we will have electronic mail, bill paying, newspapers, library access; two-way and multiplex electronic links to people, to information, to services, to entertainment. Most workers will be primarily involved with processing information; a large portion of the manufacturing and physical services will be automated or semi-automated. Appliances and production equipment will be "smart," small microprocessors giving them the equivalent of brains superior to those of most animals. Intellectual and mental capabilities will be extended. Conceptual knowledge will be the source of continuing innovation, and the guide to policy formulation.

The information society accepts as axiomatic that jobs, welfare, and education depend upon the continuing and accelerating generation of wealth in the economy. When the market approaches saturation in the areas of material goods and physical services, information is the great "renewable resource". Dedicating itself to ever-increasing processing of information, society can create the jobs needed by a workforce not so necessary as before for goods and services; jobs, in turn, create the demand to keep the economy rolling. The new version of planned obsolescence is that every few years we will need to replace our appliances for "smarter" ones.

There are a couple of flaws in this picture. There is a high correlation, in the modern economy, between economic activity (even information processing) and resource use; and a high correlation between resource use and overall impact on the environment (even with a thriving "pollution control industry"). Thus, planetary constraints on economic activity have to be taken seriously. Also, we have already seen the early signs of consumer resistance to some aspects of the information society depicted by: limited demand for information services, resistance to the cashless/ checkless society, resistance to electronic label-reading in supermarket checkout stands, etc.

Progress toward the "information society" might be headed for a slow-down.

The Knowledge Society

Let me define a different version which for our purposes today we will call a "knowledge society." Planetary limits to economic activity are recognized, and the role of consumer is perceived as not being humankind's penultimate destiny. There is "re-rationalizing" of the economy; material consumption is down and there is more emphasis on quality, including durability. Economic indicators of the past, which tended to measure throughput of energy and materials, have been replaced with more suitable measures. There is an appropriate technology emphasis, typified by the hand-held calculator and the well-made hand tool. Work sharing has brought increased leisure to all, and much of this leisure is used in the pursuit of knowledge. Informal gift and barter economies flourish, and decentralizations are the order of the day with decentralization of production, population, economic activity, and mass culture.

In the "knowledge society," priorities are rearranged. Pursuit of understanding and wisdom ranks high and mindless consumption ranks low. "Wealth creating" activities have been diminished; in a material sense, all may have somewhat less, although in quality of living, most have more. Global competition has been reduced and around the world local self-reliance has been encouraged.

This "knowledge society," too, has some potential flaws. Its successful evolvement requires a significant amount of change in individual and, particularly, in institutionalized values. There is some tendency to consider work—at least work in the mainstream economy—as a scarce commodity that had to be rationed, which is a fundamentally questionable proposition.

The Learning Society

There is still another related image of where we might move to, which was termed by Robert Hutchins "The Learning Society," in a book that attracted considerable attention in the mid-Sixties. Both Hutchins and Lewis Mumford pointed out the pertinence of the Greek concept of "Paidea." The basic premise of Paidea was that it is the whole societal matrix from which we learn. Thus, learning is not a task administered by the schools and universities, but the responsibility of every institution in society, from the family to the counterpart of the transnational corporation. Furthermore, the curriculum is not a restricted set of knowledge and skills, but the whole of living. In scholar Waner Jaeger's tome on the subject, the central task in Paidea is described in a chapter entitled "The Search for the Divine Center."

We moderns have been inclined to treat history as though we had little to learn from the past. Yet, there are numerous signs that this Greek model may be more pertinent than we might have thought, in spite of the obvious differences between ancient Greece and modern Toronto. In the culture, we see a renascence of interest in things transcendental, and calls for a re-spiritualization of our institutions. In science, on the fringe sometimes called "consciousness research" or "transpersonal psychology," issues thought dead since science explained away religion several generations ago, have re-emerged as very live issues. (One tangible sign of this is last October's international colloquium on "Science and Consciousness" in Cordoba, Spain, sponsored by the French government).

A "learning society" on the Paidea model would have many characteristics in common with the "knowledge society," with a much clearer rationale and perhaps a deeper commitment to the transcendentally based values required to make that society work. The "central project" of the "learning society" is the social and spiritual evolvement of humankind. It has what industrial society has lacked, a wholesome balance between the concern for the outer world and the deep searching of the world of inner experience. Because of this, it is less confused on value issues than the modern world.

THE GLOBAL TRANSITION TO THE SOLAR AGE

Hazel Henderson

The premise of my work over the past fifteen years was studying the transition of industrial societies from their non-renewable resource base as they shifted toward a new base of renewable resources. This transition is both inevitable and evolutionarily necessary, and the only question is whether industrial leaders will recognize this shift and work with it or continue to try to override its signals.

In fact, the wrenching shifts to sustainable and ecologically-viable forms of productivity have been manifesting themselves in many ways since the 60s. But the overall pattern of this great industrial transition, until recently, has been obscured and mis-diagnosed by obsolete analytical and policy tools. These events and changes have ranged from new forms of social pathology: such as domestic resource-based inequities, permitting old and poor people to die of lack of heat, to international conflicts and the spiralling arms race. They have included the appearance of new "post-materialist" values in industrial societies, shifting geopolitical power and terms of trade to the new Gordian knot of oil prices, Third World debt and the continuing threats they pose to the global banking system. The underlying pattern in all these events has been concealed by the myopia of traditional economics (whether market-oriented or socialistic); by industrializm's fragmented, Cartesian worldview which, in turn allowed its single-minded pursuit of mass production, undifferentiated growth of Gross National Product, its over-aggregation of energy statistics and models and its narrow definition of "efficiency", "growth" and human welfare.

Of course, the inevitability of this great transition of industrial societies to sustainable renewable resources based productivity has been evident for decades to those trained in the life sciences, as well as many thermodynamicists, chemists, engineers, physicists and systems analysts, not to mention many sociologists, anthropologists and psychologists and millions of well-rounded citizens and generalists. But as the great industrial societies reached their fossil-fueled zeniths in the 50s and the "Soaring Sixties", signs of trouble were only publicized by a courageous few, such as Rachel Carson, whose warning note in *Silent Spring, Hidden Costs and Subsidies* was dismissed in 1962 by the celebrants of industrialism's success.

So great was the euphoria that ominous social costs, from polluted air and water, to deteriorating cities, mass transit of all infrastructure were ignored. But not only were the social and environmental costs of industrialism ignored, so were its many subsidies unaccounted for in economic models.

The social subsidies hidden from analyses were based on a set of industrial values we now view as colonialism, racism and sexism. For example, the colonial value-system was perpetrated in globally inequitable terms of trade which locked Third World countries into such deals as those by which Ghana still sells its hydroelectricity for aluminium smelting, at a fraction of world energy market prices, or misguided development advice and "assistance" which created today's external energy and technological dependencies on the North. The hidden subsidies to industrial economies by domestic colonialism, i.e. racism, included categorizing many lowly but indispensable maintenance jobs as "less productive", for example, garbage collectors, industrial cleaners and janitors mass transit, road maintenance and other public services workers, hospital orderlies, domestic and farm workers as reserved for Blacks, Hispanics or other less powerful ethnic minorities. The subsidies provided by indigenous Native Americans were literally Inestimable, as their lands and resources were plundered by force, and their peace treaties abrogated each time another energy or mineral resource became commercially attractive.

Lastly, the subsidies provided to the monetized GNP sector by sexism are only now coming into full view. The energy profligate mushrooming of the "Suburban Lifestyle" was almost totally predicated on the unpaid labour of the American woman. She was relied upon to maintain the single-family suburban home and backyard, parent the children, serve on school boards, volunteer for a host of community services and most of all to fill the key job of incessant chauffering of the automobilized population, on which the whole lifestyle depended. Not only was this huge subsidy unrecognized, but also the American woman's role as "heroic consumer", trained in millions of home economics courses and advertising, supported "service" magazines for her key role in "keeping up with the jones" and thus maintaining Keynesian demand-led, economic growth.

A Model Challenged

As recently as a decade ago all of these lynch-pins of the industrial value-system were accepted with little question. Today, all of it has changed. The advent of OPEC and the subsequent private bank "recycling" of petrodollars has altered the fundamental relationship between industrial and Third World countries. The formerly unacknowledged interdependencies are now crucial agenda items in recent economic summit meetings and those of the foreseeable future. The old bankers' adage has entered the vernacular "if the bank lends you $100, it's your problem; if it lends you $100 million, it's the bank's problem". Similarly, the subsidies of racism must increasingly be accounted for in the GNP. Black voters are proving this locally, in Chicago and Philadelphia as well as in national politics, as they and Hispanic Americans change the economic rules as their clout increases. And political strategists ponder the growing "gender gap" in the voting patterns of women. While native American people battle in courts and legislatures for their land and resources rights, they are also trying to teach us how their value systems protected resources and fostered sustained yield productivity, making them almost "invisible farmers" of North America's natural ecosystem and wildlife.

By the late 60s, many of these formerly hidden environmental and social costs had become visible enough to produce citizen protest movements in most industrial societies, whether to fight pollution, or lobby for civil rights, corporate and government accountability, better mass transit, housing and to reduce the dangers of nuclear proliferation and the arms race. But still the grand pattern of the industrial transition did not become fully clear until the onset of the "Stagflation of 70s". Until then politicians had the comparatively simple task of maintaining GNP-growth, while keeping both inflation and unemployment at politically-acceptable low levels. Resources were still readily available or could be cheaply imported from Third World countries; citizen movements had not gained sufficient political clout to enforce many of the new regulations on industries that dumped toxic wastes, discriminated against women and minorities or exposed their workers to hazardous materials.

OPEC Invites Economists to Learn

Right upto 1973, economists ignored the special role of fossil energy as the flywheel of traditional industrialism. Energy was still a vague, highly-aggregated single input in most production models assumed to be inexhaustible and interchangeable as long as the price was right. So when OPEC flexed its muscles in 1973, thousands of biologists, ecologists, thermodynamicists and systems analysts rejoiced discreetly. At least OPEC would force economists to learn to respect the basic laws of physics and ground their abstractions in some base-line data from the natural world.

Economists were challenged to disaggregate their energy supply-demand models, to look at end-use efficiencies; to make net-energy analyses; and to adopt life-cycle costing comparisons for investment. Even more embarrassing, they were forced to account for social impacts, environmental costs and even acknowledge that "pollutants" and "wastes" were in reality often valuable resources misplaced and mislabelled and sometimes even with "profits" going up in smoke. At the micro-level, all this was pretty obvious, but at the macro-economic management level all these realities were still blurred by the heroic abstractions of national data-averaging national energy planners with their "supply side" models and the general schizophrenic faith in the workings of the "free market" even as they poured well over a hundred billion of taxpayers money into subsidizing coal, nuclear, oil and gas. Rather than disaggregate these national models, economists continued to ponder over the obvious symptoms of the transition to renewable resources. The two surrogate variables for all the factors economists had left out became inflation and unemployment as they pursued the old capital/energy-intensive path at the expense of jobs. But no longer were inflation and unemployment the trade-offs familiar to economists in the past as the "Phillips curve" but both marched upward in "stagflation" and during the 70s each recession left both inflation and unemployment higher than before.

Citizen's Transformational Movements

By the early 70s, citizen's movements started responding to the situation with a positive agenda. They organized for safe, renewable energy development, emphasizing its labour-intensity; conservation and weatherization programs rather than new electric plant construction; smaller-scaled democratized technologies that decentralized economic and political power; re-trofitting and renewing old center cities, revitalizing mass transit, local self-reliance and alternative economic development and enterprise. Their cause all began to flow together in their global agendas of transition to a planetary "solar age" which might reduce militaristic confrontations over non-renewable resources a saner, more equitable, ecologically-viable world order and a totally new path of "development" centered on human rights and basic unmet needs of grassroots populations, rather than continuing to chase undifferentiated, per capita-averaged, economic growth. All these "transformational" movements in industrial countries came up with remarkable similar sets of agendas, and energy alternatives were basic to all of them: different mixes appropriate to each country of solar, wind, hydro, biomass, peat, biofuels, ocean-thermal wave or tidal power, solar ponds and a ubiquitous emphasis on organic agriculture, passive architecture, redesigning communities for safe walking and cycling and overall energy conservation, and efficiency ratings for cars, appliances, production processes and waste recycling. All these alternatives began to be seen as facets of the same transition, and while still derided by the central planners and politicians and corporate giants, generally captured much public imagination as more creative, innovative and viable than continuing the old centralized, standardized march to traditional industrial goals, now only producing an ever-more debt-inflated GNP and unemployment.

The Hoax of Full Employment

There was a dawning realization that the most basic promise of industrialism: "full employment" was a cruel hoax. In 1978 the Organization for Economic Cooperation and Development (OECD) warned that due to continued, capital-intensity and automation and the micro-processor revolution, the 1980s would be an "era of jobless economic growth". Today, there are some 35 million people unemployed in OECD's twenty-four member countries. But minority groups and women began to point out an even more fundamental hoax in the promise of "full employment" — it was based on exclusion of many groups from the workforce, from black teenagers to women. In fact, industrialism's definition of "full employment" was actually predicated on excluding half the population out of the workforce: the woman-keeping the home fires burning and powering the suburban lifestyle. Today, not only over half of the workforce consists of women (mostly single breadwinners or supplementing their husbands' inadequate income or unemployment checks) but only 12 per cent of all US families conform to the statistical norm of the nuclear male-earner headed household.

New Consumption Habits

Further, as a result of the changing role of the American woman, who no longer has time to serve as the "heroic consumer", the world economies can no longer consider US to be the consumption-led "locomotive" of world recovery. As Franz Schurmann, historian of the University of California at Berkeley points out, over 60 per cent of US women who are now in the workforce have drastically changed their consumption habits to basic needs, fewer goods and more services, for example, education, day care, energy and shelter. Already we see how such shifts have changed basic patterns of production and consumption. Day-care is one of our fastest growing industries as parenting becomes monetized. Cooking is now in the money economy with fast food eateries, while all those other time-consuming chores from food shopping and cleaning to cooking and waiting for the appliance repairman, baby-sitting and home maintenance are shared by men. For example, one Madison Avenue survey leads to the conclusion that advertisers must now sell washing powders and toilet bowl cleaners with great respect, since almost 50 per cent of their users are now men.

The energy-consumption shifts that are driving and being driven by such changes and major value-shifts now transform industrial cultures. Your own market surveys attest to these trends towards the do-it-yourself, home-centered consumption, the doubling-up and "downward mobility" in the housing market. Other studies from Yankelovich, Stanford Research Institute, Harris and Roper and John Naisbitt's Trend Reports underline these value shifts. Away from traditional suburban materialism, to self-reliance and mutual aid in health care, bartering services, sharing and except for government (which has increased its energy use since Mr Reagan's supply siders took office) the overall shift to energy-conservation as a way of life. *Business Week*'s Harris poll (4 April, 1982) found that over 35 per cent of consumers said they would use less energy even if the price fell between 10 to 20 per cent while 25 per cent said they would not increase their consumption. And the biggest new energy market, now up for grabs, is that for energy-saving systems which sells currently to the tune of $ 1. 2 billion annually in building control systems alone.

Meanwhile the increasing social costs of relying on traditional energy sources is clear: from the almost total unpredictability of oil supplies and prices, to the problems of cleaning up coal's sulphur emissions, acid rain and atmospheric CO_2 levels rise to the level of international issues. Homeowners are shying away from natural gas in the faces of rising prices and deregulation. Wall Street turns away from nuclear power as the bond markets are threatened by possible massive defaults as in the case of Washington's WPPSS debacle, the new NRC crack-downs on nuclear utility operators' safety violations and new citizen drives to elect state utility commissions or further politicize their rate increase attempts. In addition, the Supreme Court's upholding of California's right to ban new nuclear plants, the recent defeat of the Clich River Breeder funding and the administration's second thoughts about funding massive coal gasification and liquification projects all raise new uncertainties that affect the traditional energy sources. Of course, government policy reverses on renewable energy research, development, commercialization and tax policies have also created a continuing nightmare of uncertainties for the renewable industries, as most industrial governments continue trying to override the signal of the transition and bail out their dinosaur industries and lobbies.

Policy Makers do not Understand

But as we moved into the 1980s, while sociologists were confirming that a social revolution had already occurred, the reactions of a "politics of the last hurrah" set in, whether Reaganomics in the US, Thatcherism in Britain or the new German Chancellor Helmut Kohl. Yet now in the 80s, we see these hapless politicians trying to steer their ships of state in reverse, while their citizens are no longer listening to them since the new issues are beyond the old formulas of both Left and Right and the old rhetoric of economists, whether Keynesian, supply-side, monetarist or that of central socialist planners seems ever more unreal to voters. All the social movements for the transition to Solar Age societies are now linking across national borders, since the conditions they address are similar, whether in socialist France, nationalistic Canada, "free market" oriented Britain and the US or in the hybrids: Sweden, Norway, Denmark, the Netherlands and Japan. In such periods of massive change, politicians and institutions react in one of two ways: either they rigidity and redouble their efforts to apply the remedies that are failing, or they re-conceptualize their whole situation. The "politics of the last hurrah" is everywhere symptomatic of basic political watershed periods, where voters reject both Left and Right and begin to realign. Meanwhile at the 1983 Williamsburg Summit, leaders tried to smooth over the intractability of their problems of industrial transition with familiar platitudes about "re-starting the engines of economic growth" as a panacea for all their woes. Mr Reagan explains away massive deficits on whose elimination he campaigned. Mrs Thatcher continues to decimate British industries under the banner of monetarism. Mr Mitterand, France's socialist

President turns out to be the world's last Keynesian. The Eastern industrial countries suffer from all the same problems from the USSR's sluggish over-centralization and low productivity to Poland, whose workers, revolt against the same dinosaur inflexibility has led to a stalemated economy. Even the "miracle" of Japan's heyday is over, as Mr Nakasone adjusts to lower growth and paying long overdue social and environmental costs overhanging its economy-while juggling Japan's external resource dependencies and bracing for the next "oil shokku".

The Nature of the Transition

As all these countries deal with the transition of industrialism, it becomes clear that this transition is multi-dimensional, non-linear, and practically unmodelable due to domestic and global interlinkages. Since energy and resource patterns form the very foundations of industrial societies their multiplier effects cannot be mapped in simple economic terms but need new interdisciplinary policy models. Only change-models from biology (rather than mechanistic models) can capture these accelerating interactive changes. Such multi-dimensional change processes are common in all living systems as morphogenesis. The processes of morphogenesis are most familiar as the changes from a caterpillar to a chrysalis, to a butterfly. No longer can political leaders be served by economists' models which are based on static, equilibrium or at best, homeostatic change, where the overall structure is stabilized by negative feedback, such as a thermostatic system. Instead, morphogenetic systems are constantly evolving unanticipated new structure, because they are governed by positive feedback loops, which push many parts of the system over thresholds simultaneously.

Once politicians begin seeing the nature of their industrial transitions they will come to see why the "politic of the last hurrah" and its simple economic remedies cannot work. They will see the vicious circles created by such remedies, for example: each additional 1 per cent of unemployment raises the deficit by some $25 billion, and each additional percentage point of real interest rate adds another $10 billion to the deficit, while lowering federal taxes only increases local and property taxes. Policies focussed on bailing out the past energy and resource patterns will only lead to higher inflation, higher unemployment and higher deficits and real interest rates, leading to an acceleration of world resource competition, the arms race and wars. Even though in the US we are now hearing some political discussion of "transitions" taking place in our economy, there is little realistic description of their nature. Some call for "re-industrialization" (clearly a rear-view mirror attempt to back into the future). Some Democrats briefly flirted with a naive "hi-tech transition scenario" fatally calling themselves Atari Democrats, only to learn earlier this year that Atari Corporation, a "Silicon Valley" employer prototypical of future job-creation, was moving off shore to Taiwan. Labour unions now are talking of industrial policy to guide investment into the "sunrise industries," but they are not talking of the transition to the Solar Age, but some unspecified, hi-tech version of industrialism, hoping that automation and robotics can be tamed to either keep people at the scene of production, if not as employees, then otherwise sharing the fruits of the per capita productivity increases. There is also talk of the transition to an "information society" based on microprocessors and automation of offices and services sector jobs, a scenario referred to as "Daniel Bell Revisited". In Bell's view of "post-industrial society", the early transition from agriculture to manufacturing would simply create plenty of new white collar jobs in the services sector. But this very explosion of the services sector (or the paper-shuffling sector) is now deemed too "unproductive" and is now the very target of the microprocessor revolution, where estimates are that 40 per cent, of all such white collar jobs can be automated. No wonder we are now being sold "space colonization" perhaps as the way to deal with the 35 million already dis-employed and the new ranks of the jobless from automated offices, restaurants, hotels, hospitals and schools. An "industrial policy" bill is now in Congress to create an Economic Cooperation Council. But it is not coming close to the more realistic transition to a sustainable Solar Age, of economic as well as political decentralization and a human-centered, skills-intensive, entrepreneurial path of development where investments are made in human development and resource conservation.

But we should not be surprised that the dinosaurs brains are the last place to get the message that conditions have changed and a grassroots revolution has already occurred. Whether it is New York's Wall Street and broadcast network headquarters or Washington with its 18th century politics, or whether it is the Kremlin, London, Brussels, Paris or Bonn, or the head offices of ever-larger corporate conglomerates, leaders still seek to manipulate the new complexities with statistical illusions, often oblivious to the disastrous local impacts of their economic-based policies. But today, their job is becoming impossible because two new barometers of distress must now be juggled, along with inflation and unemployment: high deficits and high real interest rates. Juggling these four barometers is not possible leading only to vicious circles. If a leader focuses single-mindedly on reducing inflation as have Mr Reagan and Mrs Thatcher, the other three barometers shoot up. In fact, trying to push down any one will only balloon the other three indicators. This is only an illustration of how non-linear, interactive global systems cannot be managed with linear models and tools. The displaced and delayed consequences of all such purely economic manipulation can be seen in an expanded model, where interactions and multiplier effects are familiar to all systems and life scientists, but a terrible shock to economists. Voters no longer believe that economic policy-makers can deliver on their promises, reiterated at the Williamsburg Summit: to simultaneously hold down, inflation, unemployment, interest rates and deficits, along with familiar assurances that their economics will pick up and soon resume growth. As these industrial leaders cajole voters that "things are getting better" we, in the US, must ask "better than what?". The answer is: only better than the past two years of the deepest recession since the depression. For example, the much hailed stock market rally, if corrected for inflation, still leaves the apparently soaring Dow Jones Average in the $300 range, while "full employment targets have drifted upward as they have proved unattainable, from 3 per cent to 7 per cent in the past decade.

We are moving, I contend, into a new era of "post-economic policy-making" a re-mapping of our transformed societies within a tightly interlinked global system created by our own technologies of mass communications, air travel and computer-speeded banking and currency flows. Such a system can no longer function as competing militaristic nation states and transactional corporations. Only cooperation can work in such a globally-interactive system, as bankers are learning, even as they still post "profits" on high-interest-bearing, but "non-performing" loans Defaults by Mexico and Brazil alone would wipe out 95 per cent of the capital of the nine largest US banks and 74 per cent of the capital of the next 15 largest ones. No wonder there are so few who would benefit from a large reduction in oil prices-making such a scenario rather unlikely. But we can be sure that the competition for capital will heat up, as well as the fundamental arguments about—which path public and private investments should take and even whether our projected $200 billion range government deficits will leave much for any private investments in the domestic, civilian economy or our rotting infrastructure after military budget increases are met by more government borrowings instead of tax restructuring and new priorities.

What we see emerging today in all the industrial societies are basic value and behaviour shifts, new perceptions and an emerging paradigm, based on facing up to new awareness of planetary realities and confirmed by a "post-Cartesian" scientific worldview based on biological and systemic life sciences, rather than inorganic, mechanistic models. Its principles can be summed up as:

Inter-connectedness	at every system level
Redistribution	(recycling of all elements and structures)
Heterarchy	(networks and webs of inter-communication, not fixed hierarchies. Many inter-active systems-mutual causality)
Complementarity	(beyond either/or dichotomous logic and zero-sum games, to both/and logics and win/win, cooperative games)
Certainty	(from static, equilibrium models, to probabilistic)
Change	(morphogenetic, and "self-organizing" models of living system and change as fundamental).

The Newly Interlinked Agendas of Citizen

These new worldviews are already generating better policy tools and models, beyond economics: technology assessment, social and job impact studies, environmental impact statements, future research, cross-impact studies, scenario building, global modelling and forecasting no longer based on past trend-extrapolation. At the grassroots level; in academia and all our institutions the politics of reconceptualization has begun. We see it in the newly interlinked agendas of citizens, from the Nuclear Freeze and anti-nuclear anti-war movements, and the emergence of human rights and planetary citizenship. These movements all embrace a new world order based on renewable resources and energy, sustainable forms of productivity and per capita consumption, ecologically-based science and technologies and equitable sharing of resources within and between countries as the only path to peace-keeping and redirecting the billions spent on the global arms race.

Such an agenda is still branded as "impractical" and "idealistic", whereas in truth it is more viable and realistic than those of the "realists" currently leading us toward accidental mass destruction. Today, the worlds' aware citizens are branding this kind of "realism" as demonstrably insane. This "politics of reconceptualization" will overtake the "politics of the last hurrah" and lead to massive realignments, new parties and coalitions, as already evident in several European countries, where old consensus have already splintered and the interim stage of revolving door coalition governments become common. In the US, the "Reagan landslide" and "swing to the right" was mis-diagnosed by old political observers. Mr Reagan's victory comprised only 26 per cent of the registered voters, which in other democracies would have been viewed as almost a *coup d'etat*. The real story was in the 48 per cent of registered voters who did not see any point in voting. In all between Republican or Democrat, and of the 52 per cent who did vote, over half said they voted against either Mr Reagan or Mr Carter. Those who did not vote are not apathetic (they are only cynical and unrepresented) believing that Nader's Golden Rule of Politics applies: 'Those who have gold rule'. This 48 per cent is the nucleus of the as yet nascent "transformational political party". They are doing "politics by other means" at the local level: solar and renewable resource politics, farmer's market and co-op politics, organic agriculture politics, holistic health care politics, worker-ownership and new entrepreneurial enterprise politics, environmental politics, and so on. These people can already form a winning coalition, together with human rights, corporate accountability groups, peace activists, labour and the women's movement. They are also your natural allies who lobby for the transition to the Solar Age and an "industrial policy" based on the Solar Lobby's SENSE (Solar Energy National Security and Employment Act) legislation now gaining support in Congress. But as you have learned in the roller-coaster ride your industries have experienced at the hand of legislators, reliance on these political efforts is not enough. Nor can you afford to rely on the newly-expanded capital market being created by the growing movements of stockholders investing in socially responsible mutual funds, such as Dreyfus Third Century Fund, Pax World Fund, Foursquare or the new one being launched by Shearson—American Express. The Fund for Balanced Investment of the star performer of the group, the Calvert Social Investment Fund, on whose Advisory Board on Social Criteria I serve, along with Amory and Hunter Lovins, Robert Rodale and other advocates of the transition to the Solar Age. Today your industries, in spite of all their recent and continuing difficulties, need to market directly to your customers and to educate the public and promote an understanding of the great industrial transition in the mass media. In this way you will not only assure your own place in the new economy now being born, but can actively hasten the needed "politics of re-conceptualization" to help assure the path to a peaceful, ecologically sane, more equitable world order for our children.

OCEAN FUTURES

R.M.S. Bhargava

Oceans are known to be our "last frontier". They are also termed as the "common heritage of mankind". However, it is very necessary that we should use the oceans wisely because oceans are sources for food energy, minerals including oil and gas. With these objectives in view, a workshop on "Ocean Futures" was held at NIO to prepare a scenario on how we will be using the sea in the year 2000 AD. Dr Quasim and Dr Seth were the workshops Director and Co-Director respectively.

The workshop was inaugurated on March 3, 1981 by Dr Raja Ramanna, Director, Bhabha Atomic Research Centre and Secretary Department of Atomic Energy. Dr Ramanna in his inaugural address emphasized the need for a proper management and utilization of manpower to explore the oceans which have assumed tremendous importance in recent years. Prof Maheshwar Dayal, Adviser, Department of Science and Technology, in his Presidential address stressed the need for the protection of environment from pollution and for effective monitoring of progress of R & D work in marine science.

The workshop was attended by forty invited speakers and participants. It had the following six sessions spread over three days: (1) General Aspect, (2) Resources from the sea, (3) Ocean Engineering and Technology, (4) Ocean, Education and Society, (5) Marine Environment and coastal zone management and 6) Concluding session and Panel discussion. In these sessions, 16 experts in their respective fields highlighted the state of art and the future needs for an effective use of oceans. Seven papers were also presented by the participants. All these areas were discussed at length and two Panel Groups were constituted for an indepth study of ocean futures. The futuristic study led to the identification of four priority areas to cover a span of 25 years.

Excerpts from Workshop on Ocean Futures: The next 24 years, March 3-5, 1981 held at NIO.

These are:

1. Living resources (food and biomedical).
2. Non-living resources (minerals, oil and gas).
3. New resources of energy (thermal, tide, wave and marine biomass).
4. Pollution control.

Emerging from this study by the two Panel Groups, the following recommendations were made at the concluding session of the workshop:

1. Keeping in view the living and non-living resources of the continental shelf, the limits of territorial waters should be extended.
2. Proper protection of territorial waters and economic zone is necessary.
3. Effective technologies should be developed for:
   (a) desalination of sea water;
   (b) utilizing thermal, wave and tidal energy and energy from marine biomass, for the generation of power and this should be taken on a top priority basis;
   (c) deep sea mining of polymetallic nodules;
   (d) forecasting the national marine phenomenon for fishing and for the protection of our shore line from erosion; and
   (e) fighting and combating marine pollution.
4. Increasing R & D efforts in ocean sciences which will lead to:
   (a) discovery of new fishing grounds
   (b) tapping energy
   (c) meeting defence needs
   (d) augmenting living and non-living resources including oil and gas
   (e) protection of coastal zone from erosion, tides, waves and storms.
5. Looking at the impending danger from oil pollution in future, the workshop recommended to take urgent measures including legislation to check oil pollution in our seas. India should strive for the ratification of IMCO 1974 convention to fight against hazards.

6. The workshop recommended to build up infrastructure and backup facilities like ships, boats, etc., which are the essential tools for ocean research.
7. The development of necessary instruments based on urgent needs for oil exploration, deep sea mining, fishing, etc.
8. Building of trained manpower for oceanographic research and industry since there is a complete lacuna in this area, and with acquisition of new researchships more and more trained manpower would be required. In this connection, it was felt that some accommodation in the research vessel 'Gaveshani' should also be made available, if time permits, to the universities for training the right man for the right job. There should be more liberal exchange programmes with advanced countries for training of your young talented scientists.
9. The existing Data Centre at NIC should be strenghtened to provide data and information to the user community including planners and administrators. The oceanographic data from all marine-based institutions should be deposited with data centre.
10. Formation of a Central Teaching Institute in Oceanography and Ocean technology.
11. Development of a well-coordinated system for technology transfer from laboratories to the users.
12. Formulation of a marine policy regarding:
    (a) the use of sea-bed;
    (b) the use of coastal waters by mechanized and non-mechanized fishing boats; and
    (c) pollution control

The workshop concluded with an optimistic view that India will use the oceans more wisely in the future.

30

ONGC: FOR AND TOWARDS FUTURE: THE CONCEPTUAL FRAMEWORK AS SEEN IN MID EIGHTIES

Satish C. Seth

INTRODUCTION: ASPECTS OF FUTUROLOGY, MODELLING AND LONG RANGE CORPORATE PLANNING

Introduction

Futurology helps in taking a global and long range view of various systems and operations. Future scanning helps to develop Corporate LR Plans more scientifically and systematically. Such an approach helps both the current decision making process as well enables the Board Room to make easily various mid-course corrections. Futurology helps to generate new ideas and alternatives. Such inputs should be sought by all Corporate Planners.

2. Futurology is basically the study of the Future. Future can be glimpsed in terms of Events — good or bad, a threat or an opportunity. If a Corporation has some idea of what lies ahead, it can then make investment intelligently of diversifying its operations meaningfully.Forecasting also helps in choosing the right technology and in seeking a direction for the R&D activities. Such consideration and approach should characterise any long range plan.

3. The knowledge of the Future can never be certain. Forescanning, Trend Analysis, Modelling, Expert Opinion (Delphi), Systems Analysis, Cross-Impact Matrix, Scenario Development do help us to map out Future. It is presumably better than blind guessing. From the information derived from the above mentioned techniques, we can develop likely sequence of events and generate alternative approaches to arrive at Future or set normative goals for an organisation. The long range plan can then be based on the future related data and preferred goals.

4. Historical experience also constitutes a valuable input to delineate future related scenarios-sequence of events and of preferring long range Corporate goals.

5. The study of the past planning — its success and failure — provide us with indicators, some of which have the character of a "Red Flag". No long range Corporate Planner can or should ignore these even if the Company is assured of its current and future

success on the one hand and the availability of funds to go forward on the other.

6. These "Red Flags" (Trends and Indicators) are in the nature of an Early Warning Signal. A 20 year long-range plan can be full of invisible pit-falls, if its authors do not first study in-depth the implications of the "Warning Signals" coming from the historical experience. They can help us judge the validity of the future related programmes and policies. Futurists usually confirm these judgements by carrying out "Delphi Study", the "Cross-impact Analysis" or Model simulation etc.The results of using these techniques help us to design confidence levels and to determine the probability of an event's happening or otherwise, besides knowing their long-range impact—would it be good or bad.

7. The Corporate data, after such a futuristic treatment, can then be used to develop long range scenarios in the context of the "system" under study and to prepare a 20 year or longer perspective and to generate plan options and alternatives on which work can commence from today onwards. What we seek first is the right direction of change. Thereafter, we can gear up our resource to fulfil those objectives.This is the essence of Futurology and Anticipatory Management.

Limits and Relevance of Modelling

8. In the ONGC's Twenty Year Plan, the Modelling used is primarily, a Geo-scientific, data forecast for the likely finds of Hydrocarbons. This Model is neither the one that an econometrician would build nor is it a Technological Model, which if based, on engineering cost estimates, would help develop forecast for energy supplies for either oil and gas or new sources of energy or can discover questions, such as; What, for example, will be the likely cost of gasifying coal or utilising synthetic oil, in the Indian context? For this we need to carry out separate studies.

9. However, this need not worry us, as long as the personal or collective judgements made provide the corporate planners with the "range" in the model. It should be one where, its mathematical equations, embrace the maximum inter-relationships, based on geo-scientific research, historical experience and statistical estimates.

10. No policy maker can, with any certainty, fall back on Computer Models. They are at best ideal inputs to develop broad scenarios from which policy options and an ideal "Technological-mission-route" can be chosen.

11. ONGC, presently has no Energy-Model. It needs yet to be developed. There are hundred odd formal studies based on Modelling efforts, available in places, where oil based and energy oriented exercises have been carried out world over. Here, I strongly recommend that the following three models be carefully studied, in case ONGC's Corporate Planning Group wishes to guide the Board-Room for ONGC's diversified entry into the Energy Sector.

These studies are :—

* The Kennedy-Houthakker World Oil Model.
* The MIT Energy Self-Sufficiency Study.
* The Federal Energy Administration Project (Independence Report).

12. Amongst the above three models, I would strongly recommend the study of the Project Independence (PIES-74). However, from the "World Oil Model" one can also learn a lot too. But we should study the new model that has been built around it called "World Energy Model" /*. It is a dynamic long run model that contains natural gas, coal, nuclear, hydro and electric power, in addition to oil. Any modelling of this type cannot be merely an ONGC activity. Perhaps it should be jointly sponsored by the Ministry of Petroleum and the Ministry of Energy and the work on this should be carried out by the Planning Commission of India.

13. Needless to say that in these Models USA is the Centre-piece. What the ONGC's Corporate Planners can definitely learn is that by looking at the design, mathematics and the economic analysis of these Models is the newer insights pertaining to the "Methodology" aspects of doing the same thing ourselves.

For this, we need an inter-disciplinary group. It should include numerous ONGC activity experts, econometrician, highly skilled computer programmers and future scanners and scenario builders.

14. I would suggest Corporate Planning Staff's interaction with the Policy Study Group of the MIT Energy Laboratory. Equally

important are studies carried out by The National Petroleum Council of USA on which the MIT studies have relied heavily. We could also benefit by obtaining Technical Literature from the American Gas Association and study the trends given there for gas futures.

15. Whether we acquire technical know-how of the conceptual modelling from the USSR or the USA, or do it ourselves, we should remember the classic comment made by William W. Hogon, the author of "Energy Modelling"; Building understanding for Better use". (/*) which is as follows:

> "Even though a model's predictions may be quite imprecise and, therefore, not as useful for Policy-makers, they still can be helpful in organising the information base and guiding the decisions."

16. For all this, a good information Data-base is a must which ONGC has yet to develop in a big way. Col. S.P. Wahi, Chairman, ONGC's foreword to the ONGC Annual Report (1982-83) augurs well for the future, wherein, he observes that "The Long Range Planning of ONGC has gone beyond the confines of the existing systems of procedures. It now pre-supposes the use of computers for improving efficiency in all areas of operations. Introduction of computers for business applications has since been planned" which will set up for the ONGC a Management Information System. Once it is there, all we need to add to it is an Early Warning System (EWS).

17. Finally, it is also suggested that, as early as possible, ONGC should bring all its planners, say a group of 15-20 experts, under a single independent umbrella of ONGC's "Corporate Planning Intelligence and Environmental Scanning Group". It shall incorporate expertise for both the, EWS (the Early Warning System) and the MIS (the Management Information System) consisting of Information Scanning Group and the Programmers.

18. Let it be clearly stated that Long Range Planning is not Mr. X's hobby, or a Corporate entity's Pavlow response, to do something that another Public Sector undertaking is doing across the road. It is a highly technical, hard and patient work and besides being a full time activity.

19. Let it be understood that the Futurists and forecasters are

not magicians but they do help unfold layer after layer in mapping out alternatives and provide answers to the question "What Next"? Professional forecasting is a technical work, a group effort and is not "a game of chance". Today Futurology/Forecasting has matured sufficiently. This input can be ignored by any Industry Defence or R&D system and the makers of the Public Policy only to their own serious disadvantage. Mervin Cetron and Thomas O'Toole, fellow Futurists have rightly pointed out that "There are still not workable crystal balls on our planet but we can do a lot more than cross the t's and dot the i's on the "Trends" that shape the future". In futuristic approach, part of the process is knowing what to look for. Still another part of the process is knowing what it is when we find it". An open mind usually helps in forecasting. The authors of the ONGC's Twenty-year Perspective Plan may consider paying heed to this advise when they choose their options for future with "an open mind".

NOTES

/* For the results of the Model, apart from studying Miachel Kennedy's "A World Oil Model" in Dale Jorgenson, ed. "Economic studies of US Energy Policy (Amsterdam ; North Holland, 1976). See H.S. Houthakker and Miachel Kennedy "Long Range Energy Prospects", in Ragali EI Mallakh and Dorothea HEL Mallakh, "Energy Options and Conservation (Boulder, Colo. The International Research Centre for Energy and Economic Development, 1978).

(/*) For details, See, Proceedings of the Second Lawrence Symposium on the Systems and Decision Success, Berkley, Col (Oct 3 1978).

SOCIO-ECONOMIC, POLITICAL NATIONAL AND GLOBAL FUTURE DEVELOPMENT AND ONGC'S CORPORATE GOALS

Oil Based to "Non-Oil" based Civilisation

Our times on this planet are characteristic of an oil based civilisation. Simultaneously, however, many nations and their scientists are working to delink themselves and their day-today life from "Oil". They intend to go to other sources of energy to usher in an era of "Non-Oil" civilisation.

2. It so happens that after the advent of the Industrial Revolution, as firewood was replaced by coal, the world has witnessed a 60 year cycle within which yet another source of energy has been found and put to use. This has enabled us to use several sources of energy both renewable and non-renewable, such as, the fire-wood, coal, electricity, oil, gas, atomic energy, wind energy, bio-mass, bio-gas and solar energy. It is expected that in less than 60 years of man's first using of the atomic energy, we could perhaps fully harness the solar-energy, or go over to Fusion Energy. The question of 'energy' however, continues to be high on the policy agenda of all countries. Consciously enough, since 1973, it revolves mainly around 'oil' or even 'gas'.

3. *The advent of "Oil shock":* It was in late 1973 and early 1974 that the world received the first "oil shock". The Arab oil producers (OPEC countries) stopped negotiating price of oil with the oil companies. They began to unilaterally set price on a "take-it-or leave-it" basis. The change of price was staggering in character. In 1960 a barrel of crude cost around US$ 1.00 to US $ 1.30. It was eight times higher by the end of 1974. The second shock occurred in 1979-80 after the fall of Shah of Iran. In fact, notwithstanding, the so called "oil glut" of 1982, the high oil prices seemed assured over the long run. Most international experts now opine that "as of 1983, no one knows the timing of any price-rise".

4. *The setting up of ONGC and its significant role in India:* It is against this backdop that we have to assess the significant role of the Oil and Natural Gas Commission of India (ONGC) which was set up in the year 1956. Much more significant is the question of

what lies ahead for it, during the next twenty years — a period of 7000 odd days, when India would have entered the 21st century, in terms of its likely contribution to the Indian Energy and Economic scene.

5. *Aspect of ONGC and Turbulent National and International Scenario:* ONGC can be looked at in many ways. We take the following three illustrative and important aspects to judge ONGC's emerging future scenario, in a somewhat turbulent, national and international environment.

6. *Firstly, ONGC is primarily a Government Company engaged to explore and provide to the nation two products :* Oil and Gas. That its operations are a success story can be judged by its economic contribution in saving enormous foreign exchange by providing indigenous "oil" even though, India is and may continue on several counts to be an oil importing country for quite some time to come. To understand this let us look at this scene in quantitative terms.

7. *Oil:* In 1980-81, India's demand for petroleum products was 32.26 million tonnes while ONGC's production for the same year was only 9.21 million tonnes. Since then the gap has been narrowed down substantially. While demand for petroleum products in India increased 1.15 times, production of crude oil by ONGC increased 2½ times by 1983-84. The demand projection of petroleum products during 1984-85 is estimated at 39 million tonnes, out of which ONGC would be able to produce about 27 million tonnes. Together with oil production of about 3 million tonnes, the total indigenous output is likely to be around 30 million tonnes which will meet 77 per cent of the petroleum need of India by the end of 1984.

8. ONGC's crude oil production during 1983-84 rose to 23.15 million tonnes which is 27 per cent more than the previous year's output of 18.23 million tonnes — 151 per cent improvement on 1980-81 performance — the first year of the Sixth Five Year Plan.

9. *Gas:* During 1983-84, production of natural gas increased by 20 per cent compared to the previous year. ONGC supplied 2227 million cubic metres of natural gas in 1983-84, whereas it had supplied 1861-14 million cubic metres of gas during 1982-83. ONGC has now fixed a target of gas to be supplied at 2665 million cubic metres for 1984-85.

10. *LPG :* Similarly, LPG supplied during 1983-84 was 22 per cent higher than the previous year and 168 per cent higher over the supplies in 1981-82. This exceeds the installed capacity at Uran LPG Plant of ONGC.

11. ONGC has registered a sales turn over of Rs. 3422.15 crores during the year 1983-84 and has contributed Rs.1907 crores to the state exchequer. ONGC has also generated internal resources of the order of Rs.1285 crores for meeting the plan expenditure during 1983-84 which amounts to 81 per cent of the plan requirement. ONGC has also made a profit of Rs. 791.56 crores after tax and Rs. 1670 crores before tax in the year 1983-84.

12. Judging from the ONGC's financial achievement given above it should come as no surprise to anyone that, of late, ONGC has been in a position even to extend a loan of over Rs.1907 crores or more to the Government of India, besides being one of the highest tax-payers of India. This amply reflects its sound financial health.

13. *ONGC : Science, Technology and Managerial Aspects:* Secondly, ONGC is also a large network of Science, Technology and Managerial assemblage. It is one of the biggest employer of the technical manpower of India. Its onshore and offshore operations display commendable scientific and technological achievements in geoscience, drilling and allied research and development comparable enough, for a place of pride amongst the oil producing countries. Let's look at few more technical details.

14. *Drilling :* ONGC's drilling activities have also shown an appreciable growth during 1983-84 when 205 wells were drilled which is 15 per cent higher than the wells drilled in 1982-83. During the current financial year, ONGC proposes to complete 252 wells both off-shore and onshore.

15. With a view to accelerate the programme of exploration on land ONGC proposes to have four contract drilling for Krishna-Godavari Project in addition to two under World Bank Funding. These four rigs will be deployed in Himachal Pradesh, Jammu & Kashmir, Gujarat and Cauvery Projects in the south. Various services like cementing mudlogging, electro-logging, mud engineering and drilling consultancy are also envisaged for the

contracted rigs. In addition, ONGC may also go for charter-hire of onland rigs from Indian entrepreneurs.

16. *ONGC: A fit candidate to play bigger role in energy sector:* Thirdly, ONGC's current operations make it a fit candidate for playing a significant "future" role in the Energy, Engineering Marine—Consultancy and Socio-economic Development in India, and hopefully, in some other developing countries. It has already taken the first few steps in this direction in its innovative measures and by adopting an "Aggressive Strategy for accelerated exploration" it stands committed towards fulfilling the following three objectives :

1. Self sufficiency in oil
2. Self reliance in technology
3. Promoting indigenous effort in oil related equipment and services.

17. *ONGC Contribution for Overseas Operations:* With a view to share the experience and expertise gained over two decades, ONGC successfully extended its activities overseas. Starting with exploration in the Persian Gulf, in association with three other international oil companies, ONGC later on undertook a service contract for exploration/drilling in south-western desert for Iraq and carried out seismic surveys using vibrosts techniques.

18. ONGC has also drilled gas wells in Sogo-Songo for Tanzania and undertook workover and production testing jobs, for Tanzanian Petroleum Development Corporation. ONGC has also succeeded in obtaining various types of consultancies from Abu-Dhabi, Sri Lanka and Seychelles. Experts from ONGC have also been deputed to various countries in the developing world.

19. ONGC is today in a position to assist any developing country particularly in geophysical data acquisition, its processing and interpretation, basin analysis and prospect evaluation, reservoir studies, preparation of technological schemes for developing oil and gas fields etc. and is fully equipped to impart training and undertake development programmes. ONGC is also willing to depute specialists to various countries on organisation to organisation basis. In fact, it could play in future a significant role as regards Technical Cooperation for the NAM countries.

20. *ONGC and India Societal Features:* ONGC, like any other

public sector undertaking is, however, not operating in a vaccum. As it moves towards the future, it shall have to, at the corporate level, pay attention to the likely vicissitudes and vagaries of the socio-economic and politico-environmental conditions.

21. Let's look at some of the societal features of India and some related global future trends. (These are only illustrative and not exhaustive in nature).

(1) *India: A Large Human System*

Firstly, India is a large human system. We are 730 million people today (1984). By the turn of the century, we should be around 1000 million — nearly a billion people or more. Naturally, therefore all Indian systems shall have to gear themselves from today, (it is both a challenge and opportunity) onwards to cope with the basic needs of a billion people.

(2) *India: The Poverty Conditions*

Secondly, India's problem number one is "Poverty". More than 55 per cent (an urban-rural average) of Indians live below the poverty line. In essence it means that in India millions of urban and rural poor have only Rs. 2 per head per day spending capacity. In short, millions of our citizens do not have a "consumer" personality. In two rupees per day, they have to cope with a 24 hour cycle of life and manage it in whatever way they possibly could, do so, to meet their basic needs for food, water, transportation, energy etc. In fact, majority of them suffer from mal-nutrition and other deprivations. As far as the "energy" goes, they meet this basic need on a "zero-private cost-basis". So they cut forest wood, collect cow dung, buy minimum of kerosene or even steal coal from the Railway's coal carrying wagons.

(3) *India: The Value and Technological Plurality*

The third, the fourth and fifth societal features relate to the (i) unhomogenous development of India (India simultaneously lives in Agraria, Industria and the post-industria, dis-playing) (ii) Value Plurality (Hence, the everpresent conflict in identifying a direction of change) and (iii) the technological plurality. (Sector-by-sector—we are using technologies of the 19th century or before and in some sectors, we are already in the 21st century, like our entry into electronics, atomic or space age. We have a place in our society, even on economic consideration, for a bullock-cart as well as for a jet or now even the satellites.

22. *India's Energy Consumption status vis-a-vis some other countries :* These societal factors, characterize our society today and they shall equally characterize India when it enters the first decade of the 21st century. The contrast to other countries energy consumption vis-a-vis India, it is submitted, even after twenty years, won't alter substantially. The picture of per capita energy consumption today is as follows:

Present energy use/capita	
USA	51.7 BOE/Year
GERMANY	26.9 "
USSR	22.4 "
CHINA	2.2 "
INDIA	0.9 "
World Average	6.0 "

"Source: Energy & Oil" — Paper of Dr. A.K. Malhotra, Member (Off-shore), ONGC, presented at the world energy conference.

NOTE: BOE : Barrel of oil equivalent
1 BOE : 5.8 million BTU's
= 158.7 cubic metres of natural gas
= 0.88 tonnes of coal replacement value
= 0.27 tonnes of coal equivalent
= 1700 Kwh of Electronics

Questions for ONGC

Some relevant questions for the ONGC in the context of the Indian societal features, and the picture of the per capita energy consumption of India, do arise. Three of these are interesting and important question for which the basic facts are that with reference to growing Indian population the energy need in India will increase with the times, as we move towards the future. Also, India, like many other countries shall continue to be dependent on several sources of energy as against any single source of energy. It may perhaps take years before such citizens of India, who are extremely poor and are below the so-called poverty line, could acquire a consumer personality. That is to say, that they may be able to raise their income levels to a point where they could afford to buy energy.

Question No. 1

The first question that ONGC has to ask itself is How, and if at all, its corporate policy and corporate goals require a modification, a new modality or emphasise so that ONGC could meaningfully respond to the Indian societal features in general and its 'Energy' aspects in 'particular'.

Question No. 2

Whereas ONGC's contribution to the Indian energy need will predominently rest wtih its prime strength of accelerated exploration and production of more oil and gas, could it diversify its activities to inter-related areas such as drilling for geo-thermal energy or take to intensive ocean mining to contribute both to the energy and the economic sector of India.

Question No. 3

Even if the ONGC could get a new mandate and could modify its corporate goals, apart from oil and gas, would its operations in the energy and India's economic sector help substantially the per capita energy consumption in India? and, if so, at what cost?

We shall revert to these questions later. Let's now look at the Global Environmental aspect as, the global "Trends" indicate the future unfoldings.

Global Trends

It may be useful to look at the important global trends which directly or indirectly impinge on the socio-economic and oil and gas energy scene. Some of these have been the result of extensive use of Computer analysis of world trends and indicators. They tell us which way the trend is headed.

Firstly, in the context of global threats of the many, the following seven indicators are more significant :—

(1) Food shortage in several parts of the world;
(2) High cost of energy and depletion of non-renewable sources of energy;
(3) Complexities relating to exploitation, depletion and transfer of mineral resources;
(4) Environmental degradation;
(5) International terrorism on land and piracy on sea and in space;
(6) Social turbulance leading to social fragmentation, social tensions, youth unrest, value crisis, industrial relations conflicts and cultural and technological shocks;
(7) The probability of nuclear war (Is one, it is not zero).

Secondly, in so far as the world energy use and choice of energy resources is concerned, the following trends, as catalogued by Ruth Leger Sevard are notable :—

The World Energy Situation Today

"An era of abundant energy at prices especially favourable to global expansion of industry and transportation has come to an end. Facts on the situation, like opinions on the best course of action, often differ significantly from the source of expert knowledge to another. Summarised here are salient features of the current situation on which there appears to be appreciable agreement."

"A profound change in the world's use and choice of energy resources is slowly underway."

"World supplies of oil and of fuelwood are being depleted more rapidly than alternative fuels are developed to replace them."

"Political volatility and conflict in the Middle East, source of over half the world's oil reserves, increase the chances of a sudden rupture of supply lines."

"Energy prices have been risen considerably faster than the general rate of inflation and are expected to continue to do so."

"Rising prices have induced some energy conservation but

on the whole progress in this respect has been slow compared with the potential."

"Coal and nuclear energy are still the leading official candidates to replace dwindling supplies of oil in this country (USA). Both have serious unresolved hazards in production and use."

"The world is rich in renewable energy sources which are largely untepped and their technologies for use not yet adequately developed."

"With one-fourth of the world's population, the developed nations consume three-fourths of the energy, considerably more than they produce."

"A marked disparity in income between industrialised and poor nations is associated with the intensity of energy use. The pressures to reduce this disparity are growing."

Issues for the Energy Future

"These are critical issues affecting the future on which experts are not all agreed. While expressed here in the form of challenge statements, essentially reflecting the conclusions of this writer, all of them in fact involve opinions and choices that call for wide public debate."

"In the years immediately ahead there is a risk of a very serious energy crisis unless more effective public action is taken to conserve supplies and allocate them equitably.

"On the whole, government policies have not adequately addressed the need for energy conservation and the development of a diversity of energy resources."

"No energy technologies should be put into operation without public assurance that they satisfy health and safety standards, and are environmentally sustainable."

"Unresolved safety problems and public protests have significantly diminished the future prospects for nuclear energy."

"Energy prices should reflect full social costs, including waste management, pollution controls, and casualty insurance."

"Taxes on energy should be used to promote conservation and renewable resources and to offset the burden of higher prices for those least able to bear them."

"Choices between energy use and non-use, and among energy-related technologies, should take into account the world's 455 million underemployed and unemployed."

"Smaller-scale, community oriented energy systems have economic advantages and are more adaptable to public guardianship than are large centralised system."

"Given public subsidy and policy support equal to that provided nuclear and fossil fuels, solar sources can meet a significant share of energy needs in this century."

If ONGC has to draw up a 20 year perspective plan with an eye to augment its role in the Energy sector, beyond oil and gas, its authors could profit by closely examining some of the above mentioned, Indian Societal Features and the well recognised global trends.

National and Global Trends: Implications for ONGC

If we can selectively look at the vast variety of future related trends delineated in the previous pages, then a few aspects need to be examined in depth, which both directly and indirectly, have some implications relevant to ONGC's current or future corporate goals:

Point (1): The days of easy oil are over

On this account, the imperative for India (and perhaps for the rest of the world too) is simple :—

A. In the national interest there is need to reduce permanently oil imports.

B. The straightforward implication for ONGC is that not only it should accelerate its exploration and production of oil and gas, in the minimum span of time, which it is doing anyhow, but a time has perhaps come, when ONGC should also take the first few steps to begin to bite at other sources of energy, as its legitimate corporate objective.

C. The third pertinent question is : Can India take it for granted that it shall continue to have an uninterrupted oil imports available from the Middle East and the USSR. And, if so, for how long? We need to make a futuristic assessment there.

Point (2): Oil is now a political and a strategic weapon

Middle East: Notwithstanding, apparent oil glut and oil price stability, we need to recognise the fact that the Middle East is a region of high political tensions and risk. In the last 30 years, it has witnessed about 12 wars and 12 revolutions. It has been the scene of innumerable assassinations and territorial disputes. The international experience has been that, all this leads to interruption of supplies and major price increases.

Soviet Union: This country too is not without its own energy problems. Bulk of its energy production was in coal until 1960, when the rate of growth of coal production began to decline. Oil overtook it as the predominant fuel. 'Coal' production is now virtually stagnant; the rate of production of oil has markedly declined from that of the previous two decades. The CIA's most recent forecast maintains that Soviet oil output could decline by nearly 17 per cent. British Economists though differ from this view, CIA forecasters say that by 1990, Soviet oil may decline by 40 per cent from 1980 levels (603 million Tons). Others disagree and forecast 25 per cent more oil in 1990. These predictions are all based on different views of scanty and unprocessed Soviet information. Naturally, therefore, future forecasts do vary

* Let's look at what is the Soviet Union's future orientation? They do recognise that their oil production will not rise greatly.
* In their current five year plan (FYP) based on their performance of the past gives higher priority to GAS.

Gas is the key to Soviet Energy Future

Let us look at some key features :—

* Soviets are laying heavy emphasis on new pipelines for which they import Technology from West.
* Their success however will lie in their ability to
  (i) substitute gas for oil
  (ii) convert to gas in boiler and industrial applications and
  (iii) add to pipeline-network.
* Soviet Union in 1979 devoted about 22 per cent of its trade with its major Western Trading Partners (some

US $ 3.4 billion) to energy related technology and equipment of this $2.7 billion was in Soviet oil and gas sector (mostly for Pipe and Pipeline Industries). It has though never imported "massive amount of oil field equipment."

In Petroleum sector, except for advanced computers USSR, imports bulk of items — large diameter pipe and pipeline equipment — From Japan, West Germany, Italy and France. (It may turn to USA, the world leaders for coal surface mining).

Comment 1

Considering that in 1979, 24 per cent of Italy's and 16 per cent West Germany gas came from USSR, an era of East-West Energy Inter-dependence may emerge. Although Analysts also talk of a sort of "gas-weapon" to expert Political Pressure. The key question is : how much energy (oil or gas) will USSR be willing to make available to others and how much to India? and for how long?

Comment 2

ONGC and country's Indian Energy Planners need to judge what is the 'GAS' potential for India and what is the state of our Pipeline Industry ? And will we develop it ourselves or with some one else's help ? If so, who ? how soon can our "Gas-grid" shall become a reality ?

Point (3)

The price of imported oil is bound to rise in future. The question is what are the outer limits of this price hike ? And how after 1990 and beyond will we in India, manage our oil based industrial, Transportation and Defence need ?

On price hike, there are several opinions. Some representative views are as follows :-

A. Robert Stobought and Daniel Yergin, have tried to put a figure on the real cost of a barrel of the imported oil for USA. It includes the "total social cost" — i.e. Market Price plus the cost to the society of future price hikes and economic disruptions that might result in increasing demands. According to their best estimate of the cost, it still comes at $65 to $100 a barrel, during the second oil shock.

B. Marvin Cetron and Thomas O'Toole well known Futurists talk of political price increase of oil. Their thesis is that every major incident in the Middle East has a tendency to step up the price of the barrel by $10. Scanning the middle eastern environment, they feel that if there is another embargo of the kind, that took place during 1973 Arab-Israeli War, or if there was a Pan-Islamic War between Sunni-Muslims against Shiites, it could inflame the entire Middle East. Because of this, one can expect much steeper hike in the oil price. They quote John O'Heary. One time, Dy. Energy Secretary in the United States, having remarked that - "You have a Scenario, where Middle East oil is essentially ruled out as longest to twenty years". Rule out middle east oil for 20 years, observe, Marvin Cetron and Thomas O'Toole, and you raise the world wide price of oil to $100 a barrel and drop the industrialised world into its longest and deepest recession. Since the great Depression of the 1930s".

They go on to add :—

"No body can forecast how many of these events will take place but by putting our trust in history. We think it is safe to predict that two disruptive events will happen in the Middle East in the next 15 years. (After all, there were two major disruptions in the last 10 years, the 1973 Yom Kippur War and the Iranian revolution that overthrew the Shah.There were three if you count Iraq's war with Iran. There could easily be another revolution in Iran, a second war between Iran and Iraq and an Iraqi invasion of Kuwait. There could also be a civil war in Saudi Arabia and a *coup d'etat* in Syria) Harder to forecast is the size of the price increase that follows each disruption. Five dollars a barrel is not out of the question for each major disruption which would translate to $ 10 a barrel if there were two such events. That would raise oil's price to $45 a barrel barring any further price increase of purely economic reasons will stick. For some curiously unexplained reason, when oil rises in prices these days because of political pressures, it never sinks back to its old price these days when the pressures ease up. Mexico and Venezuela both raised the price of their oil after the outbreak of the war between Iraq and Iran. Both countries appologized effusively for doing to but they stuck to their price increases. The only oil producing country that does not adhere strictly to this rule is the biggest, Saudi Arabia".

In conclusion they observe "If, by some miracle, there are no political disruptions in the Middle East, we are still forecasting higher oil prices for the next 15 years. Lets face it, the world's oil wells will continue to dry up and exploration costs will continue to escalate to put upward pressure on prices".

"In the American context, they remark that the 8.634 million barrels of oil that American wells pumped as a daily average in June 1981 marked the first time United States production was put in the lower 48 states in eight years but it also marked an upper production limit on domestic wells that the United States will never see again. Even the two million barrels USA gets every day from Alaska's North Slope will begin to drop later unless another new field the size of Prodhoe Bay is discovered in the next few years, The new fields being found in the North Sea are getting smaller in size with each new find, suggesting the North Sea has a limited oil future. Drilling costs on the North Slope and in North Sea have climbed to over $1,000 a meter, meaning that new discoveries in these two frontier regions will be harder to come by".

"There is a lot of oil exploration going on, despite the rising costs of finding oil. Oil companies are looking for oil off the western coast of Australia. In Indonesia off the coasts of Java, Sumatra, Borneo, Sarwak and Brunei, off the costs of China and Vietnam, in the Gulf of Alaska and the Canadian Arctic, off both coasts of South America and along the entire outer continental shelf, in the Atlantic Ocean.

There is even talk of exploratory drilling in the deepest depths of the ocean using the former Central Intelligence Agency submarine recovery Ship, the Glomar Explorer". The outlook for all these adventures. "say Cetron and O'Toole, is hazy and questionable".

They add "The only countries that are sure to have sizeable reserves of oil at the end of the 20th Century are the Arab countries of the Middle East, especially Saudi Arabia and Kuwait. There are three kinds of recoverable oil in the world, the oil close to the surface that just flows out, the oil not too far beneath the surface that must be jumped out and the oil far below the surface that must be forced out by the underground injection of chemical detergents and hot steam. Most of the oil in the Middle East just flows out. Kuwait alone has better than a 40 years supply of close to the surface oil. Saudi Arabia has almost half the world's recoverable oil".

"It is our estimate that the real oil crunch will be experienced somewhere in 2010A.D. and 2020A.D. We explain it in the following words :- "What will be the price of oil in the next 20 years ? Some experts think, it will be $50 a barrel by 1995 and $80 to $85 a barrel by the year 2000. We don't think that fusion power will be so close to demonstration by 1995. That is most unavoidable. What will that mean to gasoline prices? The rule of thumb is that you add two and half cents a gallon to the pump price of gasoline for every dollar add to the price of a barrel of crude oil. So figure it out. If oil costs $35 a barrel right now, $20 per barrel increase will add 50 cents to the prices of a gallon of gasoline. Will there be enough oil at the end of the Century ? There will be enough oil to fuel ships, planes and the cars that are still propelled by internal combustion engines. An oil crunch when world wide oil supplies start to dwindle rapidly will not come until 2010 or 2020. These will be the years that Middle East oil starts to dry up. The social and psychological fall out of an end to oil and gasoline will be severe".

Limits of Forecasts

To sum up, whatever be the merit of these forecasts, we do know, that they are based on different assumptions. Naturally, they then come out of different outcomes. The key uncertainty includes the following factors :—

1. Rate of economic growth in the given country and elsewhere in the world.
2. Energy usage per unit of economic output (in other words amount of conservation).

3. Oil Production in South Arabia.
4. Oil Production in other OPEC Nations.
5. Oil Production in Non-OPEC Nations.
6. Contributions for other conventional energy sources — Natural Gas, Coal and Nuclear.
7. Contributions by Non-traditional sources as shale oil, solar, tar sand, geothermal, wave power and so on.

Different assumptions can produce enormously different forecasts. For instance — by making different assumptions on two items — Rate of Economic growth and energy usage per unit of economic output, specialists have forecast world energy consumption to increase by as little as 60 per cent by the year 2000 or by as much as 230 per cent.

All forecasts should thus need to be offered with some modesty and rejudged in the special context in which we wish to examine them or use them.

Against the above scanning of the International Oil related environment (We have chosen here only a few illustrative indicators Trends on a selective basis) and in the instant context of the ONGC's future and the Indian Energy Scene, in particular, the following three comments can be made :-

Comment 1

Notwithstanding the fact that (i) the future holds in its bosom real energy crisis and that, in the long run, (ii) developing more plentiful substitutes for oil in developing countries and in India will be more important than finding or conserving oil, yet (iii) a need exists for a good assessment of present and prospective (long range) energy supply and demand picture for India as the starting point for Energy Policy Planning. Perhaps the Indian Ministry of Energy and the Planning Commission need to develop an Indian Energy Model and have a second hard look at it in terms of the National and International Parameters, National Economic growth and even life-style.

Comment 2

In terms of the long range Future implications for the ONGC, notwithstanding its current mandate relating to the Hydrocarbons, a positive need exists to relate ONGC's current and future corporate objectives to India's "Developmental Variables" that influence and at the same time make energy projections a somewhat complicated business. Once it is done a rationale for somewhat modified and extended mandate for the ONGC's role may look for more reasonable than is the case today within the ambit of the Act and what it warrants.

Comment 3

In the event of any future hike in oil price, to us in India, one can leave each system to judge for itself. The well known internationally acknowledged consequences are usually as follows:—

(i) The oil importing nation has to do more work to buy a given quantity of oil.

(ii) The payments to foreign Governments "Contract domestic demand for goods and services and in fact becomes an excise tax, a 'drag' on the economics of the importing countries".

(iii) It can also and has lead to unemployment since the Industrial nations, deflate their economies in the face of oil induced inflation and balance of payment deficits which further reduce growth and further increases unemployment.

(iv) It can also put severe strains on the international monetary system. Robert Stobaugh has estimated that, "In total, the two oil shocks cost of industrial nations $1.2 trillion in lost economic growth from 1974 to 1981".

(v) Finally, the higher oil prices can also lead to internal and international political conflict. Robert Stobaugh comments :

"Since 1973 serious clashes have developed among Western allies over oil and nuclear power, which show that energy questions — involving dependence and vulnerability, employment and growth, the stability of governments — have taken on extraordinary sensitivity. In fact, they have become security issues of paramount importance. Thus higher oil prices in the next decade—

> following a decade of tension and suspicion caused by the two oil shocks — could severely strain relations among the Western nations.
>
> About the most optimistic current forecast that can be made is that the world will drift alongwith a little slower economic growth and a little higher inflation than usual. Indeed, some of the optimists those who say not to worry about substantially higher prices in the next decade — are basing their outlook on continued low economic growth. Hardly, a satisfactory solution for this would extract a high price in the form of unemployment, diminished opportunity and, the inevitable political conflicts.

Comment 4

Indian Energy Planners, as way back as the Sixth Plan formulation time had estimated a Price Hike around US $60.00. In a recent assessment, R.K. Pachauri, in his paper entitled, "The Global Oil Market — Perspective and Prospects", has in one of his scenarios observed that the "real oil price may grow steadily at 3 per cent annually during the period 1990-2000, preceded by a sudden increase of 25 per cent in 1985 and no price increase in the remaining years covered". All organisations working in the field of Energy need to accommodate these trends to seek appropriate policy shifts. Dr. Pachauri is right when he observes that "the outlook for OPEC production and exports is fraught with uncertainties".

"Interestingly", he adds, "there appears to be greater disagreement at present on the short-term outlook for oil prices and global demand than on the long-term prospects, on which there is a fair degree of consensus based on the outlook for depletion of world oil resources as a whole".

Conclusion

Be it as it may, one conclusion for the ONGC, in its limited and focussed context defined by its current mandate (Act) and its role in the Indian Energy Sector, a good care exists to review general and specific corporate priorities. With reference to its 20 year long range perspective.

It should be borne in mind that the ONGC can barely and only somewhat indirectly influence the "Current Demand Management Consumption patterns of the country".

Col. Wahi, Chairman, ONGC, in his interview with the author of this monograph has succinctly summed up the future line of action, when he said, "Even if there are too many uncertainties and even though oil is Probablistic gamble, we have to take to Bold and Aggressive strategy for oil production go to areas which are rich taking all the care of altering higher Productivity; and work relentlessly for Big discoveries for oil and gas". He further added, "This is why we need to go for live data; prepare a long range scientific perspective Plan and examine ONGC's role in the Indian Energy Sector for today and tomorrow. ONGC, one of the premier undertakings of India is obliged to do ample thinking for ourselves and others and generate ideas in the Energy Sector. This is more important than worrying about who can or who should diversify.".

In the next section, we turn to examine the inner and outer limits, the relevance or irrelevance of diversification.

NOTES

Rute Leger Sivarl in the document "World Energy Survey"; World Priorities Inc. Virginia? USA.

Joseph A Licari "Linkage and Between Soviet Energy and Growth Prospects for 1980s. A paper presented at the 1981 NATO Economic Directorate Colloquium 1981.

L. Sawyer, the Soviet Energy Sector; Problems and Prospects Harvard University, Jan. 1978. Quoted in George "Hoffman" Energy Projections — Oil, Natural Gas and Coal in the USSR and Eastern Europe, Energy Policy, p. 232-241.

See OECD Committee, for Energy Policy.

Energy Prospects for USSR and Eastern Europe (1981)."

Chapter II entitled "After the Peak : The Threat of Hostile Oil Energy Future : Report of the Energy Project At the Harward Business hooled by "Robert Stobaugh and Danie Yergin. Wintage Books (USA) 3rd edition.

Also see, Darkwart a Rustow or, "Political Force Affecting the Price and availability of oil in the 1980's," in Petroleum Industry Research Foundation took for World oil into the 21st Century (Palo Alto, Ca, Electric Power Research Institute, June 1978).

An internal document prepared for TERI (New Delhi), Dr. Pachauri is its Director and is also Member, Energy Board headed by K.C. Pant. He was also convenor, NCST Panel on Futurology's Technical Sub-Group on "Energy". Also see R.K. Pachauri's "The Political Economy of Global Energy, Forthcoming, John Hopin University Press, Baltimore (USA).

ONGC: GROWTH NEEDS AND LIMITS TO DIVERSIFICATION

It is necessary that before we examine various options and choices which look glamorous enough for ONGC's diversification, primarily to enable ONGC to play a more positive role in its narrow context of Energy and Marine Engineering, Information and Consultancy and Rural Development Sectors, we ask the question : what kind of strength ONGC has? And what kind of diversification is based on Technological or Marketing strength?

As Peter F. Drucker has rightly commented that,

> "In diversification one has to build on strength. Diversification will be successful only if it promises a greater return on what, one can do and do well. It has to be an extension of one's proven performance capacity."*

However, all product oriented companies, even if they be a Governmental Public Sector Undertakings have to have "Growth objective" But as Drucker has observed, A management needs a rational growth policy. A management needs objectives that are based on more solid grounds than the desire to grow or the promise to grow".

Surely anyone concerned with the future of one billion plus population of India cannot remain oblivious to the fact that its energy needs will, over the next 20 years (1985-2005 A.D.) will be monumental in character. This energy has to come either from land, ocean or the space with Indian Plan obligations to build a socialistic pattern of society, energy is needed on all counts for Agriculture, Industry and Domestic use.

The authors of new world famous report on "Energy in Transition (1985-2010)" made a realistic comment regarding the energy aspects pertaining to the developing countries vis-a-vis world Financial system. They observed:

> "As we have seen, the growing demand for energy in the developing countries will make them increasingly important in the global energy picture. Some of these countries are already considerable importers of oil and other will become

> so as their transportation sectors expand. Moreover, the industrialisation that is an inescapable aspect of economic development will greatly increase their reliance on electric power, of which, they now have very little. Their agriculture will also shift from animal and human energy to tractors, harvesters and trucks and from natural to industrial fertilizers. As personal income rises in these countries, they will want better housing with more lighting and appliances, not to mention air-conditioning. The more affluent of their citizens will demand motor cycles, automobiles and air travel. In fact, the total demand for energy in these countries could conceivably rise faster than GNP. Furthermore, we must hope that their GNP does rise at a reasonable rate, not only in their own interest but also for the sake of global political stability."

They further add : "However, if present patterns of economic growth in the world continue, and if the aspirations of the developing countries for longer shares of economic activity are realised, the average long term rate of energy demand growth is unlikely to fall much below 3 per cent per year even if energy conservation in the United States accomplishes a great deal domestically, it will be more than offset by demand growth in countries at the "take off" stage of development. By the year 2010, world energy consumption will probably be 3 or 4 times as large as it is now. The developing countries will then have a larger share in world energy consumption than they have present".

They conclude, "In the absence of truly spectacular discoveries elsewhere, the OPEC countries (Especially those in the Middle East and Africa) will account for the bulk of the world's oil production in the early part of the twenty-first century. In addition to North America, Europe, East Asia, even Latin will by then probably be a large fully developed cumulative oil production between now and 2010 and is likely to exhaust all presently proved reserves of "conventional oil". Because of intervening discoveries oil reserves should be atleast as large as they are now but they will be high cost reserves".

As oil production gradually falls more firmly under OPEC

control, the opportunity for surges in oil price like those of 1973-74 and 1979 will increase. Moreover as OPEC's reserves of low cost oil are depleted, the incentive, to raise prices will intensify this would be true even the absence of a Cartel".

Against this background and as we can some of our demand data, what could be ONGC's "growth" policy? Could we through Accelerated Exploration and Production become self-reliant. If so, by what date?

Against this background and as against our own demand data, we shall have to identify what could be ONGC's "growth" perspective and policy? Could we through Accelerated Exploration and Production become self-reliant? for our oil and gas needs? If so by what date? Could ONGC also become a world-recognised "oil-exporter" for India? or do we hereto plod on as at present?

From whatever angle, we may see, our growth options or diversification has to respond to and quality to either of the following scenarios :

(1) Business as Usual Scenario
(2) Moderating Enhanced (Energy) Conditions Scenario
(3) National socio-economic development commitment scenario

Let us look at the current Indian Energy demand pattern for Hydrocarbons and its derivatives and also look at the national and international viewpoints, debate and real prospects of some alternative sources of energy only those which ONGC can bite at in its own strength.

In terms of the oil needs in India, it is now universally agreed that oil demand needs to be curbed and systematically managed in terms of the national energy needs. It is also clear that we have to rely on a judicious combination of different forms of energy. The next 20 to 30 years' period is the transition period as well as the challenging period where India needs to have an accelerated exploitation of the domestic conventional energy resources such as oil, coal, gas, Hydrocarbon and nuclear power. We have also to take steps for energy conservation and we need to develop renewable resources of energy. In terms of the management of the oil demand, strangely enough, the per capita consumption of oil in India is amongst the lowest in the world barely (48 kg. per year). 70 per cent of this oil is used for freight, public transport and agriculture. About 20 per cent is used by the domestic sector, almost entirely for lighting in rural areas and cooking in Urban Areas. An internal indicative assessment gives us an aggregated forecast picture of the commercial energy contribution towards the Indian Energy Demand, which is as follows:

	1953-54		1989-90		2000-2001	
A	Cowdung	9.85%	Non Commercial	40.38%	Non-Commercial	11.74%
	Agricul-ture waste	13.35%				
	Fire wood	44.1%				
Non-Commercial : 6.3%						
B	Electricity	4.6%	Electricity	17.10%	Electricity	33.06%
	Oil	12.75%	Oil	25.52%	Oil	33.85%
	Coal	13.35%	Coal	13.94%	Coal	20.62%
	Commercial	32.7%	Commercial	52.62%	Commercial	88.53%

Indian Sectoral Energy Consumption

The sectoral demand status for these Hydrocarbon based energy, in the absence of an accurate growth rate of consumption in sectors, such as — Industry, Agriculture, Transportation, Domestic, etc., it is hazardous to provide a future demand break up perspective vis-a-vis oil and gas. However, the global trend for energy consumption growth rate of 3 per cent per year is suggestive enough. If the past is any guide, the same energy consumption rate growth as an average — will if not more could be equally valid for India as well — in a range varying between 3 per cent to 8 per cent for different sources such as electricity, coal, oil, gas, etc.* Besides, the Plan allocations for the Indian Industry Agriculture and transport development does not seem to indicate if, oil import dependency of India shall abate over the next twenty year time frame.

The recent interim report of GOI's Advisory Board on Energy has aptly summed up this position when they point out that "The time has come to make the task of meeting the energy demand of households every where but particularly of the rural and urban poor, a principal element of our energy strategy in the Seventh and subsequent plans. The challenging task of meeting the Energy requirements of households must be accorded top priority and the necessary supportive social, technological and institutional changes effected. Unless this is done, the problem will continue to be ignored and will get out of hand. A deliberate and special effort is needed because this section of our population lacks organisational strength and often cannot conceptualised and articulate such concerns forcefully. An energy policy cannot be divorced from an inherent set of priorities that is linked to our vision of what type of society we want to establish. We believe, therefore that domestic energy requirements are a minimum need that the government should undertake to fulfil."

A. The Indian breakdown for the sectoral consumption of commercial energy for Direct use for the year 1982-83, for instance is as follows:

	Electricity (mkwh)	*Coal*	*Oil (mt)*
1. Household	11.97	3.10	5.71
2. Agriculture	17.78	-	3.61
3. Industry	61.62	60.70	4.60
4. Transport	2.68	10.98	12.41
5. Others	9.75	-	0.08
Total	103.80	74.8	26.41

NOTE: All figures are provisional and subject to revision, oil and coal used for power generation and oil products like Naptha, Bitumen Coke etc. are excluded

(*Source:* GOI, Advisory Board on Energy)

B. The Consumption of Petroleum products for the year 1982-83 is as follows:

		(Unit-000 tonnes
1. Light Distilates	5420	
LPG	601	601
Mogas		1722
Naptha		2958
2. Middle Distillates of which		19660
Kerosene		5214
ATG		1145
HSDO		12013
LDO		1067

They further add, "Demand management does not mean that energy will be denied to consumers. In a developing economy like ours there is bound to be natural growth in the demand for energy from different sectors of the economy. In this sense, one essential facet of India's energy policy will always be expansion of energy supply. The second aspect of demand management is inter-fuel substitution. Here our performance has fallen woefully short of expectations. A shift away from the use of hydrocarbons to a greater use of coal and other sources is called for ..... It is quite obvious that the implementation of our fuel substitution policy has been a failure...."

If the consumption of oil products in the year 1989-90 would be around 63 million tonnes, the Board's report observes that the "Present exercises in petroleum product management show an overwhelming concern with the problem of supplying petroleum products to a level dictated by demand from various sectors of the economy. In the short-term, this may be inevitable but it is certainly not desirable or feasible in the long run." There are several clues and indicators here to delineate the future energy demand scenario for India.

The meaningful lesson in ONGC's context, that we can draw here are simply two :—

(i) We need to augment the oil output and to turn gas as a major future source of energy.

(ii) Around oil and gas Technological-cum-Management strength, diversify in the energy sector.

Today ONGC is a "dual" product (oil and gas) undertaking and is contributing big way towards the energy sector. However, as it moves forward towards the future, it has to explore all possible ideas whether for ONGC or for other Indian Agencies primarily in the Energy and the Marine Sector. How best, in a twenty-year or more time frame, it can help India become self-reliant in energy. The diversification aspect for the ONGC, can be examined in the following two ways :

A. The Administrative-cum-Operational Aspect

(a) Firstly, in India, judgements pertaining to diversification of activities, run by the Government are not easily obtained.
Secondly, they are hard to come by.
Thirdly, even when they are granted to an organisation, they come either too delayed or come in with somewhat overlapping jurisdictions. For example, oil exploration and

oil refinery work is an illustrative example. We can't say they are a single agency operations.

As a contrast, let it be noted that oil companies in other countries have and can diversify even in un-related products. The same re-silence is not available to Indian Private or Public Sector companies. Coca Cola, primarily, a food based company, surprising as it may seem has also been selling Desalination plants to the Soviet Union. The Standard Oil Company of the USA was integrated backward from its refineries to tank farms, oil gathering railroads and pipelines and crude oil reserves in the ground and integrated forward from its refineries to plants for making oil containers, railroad cars and ships for transporting its kerosene, gasoline, naphtha, lubricants, 700 varieties of candles and other products to market and a fleet of 9 tankers to carry standard oil goods to the farthest ends of the earth. The Standard Oil Trust was broken up into some 30 odd companies in 1911, with the largest extent offspring such as Exxon, Mobil and Standard Oil of California.

Comment 1

If we need to see assured managerial success, we need to establish both horizontal and vertical integration.

Comment 2

If the Indian Public Sector Undertakings should not become Industrial giants, nevertheless they can achieve their corporate goals only through a realistic and not notional Inter-Sectoral corporation and coordination.

Comment 3

We, in India, atleast in the Public Sector realm, have a tendency to treat even coordination as a control Function which it never should be.

Let us now look at how several well-known oil companies in the USA have diversified their activities.

The oil industry did not increase its search activities, but mainly because of oil's sharply higher price. At the same time, however, the industry began a vigorous diversification campaign not only into other forms of energy such as coal, nuclear and solar, they even moved into entirely new businesses which they felt offered more promise for the futures such as telecopiers (Exxon) Department Stores (Mobil); Pharmaceutical (Sun) and Ship-building (Ashland oil). The Gulf oil company even made an offer for the Ringling Brothers, "Barnam and Bailey circus".

However, even in the US, the natural gas suppliers (following the oil industry) are today diversifying into other energy resources, as well as into completely new business i.e. Tenneco (Farm equipment) and Americal Natural.

B. Natural Diversification

Even if an Indian Public Sector Undertaking is a unique entity nevertheless, in so far ONGC goes. A natural diversification opportunity in its case does lie in the following five sectors :—

A. *Energy Sector*

Gas to Methanol
Coal liquidation
Synthetic Fuel

B. *Marine Sector*

1. Ocean mining and scorping of Modules
2. Seismic consultancy for Fisheries
3. Ocean Thermal Energy Conversion
4. Energy from Waves and Tides
5. Disposal of Nuclear Wastes in Deep Sea

C. *Engineering Sector*

1. Manufacturing activities relating to Marine based equipment.
2. Captice Annually Manufacturing
3. Other Items.

D. *The Consultancy and Allied Services Sector*

1. Participation for gas and oil exploration and production in the Third World Companies.
2. Developing a National Data Bank, based on the data today being connected with ONGC's diverse activities, relevant to Defence, Agriculture and others.

E. *Rural Development*

1. Gas network for rural energy needs.
2. Rural water management systems.
3. Energy plantations for Hydrocarbons
4. Rural Development through supply of Technical Data on soil etc.
5. Road Building, Housing etc.

Energy Sector: Alternative Fuel for Transportation

Gas: The Best Candidate for Diversified Activities

The Natural gas has enormous potentialities. Let us take Methanol. It is now routinely made from natural gas. It can also be, notwithstanding, its corrosiveness, a potential transportation and boiler fuel. To its benefit, methanol is an inexpensively priced potential transportation and boiler fuel, which has widespread use. It can dramatically reduce two things :—

(i) Critical gasoline.

(ii) Diesel-Related environmental problems: air pollution (specially, nitric oxides and hydrocarbons) and acid rain.

The key question is, leave ONGC aside, Have Indian Energy Policy maker taken any policy view on it ? Even in the USA despite Methanol's important environmental contribution, and it's support from progressive energy policy makers like Ottinger, the issue of national commitment to massive methanol production is clouded. A major liquid fuels debate, already well known within alcohol community seems inevitable.

It is interesting to learn how currently, that policy debate pits "centralists" against "decentralists" small business against big business and more specially, the coal and natural gas industries against the farm sector, in what some feel could develop into a politically volatile future-fuel showdown.

Let us look at the logic of not evolving Methanol as an alternative transportation fuel. In the context of USA it runs somewhat as follows :—

(a) All parties agree that methanol is an extremely toxic, volatile and corrosive substance. Further studies need to be conducted on suspected caricinogenic aldehyde ommission levels safety measures need to be established to address methanol's explosiveness and invisible burning characteristics.

(b) Methanol production will likely remain offshore for atleast the next decade, perhaps into the next century because of the low price of the cheap natural gas feedstock in methanol-producing countries like Saudi Arabia and Canada. In the present market, therefore, methanol might modify, but is not likely to reduce USA's dependence on imported liquid fuel.

(c) Even its advocates agree that methanol, under Reagan Policy, would not profoundly tap potential renewable feedstocks, which include woody biomass and municipal waste. Uncle Sam currently views methanol as the means to invigorate depressed high sulfur coal yearly or 40 per cent of current annual US coal production would be necessary to provide methanol fuel to only 20 per cent of the nation's current 123 million automobiles.

(d) Simple arithmetic suggests that USA would need to increase by nearly a factor of 1000 its current 4.8 million gallons per day methanol production capacity to meet the current equivalent daily use of 2.3 million gallons (one billion litres) of gas for transportation in the US (On a Btu basis, two gallons of methanol is equal to one gallon of gasoline). For this, American Energy experts suggest that massive and capital intensive coal to methanol plants like one scheduled for construction in Dunn City, North Dakota in the late 1980s would be required.

(e) Water free-fuel distribution pipelines would have to be built and existing ones retrofitted.

(f) Basic studies are needed to establish the Industry's future capital needs and its effect on methanol fuel cost in a competitive market place. And construction leadtimes for such plants are minimally estimated at 5 to 10 years hardly a comfortable timetable given the fragility of US oil supply.

(g) Finally, neat methanol is a good distance away from commercial markets despite its relative low cost ($ 50/ gallon ($0.13/litre) on the surplus market versus $1. 0/ gallon ($.45/litre) for ethanol.

The immediate rival to Methanol is Ethanol. What Ethanol's advocate have to say for it, in the context of USA, is somewhat as follows :—

(a) Ethanol, currently is warranteed by major car companies for blending.

(b) It has two major weaknesses; high cost and vagaries in the corn and other principal grain feedstock markets.

(c) But as a potential fuel source (as a gasoline blend, or as an 80-90 per cent mix with water) from agricultural and municipal wastes, ethanol has a much purer fuel pedigree; it's renewable non-toxic, non-corrosive, requires minor engine modification and is largely non-polluting. "Its the perfect fuel" says Illinois based Herb Hansen.

The biggest threat facing ethanol however has come from the recent statements made by ARCO and Dupont that significant amounts (upto 15 per cent) of methanol should be allowed to be blended into gasoline to establish a near term methanol market. Obviously, its entrance as a blend which

At least, unlike India "Methanol Vs Ethanol" is an ongoing debate in USA. Three principal US ethanol producers—Jake Wade of Kentucky Ag Energy, Wagne Eakin of America Fuel Technologies, Doug Synder of Archer Daniels Midland-view methanol with varying degrees of caution.

However, all concur that methanol's development should not be allowed to eclipse a bright future for ethanol.

Others are more outspoken. "Ethanol people are being shortchanged" says Al Mavis, President of Alenco and former Head of the National Gasohol Commission. "It is showing that big oil runs the government that it has more pull than agriculture. This is a shoot-out as far as I'm concerned."

Suffice is to say that, in terms of diversification, whatever may become the future Indian viewpoint on this matter, the central point that will have to be re-judged still remains; Is not "gas" and whatever could be done with it is the genuine field for ONGC's intensive exploration and diversification for all that "Gas" can offer? And the first claim to be in all these fields which could be the gas or its derivatives of gas:

VERSALITY OF GAS

Natural Gas

Liquify and Bottle	Methane
	Domestic Fuel
NGL	Space Heating
LPG	Industrial Fuel
Regasify for	Engine Fuel
different Uses	Power Generation
	Protein Synthesis
	Chemical Products
Use for Reinjec-	Fertilisers
tion Purpose	Cosmetics

RENEWABLE RESOURCES AND NEW TECHNOLOGIES AND THEIR POTENTIAL FOR USE IN THE THIRD WORLD COUNTRIES

Sr. No.	*Renewable Resources Geophysical Resources*	*Extent of resources/ prospect of exploration*	*Current Status Use of Technology*	*Cost and Benefits*	*Potential for Application*
1.	Geothermal Energy (including geopressurized zones)	Widespread especially in recently volcanic areas; geo-pressurized zones are very deep and contain great quantities of natural gas as well.	Geothermal dry system technology commercial some use of wet steam is in experimental/pilot stage	Unless recycled, Geothermal wastes (chemicals) harmful to local environment Geothermal technology is modular in nature so can be used on large or small scale, steam Geothermal	Local potential for space and water heating much larger potential for electricity if capital costs can be reduced and wet steam processes perfected; geothermal pressurized zones not yet exploitable.
2.	Tidal Energy	Scattered bays and estuaries with high median tides	Not fully commercial but being exploited in France and Russia, suitable for large scale electricity generation.	Very complex very high capital costs, some environmental impact	Inherently very limited application under existing vital amplitude limits.
3.	Wave Energy	Limited to coastal countries but not by climate	The practical full scale demonstration done; would be used for electricity generation	No costing available but probably similar to ocean thermal, probable slight environmental impact.	Potentially significant but probably not commercial before the end of the century.

Source: Evaluating the Third World's Energy Options, Excerpt from "An Alternative Road to the Post Petroleum Era :- North South Cooperation by Howe, J.W and Tarrant, JJ : Overseas Development Council, Washington (June 1980).

Comments

1. Considering ONGC's expertise in drilling know-how, Geo-thermal source of energy is yet another strong candidate for diversification.
2. On other items, perhaps, it could initiate R and D work in collaboration with other Indian R and D agencies.
3. In either case some research needs to be carried out to quantify and evaluate the technological feasibility and economics in terms of cost on the one hand and how will geo-thermal energy could wake a substantial impact on collective energy supply demand perspective on the other.

Coal to Oil/Gas

Coal to oil Technology and its actual application goes back to development of Liquified Coal fuel, developed before the Second World War, when it was used to power German Air Force. Commercially, it has currently being produced by South Africa.

This is, however, a cost intensive Technology. The efforts made by some of the US oil companies in this area such as Exxon, Gulf, Shell, Occidental, Continental Oil and others are merely experimental in nature. Coal Liquification like oil shale retorting requires tremendous inputs of Front-end energy. It consumes large quantities of water and results in environmental damage through the surface mining of the coal and the generation of air and water pollution during the liquification process. Every one does recognise that it is cost intensive path. US energy officials have estimated that a plant capable of producing 50,000 barrels of crude oil per day from coal less than 3/10th of 1 per cent of USA's daily consumption, would cost between US $ 800 million and US $ 1.00 Billion in 1996 dollar price.

This is one diversified role for the ONGC that even Ministry of Petroleum looks at favourably. As a representative of that Ministry observed, "Why should ONGC diversify"? If at all they have to do so they why is ONGC not working more actively in the field of coal to oil instead merely carrying out academic library research"?

Synthetic Fuels : Coal Gasification and Coal Liquification

Undoubtedly, ONGC has the expertise to go into coal to oil/ Gas as a relative diversified activity. However, all this involves costs both fiscal and environmental.

Let us look at the nature of debate on this subject with reference to the United States of America who are a world leader in this technology.

During the Joint Hearing before the sub-committee on "Energy Development and Applications" of the Committee on Science and Technology and the Sub-Committee on "Oversight and Investigations" and the sub-Committee on "Energy and Power" of the Committee on Inter-State and Foreign Commerce of US House of Representatives, the subject of US spending on

Synthetic Fuel came for intensive Scrutiny and Cross-examination of the experts.

These hearings were headed by Mr. Ottinger. In this statement before this Committee Mr. Merrow representing the Road Corporation, who had at that just finished a study for US Department of Energy on cost estimation of synthetic Fuel Technologies.

"Mr. Merrow:

When OPEC increased the prices dramatically back in 1974, the companies that had synthetic fuels processes on the drawing boards, but had done very little detailed work on them, suddenly asked themselves whether or not these plants may not now be commercially viable projects. They jumped in some cases, with very heavy commitments, to detailed engineering for the projects, only to find that when they began to acquire the information about what would be necessary to build a real plant in a real place, the costs were very much higher than they previously had estimated.

It is our understanding, although we have not done an in-depth analysis, that coal to methanol is relatively better developed technology than some of the liquification technologies that have been mentioned. We also mentioned surface oil shale retorting is also quite far advanced in terms of its development definition of one or more projects.

We believe the principal problem really is in the state of the cart cost estimation for new and very large process plants.

The coal liquids technology varies from some technologies that have been tried at commercial scale, such as the SASOL-2 technology in South Africa, all the way to technologies for which required pilot facilities have not even been designed as yet. So they essentially vary all over the map from very well developed to very early in their development stages."

Testifying before this Committee was Mr. George Mitchell, a person well acknowledged in the petro-industry in the USA. A detailed excerpt from his testimony is worth referring to here.

Mr. Mitchell:

I have been involved in geology and engineering, drilling some 4,000 wells of which 50 have been wild cats. I have been for the past six years the President and Chairman of the

Texas Independent Producers and Royalty Owners Association, which includes 4000 independent producers, so I have some knowledge.

Besides the drilling of some 4,000 oil and gas wells, or trying to find oil and gas for we don't always hit oil and gas, as you know I also have been the President and Chairman for the last 6 years of the Texas Independent Producers and Royalty Owners Association. So from that vantage point, I think I have enough knowledge of the challenge to the Nation, of what can be done and what independents can do.

As I mentioned, I have grave misgivings and real concerns about the President's Programme. I will try to elaborate why, I agree with the President on many points that conservation really has to be No. 1. The only hope we have for the next 10 years is conservation.

No. 2 in our list of priorities has to be gas, natural gas

No. 3 Oil.

No. 4 Coal, but environmental, labour and industrial concerns must be satisfied.

No. 5 nuclear, when we solve the safety problems.

No. 6 is synthetic fuels from coal and from shale.

No. 7 the so-called panacia of solar and geopressure.

This is pie in the sky right now and misleading to the public. But synthetics and solar are the resources, we should be thinking about probably for the year 2000. And yet, we should do all the proper work in the meantime of having pilot plants, like the Rand Corp. study shows. We have very questionable technology for synthetics at this time and we should really press forward with a very hard programme on pilot plants and probably several demonstration plants to see that technology is available at the price we can afford. To give you the background why I say this, our natural gas costs us in the market place now $4 barrel equivalent. Our oil is $10 per barrel equivalent. It is going up now. OPEC is $20 per barrel equivalent. Tar sand and shale oil is $30 per barrel equivalent. Oil from coal is approximately $35 per barrel equivalent. Those are the latest numbers we have received in talking to many companies and many people doing work in this. And solar panels $50 per barrel equivalent and solar photovoltaic is $200. We need breakthroughs in those last two.

There are many things that can be done with the new enhanced recovery techniques. We are fortunate in working with DOE in one of the most successful manufacturing projects in east Texas where we took at 4-inch well bore down to 11,000 feet. We had 11 pieces of large equipment and we fractured the well with 2.8 million pounds of sand that created a fissure 200 feet high in the hot tight rock, out one-half mile from the well bore. That well is now producing 3.2 million feet a day where before it was commercial. This one experiment probably will add another 2 to 4 trillion feet of gas in the whole east Texas area because a similar rock runs all the way through the east Texas area.

Enhanced recovery of gas : DOE studies have shown you can double the present known reserves, which is more than the equivalent of synthetics. You could really turn the country on and drill a lot of holes.

There are many other areas that we should work on. The technology is available offshore now to drill in 3,000 or at $ 12 per barrel for oil. And you can't do it if half of it goes back in what I call a severance tax. The major company earns 9 cents per dollar of sales, or only about 15 per cent, which is a kin to all other industries. So these are the things we must decide. Are we going to go through a capital intensive environmental programme that the President recommended or are we going to look at the facts and go through a system of priorities to do the job properly ?

Major companies work with the host nations of the Western Bloc to find oil and gas, like on the North Slope or even in Saudi Arabia, all over the world, in nations that have large populations. If we channel and souble and triple their efforts, we could break OPEC's back in 15 years, but it will take that much lead time to do this. Western Bloc nations are competing in various ways for the remaining oil. The result could be a military confrontation, we can avoid that. Without industry, we have the ability to do it. Yet we are going off into the sun, with another programme which really does not make sense to me.

I don't dismiss solar or alcohol fuels. I really think we should work on them very diligently and do one practical application, subsidies and things like that until we see how the costs are coming. Gasehol, I think is beginning to take hold. If we can get waste mass, waste products to be used in stead of grains, I think that has great promise. I think may be something will break through. An enormous volume of liquids goes into the oil market and to have that volume of liquids, if it diminishes the use of crops for food uses, that is potentially serious problem. But I think we ought to work on all the categories, get the priorities straight and move on them simultaneously.

I agree that conservation is number one : that it is the only way I know to fast track these things and figure out the priorities and figure out how much we can afford to put out on each of them.

The sum and substance of all this discussion was that a new agency entitled "Synthetic Fuels Corporation" was created for a period of 12 years and was authorised to spend US $ 20 billion during its first four years. During the next phase of eight years the SFC was to focus on developing commercial facilities based on proven technologies pertaining to coal and oil shale. When Mr Reagan took over from Mr. Carter, the falling oil prices and high interest rates, "enthusiasm for syn-fuels quickly diminished". However, this period does register stepping up of R and D investment in coal R and D both in the Federal aided and private sectors. The Oil and Gas companies there have not only evinched interest but have also sponsored twenty two projects out of thirty-six projects that US Synthetic Fuel, Bureau of Mines had identified in Mid sixties, for research and development (R and D).

Comment

A wider R and D base within ONGC, followed by pilot-plants for different energy sources, in related specialities of the ONGC is apparently the first step forward towards diversification.

If we look at the emergence of the socio-economic and political trends in India and also examine the diversification needs of the ONGC, we will have to keep in mind, two important factors which are as follows:

1. *The era of rising expectations and its political expression.*
   (i) If one closely examines the recent socio-political trends, particularly those where pressure groups and the spokesman of the economically weaker sections of the society have gone about seeking distributive justice, they had invariably emphasized and heightened their Urban-Rural chaslm. They have further juxtaposed even

centres of excellence vis-a-vis the claims of similar benefits for the Rural India and the poorer sections in "ellitist" and "non-ellitist" terms. Thus even the rational aspect of growth through merit, though competition has taken a backseat as against vociferous claims for reservations and search for allied concessions. Such a trend is not likely to abate in future.

(ii) Yet another aspect of the similar tendency can be glimpsed in as much as the centres exhibiting scientific or technological excellence have not only been branded as ellitist complex centres and networks but described and evaluated in such tendentious terms, which may mean as if the pursuit of 'excellence' is anti-people. All these trends have given to our socio-political environment, an unhealthy flavour. But since there, it has several implications for several organisations. Consequently, the country in the last decade, has itself witnessed certain policy shifts which were patently inimical to the growth of science and technology. Happily, such retrograde moves were short-term in character. Nevertheless, the damage done and scars inflicted on progress and modernisation do last. Similar tendencies persist and one can't say for certain, if, in spite of all our socio-economic progress which centralised and de-centralised planning, have really minimised the rural urban divide.

(iii) Added to this is the 'bogus' and irrelevant debate of High Technology versus Intermediate technology.

2. What Political shifts and growth modalities shall emerge during the next 20 years in this country is difficult to say. However two things are certain. All system centres of excellence and economic progress—be they educational in character or industrial in character will have to demonstrate that they are also discharging a bit of their social obligations and that their corporate personality is also committed to rural advancement and has a "visible" rural face.

All these trends have given to our socio-political environment an avoidable turbulence. But since it is there, it has several implications for several organisations.

Secondly, for many decades to come, perhaps as long as

abject poverty prevails in this country, and as long as their quality of people is not one which indicates that they have conquered over their basic minimum needs and have risen above the so called poverty line. Duel dispensations will continue to remain a disturbing factor causing servious state of social discontent. Objectively speaking, many citizens of India have good reasons to express their dissatisfaction, which to give just one example gets expressed as follows : "If a hut is good enough for a villager then it should be good enough for an urban dweller also or vice-versa? Alternatively, what this really implies has in it, in-built demand for social and economic society.

It is obvious that these are matters of state policy. But it is equally obvious that the corporate sector, be it in the private or the public domain, it better watch out. Let not an organisation be branded as if it is merely an ellitist organisation.

In brief, the question that is being posed here are as follows:

Is ONGC an ellitist organisation ? Are its efforts and products being mainly monopolised by the urban consumer ?

Has ONGC some social obligations ? If so, what are we directly doing for this ? In short, does it have a rural face ? Could it diversify some of its functions, which may step up its existing direct or indirect contribution towards rural development and the betterment of economically weaker sections of society.

Ever since its inception, the ONGC is certainly contributing directly and indirectly to the Rural side of India. Its direct contribution has come in the form of the development of remote areas, where due to ONGC's activities, new settlements have emerged which have also provided enhanced employment opportunities to the local people. Besides this, in many parts of India, ONGC has undertaken Road Building Programme — Thereby linking villages and towns and thus increasing communications. In addition to this, ONGC also provides the crude oil which comes to people in the form of Petroleum for Transportation and in the form of Kerosene for domestic cooking fuel and for lighting.

In this context, it is further obvious that several of ONGC's legitimate operations, pertaining to oil and gas, generates a great deal of information and data which through formal linkages with such agencies which are specifically concerned with the implementation of the Rural Development Schemes can be given this data against nominal payment to them.

For example, ONGC generates a lot of soil data. We can share it with Department of Agriculture or with the Ground Water Boards.

The ONGC can also take up developing of water resources on a selective basis. It will be interesting to note how a group of ONGC Geophysicist, during the repeatedly told by the local community : "What we need here is not oil. We need water."

Likewise, some of the Geoscientists in the Bombay region mentioned that ONGC's seismic data can also be used by the Fisheries Departments. Considering however that ONGC's dominant role lies in the field of oil and gas and as we move for and towards the future, ONGC can certainly play a major role through energy oriented diversification pertinent to the Rural growth. We can directly contribute our bit to the "Rural Energy Resources Basket" to help meet with the rural people's diverse energy needs.

At some distant future, some of this could be met by tapping Geothermal energy. Let us take Gas to Rural India. What is suggested here is that wherever there is an high incidence of gas, which we are today flaring — let some of this be used through our direct efforts by the installation, distribution and maintenance of rural gas networks, to cater to the rural energy needs of a cluster of 100 villages in the very local setting where gas is available.

We could demonstrate our concern for rural development by undertaking in different parts of India, atleast to begin with (during 1985-1990) 50 such projects. We should run them at least for a period of five years integral during the plan period free of cost. Thereafter, let these pilot programmes be taken over by the concerned State Governments and other agencies and be paid for by them.

An equally valid case exists for diversified activities in the field of Energy — Plantations. This is of two types : First is the growth of such plants which, like rubber have rich Hydrocarbon content. A Nobel Laurete, in California has collected 300 such species. Once even ISRO in India used Hydrocarbon from a local plant and ran a motor-vehicle on an experimental basis. The second area is what is integral to social Forestry Developing fast growing species and to permit its use as wood-fuel for domestic cooking.

One can thus multiply and catalogue several such ideas. In the national context, they may not make much economic sense but in the local context — at a povery ridden village level, they do acquire some importance.

A more balanced view on this aspect, namely ONGC and Rural Development activities was provided by Dr. A.K. Malhotra, Member (Operations) who in his discussion with the author points out many much needed facets of ONGC can flower best if ONGC becomes a more "self-contained" unit and less dependent on others and move free from external interference. Dwelling on the "Community Inter-action and community welfare activities, he observed that "ample slope exists to extend ONGC's welfare-oriented services in each region around its local formations using the regional General Manager's delegated authority as the prime building block and catalyst be it for augmenting local water-supplies or extending a 'gas' network in the people living in the neighbouring villages."

One can sum up this matter by simply stating that "We have to work a thousand miles. Let's take the first step".

Diversification towards Marine Engineering Consultancy and Third World Countries

I do not propose, in this interim report to catalogue ideas on the above mentioned aspects since most of them are already known. All that we need to do is to carry out further research to identify their (i) feasibility (ii) Economics. Already many committees Task Forces and special groups are perhaps working on these aspects. We could await their recommendations.

To sum up, all we can do here is to catalogue "Alternative steps for change / diversification for ONGC in its march for and towards future in the context of ONGC's mission and objectives.

The authors of 20 year Perspective Plan can accommodate the ideas given in the Table below, in the light of the "Priority" that commission may accord to them.

NOTES

*Peter F. Drucker "Management : Tasks, Responsibilities, Practices" Allied Publishers Private Ltd. (Bombay) First published by William Heinman Ltd. (1974) Indian Edition (1975).

See overview, Energy in Transition (1985-2010), Final Report of the Committee on Nuclear and Alternative Energy Systems" of National Research Council. National Academy of Sciences, Washington (1979) ONGC Corporate Planner will wastly gain, should they try to obtain and study and Major Report Document and that of its Panels.

See 'Energy and Oil' A paper by Dr. AK Malhotra, Member (Operations) ONGC.

See K. Dharamrajan, Director, Ministry of Energy, Shram Shakti Bhavan, New Delhi, his paper entitled "India-Energy Supply Policy and Management" presented at a U.N. Symposium 1982 published in the Natural Resources Forum (C) United Nations, New York 1983. He has given the Indian Sectoral energy consumption pattern as follows : "Industries, 48 per cent, Transport 30 per cent, Household 11 per cent, Agriculture 6 per cent. The industrial sector consumes commercial energy mainly in the form of coal and electricity. The transport sector is the major consumer of oil, accounting for more than 50 per cent of oil consumption."

"In terms of growth, electricity ranks first. The compound growth rate in the last decade has been 7 per cent. The consumption of coal which had an annual growth rate of 3 per cent during the decade 1960-70, is now rising much faster — the annual growth in the last three years being over 8 per cent. Prior to the 1973 increase in the price of oil, consumption of petroleum products was increasing at a rate of 8 per cent per year. Between 1973 and 1976, consumption remained virtually stagnant. Consumption has again begun to increase and is presently growing at the rate of 6 per cent per year."

* O Richard L Ottinger is a Congressman from New York and Chairman Sub-Committee on Energy Development and Applications (1979).

A: The Processing Route : Coal to Methanol to Gasoline

- Coal gasification with coal preparation.
- Gas Treatment
- Methanol Synthesis
- Methanol to Gasoline

B: Coal Gasification

Of the known and commercially applied coal gasification techniques, entrained flow gasification with dry-feed in processes the highest degree of application potential. It is suitable for all solid fuels occuring. No undesirable by products occur during gasification. Only minimum environmental impact is caused. A technically pure gas with a high content of $CO + H_2$ is produced. On the large commercial scale, it is carried out using the Koppers-Totzek Process.

ONGC: FOR AND TOWARDS FUTURE: DIVERSIFICATION PERSPECTIVE

Mission and key objectives of the Commission	*Alternative steps for change/ diversification*
A. To stimulate, continue and accelerate efforts to develop and maximise the contribution of the energy sector to the economy of the country.	1. Accelerate Hydrocarbon bindings through conventional and unconventional means. 2. Diversify 40 per cent of ONGC's activities in a 7000 day framework, in a phased manner. 3. Increase ONGC's direct/indirect participation in Rural Development in India.
B. To continue and expand exploration efforts to convert in the fastest time possible the country's hydrocarbons prognosticated resources to establish reserves.	1. Augment and Expand the Geo-scientific Research Base. 2. Identify steps to achieve all round economy and step up productivity.
C. Consistent with ideal reservoir practices to maximise production profile of oil and gas contained in national policy.	Master EOR Technologies of Today and Tomorrow in a time bound Programme.
D. Build up relevant technology scientific knowledge and expertise in relevant areas of exploration techniques, exploitation practices and technology, engineering, construction and maintenance.	1. R & D for Tomorrow's Technologies today. 2. Increased Inter-sectoral coordination. 3. Need exists to develop a technology material profile for future in economic terms. 4. Develop an ONGC's National Data Information Service.
E. Processing of Petroleum products for achieving self-sufficiency.	More R and D and more Aggressive marketing by concerned agencies.

Mission and key objectives of the Commission	*Alternative steps for change/ diversification*
F. Constantly updating the state of art in all relevant technology and management in the industry to the best of international standards and practices.	1. Intensive and Broad based R and D (step it up to 10 per cent investment of total company budget). 2. Need for New formations.
G. Obtaining share in the world market.	Concentrate on giving consultancy (actual operational) work to begin with the NAM countries).
H. Generation and maximisation of internal financial resources for enhancing growth consistent with environmental requirements and maximisation of the rate of return on investment.	1. Diversification to marketable sources of energy (Gas-methanol) (Methanol Hydrogen apart from the electric driven Automobiles will be the future alternative Transportation fuel). 2. Increased vertical and horizontal linkages — Depute ONGC staff to sister public sector undertakings who are manufacturing things for ONGC to oversee and coordinate the progress pertaining to our short-term and long-term corporate goals. 3. Enter Marine Sector in collaboration with Department of Ocean and other allied agencies. 4. Install captive small or medium scale entrepreneurs on the lines of HMT/BHEL for our work in "Selective" areas in engineering and allied sectors. 5. Set up a full time Environmental Scanning Group.

THE EMERGING SCENARIOS: A CONCEPTUAL FRAMEWORK

The Summing Up: Emerging Scenarios

Environmental scanning both of the National and the Global socio-economic and the energy related trends on the one hand and the objective scrutiny of the ONGC's initial, current and likely strengths, weakness and corporate obligations, in the context of India's socio-economic development variables, one can develop several scenarios. The validity of such scenarios is limited to the information exposure provided by the ONGC to the scenario-writer. Evidently, the scenarios offered here are not the result of any quantitative analysis of the ONGC's data. At best, they can be assessed as qualitative, conceptual and judgemental but definitely indicative in character. Hence relevant enough to inspire thoughts for policy shift.

Trends Analysis : (Opportunity Aspects)

If we closely look at the previous 10 years' period covering the 5th and the 6th plans and the developments relating to gas and oil that have since taken place so far, including the likely developments in the immediate future, which shall emerge from the earlier policies, ONGC has since initiated, then the following five factors do emerge prominently. They constitute ONGC's strength, opportunity filled future and are as follows:

1. ONGC is now a Science and Technology intensive organisation.
2. ONGC has, over the years, emerged as the biggest Indian employer of the professional executive and of the skilled workers in India.
3. ONGC is today and shall be much more in the future an information based organisation. It has already taken several steps to set up a Management Information System (MIS) besides developing an Environmental Scanning Early Warning Group (EWS).
4. ONGC is actively engaged and is sponsoring import substitution and indigenisation processes, which over

the next twenty years can lead to technological self-reliance in the field of location, drilling and production of oil and gas and allied Engineering Sectors.

5. ONGC's commitment to Research and Development (R and D) activities is total. Its various Research Institutes are today actively engaged both in the fundamental and the applied aspects of R and D. Its R and D efforts are also dovetailed to seek mastery over tomorrow's Science and Technology relevant to ONGC's operations.
6. In the context of its latest re-organisaion, its corporate philosophy lays emphasis on cost consciousness and productivity and growth orientation.

Trend Analysis (Threat Aspects)

Based on this writer's discussion with a corss-section of ONGC's executives, apparently there is a general recognition by them that like many other organisations, ONGC too, faces difficulties which if not checked in time, through anticipatory measures, can acquire a "threat" personality. Of course, such perceptions do vary from person to person. That's natural. Of course, there is no unanimity of views here. In many cases, if some negative trends and indicators are posed before the concerned personnel, a defensive posture emerges, which does not recognise such trends as a future threat to the ONGC. But some important selective listing needs to be made (see Appendix). The key aspects are as follows :

The Energy Aspect

This aspect too is a mixed one and has two sides to it. ONGC's performance and contribution so far has been one which can recall Jawahar Lal Nehru's reference to the Public Sector Undertakings as, "The Commanding heights of the Indian Economy". But oil is a tricky business and the problems attendent to and accompanying imported oil are endless. Will ONGC's image suffer any "distortion" in the future? How far away is that future? The Global forecasts puts it to less than 30 years or so.

Be it as it may, it is difficult to take any position in this matter, or make any definitive prognosis. As India advances, industrially, which it shall, not withstanding international pressures and conflicts, India shall need several times more an uninterrupted supplies of energy than is the case today.

What could ONGC do now onwards to contribute to the Energy future? How can it help India survive the threatening clouds of Energy Wars. Is this a crisis point? The answer is both Yes and No. Much will depend on how ONGC relates itself to the Indian societal energy and development needs. It is a moot question if this duel product company will be allowed to play a diversified role now or in the future.

Matters relating to inter-sectoral and inter-face problems of coordination, cooperation and down-stream facilities

Let this be made absolutely clear that more than others, it is ONGC's responsibility to take all such steps, imaginative and innovative measures which could instal in the short range and the long range context in the corporate plans of the BHEL, MDL, SCI, EIL and several other organisations, a commitment internal to these organisations, to sppeily fulfil the indigenised tasks entrusted to them by ONGC. The same applies to the timely development of downstream facilities, be it for the utilisation of natural gas or for corresponding development of refining capabilities.

Manpower Aspects

This aspect emerges both as a fulfilment as well as a likely future crisis. ONGC is today's India's largest employer of the technical, the professional and the skilled Manpower. In fact, most of them are also the best paid personnel in India. The professional in-take of the ONGC unlike the oil and gas companies abroad is of a very high order. The seventh five year plan (draft) document suggests three times intake of the professionals as well as that of skilled manpower during the next five years. Undoubtedly, today, all this personnel is needed.

In fact, ONGC has the capability and the financial viability of absorbing even a larger number and can offer a "spirited" defense thereof. But what about the future? What about the norms of productivity? And in case, we are moving like other Nations towards Technological culture, one has to pose the question: What is ONGC's Corporate attitude towards man-machine ratio? What about the current and future placement policy? What about their career prospects? Considering ONGC's official documents placed before the Indian Parliament, referring to the presence of stagnation what are we doing about it? Finally, would ONGC be able to retain for long its young recruits and would provide them a meaningful career prospects?

Happily these seemingly crisis laden points are not new. Nor are they being overlooked? In fact, as their writer was told in his brief interview with Mr. Srinivasan, Member (Personnel), "These are the very questions which are engaging the highest attention of the Commission".

Be it as it may, the scrutiny of the last quarter century of the growth and performance of the Commission's numerous operations, failures, successes, one can confidently say that of late, this Commission is silently passing through a silent revolution in its managerial culture, corporate philosophy and growth strategies. Let us first look at the "Conceptual framework" of its Corporate outlook, which has been summarised in the following table:

ONGC : Conceptual Framework

Comparison of Initial and Current and Emerging (Future related) Corporate Policy Orientation

Embracing context	*Initial and Current Paradigm*	*Emerging Paradigm*
Philosophical	Evaluative Ellitist assessment Incremental Policy Orientation	Future-creative Participatory Orientation Meta-Policy Orientation
Ephisemological (Theory of Method of grounds of knowledge)	Value Free	Value sensitive (social orientation)
	Change restricted to empirical enquiry	Accepting all enquiry systems
	Restricted to scientific knowledge	Admitting intinctive judgement (Greater Delegation)
Methodological	Technology as independent variable	Technology and society as interdependent variables
	Quantitative analysis orientation	Reliance on both Quantitative and Qualitative analysis
	Conventional Integration	Systemic Integration
Procedural	Bureaucratic and Centralised	Participative (but not yet fully autonomous on fully Decentralised)
	Given to aggregated cost-benefit orientation.	Disaggregated cost-benefit orientation
	Precedence dominates decision making	Consequence dominates decision making (Hence graduation to Anticipatory Management).
	Heavily dependent and outward looking	Semi-Independent and seeking diversification. Moderately dependent inward looking and working towards self-reliance.

If we further look at this paradigm in terms of alternative Growth Scenarios, spelling it out in terms of ONGC's product, attitudes and contribution towards India Economy, role of its professional groups and individual's its contribution towards employment use of service and technology, society and global role, if any, two scenarios can be projected which are as follows :

1. ONGC and the Marginal Change Scenario
2. ONGC and the Optimum Change Scenario

We can briefly capture the high points of these scenarios, as given below :

ONGC : Alternative Growth Scenarios

	A: (Conventional and Bureaucratic Orientation)	*B : Future Growth and Business Orientation*
Indicators	Accelerated Operations Scenario (1985-2005 A.D.)	Accelerated and Diversified Operations Scenario (1985-2005 A.D.)
Product	Aggressive oil and gas exploration and production	Enlarged and multiple functions in energy and other sectors
Economy	Reduction in Indian oil imports leading to limited self-reliance	Greater and sustained input beyond oil and gas to Indian economy
Organisational structure and Individual's (Role Perception Attitudinal Aspect)	Bureaucratic Centralised	Participative/Decentralised
	Power Oriented	Task oriented
	Individualised Output	Synergestic Output (Team-work : Orchestra Model)
Employment	Recruitment and Development of skilled and Technical manpower for India	Radical shift in : (1) Recruitment (2) Placement and (3) Training Policy
Science and Technology	Development of R and D network and marginal development of applied technology	Enhanced R and D Base with Inter-sectoral linkages
Society	Marginal social inputs in Rural/Urban areas	Dynamic interaction and direct contribution to Rural Development.
Global	Third world joint participation	Bigger Global Role
Nature of Change	Marginal Change Scenario	Optimum Change Scenario

In the light of above, conceptual and analytical framework outlined here, all one can say, in the qualitative and not quantitative context is that no matter how one looks at ONGC's onward march towards future, two points emerge prominantly :

Firstly: ONGC plays a far bigger role in the socio-economic development of India and for this it needs a new Mandate.

Secondly: Every conceived step should be taken to convert its "Accelerated Orientations Scenario" into a "Diversified Operations Scenario".

KEY RECOMMENDATIONS

In the light of the study made here, the following key recommendations are submitted for the due consideration of the Commission (Incidentally, these recommendations also constitute areas of further research and expert discussions).

1. As early as possible, ONGC should bring all its planners, say a group of 15-20 experts, under a single independent umbrella to constitute ONGC's "Corporate Planning Intelligence, Environmental Scanning and Energy Forecasting Group." It shall incorporate expertise for both the EWS (Early Warning System) and the MIS (Management Information System) consisting of the Information Scanning Group, the Forecasters and some Programmers.
2. All Futurists have gone on record that the price of imported oil is bound to rise in future. The Indian Socio-Economic Development, by the turn of this Century, is bound to need three times more energy inpurts than is the case today. Therefore, besides intensive oil exploration, the key source of energy of Future, with its multiple application and uses, would be the Gas Potential of India. ONGC should take all possible steps to develop augment fully the multiple uses and application of Gas. Wherever necessary commencing work with Pilot Plants.
3. Since diversification has to be built on one's strength and in response to the national needs, ONGC's 20 year plan should accommodate a phased diversification in the sectors, indicated in this report, leading to a diversification of the order of 40 per cent in ONGC's activities in a 20 year time frame.
4. The corporate success of the ONGC would lie in broad-basing its Geo-scientific Research and Allied Research, Development and Design (RD&D) activities. ONGC's R and D budget should, therefore, be stepped up to 7 per cent of the total corporate budget in the 7th plan period and be steadily increased to reach 10 to 15 per cent by 2005 A.D.
5. In order to ensure ONGC's total corporate success, it needs to seek and establish increased inter-sectoral cooperation

and coordination. ONGC should, therefore take an initiative to introduce numerous innovative, institutional and managerial concepts to foster "Mutual identity of common corporate interests" between ONGC and the sister Public Sector Undertakings including Manufacturers and users of ONGC's products.

6. The Management Development and Training Programmes of ONGC need to be thoroughly overhauled with greater emphasis on *Training in Anticipatory Managerial Culture* ONGC's training network should also be supplemented by an Internal Research Wing to be attached to its training set up.
7. ONGC may, on a selective basis, consider to gradually step up its role and contribution towards the *Rural Welfare and Development* and other *community services* in the regions of its active operations.

CONCLUSION

Satish C. Seth

Undoubtedly in the highly industrialized societies, the conquest of nature did generate a great deal of enabling powers which has, each day during the last five decades lead to a near global perception amongst the elite, the intelligentsia and the industrialists that 'future' is a resource. The remarkable developments in the field of Science and Technology, in fact, had confirmed it each day. These developments made it easier for a few amongst the, 'elites' to accept and display a near total faith that it is man's duty to go beyond all to explore anew.

Secondly, in the free developed world, the emergence of the capitalist order gave a unique importance to a, 'product'. The product in fact became the, 'master' making science, technology, engineering, market forces and everything else of the 'product' something secondary and instrumental to uphold its supremacy both qualitatively and quantitatively. The phenomenon continues. The producer and the consumer have both further accepted this phenomenon as a valid rationale to probe into the future consumerism and the doctrine of market forces. The competition ushered by the doctrine of market forces, particularly the socio-economic phenomenon and sustained by the industrial Science and Technology network might have unfolded many a seemy sides to it; yet, in each sector, it motivated the manager and the researcher alike to constantly seek the answer to the question : 'What next'? This to my mind is the genesis of modern, 'Futurology'.

Future consciousness received its highest impetus from the fact that people in most cultures realized that they have only one life and that the rest of ones life, one has to spend in future. They further realised that most of their opportunities will come only from future and not past. And, therefore, they felt that it is man's duty to anticipate, forecast and envision the likely future possibilities. The future consciousness, in the technology-society nexus, in the western world, thus found a rationale, where forecasting acquired a natural legitimacy. This is not to say that there was any universal acceptance of such a philosophy. The conservative element which in any society constitutes the majority of its people, amply demonstrated their resistance to change, and personal belief that any march towards future has to draw its thrust mainly from the past. Thus futurism and conservatism even in the advanced societies still coexist.

When we look on many of the oriental societies amongst the less developed societies (we will treat Japan little differently). They represent quite a different socio-cultural amalgam. In some cultures particularly, the Hindus of India, there was no time-frame to reflect upon matters relating to living achievement. In fact, it is a moot point if, their belief in many lives yet to come after death, and a twenty-thirty years planning for life, could be a bit of a trifle matter to be bothered about. In most of these cultures, however, the tradition of history and culture was governed by a social millieu where, feudalistic socio-political order and religion in its all pervasive form, kept these societies riveted to their traditional inheritance, as it came to people from the past. Preservation of the past and the prevailing order of the day for the majority of these societies, thus became their obvious resource. Their resource was yesterday (past) and not tomorrow (future). In these societies, technology played a minimal role. Even when it displayed its excellence, it was in the realm of art, culture, architecture, handicrafts, music, painting and other traditional forms, through which the human spirit displayed its innovation and creative excellence. Thus, the entire mood was one of relating oneself through these numerous forms of expressions to God. The supreme power which sustains people, typically in the case of India, did not accord supremacy to, 'product' but to 'God', the same supreme form from which it is believed that everything springs, and which makes life possible. The prime objective of all socio-political institutions, in fact, of the entire society, the collectivity of the people, was to preserve and carry into the future what they had inherited. To them therefore future was not a realm of deep exploration but a passage of time to be decorated with greater zeal with all that the past had bequeathed to the people in terms of their own ways of life and their locally available expressions. This can be and indeed is, a world of limited progression of change. And this is true for millions on the planet earth for whom, any thought projections in terms of future, will be delimited by the social dynamics of their own world as it stood neglected by their familiar and experienced mode of work and life, committed to several private futures and invariably controlled and confined to the community mores and its dictates as passed on by the hold of tradition from one generation to the other.

Thus, in the context of the question : What next? One can, therefore, see the contrast in the reaction and response of diverse cultures. If Mr Brown went to a river, to him, it posed an obstacle and a challenge as did a steep mountain. And before an obstacle, his prime reaction was, 'how can I go beyond it'? How to cross or bridge the river? How to scale the mountain? What do I need to do for this? What technology can help here? What alternative method can I pursue? To do so, what new management system will be needed? In the specific context, this thought proves and consequent action was to determine a future course of action: On how to go beyond a boundary condition? The question, what next? thus, acquired new legitimacy. In this process one unconsciously fixed a new goal for the future. Future in this normative context, suddenly acquired and reinforced the character of its being looked at a, 'resource'.

Whereas, in the same situation, if a person of a different culture when, he or she, came across a boundary condition, displayed acceptance and resignation to the status quo. To Mr Ram, the hills and mountains were the dwelling place of the Gods and the river a holy flow of water. It was not for him to challenge or question their existence, or even irreverentially, look at them as an 'obstacle'. On the contrary, such examples of a boundary condition was something to be concurred with and to feel humble before nature and the powers that could be behind them. Naturally, therefore, any such thing which constituted a boundary condition, was not, for a given time frame of future, meant to be changed or violated. The question of any conquest to be made over 'nature' hardly arised here. One was conditioned to live and to put up calmly with one's environment. These are other cultural patterns where for centuries and even today the question, 'What next'? is too strange and even an unnatural query.

I think, we need to reflect on the fact that the understanding of future in a sense, is indeed not quite a direct function of technological forecasting for the majority. For most people, future is nothing but an uncertain period of time which is obscure. One cannot possibly trust what is not familiar and unknown. For the majority of people in China, India, Arabia and Europe during the middle ages or even today, there are a vast majority of people who are content to relate human behaviour to the socio-political phenomena, the social actions and the various achievements more around their limited sense of cognitive compulsions. They are not given to the envisionment on a societal scale; but on a private level, may be. Traditionally, thinking about future, in most cultures perhaps, was left to the astrologers who tried to relate the life of the planet earth to the movement of other planets, the comet and other celestial bodies in the firmament.

Futurology, on the other hand, is an interdisciplinary subject which took to science and analytical mode to identify numerous future possibilities. In all this, what is important is not whether or not their predictions come true, but the fact that the majority, the collectivity of the people, looked at future as something remote and far beyond their comprehension. For centuries, it was never a matter of scientific study to seek, by volition new directions of change. Least of all, thinking about future and its study was seldom used to pre-recognize the trends in human affairs or to understand future for socio-economic development except during war and battles for defence wherein the past one did attempt to conjecture the unforeseen moves of the enemy.

As a body of interdisciplinary knowledge, therefore, futurology or futures studies is something of a very recent origin. It is not more than four or five decades old. It is a strange irony of facts that the first beginning of Technology for casting, in our times too, should commence, in the defence for the search of newer weapons in response to the question: 'What next'?

Be it as it may, the new challenges, that lie before us futurists are many. The foremost of this is: 'what should we do to comprehend and measure the different cultural patterns and allied outlook to determine indicators and parameters, of change, of different people? What methodology or anticipatory techniques can we use to assess the hopes, fears and expectations of the people who are, geographically dispersed, and who live at varying levels of exposure to modern times, objectives of living and of future.

The point is not that, most people, the majority that is, have to be future minded or, that in all societies, people should take a lead towards future as against their custom and preference to be led forward. The key point is that, in order to gain any global success, to make future consciousness a well accepted movement, we futurists have to develop new analytical tools for a deeper and better understanding of the different cultures and people's varying and quite different perceptions of 'time' and 'change'. We do not, quite yet know, why some people change quickly and some don't? What are their perceptions of change in terms of time. Some people want to change instantly and indeed they covet change. Whereas, some people want to change; but they even fear it. Even though there are also a handful of people, in all cultures, a miniscule minority, like we futurists, whose very purpose of life is to explore new frontiers and to go beyond frontier after frontier, to seek afresh anew. To them this seems to be the sole and natural purpose of life. Whereas the majority wants to be left as they are, perhaps to be themselves. We futurists, still do not yet know what are the socio-psychological motivations behind peoples attitudes, of such non-interest in future. And they who can claim to be nearer the goal of happiness—if at all happiness too could be measured. I do not yet know of anything like a happiness code.

It may look unnecessary to question the fact that people who are well-adjusted to their immediate environment and their, man made boundary conditions, ought to show a special interest towards future to seek ways and means to determine some special normative goals for future for seeking new and better socio-economic development. Let's not forget, the cynics may question and say: 'who are we to goad people to forsake their respective life-style,' Please leave people alone.

One, however, wonders if the situation is that simplistic in modern times. Many societies have amply demonstrated the people's demands for basic needs in terms of food, water, clothing, housing and education can be improved for one and all. Thanks to Science and Technology through which it is possible today to have less painful births, to produce more food grains from the same plot of land and to provide purer and cleaner drinking water, besides being able to communicate easily across the local, national and international boundaries.

All this has happened in those countries where, 'future' was treated as a resource, where new technologies, new education and new management systems worked in unison to make a vast humanity to touch a better quality of life. If knowledge is universal, if it can be shared and used to achieve results, then what justification indeed is there for perpetuating poverty and for romanticising about drudgery, illness and lack of such amenities besides calling such conditions as God's will. Future consciousness and its application in practice has shown that the path of such conquests which can give people better life care systems, lies with new education, new technologies and new management which emanate when we begin to treat future as a 'resource'.

This then does constitute a good enough rationale to advocate that future consciousness should have a wider spread and percolation to the grass root levels. We need to use every avenue to achieve this. This can be done through the educational route. It can also be done through mass media and through the participatory mode, be it for technology transfer or for dissemination or planning know-how for the socio-economic development. The important point here is that all this, we futurists have to do through our 'idiom' of futuristic thinking and Long Range Perspective Planning.

To achieve all this, we Indian futurists who are committed to the interdisciplinary, ought to perfect our tools of enquiry and non-linear thinking: Systems Probe and Analysis. In assessing the varying perceptions of time we need an anthropologist to give us the relevant inputs. In assessing the fears and hopes amongst others, perhaps, we need some inputs from psychologists. To understand the role of the personalised and private realities and the place of kinship and religion, we need several inputs from the sociologist. In order to understand why people are so linear in their thinking and so non-understanding of the merits of technology, we perhaps need inputs from our educationists, practitioners of different disciplines. And in order to understand the gross managerial illiteracy amongst the majority of people; we need to ask ourselves: Have we, society by society developed a new brand of 'leader-of-and-for-future' who can inspire people to learn to anticipate change and, thereafter to work to manage it for a better life.

Let's go over the hard case of this problem once again. Supposing that we got all these inputs from all the specialized sources, even then, the fact remains, that most cultures under the grip of inherited conditions do find it hard to break their boundary conditions. Over the years they have developed several social handicaps which disable them to relate themselves to the 'unknown' and to 'uncertainty' in short to 'change' to newer and yet achievable and possible socio-economic horizons. It is quite easy to explain such inhibited behaviour patterns in terms of people's varying perceptions of their social ethics and norms imposed on them by various institutions in society. After all, in all cultures, the social norms spring from the religious and the moral codes of do's and don'ts. As things go, for many it is easier to break boundaries, for 'crime' than to explore or forsake the possibility of societal customs for the unchartered 'growth' paths. We cannot also ignore the fact that people in the spatial context possess a limited understanding of the formalised institutions networks. Probably, for a majority of them, these institutions for welfare are too remote, too distant and even fearsome. Notwithstanding these obvious facts, people also do not want to change independently even if there was a recognised and well understood social ferment visible and acceptable to them. People prefer to change with others. Changing by oneself against strong social forces is too frightening and risky an effort for an average person. One is scared that it may militate against their prime-goals of self-preservation and survival. People don't want to build a new scenario for living, lest, it may hurt them economically. For them, all concerns for the future lie in safeguarding the numerous inbuilt securities they have found or have managed to build over the years to further safeguard the interest of their children, family, and all things that fulfil the prime need of raising the children, educating them and marrying them. The point that is being stressed here is that, for the majority of people, the social movements and the technological progress be it of today or that of tomorrow, is not, at least in the developing countries, the main concern of the masses even if the new movement and new technology were the instruments of change and the harbinger of a better life.

Even at the level of the youth, when one is idealistic, their participation in things that may influence future or things that hold a great deal of promise for a new future, is not without some obstacles. These are mainly that of the inability complex: I can't do it, let me not do it. This will induce one to look more towards the past for seeking inspiration for survival, rather than, to covet unpredictable opportunities and chances of future. After all, there are unending needs and therefore, varied responses.

Such a social behaviour, therefore, where concern for private futures, the concern for maintaining the status quo to seek safe, marginal, incremental change can be easily judged or classified as the pursuit of the 'selfish' mode of life. Be it as it may, this too is a social reality. And we need to understand it with sympathy. It is not easy for millions to relate themselves to 'unselfish' societal-change that characterises the 'what next' attitude in futurism. Every one is indeed not a leader. Majority consist of the followers. Perhaps, in passing, one can add that the socio-economic change agents ought to be also some kind of futurists.

However, this elementary analysis or any other complex explanation of this societal phenomenon only points out to the fact that even though an average man or woman does not naturally work for realizing of the social futures, people are not averse to understand, in their personalized context, the alphabets of the future. Thus, a definite need exists to gently bring people out of their self-built, self-centered cocoons to make them understand the rationale for consciously working towards a new future on the societal level, as well. It constitutes indeed a very small departure from the ongoing habit-thinking by which, consciously or unconsciously, they tend to extend the past into the present and both of this into the future. They need instead to learn not to turn their tomorrows into yesterdays. To achieve this, which I would like to call a kind of 'Societal-Quantum-Jump' does demand a herculean effort on the part of we futurists.

In the Indian context, today we stand, on a strange cross-road.

Out prime societal features namely the demographic factor, the unequal growth and many others have created a strange turbulence which is all pervasive indeed. A near billion people, suffering with acute poverty conditions, coupled with unequal reach to future opportunities, live in a curious mosaic of cultural plurality groping for a meaningful direction of change. Sometime, one feels as if time has come to a standstill in India. Under the same roof the members of a joint family live apparently so blinded that each individual member seems to belong to a different century. More than this, in the realm of technology, the Indians, like many other third world countries also find themselves in an extraordinary situation where no technology seems to fade out forever. We seem to live in all ages, from the bullock cart to the space age, though India is successfully trying to bridge up the best of the past to the best of the future. It is a unique case where one seems to be pursuing a blended future of times bygone and of times to come.

However, neither the time nor the environmental turbulence ever waits for people to change. People have to act in time in their own larger interest in particular to conquer and rise above the misery of unfulfilled basic human needs. In such a situation/ seeking a future (which may now be the past of others) whatever may be the varied perceptions of change of the elite and the non-elite, demands that the study of the future, in terms of the likely threats, opportunities and implication of the emerging technologies and allied aspects be taken more seriously. The humanity has still a fair chance to plan futuristically for the welfare and betterment of the living conditions of millions of our people. This can and should happen society after society.

If Futures Studies is also a powerful tool of planning and management, it is high time that our management stance be one where we are not totally dependent on the precedent (past) but we instead begin to look for new solutions for the age old problems, in providing people a better living standard, through Anticipatory Management.

The long range planning has to be the prime requisite of socio-economic development where decision making process has to be one which pays greater emphasis to the Normative Goal-setting and Consequences (Future). Here there are no options or choices to reject or accept this line of action because of the speed with which: (a) external environment is changing in all walks of life, (b) the resources are being depleted each day; and (c) the population pressures are demanding more food, more schools and more jobs, in such a case, linearity, boundary conditioning and the *status quo* would not help.

We have no other option but, to take recourse to management by anticipation and future scanning. In current days choice, we need to accommodate as much as we possibly can, the sectoral demands (food, housing, clothing, education, communication, culture, defence, etc.) of coming years (future).

The global and the national environment turbulence, be it of the S&T developments or the geo-political or be they due to the social fragmentation and population explosion, they all impose on any state or society new current and future related burdens.

In sum, the situation automatically demands a new 'viewing' of future consciousness and its spread at all levels. Futurology study cannot remain a mere mathematical tool replete with 'Fuzzy sets and models' being worked with the high-tech oriented think-tanks. Such future related consciousness has to percolate to all people and the masses in an appropriate and imaginative and creative mode in embracing their personalized context as well.

How do we do this is to my mind, the prime unfinished task of the Futurist community.

This situation, in the current national or global context, is too important and should be attended to.

Apparently, many well-to-do, elite champions of Industry and officials ought to involve in the Futures movement. An individual, a company and a government moves only so far and may be even less as it sees.

The environment and foresight education perhaps needs to be remodelled for them as well as for its other clients.

Alas, we futurists have ourselves still, "miles and miles to go". As a first step let a new debate commence. For how to choose a future still remains an enigma for many.